SCHAUM'S
OUTLINE OF

Italian
Grammar

SCHAUM'S
OUTLINE OF

Italian Grammar

Third Edition

Joseph E. Germano, Ph.D.
Associate Professor Emeritus of Foreign Languages
State University of New York–College at Buffalo

Conrad J. Schmitt
Foreign Language Consultant and Editor

Schaum's Outline Series

New York   Chicago   San Francisco   Lisbon
London   Madrid   Mexico City   Milan   New Delhi
San Juan   Seoul   Singapore   Sydney   Toronto

JOSEPH E. GERMANO is Associate Professor Emeritus of Foreign Languages, State University of New York College at Buffalo. He has taught both Italian and Spanish at the secondary and college level, and holds a New Jersey State Department of Education Dual Certification in Italian and Spanish, K-12, from Seton Hall University. A native of Italy, Dr. Germano received his Ph.D. in Italian, in Medieval and Renaissance Literature, wit ha concentration in Franco-Latin Literature, from Rutgers University, New Brunswick, where he coordinated the Rutgers Italian Workshop Series from 1076 through 1981. He earned his Bachelor's in French and Spanish from the University of Nebraska (Omaha), and his M.A. in Italian with a Spanish minor from the University of Colorado (Boulder). He is the founder of *NEMLA Italian Studies* which he edited/co-edited from 1977 through 1986, now published at Rutgers University. Dr. Germano is the author of articles on Italian Literature and Culture, and of four language textbooks. HE developed and taught, among others, a course of Business Italian, and completed a book manuscript of *Commercial Italian*. From 1985 through 1987 he was Resident Director of the State University of New York Italian Study Abroad Program in Siena, Italy. He is a technical and literary professional translator.

While in Siena, he was invited to translate a technical manual describing a new way to execute fresco painting: Otello Chiti, *Fresco on Cloth or Other Non-Mural Supports* (Original title: *Affresco su tela o altri supporti non murali*). Introduction by Pietro Annigoni. English Translation by Joseph E. Germano. Poggibonsi: Nencini, 1986. His many literary translations include poetry by Da Lentini, Protonotaro, Federico II, Dante, Angiolieri, Cavalcanti, Petrarca, Boccaccio, Boiardo, Lorenzo de' Medici, Poliziano, Machiavelli, Michelangelo, Groto, Foscolo, Leopardi, Pirandello, Govoni, and Jahier.

CONRAD J. SCHMITT was Editor-in-Chief of Foreign Language, ESL, and Bilingual Publishing with McGraw-Hill Book Company. Prior to joining McGraw-Hill, Mr. Schmitt taught languages at all levels of instruction from elementary school through college. He has taught Spanish at Montclair State University, Upper Montclair, New Jersey and Methods of Teaching a Foreign Language at the Graduate School of Education, Rutgers University, New Brunswick, New Jersey. He also served as Coordinator of Foreign Languages for the Hackensack, New Jersey, Public Schools. Mr. Schmitt is the author of many foreign language books at all levels of instruction, including the communicating titles in Schaum's Foreign Language Series. He has traveled extensively throughout the world. He presently devotes his full time to writing, lecturing, and teaching.

Schaum's Outline of
ITALIAN GRAMMAR

2 3 4 5 6 7 8 9 0   RHR/RHR   0 1 4 3 2 1 0

ISBN   978-0-07-163529-5
MHID   0-07-163529-7

Library of Congress Cataloguing-in-Publication Data is on file with the Library of Congress.

In memory of my parents,
Antonio Germanò and
Maria Carmela Romeo Germanò

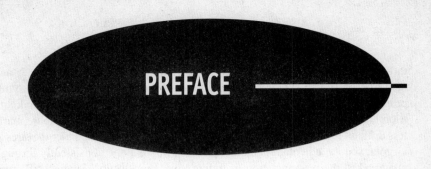

PREFACE

This Third Edition, as the previous ones, has been designed to make the study of Italian grammar easier for the learner. The book is divided into eleven chapters, each of which concéntrates on a basic problem area in Italian: the pronunciation of Italian, nouns and articles, adjectives and adverbs, comparatives and superlatives, numbers, dates, and time, verbs, negatives, interrogatives, pronouns, prepositions, and special uses of certain verbs. Each grammatical or structural point is introduced by a simple, succint explanation in English, and this explanation is further clarified by a number of examples in Italian. It is recommended that you first read the explanation, then study the illustrative examples, and only then proceed to the series of exercises provided. The best way to learn a language is to practice it—both in oral and written forms——so you should complete each exercise, checking your answers with those at the end of the book, before moving on to a new topic.

In Foreign Language Pedagogy there are certain teaching strategies (strategies that are also valid in the teaching of other subjects) which, if violated, can produce negative results. There are two bad habits that diligent foreign language instructors have always tried to avoid: 1) writing a wrong word, phrase, or sentence on the blackboard, thus teaching by using negative examples, and 2): using Anglicized phonetic transcriptions (often hyphenated) of a foreign language on the blackboard or in handouts prepared for students. The former habit is counterproductive because wrong examples compete with correct ones and no one knows which ones will be absorbed and remembered by the students. The latter habit presents a false pedagogical aid by encouraging such sound distortions that produce a phonological parody of what an acceptable pronunciation actually is. What is popularly acceptable, and perhaps even helpful, in foreign language travel books for tourists, becomes downright pernicious in foreign language classrooms and texts. In this book each example is given in its correct form, and pronunciation is never distorted with phonetic transcriptions.

In Italian, the written stress is indicated by an accent mark usually only on words that end with accented vowels; many Italian Grammar books in North America utilize only the grave (`) accent mark, and a few others offer some variation of this practice. Since the debate on accents still continues in Italy without any resolution in sight, there is a silent consensus to accept all systems grammarians use. No one in Italy has ever stated that the debate is over; trying to assert one system over any other, in Italy or elsewhere, is premature and inappropriate. In this book, the accent marks used to indicate stress on the last syllable of a word will appear as follows: the grave accent (`) will be placed on accented final vowels -à and -ò; the acute accent (´) will be placed on all final vowels (-é, -í, -ú) with the exception of the third-person singular of the verb *essere;* è (he, she, it *is;* see p. 105), of cioè *(that is)*, and a small number of words of recent foreign origin: **caffè, canapè, karatè, tè or thè**, etc. This is the same system used by Einaudi, arguably the most distinguished Publisher in Italy, and by *Italian Quarterly* (published in North America), one of the finest journals of Italian Literature and Culture outside Italy. My personal knowledge of this system is owed to Professor Luigi Romeo, former Chairman of the Department of Linguistics and Professor of Italian and Linguistics at the University of Colorado, Boulder, whose superb lectures of long ago on Italian Linguistics are still remembered and appreciated.

This Third Edition introduces a new chapter: *Chapter 4*, p. 59, which expands considerably the previous treatment afforded the comparatives and superlatives. The **IPA** *(International Phonetic Association)* alphabet symbols are added throughout the presentation of the pronunciation of Italian in *Chapter 1:* an approximate English sound is provided next to each Italian example for each letter of the alphabet and an **IPA** symbol. This should aid the reader in proper pronunciation. Additionally, other concerns are addressed and explained: single and double consonants, diphthongs, triphthongs and hiatus, syllabication, and punctuation and orthographic marks. Also, when a word is unaccented and it is difficult to determine where the stress falls, a dot is placed under the stressed vowel (i.e. aula, baule, euro, matricola, virgola, scuola, edicola, enciclopedia, etc.); this is done consistently throughout the book. In American foreign language texts, the pronunciation of Italian **'gn'**, French **'gn'**, Spanish **'ñ'**, and Portuguese **'nh'**, has traditionally been explained as an approximation of the sound of English **'onion'** and **'canyon'**. I have decided to start using the word **'poignant'** instead, because the **'gn'** in **'poignant'** is a true English sound equivalent, not an approximation, of the Italian **'gn'** (the same can be said for the other languages named above). At the end of *Chapter 1*, there are twenty-five exercises many of which were especially designed to review oral skills in writing, a feature not found, as presented herein, in any similar Italian Grammar reviews for speakers of English. Other appropriate changes and additions have also been introduced in all other chapters. Also, for the very first time in any of *Schaum's Foreign Language Grammar Outlines*, end-of-book glossaries, **Italian-English** and **English-Italian**, have been added totaling more than two thousand entries, carefully chosen from the more than ten thousand to be found in the book.

This 3rd edition of *Schaum's Outline of Italian Grammar* reflects the recent change in legal tender from **lira to euro**. On January 1, 2002, the **euro** bank notes and coins became the only legal tender circulating in Italy and some other member states. In addition to twelve **EU** (European Union) states, the new currency also circulates in Monaco, Vatican City, and San Marino, among others. The **euro (€)** is divided into **100 cents**, popularly known as **euro cents**. Italians pronounce the **c** of <u>cent</u> in English or like Italian **s** (as in **Sara**); they also refer to <u>cent</u> with its Italian equivalent **centesimo** (pl. **centesimi**). In Italian, the words **euro** and **cent** function as other foreign words do and are treated as such grammatically. Foreign words are usually masculine (i.e. **il film, l'alcol** or **l'alcool**, etc.) and are not pluralized, but are given the appropriate definite (or indefinite) articles (singular or plural, as needed) according to how they begin. Observe the following examples: **il film > i film = il cent > i cent; l'alcol > gli alcol = l'euro > gli euro**. The Italian **euro** bank notes are as follows: **€ 5 (cinque euro); € 10 (dieci euro); € 20 (venti euro); € 50 (cinquanta euro); € 100 (cento euro); € 200 (duecento euro); € 500 (cinquecento euro)**. The coins are as follows: **lc or € 0.01 (un cent); 2c or € 0.02 (due cent); 5c or € 0.05 (cinque cent); 10c or € 0.10 (dieci cent); 20c or € 0.20 (venti cent); 50c or € 0.50 (cinquanta cent); € 1.00 (un euro); € 2.00 (due euro)**.

One of the most difficult and tedious tasks in acquiring a second language is to learn the many forms that exist in the language, be they noun, adjective, or verb form, In this book all forms have been logically grouped in order to make their acquisition as simple as possible and also to minimize what at first appear to be irregularities. For example, in most Italian texts the verbs *ridere* and *rimanere* would be treated separately. In the discussion of the preterite in this book, however, these verbs are presented together because of the similarities of their endings.:

> *ridere: risi, ridesti, rise, ridemmo, rideste, risero*
> *rimanere: rimasi, rimanesti, rimase, rimanemmo, rimaneste, rimasero*

Such groupings of forms that at first may seem to have nothing in common should help you to simplify and streamline the task of acquiring large numbers of "irregular" forms, including verbs in all tenses.

Schaum's Outline of Italian Grammar can be used as a complete grammar review *text*, as a companion to any basic text, as a text in Advanced Grammar courses, in Conversation and Composition courses, in Translation courses, in other upper-level courses, or as a reference book. In order to reinforce each point you are learning in your basic text, you may wish to get additional practice by doing the clear, logically organized exercises provided throughout this book. Since the very nature of basic texts is to present the material piecemeal, this book instead provides the user a complete view of a particular grammatical point with its details and nuances as easily and patiently explained as in the best classrooms. **The latter feature, along with four hundred seventy-nine exercises (all of them with answers), makes this book also perfectly suited for self-study.**

The author wishes to thank Schaum's Senior Editor Charles Wall and Editorial Assistant Kimberly Ann Eaton for their fine work. Special thanks are due Ms. Rosalie Perrone, a teacher of Italian (Easton, PA), for her expert advice, and Dr. Rafika Merini (SUNY College at Buffalo) for her excellent work on the Glossaries. I particularly appreciated Fmr. Schaum Publisher Barbara Gilson's personal efforts on my behalf and to improve the book. The author welcomes any remarks or inquiries from readers.

JOSEPH E. GERMANO

CONTENTS

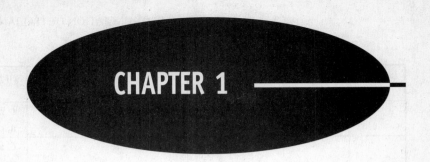

CHAPTER 1

The Pronunciation of Italian

THE ITALIAN ALPHABET AND ITS SOUNDS

The Italian alphabet has twenty-one letters: five vowels (**a**, **e**, **i**, **o**, **u**) and sixteen consonants. For the most part, Italian is *phonological*; that is, the letters of the alphabet are usually pronounced as written. The spelling of each word usually conforms with its sound. The exceptions are few: the **h** is always silent (a**h**, o**h**, **h**o, **h**ai, etc.), and the vowels **e** and **o** have closed and open sounds. Although there are standardized rules for pronunciation (under the Tuscan model), regional influences are so strong that Italians accept these slight differences in the pronunciation of these two vowels. An example of the difference is roughly the American equivalent of the initial **o** in the word *Boston* as pronounced in the city of Boston compared to its pronunciation in other parts of the country. The traditional sounds of **e** and **o**, under those rules, are as follows: closed **e** as in b**e**ne, perch**é**, s**e**te (as in English *make*), open **e** [ɛ] as in **è**, cio**è**, b**e**llo (as in English *let*), closed **o** as in d**o**ve, m**o**lto, **o**ra (as in English *cone*), open **o** [ɔ] as in c**o**sa, d**o**nna, p**o**rta (as in English *lost*).

Often, vowels may appear together to form a *diphthong* [*dittongo*] (two vowels: pi**u**ma, **u**omo, pi**a**no, Fi**e**sole), or a *triphthong* [*trittongo*] (three vowels: mi**ei**, tu**oi**, su**oi**, mai**u**scolo, zab**ai**one). In such combinations, a vowel may become a semivowel and lose its typical pronunciation. Additionally, there are some sounds that need more than one consonant for their formation: for example, **ch** = [k] (per**ch**é), **sch** = [sk] (**sch**erzo), **sc** = [ʃ] (u**sc**io), **gh** = [g] (**gh**iro), **gl** = [λ] (fi**gl**i), **gn** = [ɲ] (le**gn**o).

The *hiatus* (*lo iato*) is also the meeting of two vowels, but they are pronounced separately. For example: ma**e**stra, po**e**ta, ri**e**ntrare.

Next to each letter of the alphabet (and its Italian pronunciation), you will find a symbol of the *IPA* (*International Phonetic Association*) alphabet under the heading *Phonemes* (*Fonemi*). *Phonemes* are the sounds of the letters of the alphabet. A word is a combination of phonemes. The *IPA* symbols help in the pronunciation of a word, and they usually appear in very good dictionaries. On the right column, there are also English words that exemplify the sounds represented by the phonemes. All these details and others appear in the table below next to each vowel or consonant, as needed.

Letter	Italian Name	(IPA Symbols) Phonemes	Italian Example	Approximate English Sound
a	*a*	[a]	**padre, mamma, banana**	**A** as in English *father, car, ah!*
b	*bi*	[b]	**bar, buono, abete**	**B** as in English *bar, beer, bat.*
c	*ci*	[tʃ]	**ceci, cinema**	**Ch** as in English *chop* when followed by **e** or **i**, or

Letter	Italian Name	(IPA Symbols) Phonemes	Italian Example	Approximate English Sound
		[k]	**Carlo, cosa, Cuba**	**C** as in English *cane* when followed by **a**, **o**, or **u**; or
			chiave, anche	**C** as in English *cane*; in Italian **ch** is always followed by **e** or **i**: chi, chiuso perché.
d	*di*	[d]	**dove, divano, due**	**D** as in English *dear, duet*.
e	*e*	[ɛ] [e]	**bello, vento, è, lento** **sete, bene, pepe, vede**	An open sound as in English *let*; and a closed sound as in English *make*.
f	*effe*	[f]	**fiume, fuori**	**F** as in English *foot*.
g	*gi*	[dz]	**gente, giorno**	**G** when followed by **e** or **i**, as in English *gentleman, gist*.
		[g]	**gatto, gara, gomma, guaio, gola, gusto** **ghiro, ghetto, ghermire, ghiaccio, ghiaia, ghigliottina, gheriglio**	When followed by **a**, **o**, or **u**, as in English *goat, gap, gum*. When followed by an **h**, **gh** sounds as in English *go, gum, get*.
		[λ]	**aglio, cogliere, gli, luglio, famiglia, figlio, figlia, maglia, foglia, giglio, pigliare, egli, svegliare** **glicine, glicerina, anglicano, negligenza, negligente** **glabro, gleba, glaciale, gloria, gladiatore, gladiolo, glossa, globo, negletto, globulo, glorioso, glossario, glucosio, conglomerare**	When **gl** is followed by **i**, the sound is somewhat similar to English *million*. It is precisely as in Portugese **lh** (lhano) However, these are some exceptions: **gl** followed by **i** may also be pronounced as in English *glass*. **Gl** is always pronounced as in English *glass* when the vowels that follow are **a**, **e**, **o**, and **u**.
		[ɲ]	**bagno, bagnino, cognome, disegno, gnomo, lasagne, lavagna, legno, ragno, sdegno, segno**	**Gn** is always pronounced as in English *poignant*, as in French **champagne**, and like Spanish **ñ** as in **año**.
h	*acca*		**ho, hai, ha, hanno, ah!, eh!, oh!**	Never pronounced, like **h** in English *oh!* and *ah!*, unless together with **c** (**ch**), or **g** (**gh**): see the letters **c** and **g** above.
i	*i*	[i]	**sí, divino, Dino fiamma, fiasco, fiume, fiocco, fieno, Fiesole, fiato**	**I** as in English *police, cheese, these*. When the **i** is unstressed in a diphthong, it is pronounced like **y** in English *yes, yet*.
l	*elle*	[l]	**latte, lei, Lola, loro, filo, Colombo, lasagne, lui**	**L** as in English *love, letter*.
m	*emme*	[m]	**mamma, musica, mio, moto, mimo, mambo**	**M** as in English *mother, music*.

Letter	Italian Name	(IPA Symbols) Phonemes	Italian Example	Approximate English Sound
n	*enne*	[n]	**nonni, nuora, naso, nuoto, banana**	**N** as in English *nickel, none.*
o	*o*	[o]	**dopo, ora, mondo, molto, dove, sole**	**O** has two sounds: closed **o** as in English *cone,*
		[ɔ]	**cosa, ciò, porta, posta, costa, canto, donna,**	and open **o** as in English *lost.*
p	*pi*	[p]	**pino, padre, papa, piede, piú, piano, cuspide**	**P** as in English *pope, pin.*
q	*cu*	[kw]	**qui, qua, quadro, quindi, quando, dunque, quello, questo, cinque, quindici, quanto, qualora, squalo**	**Q**, as in English, is always followed by **u** and one or more vowels: **quando; quiete**, as in English *quiet; quorum, quince.*
r	*erre*	[r]	**Roma, aroma, rete, ieri, verde, vero, carta, parete, zero**	Similar to the English **r** in *red* (but trilled instead of rolled).
s	*esse*	[s]	**scala, Scozia, suo, ascoltare, scuola, stare, vasca, sala, sale, sole, falso, discutere, spazio, scopa, stoffa**	**S** may be unvoiced or voiced. It is unvoiced when initial, pronounced as in English *see, stay, spy.*
		[z]	**sbaglio, sbalzo, sbarbare, sdegno, sdraia, sdrucire, sgabello, sgelo, sgomento, slancio, slitta, sloggio, smacco, smagrire, smaltire, smania, snellire, snidare, sradicare, svanire, svantaggio, sveglio, svendere** **quasi, rosa, paese, centesimo, chiesa, quaresima, bisonte, invaso, caso, oasi, frase** *but* **risentire, girasole, controsenso, preside, sessantasei**	It is voiced when initial followed by **b, d, g, l, m, n, r, v,** sounding like in English **zenith: sbaglio**, etc., except when in a foreign word such as *slam, smoking, snob, smog.* The **s** is voiced also when intervocalic (between two vowels), sounding like **z** in English *zenith* with some notable exceptions: **casa, cosa, cosí, tesa,** and a few others, as well as in compounds such as **autoservizio** Note that, in general, in Italy, the **s** is mostly voiced in the North and mostly unvoiced in the South.
		[ʃ]	**sciocco, sciopero, sciovia, sciame, liscio, coscia, uscio** **scherzo, schiodare, schema, Schicchi, mosche, caschi**	**Sc** followed by **e** or **i** produces the sound **sh**, as in English *shoot.* **Sch** followed by **e** or **i** produces the sound **sk** as in English *sky* or **sc** in *escape.*

Letter	Italian Name	(IPA Symbols) Phonemes	Italian Example	Approximate English Sound
t	*ti*	[t]	**tappo, tarlo, TAC, tema, terra, topo, Topolino, artista, pasta, pista, basta**	**T** as in English *tire, take*.
u	*u*	[u]	**buco, cubo, sugo, rughe, luna, tuta**	**U** as in English *ruler* or *cool*.
			uọmo, quạndo, Guịdo, quạnto, galantuọmo, nuọvo, guẹrra, guạsto, guidare, buọno	When followed by a vowel, the **u** is pronounced as **w** in English *west*.
v	*vu*	[v]	**vulcano, vuọto, vaso, vino, veste, Vespa, vịvere, uva, vita**	**V** as in English *vote*.
z	*zeta*	[ts]	**Firenze, zịo, ọzio, paziẹnza, prezzo, grạzie, zụcchero, pazzo, terzo, zịa, calza, sạzio, stanza, conversaziọne**	**Z** is unvoiced and voiced. It is unvoiced (**ts**) as in English *vets*.
		[dz]	**mezzo, romanzo, zelo, Manzoni, Ronzoni, zero, zạino, zọö, zabaiọne, ozono, analizzare, azzurro, zodịaco, dozzina, Zạnzibar**	**Z** is voiced (**dz**) as in English *beds*.

Five additional letters of the alphabet appear in many foreign words fully integrated in the Italian language. There is an attempt to pronounce these words as in the original language; however, the results seldom conform to the original pronunciation.

Letter	Italian Name	Example
j	i lunga; i lungo	**jogurt, jolly, jụnior, jazz, judo**
k	cappa	**hockey, kimọno, poker, polka**
w	dọppia vu, vu dọppio	**Walter, watt, welter, sandwich**
x	ics	**taxi, xenofọbia, box, unisex**
y	ịpsilon; i greco	**brandy, sexy, rally, yoga, derby**

SOUNDING OUT THE ALPHABET

When we try to relay to others the correct spelling of a word, especially over the telephone, in English we say things such as: **B** as in **Boy**, **D** as in **David**, etc. In Italy, there is a list of words generally used by Italians. Variations are common. Observe the following:

A(a)	come	**Ancona**	**N(n)**	"	**Nạpoli**
B(b)	"	**Bologna**	**O(o)**	"	**Ọtranto**
C(c)	"	**Como**	**P(p)**	"	**Pạdova**
D(d)	"	**Domodọssola**	**Q(q)**	"	**Quaranta**
E(e)	"	**Ẹmpoli**	**R(r)**	"	**Roma**
F(f)	"	**Firenze**	**S(s)**	"	**Savona**

G(g)	"	Genova	T(t)	"	Torino
H(h)	"	Hotel	U(u)	"	Udine
I(i)	"	Imola	V(v)	"	Venezia
J(j)	"	Jogging	W(w)	"	Washington
K(k)	"	Cappa	X(x)	"	Ics
L(l)	"	Livorno	Y(y)	"	York
M(m)	"	Milano	Z(z)	"	Zara

Vowels (Vocali)

As we have seen, each of the five Italian vowels has one sound and is always articulated the same way. Since the **e** and the **o** can be both closed and open (if properly pronounced), the five vowels can produce seven sounds, as shown in the following diagram. Remember that **e** and **o** are open (ε and ɔ) when stressed, and closed (é and ó) when unstressed.

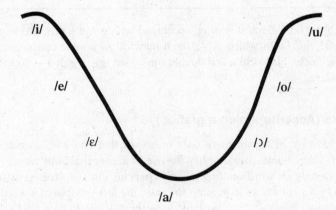

As can be seen, **i** is the first front vowel (**i** as in English *glee*), and **u** is the last back vowel (**u** as in English *cool*).

Single and Double Consonants (Consonanti singole e doppie)

In Italian, the single consonants **b, d, f, l, m, n, p, q, r, s,** and **t**, are usually pronounced as in English.

All consonants may be doubled to produce a longer and more emphatic sound. A trained ear will notice the difference between single and double consonants. Below are some words that differ only in a particular consonant (except for **quadro / soqquadro**).

Single Consonant		Double Consonant	
tufo	*tufa*	**tuffo**	*dive; plunge*
lego	*I tie*	**leggo**	*I read*
ala	*wing*	**alla**	*to the (f.s.)*
gala	*gala*	**galla**	*(a…) afloat*
pala	*shovel*	**palla**	*ball*
capello	*hair*	**cappello**	*hat*
velo	*veil*	**vello**	*fleece*
camino	*fireplace*	**cammino**	*path*
fumo	*smoke*	**fummo**	*we were*

Single Consonant		Double Consonant	
cane	*dog*	canne	*reeds*
nono	*ninth (m. s.)*	nonno	*grandfather*
sono	*I am*	sonno	*sleep*
dona	*gives*	donna	*woman*
papa	*pope*	pappa	*pap; mush*
copia	*copy*	coppia	*couple*
quadro	*picture; painting*	soqquadro	*confusion*
caro	*dear; expensive*	carro	*cart*
casa	*house*	cassa	*cash register*
tuta	*overalls*	tutta	*whole (f. s.)*
note	*notes*	notte	*night*
fato	*fate*	fatto	*fact*
bevi	*you (**tu**) drink*	bevvi	*I drank*

Remember that although the **h** is silent, it is often combined with **c** and **g** (**ch**, **gh**) in order to form guttural hard sounds, /k/ and /g/: **ch**i, per**ch**é, and la**gh**i, **gh**iro. Also, the **h** may follow double consonant -**cc**- (-**cch**-) to form a very emphatic hard /k/ sound — Schi**cch**i, abba**cch**io, and double consonant -**gg**- (-**ggh**-) — to form a very emphatic hard /g/ sound, a**ggh**iacciare, a**ggh**indare.

Stress and Accent Marks (Accento tonico e grafico)

In Italian, the stress is indicated by an accent mark only on words that end with accented vowels. The accents are called grave (`) and acute ('). Many books oversimplify the use of accent marks by always preferring a grave accent. Others utilize the acute accent only on words ending in -**ché** (**perché**, etc.), in -**tré** (**ventitré**, etc.), and others.

In this book, the system of accent marks indicating stress on the last syllable of a word is the very same one used by the Italian publisher Einaudi, arguably the most distinguished of all Italian publishers, and countless others. Considering our location, it is quite significant to note that *Italian Quarterly,* one of the finest journals of Italian literature and culture outside Italy, uses the very same system as Einaudi consistently, from cover to cover, irrespective of the individual author's preference of one system over another.

The system is as follows:

A. The grave accent (`)will be placed on accented final vowels à and ò:

città *city* **civiltà** *civilization* **università** *university* **comò** *chest of drawers*
oblò *porthole* **sarò** *I will be*
Note that the vowels **i** and **u** are closed vowels; when accented, they take the acute accent, -**í**, -**ú**: **tassí**, **tribú**.

B. The acute accent (') will be placed on all other final vowels with the exception of the third-person singular of the verb essere: è (he, she, or it is), cioè (that is), and words of foreign origin such as caffè, tè, karatè, etc:

perché *why; because* **anziché** *instead* **cosí** *so*
capí *he/she understood* **dí** *day* **Corfú** *Corfu* **piú** *more* **virtú** *virtue*
Remember that the Italian vowels **i** and **u** are closed vowels; for this reason in this book they will always appear with an acute accent, **í** and **ú** (as in **cosí** and **Corfú**), whenever they are accented.

C. The grave accent will be placed on accented final vowel -è in words of recent foreign origin:

caffè *coffee* **canapè** *settee, sofa* **karatè** *karate* **tè** *tea*
In all other instances, deciding where the stress falls is problematic. Some general guidelines are as follows:

A. In many Italian words the stress falls on the penult (the next to the last syllable):

ter-ra *earth; dirt* **te-le-gior-na-le** *TV news*
set-ti-ma-na *week* **pat-ti-nag-gio** *skating*

i-ta-lia-no	*Italian*	pa-le-stra	*gym*
An-to-nio	*Anthony*	vi-o-lon-cel-lo	*cello*
com-pra-re	*to buy*	af-fre-schi	*frescoes*
fia-to	*breath*	ca-not-tag-gio	*canoeing*

B. *On just as many other words, if not more, it is difficult to decide. When in doubt, consult a dictionary. Throughout this book, a small dot under the stressed syllable will indicate the correct stress (when the penult syllable is not stressed). Observe the following:*

Ste-fa-no	*Stephen*	ri-di-co-lo	*ridiculous*
sim-pa-ti-co	*nice, pleasant*	fra-gi-le	*fragile*
Um-bria	*Umbria*	mu-si-ca	*music*
cre-de-re	*to believe*	e-di-co-la	*kiosk*
al-be-ro	*tree*	e-no-lo-go	*oenologist*
sem-pli-ce	*simple*	in-ci-de-re	*to engrave*
gon-do-la	*gondola*		

Diphthongs and Triphthongs (Dittonghi e trittonghi)

A. *A diphthong is a syllable comprised of two vowels:*

maggio	*May*	grazie	*thanks*	cuore	*heart*	dialogo	*dialogue*
scuola	*school*	iato	*hiatus*	Fiesole	*Tuscan city*	fiato	*breath*
piuma	*feather*	uomo	*man*	già	*already*	fiamma	*flame*

B. *A triphthong is a syllable comprised of three vowels:*

maiuscolo	capitalized	zabaione (zabaglione)	*type of eggnog*	miei	*my (m. pl.)*
aiuola	*flower bed*	suoi	*her/his/its (m. pl.)*	Suoi	*your* (formal poss. of *Lei*)
guai	*troubles*	vuoi	*you* (tu) *want*	buoi	*oxen*

Hiatus (Lo iato)

The *hiatus* is, like a diphthong, the meeting of two vowels. However, in the *hiatus* the vowels are pronounced separately and constitute two syllables. This happens in the following cases:

　　A. When the vowels involved are neither **i** nor **u**. For example: aorta, museo, poeta, maestro.

　　B. When either the **i** or the **u** is present, but is accented. For example: mania, paura, poesia, zio.

　　C. When a compound verb has the prefix of **ri-**. For example: **ri**entrare, **ri**alzare, **ri**accendere, **ri**ordinare.

Syllabication (Sillabazione)

The names of Italian syllables are as follows:

　　A. Monosillaba (monosyllable): one-syllable word. For example: **tè, gru, tu, re, gnu**.

　　B. Bisillaba (bisyllable): two-syllable word. For example: **li-bro, tre-no, non-ni**.

　　C. Trisillaba (trisyllable): three-syllable word. For example: **gior-na-le, cu-gi-no, To-ri-no**.

　　D. Quadrisillaba (quadrisyllable): four-syllable word. For example: **ab-bron-zar-si, pub-bli-ci-tà, cioc-co-la-ta**.

　　E. Polisillaba (polysyllable): word with two or more syllables without specifying how many. For example: **pen-na, mac-chi-na, gram-ma-ti-ca, te-le-co-man-do, dimenticatelo**.

To divide Italian words into syllables, the following guidelines are suggested:

A. *A single consonant absorbs the vowel that follows it:*

ca-de-re	*to fall*
ce-de-re	*to give in*
pe-pe	*pepper*
ra-gio-ne	*reason*

B. The consonants l, m, n, and r are always separated from any other consonant that follows:

ạl-be-ro	*tree*
cor-sa	*race*
im-pe-ro	*empire*
mạn-cia	*tip*

C. All other groups of two consonants absorb the syllable that follows:

pa-sta	*pasta, dough*
ba-gno	*bath, bathroom*
fị-glia	*daughter*
va-nị-glia	*vanilla*

D. Double consonants are divided:

bas-so	*short*
pan-na	*cream*
son-no	*sleep*
pẹg-gio	*worse*
fet-ta	*slice*

E. When three consonants appear together other than initially, the first one is absorbed by the preceding syllable. Observe the following:

sẹm-pli-ce	*simple*
den-tro	*inside*
Lon-dra	*London*
In-ghil-ter-ra	*England*

F. When the vowels i and u are unstressed, they will be absorbed by the vowel that follows:

chiụ-so	*closed*
schiụ-ma	*foam*
uọ-mi-ni	*men*
chiẹ-sa	*church*
chiạ-ve	*key*

Punctuation and Orthographic Marks (Punteggiatura e segni ortogrạfici)

.	il punto; il punto fermo
,	la vịrgola
;	il punto e vịrgola
:	i due punti
?	il punto interrogativo
!	il punto esclamativo
...	i puntini di sospensiọne
<< >>	le virgolette
-	il trattino
–	la lineẹtta
*	l'asterisco
/	la sbarretta
()	le parẹntesi tonde
[]	le parẹntesi quạdre
`	l'accento grave
´	l'accento acuto
{	la sgraffa

,	l'apostrofo
··	la dieresi *(rarely used)*
^	l'accento circonflesso *(rarely used)*

1. Identify and write in the same order in which they appear below all those words which contain the sound ch as in English chart. Review the chart, page 1.

ciao	Cuba	continente	ciarlatano		ceppo	chiaro	cinico	perché	cencio
chiave	Vincenzo	scena	ciò		bicicletta	richiamo	cinque	baci	questo

1. _____   6. _____
2. _____   7. _____
3. _____   8. _____
4. _____   9. _____
5. _____   10. _____

2. Identify and write in the same order in which they appear below all those words which contain the sound of k as in English key or cup. Review the chart, page 1.

cena   coppa   mancia   chiave   perché   come   ceci   Corfú   cinici   chimica   parco   chiesa
aceto   credito   Chieti

1. _____   6. _____
2. _____   7. _____
3. _____   8. _____
4. _____   9. _____
5. _____   10. _____

3. Identify and write in the order in which they appear below all those words which contain the sound of e as in English bet or fake. Review the chart, page 1.

vero   faro   tenda   bella   auto   ferro   ma   cane   navi   neve

1. _____   5. _____
2. _____   6. _____
3. _____   7. _____
4. _____

4. Identify and write, keeping the word order the same, all those words from the list below which contain the sound of g as in English George. Review the chart, page 1.

gatto   Gino   laghi   gente   gonna   giovane   rogo   ragione   vaga   grigi   vanga   giacca

1. _____   4. _____
2. _____   5. _____
3. _____   6. _____

5. Identify and write, keeping the word order the same, all those words from the list below which contain the sound of g as in English go. Review the chart, pages 1–2.

gloria   Giorgio   ghiro   glicine   gemma   gioia   ghetto   gatta   foglia   laghi   aglio   ghiaccio
gomma   valige   gas   aghi

1. _____   6. _____
2. _____   7. _____
3. _____   8. _____
4. _____   9. _____
5. _____   10. _____

6. Keeping the word order the same, identify and write out, all those words from the list below contain that the sound of the IPA phoneme /‹ɲ›/. Review the chart, p. 2.

ragno   raggio   cognome   segno   bagnino   luglio   giugno   lavanderia   bagno   lavagna
rullino   disegno   mambo   lasagne   tengo   legno

1. _____   6. _____
2. _____   7. _____
3. _____   8. _____
4. _____   9. _____
5. _____   10. _____

7. Review the chart on the pronunciation of h, page 2, and write below ali the Italian examples given in the chart.

1. _____   5. _____
2. _____   6. _____
3. _____   7. _____
4. _____

8. Keeping the same word order, identify and write out all those words from the list below whose sound corresponds approximately with the ll in English million or scallion.

glaciale   luglio   globo   glutine   meglio   sbagli   gloria   ammiraglio   anglicano   svegliare
svogliato   negletto   maglione   snello   rullino   figli   gli   quelli   foglie

1. _____   6. _____
2. _____   7. _____
3. _____   8. _____
4. _____   9. _____
5. _____   10. _____

9. Identify and write all those words from the list below that contain a sound that corresponds with the vowel sound in English feet. (Keep the same word order.) Review the chart, page 2.

penna   tipo   riso   cena   fame   zio   vino   vena   Cina   Genova   Milano   diva   neve   farina

1. _____   5. _____
2. _____   6. _____
3. _____   7. _____
4. _____   8. _____

10. From the words listed below, choose and write, in the order of appearance, those words that produce the initial sound of z as in English zero (because of the voiced s in Italian). Review the chart, page 3.

sole   scopa   smaltire   sbagli   spazio   sale   smania   sbarbare   snob   sgabello   smog   svanire

1. _____   4. _____
2. _____   5. _____
3. _____   6. _____

11. From the words below showing intervocalic -s-, identify and write those words that have an unvoiced intervocalic -s- and produce the sound of s as in English son. (Keep the word order the same.) Review the chart, page 3.

quasi   cosí   cosa   rosa   caso   girasole   desiderio   controsenso   invaso   preside   frase
autoservizio   chiesa   risentire

1. _____   5. _____
2. _____   6. _____
3. _____   7. _____
4. _____   8. _____

12. From the words below, identify and write, in the same order in which they appear, those words with the sound of sh as in English shoe. Review the chart, page 3.

schiena   sci   uscita   sciopero   scherzo   boschi   lasciare   scarpa   scena   bacio   sciolto
scendere   scala   sceicco

1. _____   5. _____
2. _____   6. _____
3. _____   7. _____
4. _____   8. _____

13. From the words below, identify and write those words that contain a voiced dz, as in English beds, under Column A, and identify and write under Column B those words that contain an unvoiced ts, as in English bets. Maintain the order in which the words appear, as much as possible. Review the chart, page 4.

zio   zie   zero   zaino   zucchero   terzo   zabaione   grazie   zoö   calza   Manzoni   ozono
zodiaco   pazienza   Firenze   zelo

A	B
1. _____	1. _____
2. _____	2. _____
3. _____	3. _____
4. _____	4. _____
5. _____	5. _____
6. _____	6. _____
7. _____	7. _____
8. _____	8. _____

14. Review the chart under Sounding Out the Alphabet (p. 4) and place the appropriate word in the spaces provided.

1. F	come	_____	8. Y	come	_____
2. Z	"	_____	9. G	"	_____
3. D	"	_____	10. L	"	_____
4. U	"	_____	11. E	"	_____
5. I	"	_____	12. W	"	_____
6. O	"	_____	13. A	"	_____
7. K	"	_____	14. S	"	_____

15. Review the five foreign letters (page 4), found in Italian words of foreign origin, and write next to each bold letter below the first three words given as examples in the chart for each foreign letter.

1. j	(a) _____	(b) _____	(c)_____
2. k	(a) _____	(b) _____	(c)_____
3. w	(a) _____	(b) _____	(c)_____
4. x	(a) _____	(b) _____	(c)_____
5. y	(a) _____	(b) _____	(c)_____

16. To the right of each word with a single consonant, write a corresponding word with a double consonant as found in the chart, pages 5 and 6.

Single Consonant   *Double Consonant*
1. capello   1. _____
2. nono   2. _____
3. tuta   3. _____
4. casa   4. _____
5. cane   5. _____
6. papa   6. _____
7. pala   7. _____

8. dona   8. _____
9. copia   9. _____
10. quadro   10. _____

17. *All of the words below are stressed on the last syllable and are written on purpose without the appropriate accent. Review the section Stress and Accent Marks, pages 6 and 7, and place the correct accent as explained in parts A and B. Rewrite the words, keeping them in the order in which they appear.*

virtu   papa   e   parti   visito   carita   cosi   perche   lunedi   citta

1._____   6. _____
2._____   7. _____
3._____   8. _____
4._____   9. _____
5._____   10. _____

18. *In the spaces provided under each category, write out, in the order they appear, the words corresponding to each category. Review the diphthongs, triphthongs, and hiatus, p. 7.*

paura   luglio   aorta   buoi   guai   zabaione   Fiesole   scuola   rientrare   museo   iato
cuore   poeta   suoi   maiuscolo   zio   aiuola   uomo

Dittonghi	*Trittonghi*	*Iati*
1. _____	7. _____	13. _____
2. _____	8. _____	14. _____
3. _____	9. _____	15. _____
4. _____	10. _____	16. _____
5. _____	11. _____	17. _____
6. _____	12. _____	18. _____

19. *In the spaces provided under each category, write out, in the order they appear, the words corresponding to each category. Review the Syllabication section, pages 7 and 8.*

parentesi   gnu   Torino   caffè   tu   vaniglia   Angela   mercoledí   peggio   mancia
Inghilterra   Russia   inverno   gru   asterisco   Reggio   re   apostrofo   Firenze

Monosillaba	*Bisillaba*	*Trisillaba*	*Quadrisillaba*
1._____	6._____	11._____	16._____
2._____	7._____	12._____	17._____
3._____	8._____	13._____	18._____
4._____	9._____	14._____	19._____
5._____	10._____	15._____	20._____

20. *Rewrite the words below, keeping the same order in which they appear, showing the separation of syllables within each word (e.g., cucina cu-ci-na). Review Syllabication, page 9.*

magnifico   cugino   maggio   giugno   ragazzi   marrone   Angelo   Giuseppe   coniglio
semplicemente   fiato   Italia   mamma   padre   Firenze   Domodossola   Stefania   mercoledí
costare   scimmia

1._____   11. _____
2._____   12. _____
3._____   13. _____
4._____   14. _____
5._____   15. _____
6._____   16. _____
7._____   17. _____
8._____   18. _____
9._____   19. _____
10._____   20. _____

21. Next to each punctuation or orthographic mark below, write its Italian name. Review the chart, pages 8 and 9.

1. ! _____
2. << >> _____
3. ` _____
4. . _____
5. , _____
6. / _____
7. … _____
8. [] _____
9. ' _____
10. ^ _____

11. * _____
12. () _____
13. { _____
14. ? _____
15. ¨ _____
16. ; _____
17. - _____
18. : _____
19. — _____
20. ' _____

REVIEW

22. Enter in each space provided an appropriate word from the list below that corresponds with the underlined sound produced by the English word in parentheses, and fits well in the context of each sentence.

ciao	aceto	svogliato	caro	zio	casa	sciopero
prezzo	cencio	Gino	sci	chiesa	perché	chiavi
ghiaccio	meglio	sbarbo	sempre	scuola	sbagli	uscita

1. Anna ed io ci diciamo _____. (*chat*)
2. Nell'insalata metto solo olio e _____. (*bet*)
3. Mio _____ e mia zia sono meravigliosi. (*deed*)
4. Quando scrive, Pietro fa troppi _____. (*zero*)
5. Quel ristorante è troppo _____. (*cat*)
6. È troppo tardi! Andiamo a _____. (*son*)
7. Giorgio non studia, è molto _____. (*million*)
8. Queste _____ aprono tutte le porte. (*key*)
9. Prima di andare a sciare devo comprare un paio di _____. (*shop*)
10. In inverno qui c'è molto _____. (*get*)
11. Dammi un _____, devo pulire il banco. (*china*).
12. La _____ elementare dura per ben cinque anni. (*son*)
13. È _____ non uscire troppo tardi! (*million*)
14. Non telefono a Pietro _____ non mi risponde. (*keg*)
15. A destra c'è l'entrata e a sinistra c'è l'_____. (*ship*)
16. Paolo e _____ sono dei bravi ragazzi. (*jet*)
17. Io mi _____ ogni mattina. (*zero*)
18. Lo _____ ferroviario durerà poco. (*shop*)
19. Il _____ di queste scarpe è modico. (*bets*)
20. Vanno in _____ la domenica. (*leg*)

23. In the spaces provided indicate the appropriate symbols.

1. le parentesi quadre: _____
2. l'accento acuto: _____
3. le virgolette: _____
4. il punto (punto fermo): _____
5. la sbarretta: _____
6. l'asterisco: _____
7. l'accento grave: _____
8. il punto interrogativo: _____
9. il trattino: _____
10. le parentesi tonde: _____
11. il punto esclamativo: _____

12. l'apostrofo: _____

13. la virgola: _____

14. i due punti: _____

15. i puntini di sospensione: _____

24. *All the words below are accented on the last syllable. Supply the appropriate accents as described in this book on p. 6.*

1. universita
2. como
3. venerdi
4. servitu
5. affinche

6. purche
7. si
8. cioe
9. te
10. karate

25. *Rewrite each word and separate it into syllables.*

1. coppia: _____

2. Urbino: _____

3. meraviglioso: _____

4. babbo: _____

5. Stefano: _____

6. Marcello: _____

7. chiesa: _____

8. Siena: _____

9. marittimo: _____

10. bellissimo: _____

11. caffè: _____

12. sbarretta: _____

13. interrogativo: _____

14. uomini: _____

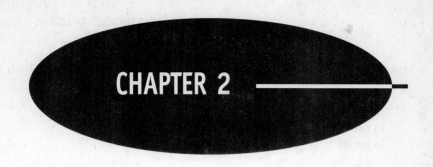

CHAPTER 2

Nouns and Articles

NOUNS

Nouns Ending in *-o* and *-a*

Singular forms

The Italian noun, unlike its English counterpart, has a gender. Those nouns that refer specifically to a man, such as *father*, *brother*, etc., are masculine. Those nouns that refer specifically to a woman, such as *mother*, *sister*, etc., are feminine.

For all other nouns it is necessary to learn the proper gender. The problem is not quite so complex as it may at first appear. Italian nouns can be classified into gender groups according to their endings. Almost all nouns that end in **-o** are masculine, and almost all nouns that end in **-a** are feminine. The Italian equivalents of the definite article *the* are **il, lo, l', la, l', i, gli, gl', le, l'**.

Masculine		*Feminine*	
il ragazzo	*boy*	**la ragazza**	*girl*
il fratello	*brother*	**la sorella**	*sister*
il nonno	*grandfather*	**la nonna**	*grandmother*
il maestro	*teacher*	**la maestra**	*teacher*
lo zio	*uncle*	**la zia**	*aunt*
il libro	*book*	**la scuola**	*school*
il quaderno	*notebook*	**la penna**	*pen*
il museo	*museum*	**la chiesa**	*church*
il negozio	*store*	**la casa**	*house*
l'attico	*attic*	**l'aula**	*classroom*
il supermercato	*supermarket*	**la campagna**	*countryside*
il bosco	*woods*	**la spiaggia**	*beach*
il centro	*center*	**la bicicletta**	*bicycle*

The definite article *the* must agree with the noun it modifies. The definite article **il** is placed before most masculine singular (m. s.) nouns.

il ragazzo	*boy*
il porto	*harbor*
il vino	*wine*

Lo is placed before all masculine singular nouns beginning with **z**, **s** plus a consonant, **ps**, or **gn**.

lo zio	*uncle*
lo studio	*study*
lo psicologo	*psychologist*
lo gnomo	*gnome*

L' is placed before all masculine singular nouns beginning with a vowel.

l'amico	*friend*
l'albero	*tree*
l'euro	*euro*
l'inverno	*winter*
l'italiano	*Italian*

The definite article **la** is placed before all feminine singular (f. s.) nouns that begin with a consonant.

la casa	*house*
la strada	*street*
la zia	*aunt*
la scuola	*school*

L' is placed before all feminine singular nouns that begin with a vowel.

l'amica	*friend*
l'aranciata	*orangeade*
l'estate	*summer*
l'entrata	*entrance*

1. **Complete the following nouns with the appropriate ending:**

   1. Il negozi o_____ è moderno.
   2. La scuol a_____ è nuova.
   3. Il ragazz o_____ è buono.
   4. L'uom o_____ è bravo.
   5. La nonn a_____ è vecchia.
   6. Lo zain _____ è rosso.
   7. La zi _____ è simpatica.
   8. Il libr _____ è piccolo.
   9. L'aul _____ è bella.
   10. Il fratell _____ è alto.
   11. La signor _____ è americana.
   12. Lo studi _____ è magnifico.
   13. Il muse _____ è bello.
   14. La sorell _____ è carina.

2. **Complete the following with the correct form of the definite article: il, la, l', or lo:**

   1. _____la_____ ragazza compra _____il_____ cappello.
   2. _____ zio porta _____ regalo.
   3. _____ maestro insegna _____ grammatica.
   4. _____ signora guida _____ macchina.
   5. _____ stadio è pieno di gente.
   6. _____ nonno fuma _____ pipa.
   7. _____ ragazzo porta _____ cravatta.
   8. _____ uomo compra _____ automobile.
   9. _____ proprietario chiude _____ negozio.
   10. _____ signorina visita _____ museo.

Plural forms

In order to form the plural (pl.) of nouns ending in **-o** or **-a**, the **-o** is changed to **-i**, and the **-a** is changed to **-e**. The definite article **il** changes to **i** (m. pl.) and **la** changes to **le** (f. pl.).

il ragazzo → i ragazzi   la ragazza → le ragazze
il maestro → i maestri   la maestra → le maestre
il nonno → i nonni   la nonna → le nonne
il museo → i musei   la zia → le zie
il libro → i libri   la casa → le case

The plural of **lo** and **l'** (with masculine nouns) is **gli**. **Gli** may be contracted to **gl'** with masculine plural nouns beginning with the vowel **i**.

lo zio	gli zii	*uncle*
lo studente	gli studenti	*student*
l'euro	gli euro	*euro*
l'amico	gli amici	*friend*
l'inverno	gli inverni (gl'inverni)	*winter*
l'abito	gli abiti	*suit*

The plural of **l'** (with feminine nouns) is **le**. **Le** may be contracted to **l'** with feminine plural nouns beginning with the vowel **e**.

l'aranciata → le aranciate
l'amica → le amiche
l'entrata → le entrate (l'entrate)
l'ora → le ore

3. Rewrite the following sentences in the plural according to the model:

Il ragazzo è bello. → I ragazzi sono belli.
La maestra è italiana. → Le maestre sono italiane.

1. La signora è alta.
2. Il libro è piccolo.
3. La nonna è vecchia.
4. La scuola è nuova.
5. Il nonno è bravo.
6. La ragazza è alta.
7. La professoressa è americana.
8. Il quaderno è giallo.
9. Il maestro è buono.
10. La cravatta è rossa.

4. Complete the following with the correct form of the definite article:

1. _____i_____ ragazzi sono italiani.
2. _____le_____ studentesse studiano molto.
3. _____gli_____ amici di Carlo sono simpatici.
4. _____i_____ dizionari sono importanti.
5. _____le_____ case sono rosse.
6. _____le_____ zie e _____gli_____ zii viaggiano molto.
7. _____gli_____ sbagli sono di Pietro.
8. _____i_____ cugini di Rosa sono in casa.
9. _____gli'_____ inverni sono molto duri.
10. _____le l'_____ entrate sono aperte.

Nouns Ending in *-e*

Nouns ending in -ore are masculine:

amore	*love*	**motore**	*motor*
rigore	*rigor; penalty* (in soccer)	**timore**	*fear*
fiore	*flower*	**rancore**	*grudge*
dottore	*doctor*	**onore**	*honor*
professore	*professor*	**rumore**	*noise*

Nouns ending in -ione are usually feminine:

azione	*action*	**attenzione**	*attention*
lezione	*lesson*	**conversazione**	*conversation*
ragione	*reason*	**stagione**	*season*
stazione	*station*	**nazione**	*nation*
manutenzione	*maintenance*	**promozione**	*promotion*

Nouns referring to human beings

Nouns ending in **-e** can be either masculine or feminine. Many of these nouns refer to people, and the gender of the noun is usually determined by the sex of the person referred to.

il parente	*relative*	**la parente**	*relative*
il cantante	*singer*	**la cantante**	*singer*
il nipote	*nephew, grandson*	**la nipote**	*niece, granddaughter*
il minorenne	*minor*	**la minorenne**	*minor*
il paziente	*patient*	**la paziente**	*patient*
il consorte	*spouse*	**la consorte**	*spouse*

Nouns referring to things

It is difficult to guess the gender of nouns ending in **-e** which do not refer to human beings. This is due to the fact that there is a vast number of both masculine and feminine nouns ending in **-e**. Below is a list of some common masculine nouns that end in **-e**. When modified by a regular adjective, the gender is seen in the adjective (see exercise 5, below).

il giornale	*newspaper*	**il fiume**	*river*
il canale	*canal*	**il fiore**	*flower*
il pane	*bread*	**il ponte**	*bridge*
il baule	*trunk*	**il mare**	*sea*
il nome	*name*	**il piede**	*foot*

Feminine nouns

Below is a list of some common feminine nouns ending in **-e**. Note that all nouns ending in **–zione** are feminine.

la frase	*sentence*	**la sete**	*thirst*
la classe	*class; classroom*	**la nave**	*ship*
la notte	*night*	**la capitale**	*capital*
la chiave	*key*	**la carne**	*meat*
la fine	*end*	**la gente**	*people*
la canzone	*song*	**la nazione**	*nation*

Forming the plural

Most nouns ending in **-e** in the singular, be they masculine or feminine, form their plural by changing **-e** to **-i**.

i padri	*fathers*	**le madri**	*mothers*
i presidenti	*presidents*	**le classi**	*classes*
gli studenti	*students*	**le chiavi**	*keys*
i nomi	*names*	**le navi**	*ships*
i dottori	*doctors*	**le notti**	*nights*
i fiori	*flowers*		

5. Complete the following sentences with the appropriate definite article:

1. _____ cantante è simpatica.
2. _____ dottore è famoso.
3. _____ padre è buono.
4. _____ presidente è vecchio.
5. _____ portone è vecchio.
6. _____ studente è bravo.
7. _____ nipote è brava.
8. _____ nome è lungo.
9. _____ carne è costosa.
10. _____ nave è grandissima.
11. _____ lezione è lunga.
12. _____ stazione ferroviaria è grandissima.
13. _____ fiore è rosso.
14. _____ manutenzione è costosa.

6. Complete the following with the correct definite article:

1. _____ pane è buono.
2. È _____ fine della pellicola (*movie*)?
3. _____ ponte attraversa_____ fiume.
4. _____ gente canta_____ canzone.
5. Come si chiama _____ canale?

7. Rewrite the following sentences in the plural according to the model:

La classe è allegra. → Le classi sono allegre.

1. La classe è allegra.
2. La madre è generosa.
3. Il dottore è famoso.
4. Il padre è generoso.
5. La canzone è melodiosa.
6. La nave è bella.
7. Lo studente è alto.
8. Il cantante è bravo.
9. La chiave è piccola.

Masculine Nouns Ending in -a

There are some masculine nouns which end in **-a**. Many of these nouns are derived from Greek roots. Below is a list of those most commonly used.

il clima	*climate*	**il pilota**	*pilot*
il programma	*program*	**il poema**	*poem*
il dramma	*drama*	**il sistema**	*system*
il poeta	*poet*	**il papa**	*pope*
il pianeta	*planet*	**il problema**	*problem*
il tema	*theme*		

The plural of such nouns ends in **-i**.

i programmi   **i drammi**

Note that many nouns ending in **-ista** refer to professions. These nouns are masculine when specifically referring to a man and feminine when specifically referring to a woman. The masculine plural ends in **-isti** and the feminine plural ends in **-iste**. Observe the following:

Masculine	*Feminine*
il dentista → i dentisti	**la dentista → le dentiste**
il violinista → i violinisti	**la violinista → le violiniste**
il giornalista → i giornalisti	**la giornalista → le giornaliste**
il farmacista → i farmacisti	**la farmacista → le farmaciste**
il pianista → i pianisti	**la pianista → le pianiste**
l'artista → gli artisti	**l'artista → le artiste**
il telecronista → i telecronisti	**la telecronista → le telecroniste**

8. Complete the following sentences with an appropriate word from the lists above. Supply also the definite article:

1. _____ di questa regione è tropicale.
2. _____ televisivo è interessante.
3. _____ suona il violino, ed è brava.
4. _____ scolastico è complicato.
5. _____ è messo in scena al teatro Roma.
6. _____ compone poesie.

9. Give the plural of the following words.

1. il poema
2. il dramma
3. la dentista
4. il farmacista
5. il pianeta

6. il pilota
7. la giornalista
8. la pianista
9. il telecronista
10. il dentista

Feminine Nouns Ending in *-o*

Several common nouns ending in **-o** are feminine. Below is a list of these nouns. Note that only the noun **mano** (*hand*) changes spelling in the plural; the others listed here do not.

la mano → le mani	*hand*
la foto [fotografia] → le foto [fotografie]	*photograph*
la dinamo → le dinamo	*dynamo*
la radio → le radio	*radio*
l'auto [automobile] → le auto [automobili]	*automobile, car*
la moto [motocicletta] → le moto (motociclette)	*motorcycle*

10. Rewrite the following sentences in the plural:

1. La radio è istruttiva.
2. La dinamo è utile.
3. La foto è bella.
4. Il bambino è carino.
5. L'auto è rossa.
6. La moto è giapponese.

Plural of Nouns Ending in *-ca* and *-ga*[1]

Feminine nouns ending in **-ca** and **-ga** form their plural in **-che** and **-ghe**, thus preserving the hard sound of the **c** and **g** of the singular.

la barca → le barche	*boat*
l'amica → le amiche	*friend*
la mosca → le mosche	*fly*
la formica → le formiche	*ant*
la pesca → le pesche	*peach*
l'oca → le oche	*duck*
la diga → le dighe	*dam*
la ruga → le rughe	*wrinkle*
la collega → le colleghe	*colleague (f)*
la tunica → le tuniche	*tunic*

11. *Pluralize the following sentences according to the model:*

L'amica è brava. → **Le amiche sono brave.**
La diga è grandissima. → **Le dighe sono grandissime.**

1. La collega è americana.
2. L'oca è grassa.
3. La pesca è deliziosa.
4. La formica è piccola.
5. La ruga è naturale.
6. La mosca è seccante.
7. La tunica è bianca.
8. La barca è rossa.

Also note that some nouns ending in **-ca** and **-ga** are masculine. Masculine nouns ending in **-ca** and **-ga** form their plural in **-chi** and **-ghi**. For example:

il monarca → i monarchi	*monarch*
il patriarca → i patriarchi	*patriarch*
il duca → i duchi	*duke*
il collega → i colleghi	*colleague (m)*

Plural of Masculine Nouns Ending in *-co* and *-go*

Most masculine nouns, but not all, ending in **-co** and **-go** form their plural in **-chi** and **-ghi**, thus preserving the hard sound of the **c** and **g** of the singular.

il cuoco → i cuochi	*cook*
il parco → i parchi	*park*
il manico → i manichi (also: manici)	*handle*
l'albicocco → gli albicocchi	*apricot tree*
il palco → i palchi	*stage*
il sacco → i sacchi	*sack*
l'arco → gli archi	*arch*
il luogo → i luoghi	*place*
l'obbligo → gli obblighi	*duty*
il prologo → i prologhi	*prologue*
il dialogo → i dialoghi	*dialog*
il catalogo → i cataloghi	*catalog*

---

[1]For a better understanding of these sounds and others, always review chapter 1.

12. Pluralize the following sentences according to the models:
Il diạlogo è breve. → I diạloghi sono brevi.
Il sacco è vuọto. → l sacchi sono vuọti.

1. Il sacco è pesante.
2. Il diạlogo è difficile.
3. Il chirurgo è giọvane.
4. Il monọlogo è tediọso.

5. Il fuọco è pericoloso.
6. Il luọgo è vicino.
7. Il catạlogo è questo!
8. L'ọbbligo è mụtuo.

You will also note that many masculine nouns ending in **-co** and **-go** form their plural in **-ci** and **-gi**.

l'amico → gli amici	*friend*	
il greco → i greci	*Greek*	
il mẹdico → i mẹdici	*doctor*	
il nemico → i nemici	*enemy*	
il pạrroco → i pạrroci	*parish priest*	
l'astrọlogo → gli astrọlogi	*astrologer*	

l'aspạrago → gli aspạragi	*asparagus*
il filọlogo → i filọlogi	*philologist*
il teọlogo → i teọlogi	*theologist*

13. Pluralize the following sentences according to the models:
Il nemico è pericoloso. → I nemici sono pericolosi.
Il filọlogo è famoso. → I filọlogi sono famosi.

1. Il mọnaco è religiọso.
2. Il teọlogo è studiọso.
3. Il pạrroco è devoto.
4. L'aspạrago è gustoso.
5. Il pọrtico è alto.

Plural of Masculine Nouns Ending in *-io*

Masculine nouns ending in **-io** usually form their plural in **-i**.

il guạio → i guại	*trouble*
lo spẹcchio → gli specchi	*mirror*
l'uffịcio → gli uffici	*office*
l'armạdio → gli armadi	*closet*
lo stụdio → gli studi	*study*
l'inịzio → gli inịzi (gl'inịzi)	*beginning*

14. Pluralize the following sentences:
1. L'uffịcio è spaziọso.
2. Il dizionạrio è grosso.
3. Lo stụdio è di Mạrio.
4. Lo stạdio è immenso.
5. L'inịzio è importante.
6. L'esẹmpio è buono.
7. L'empọrio è ben fornito.
8. L'armạdio è pieno.
9. L'ụscio è aperto.
10. L'esercịzio è difficile.

Also note that when the **-i** of **-io** is stressed, the plural of **-io** is **-ii**.

lo zịo → gli zịi	*uncle*
il fruscịo → i fruscịi	*rustle*

Nouns with Two plurals (Feminine and Masculine) and Two Meanings

There are certain masculine singular nouns that have two plurals, one masculine and one feminine, each with a different meaning. Observe the following:

Singular	*Plural Masculine*	*Plural Feminine*
l'anello (*link [of a chain]*; pl. **anella**: *hair ringlets*; *ring [wedding ring,* etc.])	**gli anelli** (di una catena) (*links of a chain*)	**le anella** (dei capelli) (*hair ringlets*)
il ciglio (*eyelash*; *border*; *side [of a road, of a wound,* etc.])	**i cigli** (della strada) (*the sides of the road*)	**le ciglia** (degli occhi) (*eyelashes*)
il dito (*finger*)	**i diti** (diti indici, diti mignoli, ecc.) (*index fingers,* etc.)	**le dita** (della mano) (*the fingers of the hand*)
il filo (*thread*; *yarn*; *wire [electric, barbed,* etc.]; *blade [of grass]*	**i fili** (della luce; d'erba) (*electric wires*; *blades of grass*)	**le fila** (della tela) (*the threads of cloth*)
il gesto (*gesture*; *deed*)	**i gesti** (movimenti) (*physical* **gestures**)	**le gesta** (le imprese) (*great deeds*)
il ginocchio (*knee*; same meaning in both plurals)	**i ginocchi** (m. pl. of ginocchio)	**le ginocchia** (f. pl. of **ginocchio**)
il grido (*the cry*)	**i gridi** (di una persona) (*the cries of one person*)	**le grida** (di molte persone) (*the cries of many people*)
il lenzuolo (*sheet*)	**i lenzuoli** (separati) (*the sheets,* when separate)	**le lenzuola** (a paia) (*the sheets,* when paired)
il membro (*limb [anat.]*; *member [of a club,* etc.]	**i membri** (di un'associazione) (*members of an association, a club, a committee,* etc.)	**le membra** (umane) (*human limbs*)
il muro (*wall [of a room]*)	**i muri** (di una stanza) (*the walls of a room*)	**le mura** (di una città) (*the walls of a city*)
l'orecchio (*ear*; same meaning in both plurals)	**gli orecchi** (anatomicamente) (*ears [anatomical]*)	**le orecchie** (anatomicamente) (*ears [anatomical]*)
il riso (*rice*; *laughter*)	**i risi** (alimentazione) (*rices [foodstuff]*)	**le risa** (umane) (*human laughter*)

15. Supply the masculine plural (A) and the feminine plural (B) of the following words (including the appropriate definite articles), taking into consideration the explanations in parentheses:

1. il muro: A: _____ (*the walls of a room*)
              B: _____ (*the walls of a city*)

2. il gesto: A: _____ (*physical gestures*)
              B: _____ (*great deeds*)

3. l'anello: A: _____ (*the links of a chain*)
              B: _____ (*hair ringlets*)

4. il ciglio: A: _____ (*the sides of a road*)
              B: _____ (*the eyelashes*)

5. il riso: A. _____ (*the rices [foodstuff]*)
              B. _____ (*human laughter,* pl.)

6. il lenzuolo: A. _____ (*sheets seen separately*)
              B. _____ (*sheets in pairs*)

7. il dito: A. _____ (*specific fingers*: i.e. *index fingers*, etc.)
                            B. _____ (*the fingers of the hand*, as a unit)
8. il grido: A. _____ (*the cries of one person*)
                            B. _____ (*the cries of many people*)
9. il membro: A. _____ (*the members of a club*)
                            B. _____ (*human limbs*)
10. il filo: A. _____ (*electric wires*; *blades of grass*)
                            B. _____ (*the threads of cloth*)

Masculine Nouns with Feminine Plurals

Certain masculine nouns ending in **-o** in the singular become feminine in the plural by changing **-o** to **-a**.

il dito → le dita	*finger*
il paio → le paia	*pair*
l'uovo → le uova	*egg*
il miglio → le miglia	*mile*
il braccio → le braccia	*arm*
il ciglio → le ciglia	*eyebrow*
il lenzuolo → le lenzuola	*sheet* (pl. paired sheets)

16. Pluralize the following sentences:

1. Il lenzuolo è bianco.
2. L'uovo è sodo.
3. Il braccio è lungo.
4. Il dito è piccolino.
5. Il ginocchio è duro.
6. Il ciglio è nero.

Plural of Feminine Nouns Ending in *-cia* and *-gia*

Feminine nouns ending in **-cia** and **-gia** usually form their plural in **-ce** and **-ge**. (Exception: **camicia → camicie**.)

la doccia → le docce	*shower*
la goccia → le gocce	*drop*
la frangia → le frange	*fringe*
la guancia → le guance	*cheek*
la pioggia → le piogge	*rain*
la valigia → le valige	*suitcase*

17. Pluralize the following sentences:

1. La coscia di pollo è deliziosa.
2. La roccia è pericolosa.
3. La doccia calda è buona.
4. La pioggia è piacevole.
5. La fascia è bianca.
6. La frangia è delicata.

Also note that when the **-i-** of **–cia** and **-gia** is stressed, the plural is **-cie** and **-gie**.

la scia → le scie	*trail*
la farmacia → le farmacie	*drugstore*
la bugia → le bugie	*lie*

Plural of Nouns Ending with a Stressed Vowel

Masculine and feminine nouns ending with a stressed vowel do not change in the plural.
Masculine:

il colibrí → i colibrí	*hummingbrid*	**il ragú → i ragú**	*meat sauce ; stew*
il comò → i comò	*chest of drawers*	**il sofà → i sofà**	*sofa; couch*
il cucú → i cucú	*cuckoo*	**il tabú → i tabú**	*taboo*

Feminine:

la città → le città	*city*	**l'università → le università**	*university*
la quantità → le quantità	*quantity*	**la verità → le verità**	*truth*
la tribú → le tribú	*tribe*	**la virtú → le virtú**	*virtue*

Nouns ending in **-i** in the singular function the same as nouns ending with a stressed vowel. They do not change in the plural.

la crisi → le crisi	*crisis*
la tesi → le tesi	*thesis*
il brindisi → i brindisi	*cheer*
la bici [bicicletta] → le bici [biciclette]	*bicycle*
l'alibi → gli alibi	*alibi*

18. *Pluralize the following sentences:*

1. La tribú è isolata.
2. L'università è necessaria.
3. Il brindisi è spiritoso.
4. Questo caffè è forte.
5. La città è affollata.
6. La crisi è severa.

Plural of Monosyllabic Nouns

Masculine and feminine one-syllable nouns do not change their spelling in the plural.

il re → i re	*king*
il tè → i tè	*tea*
il dí → i dí	*day—same as* **giorno**
la gru → le gru	*crane*

19. *Pluralize the following sentences:*

1. Il tè è delizioso.
2. Il dí è lungo.
3. La gru è alta.
4. Il re è vecchio.

Irregular Plural Nouns

The following nouns are completely irregular in the plural. Note also that **gli** accompanies **dèi** in the plural, contrary to all rules.

l'ala → le ali	*wing*
il bue → i buoi	*ox*
il tempio → i templi	*temple*
il dio → gli dèi	*god*
la moglie → le mogli	*wife*
l'uomo → gli uomini	*man*

20. *Complete each sentence with an appropriate noun from the list of irregular plural nouns above.*

1. Gli uccelli hanno le _____.
2. Non c'è solamente un bue, ci sono due _____.
3. I membri della tribú credono in molti _____.
4. I signori sono venuti con le loro _____.
5. Non parla di un uomo; parla di due _____.
6. Ad Agrigento ci sono i famosi _____ greci.

Masculine and Feminine Endings of the Same Noun

Certain masculine nouns become feminine by changing their final vowel to **-a**.

il sarto	tailor	**la sarta**	dressmaker
il figlio	son	**la figlia**	daughter
il signore	gentleman	**la signora**	lady
il marchese	marquis	**la marchesa**	marchioness
il padrone	boss, owner	**la padrona**	boss, owner
l'infermiere	nurse	**l'infermiera**	nurse

Most masculine nouns ending in **-tore** become feminine by changing **-tore** to **-trice**. (Exceptions: **tintore → tintora** *dyer*; **avventore → avventora** *customer*; **impostore → impostora** *impostor.*)

l'attore → l'attrice	actor
l'autore → l'autrice	author
lo stiratore → la stiratrice	presser
il lavoratore → la lavoratrice	worker
il traditore → la traditrice (*also:* **traditora**)	traitor

Certain masculine nouns become feminine by replacing their final vowel with **-essa**.

lo studente	student → **la studentessa**	student
l'oste	host → **l'ostessa**	hostess
il principe	prince → **la principessa**	princess
il poeta	poet → **la poetessa**	poet
il sacerdote	priest → **la sacerdotessa**	high priestess
il conte	count → **la contessa**	countess

21. *Rewrite the following sentences making the subject feminine. Change the adjective if necessary.*

1. Lo studente lavora molto.
2. Il lavoratore riceve il denaro.
3. Il principe abita nel castello.
4. L'oste parla con gli invitati.
5. L'attore canta bene.
6. Il conte è ricco.

Foreign Nouns

In Italian, foreign nouns are usually considered masculine and are always written in their singular form. The plural of foreign nouns is formed by pluralizing the definite article.

il film → i film		il cent → i cent
l'alcool → gli alcool (*also:* alcol)	alcohol	
lo sport → gli sport		l'euro → gli euro
il tram → i tram	streetcar	
il weekend → i weekend		l'album → gli album
il gas → i gas		
il bazar → i bazar		
il bar → i bar		

Compound Nouns

Many compound nouns are formed by taking a verb root along with a noun to form one word. The root is usually the third-person singular of the present indicative as in all words below, except **l'apriscatole** (second-person singular).

il paracadute → i paracadute	parachute
il portavoce → i portavoce	megaphone
il cantastorie → i cantastorie	minstrel
l'apriscatole → gli apriscatole	can opener
l'affittacamere → gli affittacamere	landlord
but l'affittacamere → le affittacamere	landlady
il portabandiera → i portabandiera	flag bearer

22. Complete the following with the appropriate definite article:

1. Adesso aspetto _____ portalettere.
2. _____ guardaroba è pieno di vestiti.
3. Devo trovare _____ apriscatole.
4. _____ giradischi di Olga è nuovo.
5. _____ parabrezza dell'automobile è rotto.
6. Il padre di Carlo è _____ guardasigilli dello Stato.

Many compound nouns are formed by uniting two separate nouns. The gender of the compound is determined by the gender of the second noun, and the plural of the compound is formed by changing only the second noun to its plural form.

il capoluogo → i capoluoghi	*capital of province*	[capo + luogo]
il cavolfiore → i cavolfiori	*cauliflower*	[cavol + fiore]
l'arcobaleno → gli arcobaleni	*rainbow*	[arco + baleno]
il capogiro → i capogiri	*dizziness*	[capo + giro]
la banconota → le banconote	*currency*	[banco + nota]
la ferrovia → le ferrovie	*railroad*	[ferro + via]
il pomodoro → i pomodori (i pomidoro)	*tomato*	[pomo + d'oro]

23. Pluralize the indicated nouns.

1. Il capogiro non è piacevole.
2. L'arcobaleno è bellissimo.
3. Il pescecane *(shark)* è pericoloso.
4. Il pomodoro è rosso.
5. La banconota è americana.
6. Il cavolfiore è saporito.
7. Il boccaporto *(hatch)* è aperto.

Note, however, that some compound nouns form their plural by changing only the first word to the plural.

il capofila → i capifila	*head of a line*	[capo + fila]
il caporeparto → i capireparto	*section head*	[capo + reparto]
il capoquadra → i capisquadra	*team captain*	[capo + squadra]
il capostazione → i capistazione	*station master*	[capo + stazione]

Some compound nouns are formed by uniting two adjectives. In the plural, only the second adjective is pluralized.

il pianoforte	i pianoforti	*piano*	[piano + forte]
il chiaroscuro	i chiaroscuri	*chiaroscuro*	[chiaro + scuro]

Some compound nouns are formed by uniting an adverb and an adjective. In the plural, only the adjective is pluralized.

il malcontento	i malcontenti	*malcontent*	[mal + contento]
la malcontenta	le malcontente	*malcontent*	[mal + contenta]

Some compound nouns are formed by uniting an adjective and a noun. In the plural, only the noun is pluralized.

il bassorilievo → i bassorilievi	*bas-relief*	[basso + rilievo]
il mezzogiorno → i mezzogiorni	*noon*	[mezzo + giorno]
l'altoparlante → gli altoparlanti	*loudspeaker*	[alto + parlante]

Some compound nouns are formed by uniting a noun and an adjective. In the plural, both the noun and the adjective are pluralized with the exception of **palcoscenico**.

la piazzaforte → le piazzeforti	*fortress, stronghold*	[piazza + forte]
la cassaforte → le casseforti	*safe*	[cassa + forte]
il palcoscenico → i palcoscenici	*stage*	[palco + scenico]

24. Pluralize only the underlined words and place them in the spaces provided.

   1. <u>Il capofila</u> è giovane. _____
   2. <u>Il caporeparto</u> arriva presto ogni giorno._____
   3. <u>Il pianoforte</u> costa cinquemila euro._____
   4. <u>Il chiaroscuro</u> di Leonardo è meraviglioso._____
   5. <u>Il malcontento</u> non è mai felice._____
   6. <u>Il caposquadra</u> ha molte responsabilità. _____
   7. <u>L'altoparlante</u> non funziona bene._____
   8. <u>La cassaforte</u> è impenetrabile._____
   9. <u>Il capostazione</u> fa partire i treni._____
   10. <u>Il palcoscenico</u> è pieno di artisti._____

Diminutives, Augmentatives, and Pejoratives

Several endings or suffixes, such as **-uccio**, **-ello**, **-ino**, and **-etto** (for masculine nouns), and **-uccia**, **-ella**, **-ina**, and **-etta** (for feminine nouns) can be added to Italian nouns to form what is called the diminutive. The diminutive may refer to actual physical size: **cavallo** (*horse*) → **cavallino** (*little horse*). The diminutive may also be used to convey a feeling of affection or endearment on the part of the speaker: **cavallo** (*horse*) → **cavalluccio** (*cute little horse*), as well as a pejorative: **film** → **filmuccio**, **filmetto** (*a movie of little importance or poor quality*).

vecchio	*old man* → **vecchietto**	*dear old man*
bimbo	*child* → **bimbetto**	*dear little child*
libro	*book* → **libretto (libriccino)**	*little book, booklet*
nonna	*grandmother* → **nonnetta**	*dear old granny*
parola	*word* → **parolina**	*little word*
uccello	*bird* → **uccellino**	*little bird*
cane	*dog* → **cagnolino**	*little puppy*
gatto	*cat* → **gattino**	*little cat, kitten*
scarpa	*shoe* → **scarpina**	*little shoe*
racconto	*tale* → **raccontino**	*little tale*
donna	*woman* → **donnuccia**	*dear little woman*
casa	*house* → **casetta (casuccia)**	*little house, "sweet home"*
asino	*donkey* → **asinello**	*little donkey*

25. Supply the diminutive of the indicated nouns, or complete the sentences according to cues.

   1. Piero ha un _____. *cane*
   2. La mia vicina è una _____. *vecchia*
   3. Silvia è una _____ simpatica. *bimba*
   4. I bambini giocano con un _____. *gatto*
   5. La nonna racconta un bel _____. *racconto*
   6. Non è un <u>libro</u> grande; è un _____.
   7. Non è una <u>scarpa</u> regolare; è una _____.
   8. É una cara piccola <u>donna</u>; è una _____.

The augmentative form of the noun is made with the suffix **-one**. The augmentative usually refers only to size or degree, and is always masculine.

l'uomo	man → **l'omone**	*large man (the* **u** *of* **'uomo'** *is dropped)*
il libro	book → **il librone**	*oversize book*
il vecchio	old man → **il vecchione**	*very old man*
il gatto	cat → **il gattone**	*tomcat*
la porta	door → **il portone**	*portal*

| la strada | *street* → **lo stradone** | *large street* |
| la scarpa | *shoe* → **lo scarpone** | *heavy boot* |

26. Complete the following sentences with the augmentative form according to the underlined cues.
1. Lo zio di Pietro è molto <u>vecchio</u>. È un _____.
2. I <u>libri</u> sono molto grandi. Sono dei _____.
3. È una <u>porta</u> alta e larga. È un _____.
4. È una <u>scarpa</u> molto grande e <u>pesante</u>. È uno _____.
5. Non è un <u>gattino</u>, è molto piú grande. È un _____.
6. È un <u>uomo</u> alto e grosso. È un _____.

The pejorative form has several endings; some of them are: **-accio, -astro, -ucolo, -iciattolo.** They are used to convey a derogatory meaning. It is advisable not to use these forms until one is completely fluent in the language.

monello	*brat* → **monellaccio**	*lousy brat, etc.*
uomo	*man* → **omiciattolo**	*poor excuse of a man, etc.*
sogno	*dream* → **sognaccio**	*bad dream, etc.*
ragazzo	*boy* → **ragazzaccio**	*mean boy, etc.*
poeta	*poet* → **poetucolo, poetastro**	*lousy poet, etc.*
verme	*worm* → **vermiciattolo**	*filthy worm, etc.*
stanza	*room* → **stanzaccia**	*lousy room, etc.*
maestro	*instructor* → **maestrucolo**	*poor instructor, etc.*
libro	*book* → **libraccio**	*lousy book, etc.*
giornale	*newspaper* → **giornalaccio**	*a rag, etc.*

THE DEFINITE ARTICLE

With General and Abstract Nouns

Unlike English, the Italian definite article must be used with all general or abstract nouns. Compare the Italian and English in the following examples.

l cani sono animali domestici.
Dogs are domestic animals.

L'oro è un metallo prezioso.
Gold is a precious metal.

ll riso fa bene a tutti.
Laughter is good for everyone.

L'odio è una cosa terribile.
Hate is a terrible thing.

27. Complete the following with the appropriate definite article:
1. _____ scienza è utile.
2. _____ amore è una cosa meravigliosa.
3. _____ smeraldi sono pietre preziose.
4. _____ gatti sono animali domestici.

With Titles

The definite article must be used with titles when talking about someone. The article is omitted, however, in direct address. Note that the definite article is never used before **don** and **donna**.

Il dottor Sperry è bravissimo e simpatico.
La signora Boni abita a Roma.
L'avvocato Ferro è nello studio.
Don Giuseppe suona il mandolino.
Donna Giuliana è molto generosa.
"Buon giorno, signora Bellini."
"Come sta, dottoressa Marini?"
"Buona sera, signor Motta."

28. Complete the following with the appropriate definite article when it is necessary:
    1. _____ dottoressa Merli è in ospedale.
    2. _____ avvocato Sereni non c'è.
    3. _____ don Carlo passeggia con gli amici.
    4. Buona sera, _____ professoressa Belli.
    5. Sa Lei chi è _____ signorina Colli?
    6. _____ donna Teresa è in America.
    7. Conosce Lei _____ professor Valle?
    8. Buon giorno, _____ signora Rossi.
    9. Conoscete _____ signori De Lena?
    10. Buona sera, _____ don Antonio.

With Languages

The definite article is used with languages unless the language immediately follows the verb **parlare** (*to speak*) or the preposition **di** (*of*) or **in** (*in*).

Parliamo molto bene l'inglese.   *We speak English very well.*
Gli studenti imparano l'italiano.   *The students learn Italian.*
I signori conoscono il tedesco.   *The gentlemen know German.*
Parlo italiano.   *I speak Italian.*
Ho un libro di francese.   *I have a French book.*
La lettera è in spagnolo.   *The letter is in Spanish.*

29. Complete the following with the appropriate definite article when necessary:
    1. La signorina Martini impara _____ inglese.
    2. Gli alunni studiano _____ tedesco.
    3. Il professor Belli insegna _____ italiano.
    4. Roberto legge un libro di _____ francese.
    5. La lettera di oggi è in _____ spagnolo.
    6. Mia madre mi scrive in _____ italiano.
    7. Stefano e Olga parlano _____ inglese.
    8. _____ italiano è una lingua romanza.
    9. _____ russo è una lingua slava.
    10. Mia nonna Rosa Maviglia conosceva _____ greco.

With Continents, Countries, Islands, Regions, and Cities

The definite article is usually used with the name of continents, countries, islands, and regions.

L'Asia è un continente grande.   *Asia is a large continent.*
L'Italia, la Francia e la Spagna sono belle.   *Italy, France, and Spain are beautiful.*
La Sicilia è un'isola italiana.   *Sicily is an Italian island.*
La Lombardia è una regione settentrionale.   *Lombardy is a northern (Italian) region.*
L'Europa è un continente occidentale.   *Europe is a Western continent.*

The definite article is omitted when the name of the continent, country, island, or region is preceded by the preposition **in** or **di**.

Mio zio è andato in Europa.	*My uncle went to Europe.*
Gli studenti vanno in Inghilterra.	*The students go to England.*
Mia sorella è in Sardegna.	*My sister is in Sardinia.*
Pietro va in Toscana.	*Peter goes to Tuscany.*
I nostri cugini abitano in Australia.	*Our cousins live in Australia.*
La capitale d'Italia è Roma.	*The capital of Italy is Rome.*
I vini di Francia sono deliziosi.	*France's wines are delicious.*
Le spiagge di Spagna sono bellissime.	*Spain's beaches are very beautiful.*

The definite article is used, however, with the prepositions **in** and **di** when the name of the country or region is masculine.

Vado nel Messico.	*I go to Mexico.*
I miei nonni sono nel Lazio.	*My grandparents are in Latium.*
La capitale del Canadà è Ottawa.	*The capital of Canada is Ottawa.*
Mi piacciono le piramidi dell'Egitto.	*I like Egypt's pyramids.*

The definite article is also used with the prepositions **di** and **in** when the name of the continent, country, island, or region is modified.

Siena è nell'Italia centrale.
Siena is in central Italy.

Il cielo della bella Italia è spesso azzurro.
The sky of beautiful Italy is often blue.

Nella splendida Firenze c'è sempre molto da vedere.
In splendid Florence there's always a lot to see.

The definite article is not used with the name of a city unless it is modified.

Firenze è in Toscana.	*Florence is in Tuscany.*
La bella Firenze è in Toscana.	*Beautiful Florence is in Tuscany.*

The definite article is omitted with the names of certain islands.

Capri, Ischia e Procida sono isole italiane.	*Capri, Ischia, and Procida are Italian islands.*
Formosa è un'isola orientale.	*Formosa is an Oriental island.*
Cuba è nei Caraibi.	*Cuba is in the Caribbean.*

When **di** means *than* in the comparative expression **piú ... di** (see page 59), the definite article is used.

La Francia è piú grande dell'Irlanda.	*France is larger than Ireland.*
L'Italia è piú piccola dell'Australia.	*Italy is smaller than Australia.*

30. *Complete the following with the appropriate definite article when necessary:*
1. _____ Africa non è un paese; è un continente.
2. _____ Africa e _____ Asia sono due continenti grandi.
3. Io viaggio molto in _____ Asia.
4. _____ Roma è una città importante.
5. Io conosco bene _____ bella Firenze.
6. _____ Torino è una città settentrionale.
7. _____ Cuba è un'isola dei Caraibi
8. _____ Sardegna è un'isola italiana.
9. _____ Capri è un'isola piccola
10. _____ Calabria è una regione meridionale.

31. Select the appropriate response to complete each of the following:

1. Io vado _____ Italia.
    (*a*) in   (*b*) nell'
2. La capitale _____ Francia è Parigi.
    (*a*) della (*b*) di
3. Mio nonno è _____ Messico.
    (*a*) in   (*b*) nel
4. L'Italia è _____ Europa.
    (*a*) nell' (*b*) in
5. L'Italia è _____ Europa meridionale.
    (*a*) nell' (*b*) in
6. Le foreste _____ Canadà sono immense.
    (*a*) del   (*b*) di
7. La capitale _____ bella Spagna è Madrid.
    (*a*) di   (*b*) della
8. La seta _____ Cina è famosa.
    (*a*) della (*b*) di

With Nouns Denoting Family Members Preceded by Possessive Adjectives

The definite article is omitted with singular nouns denoting family members and relatives preceded by possessive adjectives, except with **loro** and **Loro**. In the plural; the definite article must be included.

Mia sorella è piccola. → **Le mie sorelle sono piccole.**
My sister is little.   *My sisters are little.*

Mio nonno è vecchio. → **I miei nonni sono vecchi.**
My grandfather is old.   *My grandfathers are old.*

Questo è tuo cugino. → **Questi sono i tuoi cugini.**
This is your cousin.   *These are your cousins.*

Dov'è vostro fratello? → **Dove sono i vostri fratelli?**
Where's your brother?   *Where are your brothers?*

La loro cugina è giornalista. → **Le loro cugine sono giornaliste.**
Their cousin is a journalist.   *Their cousins are journalists.*

32. Complete the following with the appropriate definite article when necessary:

1. Antonio è _____ mio fratello.
2. _____ miei nonni sono italiani.
3. _____ tua sorella ha sedici anni.
4. _____ nostra madre è americana.
5. _____ vostre cugine abitano a Chicago.
6. Luisa va al cinema con _____ mia sorella.
7. Roberto e Stefano giocano con _____ nostri fratelli.
8. _____ loro figlio è un bravo ragazzo.

Note that the definite article is included when a singular noun denoting family members or relatives is given in its diminutive form. For example:

Silvia è la mia sorellina.   *Sylvia is my little sister.*
La nostra mammina è generosa.   *Our mommy is generous.*
Il tuo fratellino è simpatico.   *Your little brother is cute.*
Il nostro babbo è generoso.   *Our daddy is generous.*

With Days of the Week

The singular form of the definite article is used with days of the week in order to convey a recurrent action. It is usually omitted in all other instances. Study the following examples.

Andiamo sempre alla spiaggia la domenica.
We always go to the beach on Sundays.

La domenica non c'è mai scuola.
There's never any school on Sundays.

Lunedí è il primo giorno della settimana.
Monday is the first day of the week.

Facciamo le spese sabato prossimo.
We are going shopping next Saturday.

Vediamo i nonni domenica.
We are seeing our grandparents next Sunday.

33. *Complete the following with the definite article when it is necessary.*
  1. _____ mercoledí è il terzo giorno della settimana.
  2. _____ domenica andiamo sempre in campagna.
  3. _____ giovedí prossimo vado al cinema.
  4. Vanno sempre in chiesa _____ domenica.
  5. Mio padre ritorna dall'Italia _____ venerdí.

With Prepositions: Contractions

Italian prepositions and definite articles are almost always contracted when used together. These contractions are listed in the table that follows. The prepositions **a** (*at, to*), **di** (*of, belonging to*), **da** (*from, by, at*), **in** (*in, to*) and **su** (*on*) always contract when they precede the definite article. The prepositions **con** (*with*) and **per** (*for, because of, through*) are rarely contracted, and it is suggested not to contract them at all. **Tra** and **fra** (*between, among*) are never contracted. The two charts below show those prepositions that are contracted with definite articles. They are first presented in their singular form and then in their plural form. In the form of an equation, it is easy to see how the prepositions and the articles merge to form new words. An explanatory sentence follows each "equation." Note that, before merging, **di** becomes **de** and **in** becomes **ne**. The **i** of **il** is always dropped. All articles which begin with **l-** double the consonant, which becomes **-ll-** when attached to a preposition. Observe the following:

Articulated Prepositions

Masculine singular forms

a + il = al: **Diamo un regalo al ragazzo.**
                          We give a gift to the boy.

a + lo = allo: **Mandi una cartolina allo zio.**
                          You send a postcard to your uncle.

a + l' = all':   **Scrivo all' amico ogni mese.**
                          I write to my friend every month.

da + il = dal: **Gli studenti escono dal museo.**
                          The students leave the museum.

da + lo = dallo: **Ho ricevuto un pacco dallo zio.**
                          I received a package from my uncle.

da + l'= dall':   **Sono scesi dall' aereo un'ora fa.**
                          They disembarked from the airplane an hour ago.

su + il = sul:

(Sul) comò c'è una sveglia.
On the chest of drawers there is an alarm clock.

su + lo = sullo:

(Sullo) stipo ci sono dei biscotti.
On the cabinet there are biscuits.

su + l' = sull':

(Sull') abbacchio mettiamo della salvia.
We put some sage on the lamb.

di → de + il = del:

La macchina (del) mio amico è rossa.
My friend's car is red.

di → de + lo = dello:

l libri (dello) studente (*m. s.*) sono nuovi.
The student's (m. s.) books are new.

di → de + l' = dell':

l rami (dell') albero sono grossi.
The branches of the tree are large.

in → ne + il = nel:

(Nel) forno ci sono due polli.
In the oven there are two chickens.

in → ne + lo = nello:

(Nello) studio ho molti libri.
In the study I have many books.

in → ne + l' = nell':

I tuoi vestiti sono (nell') armadio.
Your suits are in the closet.

Feminine singular forms

a + la = alla:

Mandiamo un regalo (alla) nonna.
We send a gift to our grandmother.

a + l' = all':

Do il biglietto (all') amica.
I give the ticket to my girlfriend.

da + la = dalla:

Uscirò (dalla) biblioteca alle sei.
I will leave the library at six o'clock.

da + l' = dall':

La macchina è guidata (dall') amica.
The car is driven by the girlfriend.

su + la = sulla:

(Sulla) tavola c'è una bella cena.
There's a beautiful dinner on the table.

su + l' = sull':

(Sull') estate (f.s.) del 2005 non ho niente da dire!
Regarding the summer of 2005 I have nothing to say!

di → de + la = della:

Ecco i giocattoli (della) bambina.
Here are the child's (f.) toys.

di → de + l'= dell':

1 colori (dell') aurora sono spettacolari.
The colors of the sunrise are spectacular.

in → ne + la = nella:

Troverai i documenti (nel) cassetto.
You will find the documents in the drawer.

in → ne + l' = nell':

(Nell') estate del 2006 sono rimasta qui.
During the summer of 2006 I remained here.

Masculine plural forms

a + i = ai:

Sabato andremo (ai) musei della città.
Saturday we will go to the city's museums.

a + gli = agli:

Ieri abbiamo scritto agli zii.
Yesterday we wrote to our uncles (also: uncle and aunt).

a + gl' = agl':

Non penso mai (agl') inverni (also: **agli inverni**)
I never think of winter (literally, winters).

da + i = dai:

Perché non andiamo (dai) nonni?
Why don't we go to our grandparents'?

da + gli = dagli:

Sempre riceviamo lettere (dagli) zii.
We always receive letters from our uncles (also: uncle and aunt).

da + gl' = dagl':	**Dobbiamo stare lontani** dagl' **inchiostri.**
	We should stay away from the ink (literally, inks).
su + i = sui:	Sui **monti fa sempre fresco.**
	In the mountains it's always cool.
su + gi = sugli:	**L'aereo è passato** sugli **Appennini.**
	The airplane passed over the Appenines.
su + gl' = sugl':	**Non possiamo sederci** sugl' **ingressi.**
	We can't sit down in the entrances.
di → de + i = dei:	**Queste chiavi sono** dei **turisti.**
	These keys are the tourists'.
di → de + gli = degli:	**Sento il rumore** degli **aerei.**
	I hear the noise of the airplanes.
di → de + gl' = degl':	**Il freddo** degl' **inverni mi fa male.**
	The cold of winter makes me ill.
in → ne + i = nei:	Nei **romanzi dell'Ottocento ci sono molti personaggi affascinanti.**
	In the novels of the nineteenth century there are many fascinating characters.
in → ne + gli = negli:	Negli **Stati Uniti d'America ci sono molti gruppi etnici.**
	In the United States of America there are many ethnic groups.
in → ne + gl' = negl':	Negl' **inverni freddissimi i miei nonni scappano per la Florida.**
	In the coldest winters my grandparents escape to Florida.

Feminine plural forms

a + le = alle:	Alle **studentesse piacciono le lingue moderne.**
	The students (f. pl.) like modern languages.
a + l' = all':	**Penso sempre** all' **estati (also: alle estati) passate in Italia.**
	I always think about summers spent in Italy.
da + le = dalle:	**Riceve molte telefonate** dalle **sue amiche.**
	He/she receives many telephone calls from his/her girlfriends.
da + l' = dall':	**Alcune signore vanno** dall' **estetiste (also: dalle estetiste) ogni mese.**
	Some ladies go to the beautician every month (literally, beauticians).
su + le = sulle:	Sulle **pareti** del **salotto ci sono** dei **bei quadri.**
	On the walls of the living room there are many beautiful pictures.
su + l'[1] = sull':	Sull' **erbe** del **prato si dorme bene.**
	On the grass of the lawn one sleeps well.
di → de + le = delle:	**ll traffico delle città (f. pl.) è orribile.**
	The traffic of the city is horrible.
di → de + l' = dell':	**Il caldo** dell' **estati (also:** delle **estati) è afoso.**
	The heat of summer is oppressive.
in → ne + le = nelle:	Nelle **valige mettiamo troppe cose.**
	We put too many things in the suitcases.
in → ne + l' = nell':	Nell' **estati (f: pl.; also: nelle estati) umide non si può vivere in città.**
	During humid summers one can't live in the city.

Observe some additional examples:

Andiamo al palazzo delle **poste!**	*Let's go to the main post-office!*
L'automobile è dal **meccanico.**	*The car is at the mechanic's.*
Le penne sono sulla **scrivania.**	*The pens are on the desk.*
ll ragazzo è sull' **albero.**	*The boy is in the tree.*
ll libro è nel **cassetto.**	*The book is in the drawer.*
I giocatori sono nello **stadio.**	*The players are in the stadium.*
Ecco i libri degli **studenti!**	*Here are the students' books!*
La carta telefonica è sul tavolo.	*The telephone card is on the table.*

(Also: **scheda telefonica; scheda magnetica**)

34. Complete the following by supplying the contracted form of the italicized preposition.

1. Ritorniamo _____ montagna. *da*
2. L'avvocato è _____ studio. *in*
3. Ecco i quaderni _____ studentesse! *di*
4. I vestiti sono _____ armadio. *in*
5. Gli uccellini sono _____ alberi. *su*
6. Camminano _____ strade. *per*
7. Vieni _____ tuoi amici. *con*
8. Luigi è _____ dentista. *da*
9. I turisti ritornano _____ monti. *da*
10. I treni vengono _____ città. *da*

THE INDEFINITE ARTICLE

The indefinite articles (*a, an*) in Italian are **un** for most masculine nouns; **uno** for masculine nouns beginning with **z**, **s** plus a consonant, **ps**, or **gn**; **una** for feminine nouns; and **un'** for feminine nouns beginning with a vowel. There are no plural forms.

un ragazzo	*boy*	**una casa**	*house*
un albero	*tree*	**una camicia**	*shirt*
un amico	*friend*	**una zia**	*aunt*
un libro	*book*	**una cugina**	*cousin*
uno studio	*study*	**un'amica**	*friend*
uno studente	*student*	**un'estate (f.)**	*summer*
uno zio	*uncle*	**un'automobile (f.)**	*car*
uno zaino	*knapsack*	**un'ambulanza**	*ambulance*
uno psicologo	*psychologist*	**un'aranciata**	*orangeade*
uno gnomo	*gnome*	**un'arma**	*weapon*

35. Rewrite the following sentences, replacing the definite article with an indefinite article except when inappropriate:

1. Pietro compra il dizionario.
2. Paola prende l'aranciata.
3. La signora Torelli compra la casa grande.
4. Il signor Marini è lo zio di Stefano.
5. Scriviamo la lettera.
6. Roberto è l'amico di Giovanni.
7. Il dottore ha lo studio grande.
8. Vincenzo guida l'ambulanza rossa.
9. Teresa porta l'abito bianco.
10. I ragazzi comprano il giocattolo.

36. Supply the appropriate indefinite articles:

1. Carlo vuole prendere _____ aranciata fresca.
2. Napoli è _____ città molto bella.
3. Quello è _____ monumento molto antico.
4. Abbiamo ricevuto _____ lettera da Carlo.
5. Loro vanno a _____ spiaggia vicino a Genova.
6. Lei lavora in _____ ufficio nel centro della città.
7. È _____ lezione difficile.
8. Vogliono comprare _____ disco.
9. Lo studente ha fatto _____ sbaglio.
10. La professoressa insegna in _____ università grande.

Special Uses of the Indefinite Article

In Italian, unlike English, the indefinite article is omitted after the verb **ẹssere** (*to be*) when it precedes unmodified nouns describing a profession or occupation:

Il padre di Arturo è avvocato.
Arthur's father is a lawyer.

La madre di Anna è dottoressa.
Anna's mother is a doctor.

The indefinite article is used, however, when the noun that follows the verb **ẹssere** is modified:

Dante è un autore famoso.
Dante is a famous author.

Dante è un autore che ha avuto molta fama.
Dante is an author who has had a great deal of fame.

Dante è un autore di grande rinomanza.
Dante is an author of great renown.

37. Complete the following with the appropriate indefinite article when it is necessary:
  1. Lo zịo di Carla è _____ chirurgo (*surgeon*) famoso.
  2. Il cugino di Stẹfano è _____ meccạnico.
  3. Teresa è _____ studentessa.
  4. La signora Merli è _____ giornalista.
  5. Luịgi è _____ studente che stụdia molto.
  6. Mịo fratello è _____ dottore.
  7. La signorina Tinelli è _____ dottoressa.
  8. Pịetro vuọle ẹssere _____ professore.
  9. Giovanna è _____ ragazzina di sette anni.
  10. Machiavelli è _____ autore di molta rinomanza.

THE PARTITIVE

In Italian, the partitive (*some, any*) is expressed by **di** plus the indefinite article. **Di** becomes **de** before contracting. (See the chart of contractions on pp. 33–35.) The partitive articles are as follows:

	Singular	Plural
Feminine:	**della**	**delle**
Before a vowel:	**dell'**	**delle**
Masculine:	**del**	**dei**
Before a z or an s plus consonant, and before **gn**:	**dello**	**degli**
Before a vowel:	**dell'**	**degli**

Study the following:

Prendo della minestra.
I have some soup.

Vogliạmo dell'acqua.
We want some water.

Lui compra del pane.
He buys some bread.

Ecco dello zucchero.
Here is some sugar.

Compriamo dell'inchiostro.
We buy some ink.

Vuoi delle caramelle?
Do you want some candies?

Abbiamo dei libri.
We have some books.

Hanno degli zaini.
They have some knapsacks.

38. Complete the following sentences with the appropriate form of the partitive:
1. Lei prende _____ insalata.
2. Noi leggiamo _____ romanzi.
3. Tu compri _____ zucchero.
4. Lui riceve _____ riviste.
5. Io mangio _____ marmellata.
6. Vediamo _____ amici.
7. Prendete _____ caffè.
8. Compro _____ camicie.
9. Bevete _____ acqua.
10. Mandiamo _____ pacchi.

The Partitive versus the Definite Article

The partitive indicates a part of something. The definite article is used with nouns when a general or abstract meaning is intended.

Prende del caffè.
He is drinking some coffee.

Gli piace il caffè.
He likes coffee.

39. Follow the models:
Prendi del caffè?
Sí, mi piace il caffè e prendo del caffè.
Volete del tè?
Sí, ci piace il tè e prendiamo del tè.

1. Prendete del tè?
2. Mangiate della carne?
3. Vuoi dei legumi?
4. Comprate dello zucchero?
5. Bevi del latte?
6. Prendete della minestra?
7. Bevete dell'acqua minerale?
8. Mangi del pane?

Exceptions to the Rule for Using the Partitive

When the sentence is negative
In negative sentences that contain the partitive, the definite article is omitted. (For more details on forming negatives, see Chapter 7.)

Affirmative	*Negative*
Prendo dello zucchero.	**Non prendo zucchero.**
I take some sugar.	*I don't take any sugar.*
(Io) ho un'automobile.	**(Io) non ho automobile.**
I have a car.	*I don't have a car.*

Compriạmo dei libri.
We buy some books.

(Noi)mangiạmo della carne.
We eat some meat.

Non compriạmo libri.
We don't buy any books.

(Noi)non mangiạmo carne.
We don't eat any meat.

40. Rewrite the following sentences in the negative:

1. Lui compra delle penne.
2. Io prendo del tè.
3. Noi mangiạmo della minestra.

4. Mạngio del pane.
5. Beviạmo dell'ạcqua minerale.
6. Mandiạmo dei pacchi.

After expressions of quantity with di

The partitive is formed with **di** after expressions of quantity such as the following:

un chilo di	*a kilo (one kilogram) of*	**un po' di**	*a little of*
una dozzina di	*a dozen of*	**una tazza di**	*a cup of*
un litro di	*a liter of*	**un bicchiẹre di**	*a glass of*

Vọglio del latte.
I want some milk.

Compriạmo della carne.
We buy some meat.

Ecco delle uọva!
Here are some eggs!

But: **Vọglio un bicchiẹre di latte.**
       I want a glass of milk.

But: **Compriạmo un chilo di carne.**
       We buy a kilo of meat.

But: **Ecco una dozzina di uọva!**
       Here are a dozen eggs!

41. Complete the following sentences with the correct form of the partitive:

1. Ecco _____ vino!
2. Vuọi una tazza _____ caffè?
3. Carlo compra una dozzina _____ pere.
4. Noi mangiạmo _____ legumi.
5. Ordino un bicchiẹre _____ vino.
6. Voi bevete un litro _____ latte.
7. Per favore, desịdero _____ latte.
8. Compro dụe chili _____ patate.
9. Bevo un po' _____ tè.
10. Prendiạmo _____ limonata.

REVIEW

42. Complete each of the following sentences with the appropriate definite article:

1. _____ calciatori sono nello stạdio.
2. _____ amica di Rosa è in Itạlia.
3. _____ zịi di Marco lavọrano insiẹme.
4. _____ ragazze vanno alla spiạggia.
5. Mio nonno fuma _____ pipa.
6. _____ ạquile sono uccelli grandi.
7. _____ proprietạrio chiụde il negọzio.
8. _____ sbagli sono molto comuni.
9. _____ studente fa bene agli esami.
10. _____ cravatta di Stẹfano è variopinta.
11. So dove sono _____ miẹi compagni.
12. _____ spiạgge italiane sono bellịssime.
13. _____ esame di lạurea è difficile.
14. _____ film di Fellini sono interessanti.
15. _____ cantante è simpạtica.

43. Complete the following nouns with the appropriate endings:

1. La violin _____ suona molto bene.
2. La duch _____ è molto ricca.
3. I parc _____ sono pieni di gente.
4. Gli asparag _____ sono deliziosi.
5. Le formic _____ sono laboriose.
6. La citt _____ di Roma è ricca di tesori d'arte.
7. L'armad _____ è pieno di vestiti.
8. Il fagg _____ è un albero alto.
9. L'estat _____ è una bella stagione.
10. I miei zi _____ sono americani.

44. Give diminutives for each of the following words:

1. il cappello
2. la sorella
3. la vecchia
4. la donna
5. il libro
6. il fratello
7. il racconto
8. la casa

45. Rewrite the following sentences in the plural:

1. Il parco è grande.
2. L'estate è bella.
3. Il film è buono.
4. La formica è piccola.
5. Il guardasigilli è vecchio.
6. L'apriscatole è rotto.
7. La pianista è brava.
8. Lo sport è necessario.
9. La gru è un uccello grande.
10. L'università è utile.
11. La doccia è fredda.
12. La fascia è bianca.
13. La scia della nave è lunga.
14. Il teologo è studioso.
15. L'uovo è sodo.
16. La telecronista parla bene.
17. Il problema è risolto.
18. La dinamo è utile.
19. La radio è tedesca.
20. La mano è pulita.

46. Complete the following with the correct definite or indefinite article when necessary:

1. _____ scuola è una cosa importante.
2. Buon giorno, _____ signorina Zocchi.
3. Mio nonno è _____ chirurgo.
4. _____ cani sono animali domestici.
5. _____ don Pietro è _____ nonno di Piero.
6. _____ diamanti sono pietre preziose.
7. La madre di Teresa è _____ dottoressa famosa.
8. _____ Ariosto è _____ poeta molto conosciuto.

9. _____ scienze sono importanti.
10. Mario scrive in _____ tedesco.
11. Olga è _____ violinista.
12. Stefano è _____ giornalista serio.
13. _____ Sicilia è _____ isola grande.
14. Roma è _____ Italia centrale.
15. _____ Italia è in Europa.
16. _____, Capri è _____ isola piccola.
17. _____ donna Teresa è _____ farmacista.
18. _____ tuniche sono bianche.
19. _____ foto sono memorabili.
20. _____ radio sono giapponesi.

47. Complete the following with the correct forms of the appropriate preposition and verbs:
   1. Il mercato è _____ centro _____ città.
   2. Il signore prende una tovaglia _____ credenza e la mette _____ tavola.
   3. Io vado _____ università _____ mio amico.
   4. Sono andato a piedi _____ scuola _____ museo.
   5. I libri sono _____ banco _____ studente.
   6. Tutti i membri _____ gruppo sono arrivati _____ atrio _____ albergo _____ loro bagagli.
   7. _____ pescatori _____ partiti presto _____ andare _____ pescare.
   8. _____ don Antonio non _____ a casa perché _____ andato _____ campagna.
   9. Oggi _____ ragazzi _____ andati _____ cinema, non _____ teatro Verdi.
   10. _____ giornalista lavora per _____ giornale *La Stampa* e scrive _____ articoli _____ politica.

48. Complete the following sentences with the appropriate form of the partitive, when necessary:
   1. Stasera mangiamo _____ minestrone.
   2. Noi non prendiamo _____ zucchero.
   3. Io leggo _____ libri nuovi.
   4. Prendi _____ tè?
   5. I bambini vogliono _____ caramelle.
   6. Tu non scrivi _____ lettere.
   7. Voglio comprare una dozzina _____ mele.
   8. Il bambino beve un po' _____ latte.
   9. Luigi compra un chilo _____ asparagi.
   10. Elena mangia _____ cioccolatini.
   11. Io compro un litro _____ vino per la cena.
   12. Mio fratello non beve _____ caffè.
   13. Per dormire bene bisogna cambiare _____ lenzuola.
   14. _____ obblighi non sono sempre facili.
   15. _____ collega di Paolo lavora troppo.

49. Rewrite the following sentences in the singular.
   1. I colleghi degli ingegneri sono intelligenti.
   2. Le amiche di Gina sono giovani.
   3. I motori sono rumorosi.
   4. A volte i dialoghi sono molto lunghi.
   5. I lavori degli astrologi sono affascinanti.
   6. I cataloghi sono questi!
   7. I medici di questi paesi sono vecchi.
   8. I dizionari sono grossi.

9. Gli studi dei professori sono pieni di libri.
10. Gli usci sono quasi sempre aperti.
11. I templi greci sono maestosi.
12. I signori sono in ritardo, le signore no.

50. Supply both plurals (A: masculine; B: feminine) of the following nouns including the appropriate plural definite articles.

1. Il ginocchio: A: _____   B: _____
2. L'anello: A: _____   B: _____
3. Il dito: A: _____   B: _____
4. Il gesto: A: _____   B: _____
5. Il muro: A: _____   B: _____
6. Il filo: A: _____   B: _____
7. Il riso: A: _____   B: _____
8. Il ciglio: A: _____   B: _____
9. Il grido: A: _____   B: _____
10. Il muro: A: _____   B: _____
11. Il lenzuolo: A: _____   B: _____
12. L'orecchio: A: _____   B: _____

CHAPTER 3

Adjectives and Adverbs

ADJECTIVES ENDING IN -*o*

Many of the most common Italian adjectives end in **-o**. Each adjective must agree in gender and number with the noun it modifies. Adjectives that end in **-o** have four forms: masculine singular (m. s.), masculine plural (m. pl.), feminine singular (f. s.), and feminine plural (f. pl.). Study the following:

> **l'appartamento moderno → gli appartamenti moderni**
> **la casa moderna → le case moderne**
> **il ponte moderno → i ponti moderni**
> **la canzone moderna → le canzoni moderne**

Note that descriptive adjectives usually follow the noun in Italian. Below is a list of some commonly used adjectives.

acerbo	*unripe, sour*	**maturo**	*mature, ripe*
allegro	*cheerful, happy*	**moderno**	*modern*
alto	*tall*	**nero**	*black*
ampio	*wide*	**nuovo**	*new*
antico	*old, ancient*	**oscuro**	*dark*
avaro	*stingy*	**pieno**	*full*
basso	*short, low*	**povero**	*poor*
bravo	*good, able*	**primo**	*first*
buono	*good, kind*	**ricco**	*rich*
caldo	*warm, hot*	**rosso**	*red*
cattivo	*bad, wicked*	**stretto**	*narrow*
dannoso	*harmful*	**timido**	*timid, shy*
delizioso	*delicious*	**ultimo**	*last*
domestico	*domestic*	**vasto**	*vast*
duro	*hard*	**vecchio**	*old*
freddo	*cold*	**vero**	*true, real*
generoso	*generous*	**vuoto**	*empty*
leggero	*light*		

1. Complete the following with the appropriate form of the indicated adjective(s):

1. La casa non è _____, è _____. *vecchio, nuovo*
2. Le mele di quell'albero non sono_____, sono_____. *maturo, acerbo*
3. Gli zii di Carlo non sono_____, sono_____. *avaro, generoso*
4. Le frittate di quel cuoco sono_____. *delizioso*
5. La minestra è_____, non è_____. *caldo, freddo*
6. Lunedí è il_____giorno della settimana. *primo*
7. Carlo e Pietro sono_____, ma Stefano è_____. *alto, basso*
8. Le bambine non sono_____, sono_____. *cattivo, buono*
9. Il cane è un animale_____, ma il leone è_____. *domestico, selvatico (wild)*
10. La bandiera è_____ e _____. *bianco, giallo*
11. Il baule non è_____, è_____di libri. *vuoto, pieno*
12. I grattacieli sono degli edifici_____. *moderno*
13. La radio di Paolo è sempre_____. *acceso*
14. Il cerchio è una forma geometrica_____, non_____. *rotondo, quadrato*
15. La tua soluzione del cruciverba è_____, non è_____. *sbagliato, corretto*
16. I fiori sono_____, non_____. *rosso, giallo*
17. Le strade di questa città sono_____, non_____. *ampio, stretto*
18. Il padre di Luigi è_____e_____. *ricco, generoso*
19. Le canzoni antiche sono molto_____. *melodioso*
20. La camicia di Silvia non è_____, è_____. *nero, rosso*

ADJECTIVES ENDING IN -*e*

Many adjectives, like many nouns, end in the vowel -**e**. Such adjectives have only two forms, singular and plural. The singular ending -**e** becomes -**i** in the plural.

il signore elegante → i signori eleganti   *elegant gentleman*
la signora elegante → le signore eleganti   *elegant lady*

Below is a list of commonly used adjectives that end in -**e**.

abile	*able*	**importante**	*important*
acre	*sour*	**intelligente**	*intelligent*
breve	*brief, short*	**interessante**	*interesting*
celebre	*famous*	**nobile**	*noble*
difficile	*difficult*	**triste**	*sad*
eccellente	*excellent*	**umile**	*humble*
efficace	*effective*	**universale**	*universal*
facile	*easy*	**utile**	*useful*
felice	*happy*	**valente**	*skillful, clever*
forte	*strong*	**veloce**	*fast, speedy*
generale	*general*	**verde**	*green*
grande	*big, large, great*		

2. Complete the following with the appropriate form of the indicated adjective:

1. Le studentesse sono_____. *intelligente*
2. Lo zio di Stefano è un uomo_____. *importante*
3. Per molte persone l'aria di montagna è_____. *salubre*
4. Gli amici di Pietro sono_____. *triste*
5. È una decisione_____. *nobile*
6. Le lettere sono_____. *interessante*
7. I giovani sono _____e_____. *forte, agile*

8. Le tue domande sono _____. *inutile*
9. I pacchi sono _____. *grande*
10. Il signor Merli è un uomo molto _____. *umile*
11. Queste lezioni sono _____. *difficile*
12. Le foglie sono _____. *verde*

ADJECTIVES OF NATIONALITY

Many adjectives of nationality end in **-o**. These adjectives function as any regular adjective ending in **-o** and have four forms: masculine singular (m. s.), masculine plural (m. pl.), feminine singular (f. s.), and feminine plural (f. pl.).

They always follow the nouns they modify.

l'uomo africano	**gli uomini africani**	*African man*
La donna africana	**le donne africane**	*African woman*
il ragazzo americano	**i ragazzi americani**	*American boy*
la ragazza americana	**le ragazze americane**	*American girl*
il caffè brasiliano	**i caffè brasiliani**	*Brazilian coffee*
la spiaggia brasiliana	**le spiagge brasiliane**	*Brazilian beach*
il tempio greco	**i templi greci**	*Greek temple*
l'architettura greca	**le architetture greche**	*Greek architecture*
il tempio israeliano	**i templi israeliani**	*Israeli temple*
la sinagoga israeliana	**le sinagoghe israeliane**	*Israeli synagogue*
lo scultore italiano	**gli scultori italiani**	*Italian sculptor*
la pittrice italiana	**le pittrici italiane**	*Italian painter*
il cappello marocchino	**i cappelli marocchini**	*Moroccan hat*
la moschea marocchina	**le moschee marocchine**	*Moroccan mosque*
l'artista messicano	**gli artisti messicani**	*Mexican artist*
l'artista messicana	**le artiste messicane**	*Mexican artist*
il nonno polacco	**i nonni polacchi**	*Polish grandfather*
la nonna polacca	**le nonne polacche**	*Polish grandmother*
il ballerino russo	**i ballerini russi**	*Russian ballet dancer*
la ballerina russa	**le ballerine russe**	*Russian ballet dancer*
il vino spagnolo	**i vini spagnoli**	*Spanish wine*
la danza spagnola	**le danze spagnole**	*Spanish dance*
il tennista tedesco	**i tennisti tedeschi**	*German tennis player*
la tennista tedesca	**le tenniste tedesche**	*German tennis player*

Here are additional nationalities showing the names of each country with its appropriate adjective: **Argentina > argentino** (*Argentine*); **Australia > australiano** (*Australian*); **Austria > austriaco** (*Austrian*); **Corea > coreano** (*Korean*); **Cuba > cubano** (*Cuban*); **Iraq > iracheno** (*Iraqi*); **Libia > libico** (*Lybian*); **Portorico > portoricano** (*Puerto Rican*); **Svizzera > svizzero** (*Swiss*); **Tunisia > tunisino** (*Tunisian*); **Turchia > turco** (*Turkish*).

Many other adjectives of nationality end in **-e**. These adjectives have only two forms: **-e** in the singular for both masculine and feminine, and **-i** in the plural for both masculine and feminine.

il ministro canadese	**i ministri canadesi**	*Canadian minister*
la birra canadese	**le birre canadesi**	*Canadian beer*
il cibo cinese	**i cibi cinesi**	*Chinese food*
la statua cinese	**le statue cinesi**	*Chinese statue*
il vino francese	**i vini francesi**	*French wine*
l'acqua minerale francese	**le acque minerali francesi**	*French mineral water*
il teatro giapponese	**i teatri giapponesi**	*Japanese theatre*
l'arte giapponese	**le arti giapponesi**	*Japanese art*
l'esploratore portoghese	**gli esploratori portoghesi**	*Portuguese explorer*
la ceramica portoghese	**le ceramiche portoghesi**	*Portuguese pottery*

Here are additional nationalities showing the names of each country with its appropriate adjective: **Inghilterra > inglese** (*English*); **Irlanda > irlandese** (*Irish*); **Olanda > olandese** (*Dutch*); **Scandinavia > scandinavo** (*Scandinavian*); **Scozia > scozzese** (*Scottish*); **Svezia > svedese** (*Swedish*); **Ungheria > ungherese** (*Hungarian*).

3. Complete the following with the appropriate form of the indicated adjective:
1. Teresa è_____. *italiano*
2. I monumenti sono _____. *greco*
3. La signora è_____. *inglese*
4. I nostri amici sono _____. *messicano*
5. I formaggi sono _____. *svizzero*
6. Le signorine sono _____. *svedese*
7. I turisti sono _____. *francese*
8. La chitarra è_____. *spagnolo*
9. Le cugine di Pietro sono _____. *canadese*
10. I miei ospiti sono _____. *scandinavo*

4. Complete the following with the appropriate form of the indicated adjective.
1. I ragazzi sono _____. *messicano*
2. Le biciclette sono _____. *americano*
3. Le acciughe sono _____. *portoghese*
4. Le radio sono _____. *giapponese*
5. Le stoffe sono _____. *scozzese*
6. Olga è_____. *greco*
7. I vini sono _____. *spagnolo*
8. Mia zia è_____. *irlandese*
9. Le canzoni sono _____. *italiano*
10. Le merci sono _____. *canadese*

5. Answer the following questions according to the model:
Sono dell'Olanda i calciatori? → Sí, i calciatori sono olandesi.
1. È della Svezia la ragazza?
2. È del Canadà il signore?
3. Sono della Francia i vini?
4. Sono del Portogallo le signore?
5. È dell'Inghilterra la cantante?
6. È del Messico il tuo amico?
7. Sono dell'Irlanda i turisti?
8. Sono della Spagna le chitarre?
9. È dell'Italia l'automobile?
10. Sono dell'America gli ospiti?

ADJECTIVES ENDING IN -co, -ca, -go, -ga

All feminine adjectives ending in **-ca** and **-ga** form their plural in **-che** and **-ghe**, thus preserving the hard sound of the **c** and **g** of the singular.

antica	**antiche**	*ancient*	**carica**	**cariche**	*loaded*
atomica	**atomiche**	*atomic*	**comica**	**comiche**	*comical*
larga	**larghe**	*wide*	**lunga**	**lunghe**	*long*
poetica	**poetiche**	*poetic*	**sporca**	**sporche**	*soiled*
stanca	**stanche**	*tired*	**vaga**	**vaghe**	*vague*

6. Rewrite the following sentences in the plural.
1. La storia è lunga.
2. La bambina è stanca.
3. È un'espressione poetica.
4. La camicia è sporca.
5. È un'usanza antica.
6. Quel discorso è lungo.
7. La bomba è atomica.
8. Questa è la tariffa turistica.
9. È una battuta comica.
10. L'auto è carica di giocattoli.

Masculine adjectives ending in **-co** and **-go** usually form their plural in **-chi** and **-ghi**.

antico	**antichi**	*ancient*	**bianco**	**bianchi**	*white*
largo	**larghi**	*wide*	**lungo**	**lunghi**	*long*
sporco	**sporchi**	*soiled*	**stanco**	**stanchi**	*tired*
tedesco	**tedeschi**	*German*	**vago**	**vaghi**	*vague*

However, almost all adjectives with more than two syllables and ending in **-co** (commonly **-ico**) with their stress on a syllable other than the next to the last (penultimate) form their plural in **-ci**.

automatico	**automatici**	*automatic*
drastico	**drastici**	*drastic*
poetico	**poetici**	*poetic*
simpatico	**simpatici**	*cute*
drammatico	**drammatici**	*dramatic*
magnifico	**magnifici**	*magnificent*
romantico	**romantici**	*romantic*
unico	**unici**	*unique*

7. Complete the following sentences with the correct forms of the adjective stanco:
1. Il bambino è_____.
2. La ragazza è_____.
3. Roberto, sei_____.
4. Signora Merini, Lei è_____.
5. Luisa e Mario, siete_____.
6. I signori sono_____.
7. Le bambine sono_____.
8. Ragazzi, siete_____.
9. Professor Marietti, Lei è_____.
10. Mi chiamo Marianna e sono _____.

8. Complete the following sentences with the correct forms of simpatico:
1. Che bambina _____!
2. I nostri amici sono _____.
3. Marisa e Silvana sono _____.
4. Ragazzi, non siete sempre _____.
5. Le amiche di Luigi sono _____.
6. Tonio e Paolo sono dei ragazzi _____.
7. Silvia e Giovanni sono _____.
8. È un gattino veramente_____.
9. Signore, Loro sono _____.
10. Signori, Loro sono _____.

9. Write the following sentences in the plural:
1. Il ragazzo è simpatico.
2. Il vino è bianco.
3. L'autobus è carico.
4. Il monumento è antico.
5. Il vestito è sporco.
6. La veduta è magnifica.
7. Il signore è stanco.
8. Il fiume è largo.
9. L'uomo è buono.
10. La strada è larga.
11. La storia è lunga.
12. Il romanzo è lungo.

ADJECTIVES ENDING IN -cio, -cia, -gio, -gia

Note that all adjectives ending in **-cio**, **-gio**, **-cia**, and **-gia** form their plural in **-ci**, **-gi**, **-ce**, and **-ge**. The adjectives belonging to this category are very few, such as:

bigio→bigi	*grayish*	bigia→bige	
grigio→grigi	*gray*	grigia→grige	
marcio→marci	*rotten*	marcia→marce	

IRREGULAR ADJECTIVES OF COLOR

The following adjectives of color do not change form regardless of the noun they modify. They are **arancione** (*orange*), **blu** (blue), **marrone** (*brown*), **rosa** (*pink*), and **viola** (*purple*), and are referred to as *invariable adjectives*. Study the following:

il vestito blu → i vestiti blu	*blue suit*
il fazzoletto rosa → i fazzoletti rosa	*pink kerchief*
la gonna blu → le gonne blu	*blue skirt*
la giacca marrone → le giacche marrone	*brown jacket*
la copertina arancione → le copertine arancione	*orange cover*
la cravatta viola → le cravatte viola	*purple tie*

10. *Pluralize the following sentences:*

1. Il disegno è rosa.
2. La porta è marrone.
3. Il vestito è blu.
4. Il quaderno è arancione.
5. La poltrona è viola.

6. La parete è blu.
7. Il cappello è marrone.
8. La cravatta è rosa.
9. La maglia è arancione.
10. Il gilè è viola.

ADJECTIVES WITH SHORTENED FORMS

The adjectives **bello** (*beautiful, handsome*), **grande** (*great, large*), **santo** (*holy*), **buono** (*good*), and **nessuno** (*no, not one*) have shortened forms when they precede a noun.

Bello

Study the following forms of the adjective **bello** when it precedes a noun. Note the similarity between the endings of the adjective and the forms of the definite article.

lo zio	il bello zio	la zia	la bella zia
l'uomo	il bell'uomo	l'estate	la bell'estate (la bella estate)
il ragazzo	il bel ragazzo	la ragazza	la bella ragazza
gli zii	i begli zii	le zie	le belle zie
gli uomini	i begli uomini	le amiche	le belle amiche
i ragazzi	i bei ragazzi	le ragazze	le belle ragazze

Conforming to the rule for definite articles, **bello** is used before masculine nouns beginning with **z**, **s** plus a consonant, and **ps**. **Bello** is shortened to **bell'** before masculine nouns beginning with a vowel. It is shortened to **bel** before all regular masculine nouns. **Bella** is used with all feminine nouns beginning with a consonant. **Bella** is shortened to **bell'** before feminine nouns beginning with a vowel.

In the plural, **belle** is used with all feminine plural nouns but can be shortened to **bell'** with a plural noun beginning with **e**. **Begli** is used before all masculine plural nouns beginning with **z**, **s** plus a consonant, **ps**, or a vowel. **Bei** is used with all other plural masculine nouns.

For nouns beginning with **e** in the plural, there are optional forms: **l'estati**, **le bell'estati**; **le estati**, **le belle estati**.

11. Complete the following with the correct form of the adjective bello:
1. È un _____ giọrno.
2. Teresa canta una _____ canzone.
3. Ho veduto dei _____ uccelli nel giardino.
4. Carlo ha comprato un _____ spẹcchio.
5. Noi abbiạmo due _____ poltrone nel salotto.
6. I Loro figli sono due _____ ragazzi.
7. C'è un _____ vaso con due _____ fiọri (m. pl.) sul tạvolo.

Grande

The adjective **grande** may be shortened to **gran** before masculine and feminine nouns that begin with a consonant other than **z**, **s** plus a consonant, and **ps**. With all nouns beginning with **z**, **s** plus a consonant, **ps**, or a vowel, **grande** is used.

un gran signore	*a great gentleman*	una gran signora	*a great lady*
un gran maẹstro	*a great master (teacher)*	una gran maẹstra	*a great teacher*
un grande artista	*a great artist*	una grande artista	*a great artist*
un grande zịo	*a great uncle*	una grande zịa	*a great aunt*
un grande studente	*a great student*	una grande studentessa	*a great student*
un grande psicọlogo	*a great psychologist*	una grande psicọloga	*a great psychologist*

However, note that **grande** becomes **grand'** before a masculine noun beginning with **u**:

un grand'uomo	*a great man*

The plural form of **grande** is **grandi** for all nouns.

12. Complete the following with the correct form of the adjective grande:
1. La signora Torre è una_____ donna.
2. Garibaldi fu un_____ uọmo.
3. Milano è una_____ città.
4. La signora Fellini è una_____ artista.
5. Mio padre è un_____ psicọlogo.

Santo

Santo[1] is shortened to **San** before masculine nouns, including proper names, beginning with any consonant other than **z** or **s** plus a consonant. **Sant'** is used before all masculine and feminine names and other nouns beginning with a vowel. **Santa** is used for all other singular feminine names.

Santo:	**Santo Spịrito**	**Santo Zeno**
	Santo Stẹfano	**Santo Zọsimo**
San:	**San Giovanni**	**San Marino**
	San Giuseppe	**San Paolo**
	San Marco	**San Pịetro**
Sant':	**Sant'Anna**	**Sant'Anselmo**
	Sant'Assunta	**Sant'Antimo**
	Sant'Elvira	**Sant'Antọnio**
	Sant'Eufẹmia	**Sant'Onọrio**
Santa:	**Santa Cecịlia**	**Santa Rosalịa**
	Sant Lucịa	**Santa Rosạria**
	Santa Marịa	**Santa Teresa**

---

[1] It is not unusual to see, because of regional usage, **San** in front of names beginning with **Z-** or **S-** plus a consonant: **San Zaccarịa**, **San Stạe**, **San Zeno**, etc. This is particularly so in Venice.

13. Write the correct form of Santo before each of the following names.

1. _____ Alessio
2. _____ Zosimo
3. _____ Teresa
4. _____ Stefano
5. _____ Annunziata
6. _____ Rocco

7. _____ Matteo
8. _____ Zeno
9. _____ Giovanni
10. _____ Maria
11. _____ Andrea
12. _____ Benedetto

Buono and Nessuno

Buono and **nessuno** have forms that are very similar to the forms of the indefinite article. Study the following and note the similarities:

uno zio	*an uncle* → **un buono zio**	*a good uncle*
una zia	*an aunt* → **una buona zia**	*a good aunt*
un ragazzo	*a boy* → **un buon ragazzo**	*a good boy*
una ragazza	*a girl* → **una buona ragazza**	*a good girl*
un amico	*a friend* → **un buon amico**	*a good friend*
un'amica	*a girlfriend* → **una buon'amica**	*a good girlfriend*

Note that **buono** and **nessuno** are shortened to **buon** and **nessun** before all masculine nouns except those beginning with **z**, **s** plus a consonant, or **ps**. **Buona** and **nessuna** are used with all feminine nouns beginning with a consonant and elided to **buon'** and **nessun'** before feminine nouns beginning with a vowel.

Nessuno has no plural forms. The plural of **buono**, **buona** is always **buoni**, **buone**.

14. Complete the following with the correct form of the indicated adjective:

1. Il signor Martini è un _____ maestro. *buono*
2. Questo rimedio non fa _____ male. *nessuno*
3. Pietro non mandò _____ notizia. *nessuno*
4. Maria è una _____ amica. *buono*
5. Carlo e Stefano sono _____ amici. *buono*
6. Lo studente non ha _____ libro. *nessuno*
7. Giuseppe è un _____ studente. *buono*
8. Questo _____ uomo è molto generoso. *buono*
9. È una _____ idea. *buono*
10. _____ anno nuovo! *buono*

TITLES ENDING IN -*e*

Titles ending in -**e**, such as **dottore** and **signore,** drop the final -**e** before proper names. Study the following:

Buongiorno, dottore.	*But:*	**Buongiorno, dottor Marini.**
Goodmorning, doctor.		*Good morning. Dr. Marini.*
L'ingegnere è canadese.	*But:*	**L'ingegner Martin è canadese.**
The engineer is Canadian.		*Engineer Martin is Canadian.*
Il professore è americano.	*But:*	**Il professor Smith è americano.**
The professor is American.		*Professor Smith is American.*
ArrivederLa, signore (m. s.)	*But:*	**ArrivederLa, signor De Lena.**
Goodbye, sir.		*Goodbye, Mr. De Lena.*

15. Supply the correct form of the titles provided.

1. Il _____ Pirri è specializzato in chirurgia. *dottore*
2. Buongiorno, _____ Monti. *professore*
3. Buona sera, _____ De Lena. *professore*
4. L'_____ è italiano. *ingegnere*
5. Quel_____ è dentista. *signore*
6. Come sta l'_____ Trevi? *ingegnere*
7. Il _____ Marchi arriva alle cinque. *signore*
8. _____, come sta mio figlio? *dottore*
9. L'_____ Brunetti abita a Venezia, *ispettore*
10. Il _____ Sacco è bravissimo. *dottore*
11. Il _____ Martini insegna storia. *professore*
12. ArrivederLa, _____. *ispettore*
13. Buongiorno, _____ Taviani. *ingegnere*
14. Questo _____ arriva sempre tardi. *signore*
15. Come sta, _____ Fabbri? *dottore*

FORMATION OF NOUNS FROM ADJECTIVES

Most adjectives can become nouns when they are accompanied by the definite article.

I giovani viaggiano dappertutto.
Young people travel all over.

I vecchi hanno molto da raccontare.
Old people have a lot to tell.

I cattivi non piacciono a nessuno.
Nobody likes bad people.

16. Change the following adjectives into nouns according to the model:
i ragazzi ribelli → i ribelli

1. il signore ricco
2. le ragazze giovani
3. i tipi cattivi
4. le signorine americane
5. il ragazzo povero
6. la signora italiana
7. il fratello minore

POSSESSIVE ADJECTIVES

Possessive adjectives indicate ownership or possession. All possessive adjectives must agree in gender and number with the noun they modify with the exception of **loro** (their) and **Loro** (your, formal plural). In order to avoid ambiguity, it is recommended to use capital **S-** for formal **Suo, Suoi, Sua, Sue,** and capital **L-** for formal **Loro**. The possessive adjectives are preceded by the appropriate definite article. Study the following:

il mio vestito	i miei vestiti	*my suit*
la mia cravatta	le mie cravatte	*my tie*
il tuo amico	i tuoi amici	*your (tu) friend, m.*
la tua amica	le tue amiche	*your (tu) friend, m.*
il suo cappotto	i suoi cappotti	*his/her overcoat*
la sua maglia	le sue maglie	*his/her sweater*
il Suo cappotto	i Suoi cappotti	*your (Lei) overcoat*
la Sua maglia	le Sue maglie	*your (Lei) sweater*

il nostro vicino	i nostri vicini	*our neighbor, m.*
la nostra vicina	le nostre vicine	*our neighbor, f.*
il vostro giardino	i vostri giardini	*your (voi) garden*
la vostra bicicletta	le vostre biciclette	*your (voi) bicycle*
il loro libro	i loro libri	*their book*
la loro rivista	le loro riviste	*their magazine*
il Loro computer	i Loro computer	*your (Loro) computer*
la Loro casa	le Loro case	*your (Loro) house*

17. Complete the following sentences by supplying the appropriate possessive pronouns according to the italicized subject pronouns:

1. _____ vestiti sono nuovi. *noi* (we)
2. _____ camicia è verde. *io* (I)
3. _____ amici sono bravi. *tu* (you, s.)
4. _____ amiche sono brave. *tu* (you, s.)
5. _____ vicini sono italiani. *lui* (he)
6. _____ bicicletta è rossa. *voi* (you, pl.)
7. _____ riviste sono interessanti. *loro* (they)
8. _____ cravatte sono belle. *io* (I)
9. _____ libri sono grossi. *noi* (we)
10. _____ cappotti sono pesanti. *lei* (she)
11. Signora, _____ vestito e_____ scarpe sono eleganti. *Lei* (you formal s.)
12. Signor Bertoni, _____cravatta e_____ pantaloni sono di Versace. *Lei* (you formal s.)
13. Signori, _____figli sono educati. *Loro* (you formal pl.)
14. Signorine, _____amiche sono arrivate. *Loro* (you formal pl.)
15. Signor Pirri e signora Torre, _____ amica è qui. *Loro* (you formal pl.)
16 Signorina, _____genitori La chiamano. *Lei* (you formal s.)
17. Signori De Lena, _____tavolo è pronto. *Loro* (you formal pl.)
18. _____ vicina è malata. *noi* (we)
19. Roberto, _____ telecomando è sul tavolo. *tu* (you s.)
20. _____ automobile è dal meccanico. *lui* (he)

With Nouns Denoting Family Members or Relatives

Possessive adjectives followed by singular nouns denoting family members or relatives do not use the definite article with the exception of **loro** (e.g., **la loro madre,** *their mother*). Study the following:

Singular	*Plural*
Mia sorella è a scuola.	**Le mie sorelle sono a scuola.**
My sister is at school.	*My sisters are at school.*
Tuo cugino è americano.	**I tuoi cugini sono americani.**
Your cousin is American.	*Your cousins are American.*
Il loro fratello è in Italia.	**I loro fratelli sono in Italia.**
Their brother is in Italy.	*Their brothers are in Italy.*

18. Complete the following sentences by supplying the appropriate possessive adjectives according to the indicated subject pronouns:

1. _____ madre è dottoressa. *io*
2. _____ sorelle studiano molto. *noi*
3. _____ cugina viaggia spesso. *voi*
4. _____ fratelli lavorano in città. *tu*
5. _____ padre è maestro. *lei*

6. _____ nonni sono in Italia. *loro*

7. _____ zia parla molte lingue. *loro*

8. _____ zio ha sessantadue anni. *lui*

9. _____ nonna è molto saggia. *io*

10. _____ fratelli frequentano l'università. *noi*

Note that the formal possessive adjectives **Suo** (*your*) and **Loro** (*your*) begin with capital letters. This practice, however, is frequently not observed.

il Suo libro	*your book* → **i Suoi libri**	*your books*
la Sua penna	*your pen* → **le Sue penne**	*your pens*
il Loro cane	*your dog* → **i Loro cani**	*your dogs*
la Loro vacanza	*your vacation* → **le Loro vacanze**	*your vacations*

Study the following sentences:

Signora, il Suo cappello è elegantissimo.
Madame, your hat is very elegant.

Dottor Martini, i Suoi pazienti sono qui.
Dr. Martini, your patients are here.

Signor Valetti e Signorina Torre, i Loro libri sono arrivati.
Mr. Valetti and Miss Torre, your books have arrived.

Signori, le Loro prenotazioni sono confermate.
Gentlemen, your reservations are confirmed.

19. Complete the following sentences with the appropriate possessive adjectives. In some sentences, a subject pronoun indicates the possessive adjective to be used.

1. Mi vuoi prestare _____ motocicletta?

2. Luigi desidera vedere _____ nonni.

3. _____ sorella studia lingue straniere (*foreign*). *io*

4. Andiamo al teatro Rossini con _____ amici.

5. _____ zii arrivano domani. *tu*

6. Signor Spinelli, _____ biglietto è pronto.

7. Gli studenti preparano _____ lezioni.

8. Signori, dove sono _____ valige?

9. _____ madre lavora in un ospedale. *noi*

10. Luisa va in Italia con _____ fratelli.

11. Signorina Marini, può chiamare _____ padre?

12. _____ amiche vanno alla spiaggia tutti i giorni. *noi*

13. I bambini giocano con _____ giocattoli.

14. Le studentesse leggono _____ riviste.

15. Don Giuseppe, _____ caffè espresso è sul tavolino.

16. _____ zia Angelina è molto brava. *io*

17. Roberto accompagna _____ cugine a casa.

20. Rewrite the following sentences substituting the words in italics with the appropriate possessive adjectives. Make all necessary changes, and include the definite article when needed.

1. Gli amici *di Paolo* telefonano spesso.

2. La sorella *di Luisa e di Carlo* studia molto.

3. Lo zio *di Stefano* è molto ricco.

4. La madre *di Antonio* è giovane.

5. Le amiche *di Olga* sono greche.

DEMONSTRATIVE ADJECTIVES

The demonstrative adjective **questo** (*this*) has four forms—**questo**, m. s.; **questa**, f. s.; **questi**, m. pl.; and **queste**, f. pl.—and agrees in gender and number with the noun it modifies. Note that, before nouns beginning with a vowel, **quest'** (**quest'amico**) may be used. The use of the latter is optional. The definite article is not used with demonstrative adjectives.

questo cavallo	*this horse*	**questi cavalli**	*these horses*
questa macchina	*this car*	**queste macchine**	*these cars*

The forms of the demonstrative adjective **quello** (*that*) are very similar to the forms of the definite article. To the letters **'que'** are added the appropriate definite articles. Review the articulated prepositions, Chapter 2, page 33. Also, **quello** takes the same forms as **bello** (*handsome*, *beautiful*), see page 48.

lo	quello studente	la	quella studentessa
	quello zio		quella zia
	quello psicologo		quella psicologa
l'	quell'amico	l'	quell'amica
	quell'inverno		quell'estate
il	quel ragazzo	la	quella ragazza
	quel libro		quella rivista
gli	quegli studenti	le	quelle studentesse
	quegli zii		quelle zie
	quegli psicologi		quelle psicologhe
	quegli amici		quelle amiche
	quegli (quegl') inverni		quelle (quell') estati
i	quei ragazzi	le	quelle ragazze
	quei libri		quelle riviste

21. Rewrite the following sentences in the singular:

1. Quegli studenti sono studiosi.
2. Queste cravatte sono blu.
3. Quelle spiagge sono bellissime.
4. Quei signori sono americani.
5. Questi amici sono generosi.
6. Quelle amiche sono italiane.
7. Questi zii sono vecchi.
8. Quegli alberi sono alti.
9. Queste macchine sono veloci.
10. Quei libri sono vecchi.
11. Questi giornali sono interessanti.
12. Quegli zaini sono pieni.
13. Queste estati sono meravigliose.
14. Quegli psicologi sono giovani.

22. Complete the following with the appropriate demonstrative adjective:

1. (*These*)_____paesaggi sono pittoreschi.
2. (*Those*)_____fotografie sono lucide.
3. (*That*)_____inverno è duro.
4. (*This*)_____amica è inglese.
5. (*That*)_____albero è alto.
6. (*These*)_____studentesse sono brave.
7. (*Those*)_____gnocchi sono deliziosi.
8. (*This*)_____signora è dell'Irlanda.
9. (*That*)_____psichiatra (m.) è giovane.
10. (*That*)_____dottoressa è brava.
11. (*That*)_____zio è scherzoso.
12. (*Those*)_____asparagi sono gustosi.
13. (*This*)_____tavolo è marrone.
14. (*That*)_____ragazzo gioca sempre.
15. (*That*)_____biblioteca è grande.

EXPRESSIONS *Che!* AND *Quanta!*

The exclamation *What a ...!* in Italian is expressed by the word **Che** ...! Study the following:

Che folla!	*What a crowd!*
Che bella giornata!	*What a beautiful day!*
Che belle giornate!	*What beautiful days!*
Che bel paesaggio!	*What a beautiful landscape!*
Che bei paesaggi!	*What beautiful landscapes!*

The exclamation **Quanto!** (**Quanti!, Quanta!, Quante!**) expresses a number or a quantity of people or things. It literally means *So much!* or *So many!* **Quanto!** agrees in gender and number with the noun it modifies. Study the following:

Quanto rumore!	*So much noise!*
Quanti bravi giocatori!	*So many excellent players!*
Quanta gente!	*So many people!*
Quante belle barche!	*So many beautiful boats!*

23. Rewrite the following in Italian:
1. What a game (*partita*)!
2. What pretty flowers!
3. So many books!
4. So much happiness (*gioia*)!
5. What a fantastic idea!
6. So many friends!
7. What a beautiful day!
8. What beautiful cities!

FORMATION OF ADVERBS

In Italian adverbs are formed by adding the suffix **-mente** to the singular feminine form of the masculine adjective ending in **-o**.

meraviglioso	*marvelous* → **meravigliosa** → **meravigliosamente**	*marvelously*
disastroso	*disastrous* → **disastrosa** → **disastrosamente**	*disastrously*
ottimo	*excellent* → **ottima** → **ottimamente**	*excellently*
bonario	*good-natured* → **bonaria** → **bonariamente**	*good-naturedly*
valoroso	*courageous* → **valorosa** → **valorosamente**	*courageously*

Many adjectives ending in **-e** simply add **-mente** without any change. Adjectives ending in **-le** and **-re** drop the final **-e** before **-mente** is added.

enorme	*enormous* → **enormemente**	*enormously*
corrente	*current* → **correntemente**	*currently*
legale	*legal* → **legalmente**	*legally*
orribile	*horrible* → **orribilmente**	*horribly*
regolare	*regular* → **regolarmente**	*regularly*
basilare	*basic* → **basilarmente**	*basically*
particolare	*particular* → **particolarmente**	*particularly*

24. Change the following into adverbs:
1. difficile
2. grazioso
3. forte
4. terribile
5. interno
6. mirabile
7. caro
8. militare
9. urgente
10. veloce
11. leale
12. aristocratico
13. liberale
14. paziente
15. magistrale
16. facile

17. raro   20. lento
18. breve   21. singolare
19. parziale   22. preliminare

REVIEW

25. Supply the appropriate forms of the following adjectives in parentheses in the spaces provided.

   1. Olga è una ragazza molto_____. (*buono*)

   2. Lo zio di Paolo è un _____cuoco. (*grande*)

   3. Le loro lettere sono troppo_____. (*lungo*)

   4. Tutte le mie camicie sono_____. (*bianco*)

   5. I suoi pantaloni sono_____. (*marrone*)

   6. Tuo padre è un_____uomo. (*bello*)

   7. Quei fazzoletti sono_____. (*viola*)

   8. Quelle srudentesse sono_____. '(*intelligente*)

   9. Gli esercizi sono_____. (*facile*)

  10. I miei amici sono_____. (*generoso*)

  11. Il gatto e il cane sono animali_____. (*domestico*)

  12. Questo formaggio è_____. (*francese*)

  13. Quelle riviste sono_____ (*vecchio*)

  14. I tuoi vestiti sono tutti_____. (*blu*)

  15. Quei televisori (*television sets*) sono_____. (*tedesco*)

  16. Teresa e Maria sono_____. (*greco*)

  17. Oggi ci sono_____studenti. (*poco*)

  18. Fermiamoci! Siamo_____! (*stanco*)

  19. I libri sono sempre_____. (*utile*)

  20. La madre di Aldo è una persona_____. (*importante*)

  21. Oggi è la festa di_____Stefano. (*Santo*)

  22. La basilica di_____Antonio è a Padova. (*Santo*)

  23. Lui non ha_____amico. (*nessuno*)

  24. Stefano è un_____amico. (*buono*)

  25. È una_____idea, (*buono*)

26. Give the Italian equivalents of the following sentences.

   1. Good morning, Inspector Brunetti!

   2. Professor Rossi lives (*abita*) in Rome.

   3. What a beautiful view (*veduta*)!

   4. Those students are from foreign countries (*paesi stranieri*).

   5. Paul's friends are English.

   6. So many people!

   7. That beach is long and wide.

   8. That horse is a champion.

   9. Luisa, where are your books?

  10. Mr. Peruzzi, when are you buying your new suits?

27. Change the following adjectives into adverbs in the spaces provided:

   1. facile_____

   2. feroce_____

   3. coraggioso_____

   4. raro _____

   5. sleale (*disloyal*)_____

   6. triste_____

7. irregolare_____
8. breve_____
9. esterno _____
10. flẹbile (*feeble*)_____

28. Rewrite the following sentences in the plural.
1. Il corridọio è lungo e largo.
2. La casa è biạnca e magnịfica.
3. Mịo zịo è simpạtico.
4. Il lavoratore è stanco.
5. Compro una giacca blu e una camịcia grịgia.
6. Quell'uọmo è un gran calciatore.
7. Il grande artista è sempre originale.
8. Il professore americano vịsita l'Itạlia.
9. L'amico di Pạolo è islandese.
10. La nostra amica è simpạtica e intelligente.

29. Supply the appropriate forms of santo, grande, buọno, and quẹllo as indicated.
1. La festa di_____Stẹfano è il ventisẹi dicembre. *santo*
2. Pạolo e Renzo sono dei_____ragazzi. *buọno*
3. _____alberi sono molto pregiati. *quẹllo*
4. Il padre di Mạrio è un_____signore. *grande*
5. _____Anna ha molti devoti. *santo*
6. Teresa è una_____amica, *buọno*
7. Pịetro Annigoni è un_____artista. *grande*
8. _____ragazzi giọcano tutto il giọrno. *quẹllo*
9. Pịetro e Pạolo sono dei_____importanti. *santo*
10. Il signor Freni è un_____uọmo. *buọno*

CHAPTER 4

COMPARATIVES AND SUPERLATIVES

COMPARATIVES

In Italian, comparatives are expressed with the following words:

Comparatives of equality:

(cosí) … come	*as … as*
(tanto) … quanto	*as … as; as much as*
non meno che	*not less than*
non meno di	*not less than*

Comparatives of inequality:

piú … di; piú … che	*more than*
meno … di; meno … che	*less than*

Comparatives of equality with adjectives

The comparative of adjectives may be one of equality or inequality. The comparison of equality means two items being compared have equal characteristics (**as … as**). In Italian the words **cosí … come** or **tanto … quanto** are used. Note that in the examples that follow, **cosí** and **tanto** appear in parentheses; that's because their use is optional. **Cosí … come** and **tanto … quanto** are interchangeable.

Roberto è (cosí) alto quanto Luisa.
Roberto è (tanto) alto quanto Luisa.
Robert is as tall as Louise.

Luisa è (cosí) alta come Roberto.
Luisa è (tanto alta) quanto Roberto.
Louise is as tall as Robert.

Questi libri sono (cosí) interessanti come gli altri.
Questi libri sono (tanto) interessanti quanto gli altri.
These books are as interesting as the others.

Note that the disjunctive personal pronouns are used following a term of comparison. (The disjunctive personal pronouns appear on page 228.)

Luisa è $\genfrac{}{}{0pt}{}{\text{(cosí)}}{\text{(tanto)}}$ **alta** $\genfrac{}{}{0pt}{}{\text{come}}{\text{quanto}}$ **lui.**

Louise is as tall as he.

Teresa è $\genfrac{}{}{0pt}{}{\text{(cosí)}}{\text{(tanto)}}$ **intellignte** $\genfrac{}{}{0pt}{}{\text{come}}{\text{quanto}}$ **me.**

Theresa is as intelligent as I.

Note **that** comparisons concerning verbs use **(tanto) quanto.**

Mario lavora (tanto) quanto Luigi.
Mario works as much as Louis.

Note that **cosí** and **tanto** may be also omitted before adverbs.

Gianna scia (cosí) bene come Ezio.
Gianna skies as well as Ezio.

Luisa canta (tanto) bene quanto Mario.
Louise sings as well as Mario.

1. *Complete the following with the appropriate words to express the comparative of equality*
1. Maria è cosí brava_____Stefano.
2. Questi ragazzi son tanto alti_____quelli.
3. Noi siamo cosí intelligenti_____loro.
4. Io sono cosí biondo_____mio cugino.
5. Questa pittura è tanto bella_____l'altra.

2. *Complete the following with the appropriate words to express the comparative of equality*
1. Questa forchetta è_____ leggera come l'altra.
2. Carlo è_____ricco quanto suo fratello.
3. Queste spiagge sono_____belle come le altre.
4. Questi libri sono_____interessanti quanto gli altri.
5. Queste lezioni sono_____difficili quanto tutte le altre.

3. *Complete the following with appropriate words to express the comparative of equality.*
1. Antonio guida (tanto) bene_____Teresa.
2. Quei giocatori giocano (cosí) bene_____questi.
3. Voi cantate (tanto) male_____noi.
4. Questi computer funzionano (cosí) bene_____quelli.
5. Tu falci l'erba (tanto) bene_____loro.

Comparative of Equality with Nouns

The comparative of equality can also be expressed with nouns (as *many…as; as much … as*). In Italian the words **tanto …quanto** are used with nouns. Note that **tanto** must agree with the noun it modifies and cannot be placed in parentheses.

Noi abbiamo tanti euro quanto voi.
We have as many euros as you (voi) do.

Maria ha tanta energia quanto sua sorella.
Mary has as much energy as her sister.

Questo museo ha tante statue quanto l'altro.
This museum has as many statues as the other one.

Quel manoscritto ha tanto valore quanto questo.
That manuscript has as much value as this one.

When both **tanto** and **quanto** are followed by nouns, the former must agree in gender and number with the nouns they modify.

> **Nel cassetto ci sono tanti coltelli quante forchette.**
> *In the drawer there are as many knives as forks.*

> **Sul tavolo c'è tanta farina quanto zucchero.**
> *On the table there is as much flour as sugar.*

4. Complete the following with the appropriate words to express the comparison of equality:
1. Lui mangia_____verdure_____noi.
2. Io leggo_____libri_____mio fratello.
3. Teresa riceve_____lettere_____loro.
4. Questa signora guadagna_____soldi_____quella.
5. Ci sono_____forchette_____coltelli sulla tavola.
6. Genova non ha_____abitanti_____Napoli.
7. Quel signore ha tanti dollari_____euro.

Note that **cosí … come** and **tanto … quanto** can be used alone without modifying any other word. **Cosí** and **tanto** are often omitted from the comparisons. Observe the following:

> **Tu ti vesti cosí come me.**
> **Tu ti vesti come me.**
> *You dress as I do.*

> **Antonio lavora tanto quanto lui.**
> **Antonio lavora quanto lui.**
> *Anthony works as much as he does.*

5. Complete the following with the appropriate words:
1. Carlo studia_____quanto me.
2. Io mi vesto_____come lui.
3. Voi correte_____me.
4. Loro lavorano_____noi.

Comparative of Inequality

The comparatives of inequality are **piú … di, piú … che, meno … di, meno … che** (*more … than, less … than*). When using **piú … di** or **meno … di**, note that **di** contracts with the definite articles it precedes when two entities are being compared.

> **Stefano ha piú libri di Luigi.**
> *Stephen has more books than Louis.*

> **La ragazza ha piú amici del ragazzo.**
> *The girl has more friends than the boy.*

> **Pietro ha meno cugini della sua amica.**
> *Peter has fewer cousins than his friend.*

The comparatives **piú … che** (*more … than*) and **meno … che** (*less … than*) are used when describing one entity (with two adjectives, two nouns, or two verbs). Observe below:

> **Questa città è piú sporca che bella.**
> *This city is more dirty than (it is) beautiful.*

> **A Roma ci sono meno chiese che fontane.**
> *In Rome there are fewer churches than (there are) fountains.*

> **È piú facile giocare che studiare.**
> *It is easier to play than to study.*

Roberto è meno ricco che bello.
Robert is less rich than (he is) handsome.

Piú di … and **meno di** … are used when the comparison is followed by a number.

Abbiạmo piú di diẹci ẹuro.
We have more than ten euros.

Il libro costa meno di sette dọllari.
The book costs less than seven dollars.

Non ho piú di cịnque dọllari.
I don't have more than five dollars.

Non cọstano meno di venti ẹuro.
They don't cost less than twenty euros.

Di is also used before the adverbs **piú** and **meno** when they follow a verb at the end of a sentence.

Ti piạce il vino? Perciò hai bevuto di piú.
Do you like wine? That's why you (tu) drank more.

Non mi sento bene; ho mangiạto di meno.
I don't feel well; I ate less.

Piú … di and **meno … di** are used before pronouns.
Il mịo cane è piú grande del tụo.
My dog is bigger than yours (tu).

La sụa moto è meno veloce della tụa.
His/her bike is less fast than yours (tu).

Quẹl vestito è piú elegante di quẹsto.
That suit is more elegant than this one.

Vọi siẹte piú cạuti di noi.
You (voi) are more cautious than us.

6. *Complete the following sentences with the appropriate words for the comparative. The comparatives meaning more … than and less … than are indicated with the signs + and - on the right side.*
   1. Carlo e Piẹtro fanno_____rumore_____loro cugini.   +
   2. Piẹtro mangia_____te.   -
   3. Noi studiamo_____loro.   +
   4. Voi comprate_____libri_____signora.   -
   5. Le bambine vọgliono_____regali_____noi.   +
   6. A Nuọva York ci sono_____negozi_____grattaciẹli.   +
   7. È_____difficile camminare_____saltare.   -
   8. Sịlvia è_____intelligente_____buọna.   +
   9. Noi abbiạmo_____amici_____Luịsa. -
   10. Luigi è_____alto_____Piẹtro. +
   11. Luigi ha_____cịnque dọllari.   +
   12. Tu hai_____diciannove anni.   -
   13. Quẹsta penna è_____bella_____buọna.   +
   14. Questi giocạttoli sono_____utili_____belli. -
   15. Io ho_____quịndici anni.   +

7. *Give the Italian equivalents of the following sentences.*
   1. My little cat is cuter than yours (tu).
   2. His/her car is faster than ours.

3. Those home appliances are less modern than these.
4. Today the children felt well and ate more.
5. With that headache I slept less.
6. Gino's sister is more athletic than all of us.
7. I'm always tired (m.); I play less than you (voi).
8. In Rome there are more cars than buses.
9. The professor has more books than us.
10. In Venice there are more bridges than canals.
11. Mary is rich! She has more than one hundred euros!
12. I'm very poor! I have fewer than ten euros.

RELATIVE SUPERLATIVE OF ADJECTIVES

The relative superlative of adjectives (*most, -est, least*) is formed by using the appropriate definite article and the word **piú** (or **meno**) before the adjective and the preposition **di** contracted with the definite article before the noun.

Teresa è la (ragazza) piú brava della classe.
Theresa is the smartest (girl) in the class.

Roberto è il (ragazzo) meno atlętico del gruppo.
Robert is the least athletic (boy) of the group.

Nuọva York è la città piú grande degli Stati Uniti.
New York is the largest city in the United States.

Stęfano e Antọnio sono i piú alti della famiglia.
Stephen and Anthony are the tallest in the family.

Marịa e Rosa sono le piú brave del riọne.
Mary and Rose are the smartest in the neighborhood.

8. Complete the following with the appropriate words for the relative superlative:
1. Loro sono_____studentesse_____brave_____classe.
2. Carlo e Pięto sono_____ragazzi_____bassi_____gruppo.
3. Quẹsta scuola è_____moderna_____città.
4. Il padre di Olga è_____dottore_____famoso_____Roma.
5. La Sicịlia è_____grande isola_____Mediterraneo.
6. Pelé è_____calciatore_____famoso_____mondo.
7. Quẹsti ragazzi sono_____atlętici_____scuọla.
8. Marịa è_____atlętica_____tutte.
9. Quẹlle studentesse sono_____intelligenti.
10. Il signor Martini è_____ingegnere_____abile_____fạbbrica.

ABSOLUTE SUPERLATIVE OF ADJECTIVES AND ADVERBS

The absolute superlative is formed by adding the suffix **-ịssimo** to an adjective or an adverb after dropping the last vowel of both the adjective and the adverb. It gives the meaning of *most, very,* and *extremely*.

bello	handsome → **bellịssimo**	*most handsome*
intelligente	*intelligent* → **intelligentịssimo**	*extremely intelligent*
capace	*able* → **capacịssimo**	*very able*
ricco	*rich* → **ricchịssimo**	*very rich*
bene	*well* → **benịssimo**	*very well*
male	*badly* → **malịssimo**	*very badly*

Note that the absolute superlative behaves like a regular (or positive) adjective and must agree in gender and number with the noun it modifies.

una signora intelligentissima → delle signore intelligentissime	*a very intelligent lady*
un giovane ricchissimo → dei giovani ricchissimi	*a very rich young man*
una lezione utilissima → delle lezioni utilissime	*a very useful lesson*
un ragazzo poverissimo → dei ragazzi poverissimi	*a very poor boy*

In order to preserve the hard sound of the positive adjective, an **h** must be added to the adjective ending in **-co, -go, -ca**, and **-ga** before **-issimo**.

un uomo stanco	*a tired man* → **un uomo stanchissimo**	*a very tired man*
una donna ricca	*a rich woman* → **una donna ricchissima**	*a very rich woman*
un fiume largo	*a wide river* → **un fiume larghissimo**	*a very wide river*
una strada larga	*a wide street* → **una strada larghissima**	*a very wide street*

The absolute superlative may also be formed by placing the adverbs **assai** (*very, much*) and **molto** (*very*) before the adjective or the adverb.

buono	*good* → **molto buono**	*very good*
bene	*well* → **molto bene**	*very well*
abile	*able* → **assai abile**	*very able*
facilmente	*easily* → **molto facilmente**	*very easily*
male	*badly* → **molto male**	*very badly*
bella	*beautiful* → **molto bella**	*very beautiful*

9. Follow the model:
> **È un giovane molto povero → È un giovane poverissimo.**
> *He is a very poor young man.*

1. Il signor Rossi è molto sensibile.
2. Teresa sta molto bene.
3. La stanza è molto grande.
4. La rivista è molto utile.
5. Gli stadi sono molto grandi.
6. È un lavoro molto difficile.

10. Follow the model:
> **È una signora ricchissima → È una signora molto ricca.** *She is a very rich lady.*

1. Il teatro è affollatissimo.
2. L'esame è facilissimo.
3. Roberto sta malissimo.
4. L'appartamento è modernissimo.

IRREGULAR COMPARATIVES AND SUPERLATIVES

The adjectives **buono**, **cattivo**, **grande**, and **piccolo** have irregular forms for the comparative and superlatives.

Positive		Comparative		Relative superlative		Absolute superlative	
buono	*good*	migliore	*better*	il migliore	*the best*	ottimo	*very good*
cattivo	*bad*	peggiore	*worse*	il peggiore	*the*	pessimo	*very bad*
grande	*big*	maggiore	*older*	il maggiore	*the oldest*	massimo	*best, most*
piccolo	*small*	minore	*younger*	il minore	*the youngest*	minimo	*worst*

The comparative forms are expressed without an article. The appropriate definite article is used with the relative superlative. Study the following:

Comparative:	**Quęsto studente è migliǫre (peggiǫre) dell'altro.**
	This student is better (worse) than the other.
Relative Superlative:	**Quęsto studente è il migliǫre (il peggiǫre) di tutti**.
	This student is the best (the worst) of all.
Comparative:	**Quęsta casa è migliǫre dell'altra.**
	This house is better than the other one.
Relative Superlative	**Quęste strade sono le peggiǫri di tutte**.
	These streets are the worst of all.

When they refer to people, the words **maggiǫre** and **minore** express the meaning of age rather than size.

Luigi è il fratello minore.
Louis is the younger brother.

Roberto è maggiǫre di suo fratello.
Robert is older than his brother.

Luisa è minore di sua sorella.
Louise is younger than her sister.

Olga è la maggiǫre della famiglia.
Olga is the oldest in the family.

In order to convey the meaning of size, **grande** and **piccolo** are used.

Quęsto pacco è piú grande di quello.
This package is bigger than that one.

Carlo è il piú piccolo del gruppo.
Charles is the smallest (one) in the group.

11. Complete the following with the appropriate form of the comparative or relative superlative according to the indicated expressions:

1. Maria è_____sua sorella.　　　*Ha piú anni.*
2. Quęsto musęo è_____della città.　　*È molto grande.*
3. Roberto è_____suo amico.　　　*È piú alto.*
4. Carlo è_____.　　　　　*È molto piccolo.*
5. Mio nonno è_____mia nonna.　　*Ha piú anni.*
6. Luisa è_____sua cugina.　　　*Ha meno anni.*
7. Olga è_____della classe.　　　*È la piú buǫna.*
8. Stęfano è_____suo fratello.　*È piú basso.*

12. Write the following in Italian.

1. Who is the youngest girl here?
2. I am older than you (*te*), but Anthony (*Antǫnio*) is the oldest.
3. They are good, but we are better.
4. George (*Giǫrgio*) and Gabriel (*Gabrięle*) are the best.
5. This book is better than that one (*quęllo*).
6. Teresa (*Theresa*) is my younger sister.
7. Stephen (*Stęfano*) is our best cousin.
8. Joseph (*Giuseppe*) is her older brother.

IRREGULAR COMPARATIVES AND SUPERLATIVES OF ADVERBS

The adverbs **bene**, **male**, **molto**, and **poco** have irregular forms in the comparative and relative superlative. All of these adverbs have regular absolute superlative forms: **bene** → **molto bene, benịssimo; male** → **molto male, malịssimo; molto** → **moltịssimo; poco** → **pochịssimo.**

Positive		Comparative		Relative Superlative	
bene	well	**mẹglio**	better	**il mẹglio**	the best
male	badly	**pẹggio**	worse	**il pẹggio**	the worst
molto	a lot	**piú (di piú)**	more	**il piú**	the most
poco	a little	**meno (di meno)**	less	**il meno**	the least

Study the following examples:

Come stại? Sto mẹglio.
How are you? I am better.

Come sta Luịsa? Sta pẹggio.
How is Louise? She is worse.

È mẹglio tornare a casa adesso.
It's better to go back home now.

È pẹggio di prima.
It's worse than before.

Se Carlo stụdia, fa mẹglio a scuọla.
If Charles studies, he does better in school.

Piú studiạmo, piú imparịamo.
The more we study, the more we learn.

Meno mangiạmo, piú dimagriạmo.
The less we eat, the more weight we lose.

Lo vedo il meno possịbile.
I see him as little as possible.

Stụdio il piú possịbile.
I study as much as possible.

13. **Compare the following sentences in the comparative or superlative using the indicated expressions as a guide:**
    1. Luịgi sta_____di prima.   *non bene come prima*
    2. Luịsa studia_____possịbile.   *moltịssimo*
    3. Non sto male, sto_____di iẹri.   *non male come prima*
    4. È tardi, è_____tornare a casa.
    5. Piú lavoro,_____mạngio.   *mạngio poco*
    6. Alberto sta_____.   *molto male*
    7. I ragazzi stanno_____.   *molto bene*

REVIEW

14. **Give the Italian equivalents of the following sentences.**
    1. We (f.) are as tall as they.
    2. Paul is as studious as Mary.

3. In this classroom there are more boys than girls.
4. They have as many friends as we do.
5. He is older than forty.
6. Theresa studies as much as Marco.
7. Olga and Theresa are the smartest in the class.
8. Robert is the least studious in the class.
9. I have fewer friends than you (*tu*).
10. They run (*corrono*) more than us.
11. We sing as she does.
12. Charles is as short as his cousin.
13. This bread is better than the other.
14. Those shoes are worse than these.
15. Carmelina is the younger sister.
16. Peter is the smallest in the class.
17. This cheese (*formaggio*) is very bad.
18. Who is the oldest boy?
19. Her coat is very heavy (*pesante*).
20. In Venice there are more churches (*chiesa*) than stadiums (*stadio*).

15. Supply the appropriate words as needed.

1. Paul has more shoes than ties.
2. Louise sends more e-mails than me.
3. You (*voi*) write better than them.
4. Ezio is less tall than you (*tu*).
5. These dogs bark (*abbaiano*) as much as those.
6. Marisa speaks Spanish as well as he does.
7. He has more euros than us.
8. These children (m.) have as many toys as those.
9. Those children (f.) have as many toys as shoes.
10. We have more euros than dollars.
11. She is not hungry; she eats less.
12. They (f.) are not tired; they play more.
13. This cat (m.) is bigger than his.
14. His sisters are older than mine.
15. Mario is the smartest (boy) in the class.
16. Olga and Mary are the most athletic of the group (*gruppo*).
17. Those ladies are very rich; in fact, they are the richest.
18. I feel (*mi sento*) very badly!
19. That statue is very beautiful; it is the most beautiful in the museum.
20. It was (*è stata*) a very long lesson!

16. In the spaces provided, supply A: the relative superlative and B: the absolute superlative of each adjective or adverb.

1. bello: A: _____   B: _____
2. intelligente (f.): A: _____   B: _____
3. ricchi: A: _____   B: _____
4. larga: A: _____   B: _____
5. utile (f. pl.):   A: _____   B: _____
6. stanche: A: _____   B: _____

CHAPTER 5

Numbers, Dates, and Time

NUMBERS

Cardinal Numbers

The Italian cardinal numbers are as follows:

1	uno	*8*	otto	*15*	quindici
2	due	*9*	nove	*16*	sedici
3	tre	*10*	dieci	*17*	diciassette
4	quattro	*11*	undici	*18*	diciotto
5	cinque	*12*	dodici	*19*	diciannove
6	sei	*13*	tredici	*20*	venti
7	sette	*14*	quattordici		

After **venti, trenta, quaranta**, etc., the numbers **uno** through **nove** are added and attached. Note that the final vowel of **venti, trenta, quaranta**, etc., is dropped when the numbers **uno** and **otto** are added. Also, when the number **tre** is added to **venti**, etc., the final **-e** of **tre** is accented: **ventitré**, etc. The final vowel of **ventuno, trentuno**, etc., is dropped before nouns: **ventun llbri, trentun cavalli, sessantun ragazze**, etc. Observe the following numbers:

21	ventuno	*41*	quarantuno	*73*	settantatré
22	ventidue	*43*	quarantatré	*75*	settantacinque
23	ventitré	*48*	quarantotto	*78*	settantotto
24	ventiquattro	*50*	cinquanta	*80*	ottanta
25	venticinque	*51*	cinquàntuno	*81*	ottantuno
26	ventisei	*53*	cinquantatré	*83*	ottantatré
27	ventisette	*58*	cinquantotto	*86*	ottantasei
28	ventotto	*60*	sessanta	*88*	ottantotto
29	ventinove	*61*	sessantuno	*90*	novanta
30	trenta	*63*	sessantatré	*91*	novantuno
31	trentuno	*68*	sessantotto	*92*	novantadue
33	trentatré	*69*	sessantanove	*93*	novantatré
38	trentotto	*70*	settanta	*98*	novantotto
40	quaranta	*71*	settantuno	*99*	novantanove

The word **cento** is invariable. Note that the word *one*, which in English appears before *hundred (one hundred)*, is not included in Italian. The numbers indicating *tens* and *units*_____*one, two, etc.*_____are usually added and attached. The compounds of **cento** are attached: **duecento**, **trecento**, etc.

100	**cento**	*118*	**centodiciotto**	*160*	**centosessanta**
101	**centouno**	*119*	**centodiciannove**	*165*	**centosessantacinque**
102	**centodue**	*120*	**centoventi**	*170*	**centosettanta**
103	**centrotré**	*121*	**centoventuno**	*180*	**centottanta**
104	**centoquattro**	*122*	**centoventidue**	*190*	**centonovanta**
105	**centocinque**	*123*	**centoventitré**	*191*	**centonovantuno**
106	**centosei**	*124*	**centoventiquattro**	*193*	**centonovantatré**
107	**centosette**	*125*	**centoventicinque**	*198*	**centonovantotto**
108	**centootto**	*126*	**centoventisei**	*200*	**duecento**
109	**centonove**	*127*	**centoventisette**	*300*	**trecento**
110	**centodieci**	*128*	**centoventotto**	*400*	**quattrocento**
111	**centoundici**	*129*	**centoventinove**	*450*	**quattrocentocinquanta**
112	**centododici**	*130*	**centotrenta**	*500*	**cinquecento**
113	**centotredici**	*131*	**centotrentuno**	*600*	**seicento**
114	**centoquattordici**	*140*	**centoquaranta**	*700*	**settecento**
115	**centoquindici**	*143*	**centoquarantatré**	*800*	**ottocento**
116	**centosedici**	*150*	**centocinquanta**	*900*	**novecento**
117	**centodiciassette**	*158*	**centocinquantotto**	*999*	**novecentonovantanove**

The word **mille** (*one thousand*) does not use the word *one* in Italian. However, **un** (*one*) is always used with **milione** (*million*) and **miliardo** (*billion*). **Mille, milione,** and **miliardo** have plurals. Note that the English *eleven hundred, twelve hundred*, etc., are expressed in Italian by dividing the number into thousands and hundreds.

1.000	**mille**	*2.000*	**duemila**
1.001	**milleuno**	*3.000*	**tremila**
1.010	**milledieci**	*4.000*	**quattromila**
1.100	**millecento**	*20.000*	**ventimila**
1.200	**milleduecento**	*100.000*	**centomila**
1.300	**milletrecento**	*1.000.000*	**un milione**
1.400	**millequattrocento**	*2.000.000*	**due milioni**
1.500	**millecinquecento**	*10.000.000*	**dieci milioni**
1.600	**milleseicento**	*1.000.000.000*	**un miliardo**
1.700	**millesettecento**	*2.000.000.000*	**due miliardi**
1.800	**milleottocento**	*9.000.000.000*	**nove miliardi**
1.900	**millenovecento**	*1.000.000.000.000*	**un trilione**
1.980	**millenovecentottanta**	*2.000.000.000.000*	**due trilioni**

Note that **un milione, due milioni, un miliardo, due miliardi**, etc., take the preposition **di** before a noun:

un milione di dollari
a million dollars

due milioni di euro.
two million euros

un miliardo di dollari
a billion dollars

cinque miliardi di euro.
five billion euros

Note that in Italian, a period is used when English uses a comma, and a comma is used when English uses a decimal point. Observe the following:

Italian	English
1.236.000	*1,236,000*
1.236,60	*1,236.60*
8,50	*8.50*

1. Write the following numbers in Italian:

1. 5
2. 13
3. 17
4. 21
5. 28
6. 33
7. 40
8. 48
9. 51
10. 53
11. 67

12. 78
13. 79
14. 82
15. 88
16. 90
17. 91
18. 100
19. 300
20. 1,000
21. 8,533
22. 3,000,000

2. Translate the following words:

1. one hundred men
2. four thousand books
3. one million people
4. six billion dollars
5. nine hundred euros
6. one thousand euros
7. two thousand euros
8. one million euros
9. three hundred thousand euros
10. one thousand three hundred forty-five euros

Special use of Duecento, Trecento, etc.

When referring to centuries, the ordinal numbers are used: **dodicęsimo**, **tredicęsimo**, etc. (*twelfth, thirteenth*, etc.). However, it is very common to use the cardinal numbers within the context of art, history, or literature. Note that **Duecento, Trecento**, etc., are capitalized when used in this context. They are also preceded by the appropriate masculine singular definite article. Observe:

il sęcolo tredicęsimo **(il tredicęsimo sęcolo)**	**il Duecento**	*the 13th century* *(the twelve hundreds)*
il sęcolo quattordicęsimo **(il quattordicęsimo sęcolo)**	**il Trecento**	*the 14th century* *(the thirteen hundreds)*
il sęcolo quindicęsimo **(il quindicęsimo sęcolo)**	**il Quattrocento**	*the 15th century* *(the fourteen hundreds)*
il sęcolo sedicęsimo **(il sedicęsimo sęcolo)**	**il Cinquecento**	*the 16th century* *(the fifteen hundreds)*
il sęcolo diciassettęsimo **(il diciassettęsimo sęcolo)**	**il Seicento**	*the 17th century* *(the sixteen hundreds)*

il sęcolo diciottęsimo (il diciottęsimo sęcolo)	**il Settecento**	*the 18th century* *(the seventeen hundreds)*
il sęcolo diciannovęsimo (il diciannovęsimo sęcolo)	**l'Ottocento**	*the 19th century* *(the eighteen hundreds)*
il sęcolo ventęsimo (il ventęsimo sęcolo)	**il Novecento**	*the 20th century* *(the nineteen hundreds)*

3. *Using cardinal numbers, give the Italian equivalents of the following centuries. Use the definite article.*

1. 20th century
2. 13th century
3. 16th century
4. 19th century
5. 15th century

Ordinal Numbers

The Italian ordinal numbers function as adjectives and must therefore agree in gender and number with the nouns they modify. They are

1st   **primo, prima, primi, prime**
2nd   **secondo (-a, -i, -e)**
3rd   **terzo (-a, -i, -e)**
4th   **quạrto (-a, -i, -e)**
5th   **quịnto (-a, -i, -e)**
6th   **sesto (-a, -i, -e)**
7th   **sęttimo (-a, -i, -e)**
8th   **ottavo (-a, -i, -e)**
9th   **nono (-a, -i, -e)**
10th   **dęcimo (-a, -i, -e)**
11th   **undicęsimo (-a, -i, -e)**   *also:* **undęcimo**
12th   **dodicęsimo (-a, -i, -e)**   *also:* **duodęcimo**
13th   **tredicęsimo (-a, -i, -e)**   *also:* **dęcimoterzo**
14th   **quattordicęsimo (-a, -i, -e)**   *also:* **decimoquạrto**
15th   **quindicęsimo (-a, -i, -e;)**   *also:* **decimoquịnto**
16th   **sedicęsimo (-a, -i, -e)**   *also:* **decimosesto**
17th   **diciassettęsimo (-a, -i, -e)**   *also:* **decimosęttimo**
18th   **diciottęsimo (-a, -i, -e)**   *also:* **decimottavo**
19th   **diciannovęsimo (-a, -i, -e)**   *also:* **decimonono**
20th   **ventęsimo (-a, -i, -e)**   *also:* **vigęsimo**
21st   **ventunęsimo (-a, -i, -e)**   *also:* **ventesimoprimo**

As you have noticed above, beginning with **undicęsimo** *(eleventh)*, the suffix **-ęsimo** is added to the cardinal numbers (**ụndici, dọdici,** etc.) by dropping the final vowel of the cardinal number with the exception of the numbers ending in **-tré** (**ventitré,** etc.) The cardinal numbers ending in **-tré** drop their accent (**-tre**) and remain intact when **-ęsimo** is added. Observe the following:

23rd   **ventitreęsimo (ventesimoterzo)**
25th   **venticinquęsimo (ventesimoquịnto)**
30th   **trentęsimo (trigęsimo)**
40th   **quarantęsimo (quadragęsimo)**
50th   **cinquantęsimo (quinquagęsimo)**
60th   **sessantęsimo (sessagęsimo)**
70th   **settantęsimo (settuagęsimo)**
80th   **ottantęsimo (ottuagęsimo)**
90th   **novantęsimo (nonagęsimo)**
100th   **centęsimo**

200th	duecentẹsimo
300th	trecentẹsimo
1,000th	millẹsimo
2,000th	duemillẹsimo
3,000th	tremillẹsimo
1,000,000th	milionẹsimo

Ordinal numbers with titles

With the numerical sucession of kings, emperors, and popes, the ordinal numbers are used, and they are capitalized.

Umberto I:	**Umberto Primo**
Carlo V:	**Carlo Quịnto**
Elisabetta I:	**Elisabetta Prima**
Elisabetta II:	**Elisabetta Seconda**
Luịgi XIV:	**Luịgi Quattordicẹsimo**
Leọne X:	**Leọne Dẹcimo**
Pịo XII:	**Pịo Dodicẹsimo**
Benedetto XVI:	**Benedetto Sedicẹsimo**

4. Complete the following sentences with the appropriate ordinal numbers according to the cues in English.

1. Marzo è il _____ mese dell'anno,　　　　　　　*third*
2. Giụgno è il _____ mese dell'anno,　　　　　　*sixth*
3. Leone _____ è un papa del Rinascimento.　　*X*
4. Pịo _____ è un papa del Novecento.　　　　*XII*
5. Martedí è il _____ giọrno della settimana.　*second*
6. È la _____ volta che ti chiamo.　　　　　　*hundredth*
7. Oggi è il _____ anniversạrio del nostro matrimọnio.　*twenty-fifth*
8. Francesco _____ è un re francese.　　　　　*I*
9. Elisabetta _____ è l'attuạle regina d'Inghilterra.　*II*
10. Benedetto _____ è l'attuale papa dei cattọlici.　*XVI*

Note that when the ordinal and cardinal numbers are used together, the ordinals precede the cardinals.

Quẹsti sono i primi cịnque ragazzi.
These are the first five boys.

Sono passati i primi dụe giọrni.
The first two days are over.

Fractions

Usually, fractions consist of both cardinal and ordinal numerals.

2/3	**dụe terzi**	*two-thirds*
1/4	**un quạrto**	*one-fourth*
1/8	**un ottavo**	*one-eighth*
2/5	**dụe quịnti**	*two-fifths*
1/10	**un dẹcimo**	*one-tenth*
10/100	**diẹci centẹsimi**	*ten-hundredths*
1/1000	**un millẹsimo**	*one-thousandth*

Some special forms are:

1/2	**mezzo; mezza; una metà; la metà**	*half; one half*
8 1/2	**Otto e mezzo**	*eight and one-half*
9 1/3	**nove e un terzo**	*nine and one-third*

Ne ho comprato la metà
I bought half of it.

Abbiamo consumato una mezza-bottiglia di vino.
We drank a half bottle of wine.

Non ricorda nemmeno un decimo della lezione.
He doesn't even remember a tenth of the lesson.

5. Write the following fractions in Italian:

1. 1/8
2. 2/10
3. 5/100
4. 3/1000
5. 9 1/2
6. 10 3/4

7. 1/3
8. 2/5
9. 1/10
10. 2/6
11. 4 1/4

6. Complete the following sentences with the correct Italian form of the number supplied:

1. Mio zio ha _____ libri.   *two thousand*
2. Questa è la _____ volta che ti telefono.   *tenth*
3. Stefano ha _____ anni.   *twenty-three*
4. Durante le vacanze riceverò _____ del mio salario.   *two-thirds*
5. Il secolo _____ è anche detto il_____.   *sixteenth*
6. Luigi _____ fu un re francese.   *fourteenth*
7. Lunedí è il _____ giorno della settimana.   *first*
8. Quell'edificio costa più di _____ di dollari.   *two million*
9. Mia cugina è nata nel _____.   *1978*
10. Ecco i _____ clienti.   *first two*
11. Questa macchina (Quest'automobile) è costata più di _____.   *40,000 euros*
12. Il _____ gennaio è Capo d'Anno.   *1(Capodanno)*
13. Il _____ agosto è Ferragosto.   *15*
14. Natale è il _____ dicembre.   *25*
15. L'Epifania è il _____ gennaio.   *6*
16. Con _____ si può comprare una bicicletta.   *three hundred fifty euros.*
17. Il _____ giugno del _____ è la nascita della Repubblica Italiana.   *2; 1946*
18. Domani celebreranno il loro _____ anniversario di matrimonio.   *33*
19. Non ricordiamo neanche _____ del discorso.   *1/3*
20. Amici miei, questi sono i _____ _____ euro che vedo in vita mia.   *1st*

7. Complete the following with the correct form of the indicated adjective.

1. Gli appartamenti sono _____ e _____.   *moderno, grande*
2. La motocicletta è _____ e _____.   *piccolo, veloce*
3. Il cibo è _____ e _____.   *caldo, delizioso*
4. I signori sono _____ e _____.   *ricco, generoso*
5. Le gonne _____ sono nell'armadio.   *blu*
6. Luisa è una ragazza _____.   *timido*
7. Dante è un _____ poeta.   *grande*
8. Gli studenti sono _____ e_____.   *intelligente, studioso*
9. _____ signorine _____ sono turiste.   *quello, svedese*
10. I _____ cugini hanno la radio _____.   *mio, acceso*
11. _____ zia Maria è _____.   *mio, italiano*
12. _____ vini _____ sono _____.   *quello, bianco, dolce*

13. _____ pera è _____ però non è _____,   *questo, bello,*
    è _____.   *maturo, acerbo*
14. _____ studenti sono i _____ della classe,   *quello, migliore*
15. Le sorelle _____ di Luigi sono _____.   *minore, simpatico*
16. I _____ vestiti non sono_____, sono _____. *tuo, sporco, pulito*
17. In Italia, la festa di _____ Giuseppe è molto _____. *Santo, importante*
18. _____ calciatore non ha _____ talento,   *quello, nessuno*
19. Teresa è piú _____ che _____.   *intelligente, studioso*
20. Le lezioni sono _____, non sono _____.   *difficile, facile*

8. Answer the following questions according to the indicated response.

1. Qual è (Quale è) il fiume piú lungo d'Italia?   *Il Po*
2. Qual è l'isola piú grande del Mediterraneo?   *La Sicilia*
3. Chi è piú brava, Olga o Luisa?   *Olga*
4. Chi sono i piú alti, questi o quelli?   *Quelli*
5. Dove sono i cugini di Mario?   *in Italia*
6. Chi è (cosi) intelligente come Stefano?   *Antonio*
7. Qual è la capitale d'Italia?   *Roma*
8. Chi è il calciatore piú famoso del mondo?   *Pelé*
9. Chi è (tanto) brava quanto Silvia?   *Maria*
10. Dove sono i giocatori?   *nello stadio*

DATES

The days of the week, the months, and the seasons of the year are not capitalized in Italian.

Days of the Week

All the days of the week are masculine except **domenica** (Sunday).

lunedí	*Monday*	(Fra gli antichi romani, lunedí era il giorno dedicato alla LUNA.)
martedí	*Tuesday*	(Martedí deriva da MARTE, il dio romano della guerra.)
mercoledí	*Wednesday*	(Mercoledí era il giorno sacro a MERCURIO, un altro dio romano.)
giovedí	*Thursday*	(Giovedí deriva da GIOVE, il dio di tutti gli dèi romani.)
venerdí	*Friday*	(Venerdí era il giorno dedicato a VENERE, la piú bella delle dee)
sabato	*Saturday*	(Sabato è una parola ebraica che vuol dire *riposo.)*
domenica	*Sunday*	(Domenica deriva dal latino *dominus* [= signore].)

Months of the Year

All the months of the year are masculine.

gennaio	*January*
febbraio	*February*
marzo	*March*
aprile	*April*
maggio	*May*
giugno	*June*
luglio	*July*
agosto	*August*
settembre	*September*
ottobre	*October*
novembre	*November*
dicembre	*December*

Seasons of the Year

In Italian, *spring* and *summer* are feminine; *fall* and *winter* are masculine.

la primavera	*spring*
l'estate	*summer*
l'autunno	*fall*
l'inverno	*winter*

Observe the following expressions:

Che giorno è oggi?	*What day is today?*
Oggi è lunedí.	*Today is Monday.*

Quanti ne abbiamo oggi?	*What's today's date?*	*(not the full date)*
Oggi ne abbiamo cinque.	*Today is the fifth.*	
(or **Oggi è il cinque.***)*		

Qual è la data di oggi?	*What's today's date?*
(Also: **Quale è …?***)*	*(the full date)*
Oggi è lunedí, il sei settembre, duemilasei.	
Today is Monday, September 6, 2006.	

Note that the year is masculine; when appropriate, the masculine definite article (or the articulated preposition **nel**) is used:

Il duemilacinque è stato un ottimo anno.
2005 was an excellent year.

Dante nacque nel mille duecento sessantacinque. (*also*: **milleduecentosessantacinque**)
Dante was born in 1265.

Note that in a date the English *on* is translated with **il** (the masculine singular definite article). All the numbers used in a date are cardinal numbers except for the first day of each month. Observe the following:

Quando ci vedremo di nuovo?
When shall we see each other again?

Ci vedremo il dieci ottobre.
We'll see each other on October tenth,

or:

Ci vedremo il primo dicembre.
We' ll see each other on December first.

Note that all the seasons take the preposition **in**, as follows:

Che tempo fa in primavera?	**Che tempo fa in autunno?**
How's the weather in the spring?	*How's the weather in the fall?*
In primavera fa bel tempo.	**In autunno piove molto.**
In the spring the weather is good.	*In the fall it rains a lot.*
Che tempo fa in estate?	**Che tempo fa in inverno?**
How's the weather in the summer?	*How's the weather in the winter?*
In estate fa caldo.	**In inverno nevica sempre.**
In the summer it's hot.	*In the winter it always snows.*

Note that when there is a specific reference to a season in a specific year, the articulated preposition (**in** plus the appropriate definite article) is used. For example:

Siamo andati in Italia nella primavera del millenovecentonovantanove.
We went to Italy in the spring of 1999.

Ho visitato i miei nonni nell'estate del duemilatré.
I visited my grandparents in the summer of 2003.

I genitori di Luisa hanno comprato una macchina sportiva nell'autunno del duemila.
Louise's parents bought a sports car in the fall of 2000.

Nell'inverno dell'anno scorso ci sono stati molti incidenti stradali.
In the winter of last year there were many traffic accidents.

Note that a definite article before a day of the week suggests a recurrent event. For example:

Domenica andiamo allo zoo.
Sunday (this coming Sunday) we go to the zoo.

but:

La domenica andiamo allo zoo.
On Sundays (every Sunday) we go to the zoo.

Il sabato usciamo con gli amici.
On Saturdays we go out with our friends.

9. *Answer the following questions with complete sentences using the indicated words, where given, as guides:*

1.	Che giorno è oggi?	*lunedí*
2.	Cosa è mercoledí?	
3.	Che tempo fa in inverno?	
4.	Che anno è questo?	*2006*
5.	Quanti mesi ha un anno?	
6.	Quando nacque Dante?	*1265*
7.	Quanti ne abbiamo oggi?	*15*
8.	Quando nevica?	
9.	Vai al cinema la domenica?	*Sí*
10.	Qual è (Quale è) la data di oggi?	*October 1, 2006*
11.	Quali sono i primi tre giorni della settimana?	
12.	Quali sono i mesi dell'estate?	
13.	Fa caldo in estate?	*Sí*
14.	Quando piove?	*fall*
15.	Cosa fai il sabato?	*studiare*
16.	Qual è l'ultimo *(last)* mese dell'anno?	
17.	Quale mese viene dopo giugno?	
18.	Fra gli antichi romani, quale giorno era dedicato a Venere?	*Friday*
19.	A quale dio romano era dedicato mercoledí?	*Mercury*
20.	Da quale parola latina deriva domenica?	*dominus*

10. *Write the following in Italian:*
1. Tomorrow is Sunday, December 19, 2006.
2. We'll travel *(viaggeremo)* in the summer.
3. March is crazy *(pazzo)*.
4. On Wednesday we eat pizza.

5. Today is Tuesday.
6. Tomorrow is the eighth.
7. There are seven days in a week.
8. Yesterday was *(era)* October first.
9. I was born *(Sono nato[-a])* in 1991.
10. Monday is the first day of the week.

11. *Complete the following with the appropriate word or words:*

1. _____ è il sesto mese dell' _____.
2. Oggi _____ abbiamo due; domani sarà il _____.
3. Le quattro stagioni sono la _____, l' _____, l' _____, e l' _____.
4. Un anno ha _____ mesi.
5. Di solito in _____ fa freddo.
6. _____ è il quinto _____ della settimana.
7. Oggi è il diciotto; ieri era _____.
8. È *(2006)* _____.
9. _____ domenica andiamo sempre dai nonni.
10. La mia _____ preferita è l'autunno.

TIME

Colloquial Time

In Italian, the question *What time is it?* has two equivalents: **Che ora è?** and **Che ore sono?** The answer is in the singular if the time is one o'clock, noon, or midnight; it is in the plural with all other hours. Observe the following:

Q. – Che ora è?	*What time is it?*	
Che ore sono?	*What time is it?*	
A. – È l'una.	*It's one o'clock.*	
È mezzogiorno.	*It's noon.*	
È mezzanotte.	*It's midnight.*	
Sono le due.	*It's two o'clock.*	
Sono le dieci.	*It's ten o'clock.*	

Note that minutes are added to the hour after the conjunction **e** (*and*) up to half past the hour. The quarter hour and the half hour may be expressed in two ways. Observe the following:

È l'una e cinque,	*It's 1:05.*
È mezzogiorno e venti	*It's 12:20.*
Sono le due e quindici.	*It's 2:15.*
Sono le due e un quarto.	*It's 2:15.*
È l'una e trenta.	*It's 1:30.*
È l'una e mezza (mezzo).	*It's 1:30.*
Sono le undici e mezzo (mezza).	*It's 11:30.*
Sono le nove e mezza (mezzo).	*It's 9:30.*

Usually, after the half hour, the minutes are subtracted from the next hour by using the word **meno** (*minus*). For example:

È l'una meno venti.	*It's 12:40.*
Sono le otto meno un quarto.	*It's 7:45.*

Although it is not incorrect, one rarely hears the minutes added after the half hour. Here are some examples:

Sono le dodici e quaranta.	*It's 12:40.*
Sono le sette e quarantacinque.	*It's 7:45*
Or: **Sono le sette e tre quarti**.	

Often, the verb **mancare** (lit., *to lack*) is used in the third-person singular (**manca**) or plural (**mancano**) to subtract minutes. For example:

> **È l'una meno un quarto.**
> **Manca un quarto all'una.**
> *It's 12:45.*

> **Sono le nove meno quindici.**
> **Mancano quindici minuti alle nove.**
> *It's 8:45.*

The question *At what time?* is asked with **A Che ora?** The answer utilizes the preposition **a** (*at*) before **mezzogiorno** (*noon*) and **mezzanotte** (*midnight*), and the articulated preposition (**a** plus an appropriate definite article) before the specified time. Only one o'clock takes **all'** (**all'una** being singular); all other hours take **alle** (**alle due**, **alle tre**, etc.). Observe the following:

A Che ora parte il treno?	*At what time does the train leave?*
Il treno parte a mezzogiorno.	*The train leaves at noon.*
Il treno parte a mezzanotte.	*The train leaves at midnight.*
Il treno parte all'una.	*The train leaves at 1:00.*
Il treno parte alle due.	*The train leaves at 2:00.*

In Italian, the expressions A.M. and P.M. are indicated with **di mattina** (A.M.), **del pomeriggio** (P.M. equals from about 1 P.M. through about 4 P.M.), and **di sera** (P.M. equals from about 5 P.M. till late P.M.). The expression *sharp* is **in punto**. Observe the following:

Sono le sette di mattina.	*It's 7:00 A.M.*
Sono le sette di sera.	*It's 7:00 P.M.*
È l'una di mattina.	*It's 1:00 A.M.*
È l'una del pomeriggio.	*It's 1:00 P.M.*
Mi alzo alle otto in punto di mattina.	*I get up at 8:00 A.M. sharp.*

Official Time

For schedules pertaining to trains, airplanes, office hours, radio, TV, movies, and theatrical performances, the so-called official time is widely used. It corresponds approximately with the American "military time" (e.g., 11:00 A.M. equals eleven hundred hours; 3:00 P.M. equals fifteen hundred hours, etc.). The Italian 24-hour system simply mentions the numbers from 1 to 24 without indicating the *hundreds* or the *hours*. With this system, the use of A.M. and P.M. is unnecessary. Minutes are always added; they are never subtracted. Observe the following comparisons between colloquial time and official time:

Colloquial Time	*Official Time*
Sono le sette di mattina. *It's 7:00 A.M.*	**Sono le sette.** *It's 7:00 A.M.*
È l'una del pomeriggio. *It's 1:00 P.M.*	**Sono le tredici.** *It's 1:00 P.M.*
Sono le dieci di sera. *It's 10:00 P.M.*	**Sono le venti.** *It's 10:00 P.M.*
Sono le nove meno un quarto di mattina. *It's 8:45 A.M.*	**Sono le otto e quarantacinque.** *It's 8:45 A.M.*

Observe the full 24-hour system:

1.	**È l'una.**	*It's 1:00 A.M.*
2.	**Sono le due.**	*It's 2:00 A.M.*

3. **Sono le tre.**	*It's 3:00 A.M.*
4. **Sono le quattro.**	*It's 4:00 A.M.*
5. **Sono le cinque.**	*It's 5:00 A.M.*
6. **Sono le sei.**	*It's 6:00 A.M.*
7. **Sono le sette.**	*It's 7:00 A.M.*
8. **Sono le otto.**	*It's 8:00 A.M.*
9. **Sono le nove.**	*It's 9:00 A.M.*
10. **Sono le dieci.**	*It's 10:00 A.M.*
11. **Sono le undici.**	*It's 11:00 A.M.*
12. **Sono le dodici.**	*It's 12:00 A.M.*
13. **Sono le tredici.**	*It's 1:00 P.M.*
14. **Sono le quattordici.**	*It's 2:00 P.M.*
15. **Sono le quindici.**	*It's 3:00 P.M.*
16. **Sono le sedici.**	*It's 4:00 P.M.*
17. **Sono le diciassette.**	*It's 5:00 P.M.*
18. **Sono le diciotto.**	*It's 6:00 P.M.*
19. **Sono le diciannove.**	*It's 7:00 P.M.*
20. **Sono le venti.**	*It's 8:00 P.M.*
21. **Sono le ventuno.**	*It's 9:00 P.M.*
22. **Sono le ventidue.**	*It's 10:00 P.M.*
23. **Sono le ventitré.**	*It's 11:00 P.M.*
24. **Sono le ventiquattro.**	*It's 12:00 P.M.*

Note that official time is very popular with the Italians, who use it at all times and for a variety of reasons in addition to the original ones noted above. In the United States, this is the time always used by the military.

12. *Answer the following questions with complete sentences. Follow the indications given in parentheses. Always use colloquial time unless otherwise instructed.*

1. Che ora è?   *11:00 A.M. sharp*
2. Che ore sono?   *1:00 P.M. official time*
3. A che ora ti alzi?   *6:15 A.M.*
4. A che ora parte il treno?   *9:50 P.M. official time*
5. A che ora arriva Luisa?   *10:50 A.M.*
6. Quanto manca alle dieci?   *20 minutes*
7. Quanto manca all'una?   *A quarter*
8. Quando c'incontriamo tu ed (*and*) io?   *At noon*
9. Che ore sono?   *3:00 P.M.*
10. È mezzanotte?   (Sí, ... [*Repeat, indicating the official time*])

13. *Complete the following sentences in Italian. All numbers must be written out in Italian, not in Arabic numerals. (Do not use official time.)*

1. Antonio arriva (*at 8:15 A.M. sharp*)_____.
2. No, non è (*noon*)_____, è (*1:15 P.M.*)_____.
3. Partiamo (*at midnight*)_____.
4. Nessuno si alza (*at 5:00 A.M.*) _____.
5. Dobbiamo essere all'aeroporto (*at 2:30 P.M.*) _____.
6. Fanno la prima colazione (*at 7:50 A.M.*) _____.
7. Sí, Giorgio e Piero ci telefoneranno (*at 10:45 P.M.*) _____.
8. La festa comincia (*at 6:40 P.M.*) _____.
9. Sono (*11:10 P.M.*)_____.
10. Non so, saranno (*5:00 P.M.*) _____.

14. Rewrite the sentences of exercise 13 above using official time. All numbers must be written out in Italian.

1. _____
2. _____
3. _____
4. _____
5. _____
6. _____
7. _____
8. _____
9. _____
10. _____

REVIEW

15. Write out in Italian the following arabic numerals:

1. 1.000 _____
2. 63 _____
3. 2.000.000 _____
4. 1994 _____
5. 107 _____

6. 58 _____
7. 91 _____
8. 17 _____
9. 11 _____
10. 100 _____

16. Supply an equivalent expression for each of the following:

1. il secolo ventesimo _____
2. il secolo diciassettesimo _____
3. l'Ottocento _____
4. il Trecento _____
5. il secolo tredicesimo _____

17. Change the following into ordinal numbers. (Use only the masculine singular form.)

1. tre_____
2. cento_____
3. mille_____
4. nove_____

5. ventuno_____
6. quarantatré_____
7. sedici_____
8. otto_____

18. Write out in Italian the following fractions:

1. 2/8_____
2. 1/10_____
3. 8 1/2_____
4. 5/100_____

5. 4/1000_____
6. 1/3_____
7. 9 3/4_____
8. 5 2/3_____

19. Answer the following questions with complete sentences; use the indicated guides when appropriate:

1. Qual è il terzo mese dell'anno?
2. Cosa viene dopo (*comes after*) lunedí?
3. Qual è il settimo giorno della settimana?
4. In quale stagione c'è la neve?
5. Quali sono le quattro stagioni dell'anno?
6. Quale mese viene dopo giugno?
7. A che ora ti alzi (*do you get up*) la mattina?　　　(*7.00*)
8. A che ora parte il treno?　　　　　　　　　(*2:00 P.M., official time*)

20. *Complete the following sentences by supplying the Italian equivalents of the time in parentheses (use colloquial time only):*

1. Pietro arriva verso_____. *(2:00 P.M.)*
2. Il treno per Milano parte_____. *(at midnight)*
3. È troppo tardi! Già sono_____. *(8:30 P.M.)*
4. Roberto, incontriamoci_____. *(at 9:45 A.M.)*
5. Loro fanno la prima colazione_____. *(at 7:10 A.M.)*
6. – Che ora è?– E_____. *(1:00 sharp)*

21. *Rewrite the following sentences, using the official time equivalents:*

1. Sono le tre del pomeriggio.
2. È mezzanotte.
3. Sono le undici di mattina.
4. Sono le nove di sera.
5. Sono le sei di mattina.
6. Sono le tre e un quarto del pomeriggio
7. È l'una e trenta del pomeriggio.
8. Sono le dieci meno cinque di sera.

22. *Complete the following sentences with the Italian equivalents of the words in italics.*

1. Questo pranzo costa_____.   *twenty-five euros*
2. Con_____possiamo fare un bel viaggio insieme.   *two thousand euros*
3. Per Donald Trump_____ non è quasi niente.   *one million euros*
4. Quella corporazione ha perduto_____.   *two billion euros*
5. Mario, mi presti_____?   *fifty-three euros*

CHAPTER 6

Verbs

A verb is a word that indicates an action or a state of being. Italian verbs function in quite a different way from English verbs. In English, a subject pronoun such as *I, you, he,* or *she* is used. In Italian, the subject pronouns (see pages 205 to 208) are usually omitted since the ending of the verb changes in order to indicate the doer of the action. However, subject pronouns must be used for emphasis. For example: **Oggi io compro il gelato** (*Today I* [meaning: no one else] *am buying the ice cream*). They must also be used for contrast, when two or more subjects perform various actions in the same sentence. For example;. **Io** *leggo,* **Maria** *scrive, e* **loro** *parlano* (*I am reading,* Maria *is writing, and they are speaking*). In order to form tenses, English uses auxiliary verbs such as *have* and *had,* and words such as *will, would, may,* or *might* before verbs. In Italian, a suffix or ending is usually added to the verb in order to indicate the appropriate tense (it is never done with compound tenses).

As in English, in Italian verbs are also either *transitive* or *intransitive*. Transitive verbs take a direct object (answering a hypothetical question of *Whom?* or *What?*). For example: **A**: The sentence, **Mario vede i nonni** (*Mario sees his grandparents*) may be the answer to the hypothetical question, *Whom is Mario seeing?* **B**: The sentence **Silvana compra una maglia** (*Silvana is buying a sweater*) may be the answer to the hypothetical question, *What is Silvana buying?* **I nonni** in sentence **A**, and **la maglia** in sentence **B**, are both direct objects. *Whom* and *What,* used in the hypotheticals, are direct object pronouns (they substitute the nouns). By using *Whom* and *What,* one can test a verb to see whether or not it is *transitive* or *intransitive*. Conversely, intransitive verbs do not take direct objects. For example: the sentence, **Renzo abita in Sardegna** (*Renzo lives in Sardinia*) cannot be tested with the hypotheticals *Whom or What.* Therefore the verb **abita** is intransitive.

Each verb, however, does not function as an entity unto itself. Many verbs that are formed in the same way can be grouped together into classes or conjugations. In Italian there are three regular conjugations of verbs. The infinitives of first-conjugation verbs end in **-are**, second-conjugation verbs in **-ere**, and third-conjugation verbs in **-ire**. When the endings are dropped, the remaining roots (or stems) are added to the appropriate endings of the different conjugations. As you will observe in subsequent parts of this chapter, even many so-called irregular verbs have characteristics in common and can be grouped together to facilitate learning.

MOODS AND TENSES (I MODI DEL VERBO)

In Italian the verb has seven moods: 1 - **indicative** (*l'indicativo*); 2 - **subjunctive** (*il congiuntivo*); 3 - **conditional** (*il condizionale*); 4 - **imperative** (*l'imperativo*); 5 - **infinitive** (*l'infinito*); 6 - **participle** (il participio); 7 - **gerund** (*il gerundio*).

1. The **indicative** expresses an action in the making or a state of being. It is used for general sayings and proverbs: **Chi dorme non piglia pesci**: literally: *He who sleeps doesn't catch any fish,* and for what is called the historical present: **Dormiamo, mangiamo, beviamo, e ci riposiamo**: *We sleep, eat, drink, and relax.*
2. The **subjunctive** expresses an action that may happen, and always depends on another verb or expression that indicates volition, emotion, doubt, wish, etc.: **I miei amici vogliono che io sia sempre pronto a giocare**: *My friends want me to be always ready to play.*

3. The **conditional** expresses a conditioned response: **Saremmo infelici se non avęssimo amici!**: *We would be unhappy if we didn't have friends!*
4. The **imperative** expresses volition, orders, wish, prayer, etc.: **Ragazzi, non gridate tanto!**: *Boys, don't yell so much!* **Per piacere, sięte bụoni!**: *Please, be good!*
5. The **infinitive** expresses an indeterminate action or state of being: **Lavorare stanca!**: *To work is tiresome!*
6. The **participle** assumes the qualities of the verb and the adjective: **Ecco i gịovani credenti**: *Here are the young men who believe.*
7. The **gerund**, like the infinitive, is invariable without number and gender: **Studịando s'impara**: *One learns by studying.*

INDICATIVE (L'INDICATIVO)

Below are some examples for each tense using regular **-are**, **-ere**, and **-ire** verbs: **parlare** (to speak), **crędere** (to believe), **partire** (to leave; to depart, to go on a trip). In compound tenses, **parlare** and **crędere** take the auxiliary **avere**, and **partire** (a verb of motion) takes the auxiliary **ęssere**. For complete conjugations and details, study the full chapter.

Simple Tenses (Tempi sęmplici)

Present	**io parlo,**	**tu credi,**	**lui parte**
Presente	*I speak; I am speaking,*	*you (fam. s.) believe,*	*he leaves; he is leaving,*
Imperfect	**noi parlavamo,**	**voi credevate,**	**loro partịvano**
Imperfetto	*we used to speak, we were speaking,*	*you (fam. pl.) used to believe, you were believing,*	*they were leaving, they used to leave,*
Preterite	**io parlai**	**Lei (formal s.) credé (credette)**	**Loro (formal pl.) partịrono**
Passato remoto	*I spoke*	*you (formal s.) believed*	*you (formal pl.) left*
Future	**tu parlerai**	**noi crederemo**	**voi partirete**
Futuro	*you will speak*	*we will believe*	*you will leave*
Conditional	**lei parlerebbe**	**Loro crederębbero**	**io partirei**
Condizionale	*she would speak*	*you (formal pl.) would believe*	*I would leave*

SUBJUNCTIVE: (IL CONGIUNTIVO)

Present subjunctive	**che io parli**	**che lui creda**	**che loro pạrtano**
Presente congiuntivo	*that I speak*	*that he believe*	*that they leave*
Imperfect subjunctive	**che tu parlassi**	**che noi credęssimo**	**che voi partiste**
Congiuntivo imperfetto	*that you might speak,*	*that we might believe*	*that you might leave*

IMPERATIVE (L'IMPERATIVO)

Present imperative	**(tu) parla!**	**(voi) credete!**	**(noi) partịamo!**
Presente imperativo	*(you) speak!*	*(you) believe!*	*(we) let's leave!*
Future imperative	**(tu) parlerai!**	**(Lei) crederà!**	**(voi) partirete!**
Imperativo futuro	*(you) will speak!*	*(you) will speak!*	*(you) will leave!*

GERUND (IL GERỤNDIO)

Present gerund	**parlando**	**credendo**	**partendo**
Gerụndio presente	*speaking*	*believing*	*leaving*

FORMAL VERSUS FAMILIAR FORMS

In Italian, there are four ways to express the subject pronoun *you*. When addressing a friend, some relatives, a child or a close associate, the pronoun **tu** (*you*) is used most of the time. **Tu** is called the familiar singular form. The plural of **tu** is **voi**. **Voi** is used when addressing two or more friends, relatives, children, or close associates, and often even strangers. **Voi**, however, can also be used when addressing only one person, such as an older friend, relative, or associate. This is particularly true in some parts of Tuscany and central Italy, and generally in southern Italy. (**Voi**, always with a capital **V**-, is also widely used in business correspondence when addressing a single person or persons).

When addressing a stranger, an acquaintance you do not know very well, or an older person, the pronoun **Lei** (*you* formal s.) is used. **Lei** is called the *formal singular* and is often capitalized. The plural of **Lei** is **Loro** (*you* formal pl.) and it, too, is often capitalized. Note that many Italians prefer not to capitalize **Lei** and **Loro**. Capitalization of **Lei** and **Loro** prevents ambiguity, thus avoiding confusing them with the third person singular form **lei** (*she*), and the third person plural form **loro** (*they*).

Subject Pronouns (I pronomi soggetto)

Singular (Singolare)

1) First person singular (Prima persona singolare):

    io: **Io mi** chiamo Graziana.   *My name is Graziana.*

2) Second person singular (Seconda persona plurale):

    tu: **Tu** sei Giorgio.   *You are Giorgio.*

3) Third person singular (Terza persona singolare):

    lui: **Lui** si chiama Piero.   *His name is Piero.*
    lei: **Lei** è mia figlia.   *She is my daughter.*

    Formal *you* singular (m. & f.):

    Lei: Signora De Lena, **Lei** sta bene?   *Mrs. De Lena, are you well?*
    Lei: Signor De Lena, dove abita **Lei**?   *Mr. De Lena, where do you live?*

Plural (Plurale)

1) First person plural (Prima persona plurale):

    noi: **Noi** siamo Piero e Olga.   *We are Piero and Olga.*

2) Second person plural (Seconda persona plurale):

    voi: **Voi** vi chiamate Mario e Paola.   *Your names are Mario and Paola*

3) Third person plural (Terza persona plurale):

    loro: **Loro** studiano l'italiano.   *They study Italian.*
    Loro: Signori, dove abitano **Loro**?   *Gentlemen, where do you live?*
    Loro: Signorine, cosa prendono **Loro**?   *Misses, what are you having?*

Note that, although all subject pronouns show number, only **lui** (*he*) and **lei** (*she*) show gender.
Note also how capitalization of **Lei** and **Loro** distinguishes them from **lei** and **loro**.

PRESENT INDICATIVE TENSE (PRESENTE INDICATIVO)

Regular First-Conjugation Verbs

The first-conjugation verbs end in **-are**. Many of the most frequently used verbs in Italian belong to this conjugation, and a short list of some of them appears below.

abitare	*to live*	**giocare**	*to play (a game, etc.)*
alzare	*to raise, lift, pick up*	**guardare**	*to look*
amare	*to love*	**guidare**	*to drive, to guide*
arrivare	*to arrive*	**imparare**	*to learn*
ascoltare	*to listen*	**informare**	*to inform*
ballare	*to dance*	**insegnare**	*to teach*
cambiare	*to change*	**invitare**	*to invite*
camminare	*to walk*	**lavare**	*to wash*
cantare	*to sing*	**lavorare**	*to work*
chiamare	*to call*	**mandare**	*to send*
comprare	*to buy*	**nuotare**	*to swim*
contare	*to count*	**parlare**	*to speak*
cucinare	*to cook*	**pensare**	*to think*
desiderare	*to desire*	**preparare**	*to prepare*
firmare	*to sign*	**raccontare**	*to tell, to relate*
formare	*to form*	**salutare**	*to greet*
sposare	*to marry*	**telefonare**	*to telephone*
studiare	*to study*	**visitare**	*to visit*
suonare	*to play (an instrument), to ring (as a telephone rings)*		

The present indicative tense of **-are** verbs is formed by dropping the infinitive ending **-are** and adding to the result-ing root the personal endings **-o**, **-i**, **-a**, **-iamo**, **-ate**, **-ano**. Observe the following:

Infinitive:	**chiamare**	**mandare**	**parlare**
Root:	**chiam-**	**mand-**	**parl-**
io	chiamo	mando	parlo
tu	chiami	mandi	parli
lui,[1] lei,[2] Lei	chiama	manda	parla
noi	chiamiamo	mandiamo	parliamo
voi	chiamate	mandate	parlate
loro,[3] Loro	chiamano	mandano	parlano

Lui chiama i ragazzi.	*He calls the boys.*
Loro mandano i pacchi.	*They send the packages.*
Io parlo agli amici.	*I speak to my friends.*
Noi firmiamo il documento.	*We sign the document.*
Tu nuoti molto bene.	*You swim very well.*
Voi cantate ad alta voce.	*You [voi] sing aloud.*
Telefona molto Lei?	*Do you telephone a lot?*
Lavorano molto Loro?	*Do you work a lot?*

Since each verb form changes to indicate the person referred to, the subject pronouns are usually omitted. The sub-ject pronouns must be included for emphasis or contrast, however:

Compro i biglietti.
I buy the tickets. or I am buying the tickets.
Emphasis: **Io compro i biglietti.**
I buy the tickets. or I am the one who buys the tickets.
Contrast: **Tu compri i biglietti e io compro i panini.**
You buy the tickets and I buy the bread rolls.

---

[1] **Egli** is used infrequently but it is not obsolete.
[2] **Ella** *(she)* and **essa** *(she)* are alternate forms of **lei** but are rarely used.
[3] **Loro** *(they)* has no gender. **Essi** *(they,* m. pl.) and **esse** *(they,* f. pl.) are alternate forms of **loro** and show gender; they are used when gender must be shown.

1. Complete the following with the appropriate present indicative verb endings:

1. Roberto impar_____la lezione.
2. Rosanna lavor_____in un negozio.
3. I ragazzi parl_____italiano.
4. Le signorine cant_____delle belle canzoni.
5. Quei signori nuot_____ molto bene.
6. Noi cammin_____lentamente.
7. Tu alz_____il ricevitore.
8. Antonio guard_____l'orologio.
9. Voi invit_____gli amici.
10. Lei firm_____la lettera.

2. Complete the following with the appropriate present indicative forms of the indicated verbs:

1. Noi_____in un ristorante.   *pranzare (to dine, to have lunch)*
2. Il cameriere_____il caffè.   *portare*
3. Tu _____l'automobile.   *lavare*
4. Loro_____in ritardo.   *arrivare*
5. Voi_____i vostri vicini.   *invitare*
6. Dove_____lui?   *lavorare*
7. Quando_____ Loro?   *telefonare*
8. Che cosa_____Lei?   *cantare*
9. Io_____nella mia piscina.   *nuotare*
10. Lui_____molto denaro.   *guadagnare (to earn)*

3. Rewrite the following in the singular:

1. I ragazzi guardano la partita.   4. Noi ceniamo (*to have dinner*) tardi.
2. Voi imparate le lezioni.   5. Le studentesse tornano a casa.
3. Loro arrivano presto.

4. Rewrite the following in the plural:

1. Io chiamo il mio amico.   4. Il cameriere porta la bevanda.
2. Lei compra il biglietto.   5. La signora compra il giornale.
3. Tu nuoti molto bene.

Verbs in -ciare, -giare, -chiare, and -ghiare

Like all regular **-are** verbs, the verbs ending in **-Ciare**, **-giare**, **-chiare**, and **-ghiare** drop the **-are** ending before they are conjugated. However, they also drop the **-i-** in the **tu** and **noi** forms before the regular endings (**-i** and **-iamo**) are added. Observe the following:

Infinitive:	**cominciare**	**viaggiare**	**invecchiare**	**avvinghiare**
Root:	**cominci-**	**viaggi-**	**invecchi-**	**avvinghi-**
Root for the tu and noi forms:	**cominc-**	**viagg-**	**invecch-**	**avvingh-**
io	comincio	viaggio	invecchio	avvinghio
tu	cominci	viaggi	invecchi	avvinghi
lui, lei, Lei	comincia	viaggia	invecchia	avvinghia
noi	cominciamo	viaggiamo	Invecchiamo	avvinghiamo
voi	cominciate	viaggiate	invecchiate	avvinghiate
loro, Loro	cominciano	viaggiano	Invecchiano	avvinghiano

Below are some verbs ending in **-ciare**, **-giare**, **-chiare**, and **-ghiare**.

cominciare	*to start*	**parcheggiare**	*to park*
marciare	*to march*	**viaggiare**	*to travel*
racconciare	*to fix, to mend*	**arrischiare**	*to risk*

| **assaggiạre** | *to taste* | **invecchiạre** | *to grow old* |
| **noleggiạre** | *to rent (a car, etc.)* | **avvinghiạre** | *to grip, to clutch* |

5. Complete each sentence with the correct present indicative form of the indicated verb.

1. Tu_____la mạcchina.   *noleggiạre*
2. Noi_____i pantaloni.   *racconciạre*
3. Voi_____forte.   *avvinghiạre*
4. Io_____tutto per te.   *arrischiạre*
5. Lui_____la motocicletta.   *parcheggiạre*
6. Loro_____per molte ore.   *marciạre*
7. Tu_____molto.   *invecchiạre*
8. Noi_____la minestra.   *assaggiạre*

Verbs in -care and -gare

All verbs with infinitives ending in **-care** and **-gare** add an **-h-** to the root in the **tu** and **noi** forms of the verb. This is done in order to preserve the hard sound of the **c** or **g** of the infinitive. Observe the following:

Infinitive:	**cercare**	**pagare**
Root:	**cerc-**	**pag-**
Root for the **tu** *and* **noi** *forms:*	**cerch-**	**pagh-**
io	cerco	pago
tu	cerchi	paghi
lui, lei, Lei	cerca	paga
noi	cerchiạmo	paghiạmo
voi	cercate	pagate
loro, Loro	cẹrcano	pạgano

Below is a partial list of verbs ending in **-care** and **-gare**.

allargare	*to widen*	**impaccare**	*to pack*
allungare	*to lengthen*	**indagare**	*to investigate*
attaccare	*to attack, to glue*	**sbarcare**	*to disembark*
divagare	*to amuse*	**toccare**	*to touch*
frugare	*to rummage*	**troncare**	*to break, to cut off*
giocare	*to play*	**pagare**	*to pay*

6. Supply the tu and noi present indicative forms of the indicated verbs.

1. Tu_____le cause dell'incidente.   *indagare*
2. Noi_____i bambini.   *divagare*
3. Tu_____quella teorịa.   *attaccare*
4. Noi_____i libri nella valịgia.   *impaccare*
5. Tu_____i pantaloni.   *allargare*

7. Complete each sentence with the correct present indicative form of the indicated verb.

1. Loro_____la strada.   *allargare*
2. Io_____la situazione.   *indagare*
3. Mịo fratello_____le valige. *impaccare*
4. Loro_____stasera.   *sbarcare*

8. Supply the appropriate subject pronouns.

1. Signorina,_____è italiạna o americana.
2. Antọnio,_____dove ạbiti?
3. Ragazzi,_____cosa cercate qui?

4. Signori,_____quando cominciano le vacanze?

5. Parli di Mario? Sí, _____ è un mio amico.

Regular Second-Conjugation Verbs

The infinitives of second-conjugation verbs end in **-ere**. The present indicative of regular **-ere** verbs is formed by dropping the infinitive ending and adding to the root the personal endings **-o, -i, -e, -iamo, -ete**, and **-ono**. Observe the following:

Infinitive:	**correre**	**leggere**	**scrivere**
Root:	**corr-**	**legg-**	**scriv-**
io	corro	leggo	scrivo
tu	corri	leggi	scrivi
lui, lei, Lei	corre	legge	scrive
noi	corriamo	leggiamo	scriviamo
voi	correte	leggete	scrivete
loro, Loro	corrono	leggono	scrivono

Most regular and irregular **-ere** and **-ire** verbs form the **loro** ending by adding **-no** to the first-person singular form. For example:

leggere:	**io leggo → loro leggono**
potere:	**io posso → loro possono**
capire:	**io capisco → loro capiscono**
dire:	**io dico → loro dicono**
venire:	**io vengo → loro vengono**

Below is a list of commonly used second-conjugation verbs:

apprendere	*to learn*	**nascere**	*to be born*
battere	*to beat, to hit*	**offendere**	*to offend*
cadere	*to fall*	**perdere**	*to lose*
chiedere	*to ask*	**piangere**	*to cry*
conoscere	*to know*	**prendere**	*to take*
correre	*to run*	**promettere**	*to promise*
credere	*to believe*	**radere**	*to shave*
descrivere	*to describe*	**ricevere**	*to receive*
eleggere	*to elect*	**ripetere**	*to repeat*
friggere	*to fry*	**rispondere**	*to answer*
involgere	*to wrap*	**scrivere**	*to write*
leggere	*to read*	**uccidere**	*to kill*
mettere	*to put, to place*	**vendere**	*to sell*
mordere	*to bite*	**vivere**	*to live*

Observe the following sentences:

Gli studenti apprendono la lezione	*The students learn the lesson.*
Il bambino piange sempre.	*The child is always crying.*
Noi leggiamo il giornale.	*We read the newspaper.*
Io scrivo una lettera.	*I write a letter.*
Voi vivete in città.	*You live in the city.*
Tu conosci varie lingue.	*You know various languages.*

9. *Complete the following verbs with the appropriate present indicative endings:*

1. Gino descriv_____le sue vacanze.

2. Tu mett_____i libri nel cassetto.

3. Il barbiere rad_____i clienti.

4. I ragazzi vend_____giornali.

 5. Voi ripet_____la domanda.
 6. Gli elettori elegg_____i candidati politici.
 7. Noi non offend_____nessuno.
 8. Giorgio promett_____un regalo al fratellino.
 9. Quel cane mord_____la gente.
10. Loro perd_____sempre le chiavi.

10. Complete the following with the appropriate present indicative forms of the indicated verbs:

 1. I giornalai_____molti giornali.   *vendere*
 2. I bambini_____spesso.   *piangere*
 3. Il padre_____molte cose ai figli.   *promettere*
 4. I ragazzi_____per la strada.   *correre*
 5. Noi_____molte lettere.   *ricevere*
 6. Tu_____la partita di calcio.   *perdere*
 7. Le studentesse_____la lezione.   *apprendere*
 8. Io_____il mio viaggio.   *descrivere*
 9. Voi_____quell'articolo.   *leggere*
10. Le pere mature_____dall'albero.   *cadere*

Verbs ending in -cere

Note the spelling changes when verbs ending in **-cere** are conjugated in the present indicative: **piacere** (*to please*) and **tacere** (*to be quiet*).

Infinitive:	**piacere**	**tacere**
Root:	**piac-**	**tac-**
Root for **io**, **noi**, *and* **loro**:	**piacci-**	**tacci-**
io	piaccio	taccio
tu	piaci	taci
lui, lei, Lei	piace	tace
noi	piacciamo (piaciamo)	tacciamo (taciamo)
voi	piacete	tacete
loro, Loro	piacciono	tacciono

Below is a partial list of verbs ending in **-cere**.

compiacere *to gratify, to please*
dispiacere *to displease*
giacere *to lie down*

11. Complete the following sentences with the appropriate present indicative form of the indicated verb:

 1. Questo discorso non_____a Giulio.   *piacere*
 2. Quel signore_____sul divano.   *giacere*
 3. Tutti gli studenti_____in classe.   *tacere*
 4. Tu non_____mai.   *tacere*
 5. Voi_____sul tappeto.   *giacere*
 6. Io_____il nome.   *tacere*

12. Rewrite the following sentences in the singular.

 1. I ragazzi piacciono alle ragazze.
 2. Giacete sul sofà.
 3. Noi tacciamo quasi sempre.
 4. Voi piacete a noi.

Regular Third-Conjugation Verbs

The infinitives of regular third-conjugation verbs end in **-ire**.

The present indicative of regular **-ire** verbs is formed by dropping the infinitive ending and adding to the root the personal endings **-o, -i, -e, -iamo, -ite,** and **-ono**. Observe the following:

Infinitive:	**coprire**	**sentire**
Root:	**copr-**	**sent-**
io	copro	sento
tu	copri	senti
lui, lei, Lei	copre	sente
noi	copriamo	sentiamo
voi	coprite	sentite
loro, Loro	coprono	sentono

Below is a list of some of the most commonly used third-conjugation verbs.

acconsentire	*to acquiesce, to agree*	**riaprire**	*to reopen*
aprire	*to open*	**scoprire**	*to discover, to uncover*
bollire	*to boil*	**seguire**	*to follow*
coprire	*to cover*	**sentire**	*to hear, to feel, to smell*
dormire	*to sleep*	**servire**	*to serve*
fuggire	*to flee*	**sfuggire**	*to escape*
offrire	*to offer*	**soffrire**	*to suffer*
partire	*to leave*	**vestire**	*to dress, to wear*

Please note that the personal indicative endings of the second- (**-ere**) and third-conjugation (**-ire**) verbs are the same with the exception of the **voi** form:

correre: Correte per la strada.
aprire: Aprite la porta.

13. ***Complete the following with the appropriate present indicative endings:***
    1. I miei zii sempre acconsent_____facilmente.
    2. Il malato soffr_____molto.
    3. Noi apr_____la scatola.
    4. I signori vest _____elegantemente.
    5. Luisa offr_____il caffè alle amiche.
    6. Gli studenti segu_____l'esempio del maestro.
    7. Voi sent_____il campanello.
    8. Noi scopr_____la verità.
    9. Boll_____le patate Loro?
    10. Il cameriere serv_____il tè.

14. ***Follow the model:***

    Seguire la moda? Noi?
    Sí, noi seguiamo la moda.

    1. Aprire la finestra? Io?
    2. Sfuggire il pericolo? Voi?
    3. Scoprire la verità? Loro?
    4. Vestire bene? Mario?
    5. Bollire le verdure? Il cuoco?

    6. Soffrire molto? I malati?
    7. Riaprire il negozio? Noi?
    8. Servire le bevande? Io?
    9. Coprire la pentola? Lei?
    10. Aprire la porta? Teresa?

Third-Conjugation Verbs with -isc-

Many **-ire**, or third-conjugation, verbs add **-isc-** to the root in all forms of the present indicative with the exception of **noi** and **voi**. Study the following forms of the verb **capire** (*to understand*) as a model:

Infinitive:	**capire**
Root for **noi** *and* **voi**:	**cap-**
Irregular Root:	**capisc-**
io	capisco
tu	capisci
lui, lei, Lei	capisce
noi	capiamo
voi	capite
loro, Loro	capiscono

The following is a partial list of **-isc-** verbs:

apparire	*to appear, to seem*		**impedire**	*to prevent*
capire	*to understand*		**ingrandire**	*to enlarge*
comparire	*to appear, to cut a good figure*		**preferire**	*to prefer*
costruire	*to build, to construct*		**pulire**	*to clean*
differire	*to differ, to be different*		**riferire**	*to relate, to refer*
dimagrire	*to lose weight*		**ubbidire**	*to obey*
finire	*to end, to finish*			

15. Complete the following with the appropriate present indicative forms of the indicated verbs:

1. Gli studenti_____il maestro.   *capire*
2. La ditta (*company*) _____un grattacielo.   *costruire*
3. Noi_____gli esami.   *finire*
4. Tu_____durante l'estate.   *dimagrire*
5. Io_____la primavera all'estate.   *preferire*
6. Antonio_____le parole.   *capire*
7. Voi_____al professore.   *ubbidire*
8. Il fotografo_____le fotografie.   *ingrandire*
9. Io_____la casa.   *pulire*
10. Loro_____rimanere qui.   *preferire*

16. Write the following sentences, putting the subjects and verbs in the plural:

1. Tu preferisci questo disco.
2. Io riferisco il suo messaggio.
3. Lo studente capisce la lezione.
4. Tu capisci tutto.
5. Io costruisco una scatola (*box*) di legno.
6. Il bambino ubbidisce sempre.

Note that **apparire** (*to appear*), **comparire** (*to appear*), and **scomparire** (*to disappear*) have two different sets of endings in the present indicative (except the **noi** and **voi** forms). Although they can be conjugated like other **-isc-** verbs, they also have alternate endings. Note that these three verbs drop the letters **-rire** and add **-i-** to the root in the **io** and **loro** forms. Observe the following:

Infinitive:	**apparire**	**comparire**	**scomparire**
io	appaio (apparisco)	compaio (comparisco)	scompaio (scomparisco)
tu	appari (apparisci)	compari (comparisci)	scompari (scomparisci)
lui, lei, Lei	appare (apparisce)	compare (comparisce)	scompare (scomparisce)
noi	appariamo	compariamo	scompariamo

voi	apparite	comparite	scomparite
loro, Loro	appaiono (appariscono)	compaiono (compariscono)	scompaiono (scompariscono)

Irregular Verbs

Dare, stare, andare

The verbs **stare** (*to stay, to be*) and **dare** (*to give*) are irregular in the present indicative. You will note, however, that the vowel endings of these verbs are almost the same as those of regular first-conjugation verbs. Study the following forms:

Infinitive:	**dare**	**stare**
io	do	sto
tu	dai	stai
lui, lei, Lei	dà[4]	sta
noi	diamo	stiamo
voi	date	state
loro, Loro	danno	stanno

Study also the verb **andare** (*to go*). Note that all three verbs double the **n** in the third-person plural: **danno, stanno, vanno.**

Infinitive:	**andare**
io	vado
tu	vai
lui, lei, Lei	va
noi	andiamo
voi	andate
loro, Loro	vanno

17. Rewrite the following in the singular (io):

1. Stiamo bene.
2. Stiamo qui.
3. Diamo gli esami.
4. Andiamo al cinema.
5. Stiamo per partire.
6. Diamo i regali.
7. Diamo il benvenuto.
8. Andiamo in salotto.

18. Complete the following with the appropriate present indicative forms of the indicated verbs:

1. Maria _____ al centro in autobus.   *andare*
2. Oggi io_____ a casa.   *stare*
3. I ragazzi _____ dagli zii.   *stare*
4. Luigi_____ il numero telefonico a Carlo.   *dare*
5. Noi_____ gli esami.   *dare*
6. Io_____ dai nonni.   *andare*
7. Tu ed io_____ al mare.   *andare*
8. Loro_____molto bene.   *stare*

Bere

In Italian, several verbs have infinitives that have been shortened from their earlier versions. The verb **bere** (*to drink*) is a good example. **Bere** is a shortened form of the old Italian infinitive *bevere*. In the formation of the present indicative, the root comes from this old Italian infinitive. In all other aspects the verb is completely regular in the present

---

[4]Note the accent in **dà**, which is used to distinguish this form of the verb **dare** from the preposition **da**. The accents on **dài, dàte,** and **dànno** are no longer in use.

indicative, and the personal forms are the same as those of any other regular verb of the second conjugation. You will find this to be the case with other irregular verbs you will study.

Infinitive:	**bere**[5]
Root:	bev-
io	bevo
tu	bevi
lui, lei, Lei	beve
noi	beviamo
voi	bevete
loro, Loro	bevono

19. *Complete the following with the appropriate present indicative form of the verb bere:*
1. Durante l'estate io_____troppo.
2. I bambini_____il latte.
3. Pietro_____un tè freddo.
4. Noi_____il vino durante la cena.
5. Cosa_____Loro?
6. Voi_____birra o vino?
7. Antonia, cosa_____oggi?
8. Mia madre_____soltanto (*only*) acqua minerale.

Irregular Verbs with -co

Infinitives ending in -durre

Italian verbs with their infinitives ending in **-durre**, such as **condurre** (*to lead, to drive, to conduct*) and **produrre** (*to produce*), have their origins in the longer Latin infinitive forms *condūcĕre* and *prodūcĕre*. The roots for the present indicative of these verbs come from the original Latin infinitives. Note that the endings are the same as the endings of any regular **-ere** verb. Study the following forms:

Infinitive:	**produrre**	**condurre**
Root:	**produc-**	**conduc-**
io	produco	conduco
tu	produci	conduci
lui, lei, Lei	produce	conduce
noi	produciamo	conduciamo
voi	producete	conducete
loro, Loro	producono	conducono

Below is a list of some verbs ending in **-durre**.

condurre	*to lead, to drive, to conduct*	**ridurre**	*to reduce, to curtail*
introdurre	*to introduce*	**tradurre**	*to translate*
produrre	*to produce*		

20. *Rewrite the following sentences in the singular:*
1. Introducete gli amici.
2. Producono molto.
3. Traduciamo in inglese.
4. Conducete i treni.

---

[5] From the Latin *bĭbĕre (to drink)*. *Bevere* still exists in its full form in some dialects, such as Neapolitan.

5. Riducono le frasi (*sentences*).
6. Produciamo poco.

21. Complete the following with the appropriate present indicative forms of the indicated verbs:
1. Gli agricoltori_____molte cose.   *produrre*
2. Il professor Martini_____molte poesie.   *tradurre*
3. Il padre di Giorgio_____l'autobus.   *condurre*
4. Io_____i miei cugini.   *introdurre*
5. Noi_____il prezzo.   *ridurre*
6. Tu_____un romanzo.   *tradurre*

22. Supply the subject pronouns and/or the verb forms as indicated.
1. Signorina Meli, _____da molte lingue.   *You; tradurre*
2. Ragazzi, _____tutto a uno scherzo?   *You; ridurre*
3. Questi campi _____molto granturco.   *produrre*
4. Olga, _____non_____mai niente.   *You; disdire*
5. Signori, _____ci_____sempre.   *You; contraddire*

Dire and verbs ending in -dire

The root for the present indicative of the verb **dire** (*to say, to tell*) comes from its original Latin infinitive *dicĕre*. The same is true of other verbs made up of a prefix and **-dire**, such as **contraddire** (*to contradict*). You will note from the following that the endings are the same as those of a regular **-ere** verb, but the **voi** form is **dite** or the prefix and **-dite**.

Infinitive:	**dire**	**contraddire**
Root:	**dic-**	**contraddic-**
io	dico	contraddico
tu	dici	contraddici
lui, lei, Lei	dice	contraddice
noi	diciamo	contraddiciamo
voi	dite	contraddite
loro, Loro	dicono	contraddicono

Below is a partial list of verbs ending in **-dire**.

contraddire	*to contradict*
disdire	*to retract, to cancel*
indire	*to announce publicly, to declare*
interdire	*to prohibit*
maledire	*to curse*

23. Pluralize the following sentences:
1. Disdice la promessa.
2. Tu contraddici il tuo amico.
3. L'organizzazione indice il concorso.
4. Non maledico nessuno.
5. Dici tutto.
6. Che dici?

24. Complete the following with the appropriate forms of the present indicative of the indicated verbs:
1. Loro_____la nostra partecipazione.   *interdire*
2. Tu_____la mia risposta.   *contraddire*
3. Maria_____la verità.   *dire*
4. Loro non_____nessuno.   *maledire*

    5. Voi_____la vostra promessa.   *disdire*
    6. Il comitato (*committee*) _____una riunione.   *indire*
    7. Noi_____poche cose.   *dire*
    8. Loro non_____nessuno.   *contraddire*

25. Answer the following questions in full as indicated.
    1. Roberto, io dico sempre la verità?   *No; never*
    2. Quest'anno quelle città_____un nuovo concorso di poesia?   *Yes; indire*
    3. Ragazzi, voi contraddite le nostre proposte?   *Yes, sometimes*
    4. Ingegnere, Lei contraddice sempre i Suoi soci?   *No, not always*
    5. Signori, Loro maledicono i Loro nemici?   *No*
    6. Che dite voi quando non avete niente da dire?   *Nothing*

Verbs with -go

Porre and verbs ending in -porre

The verb **porre** (*to put, to place*) comes from the original Latin *ponĕre*, from which it gets its root for the formation of the present indicative. You will note that there is a **-g-** in the **io** and **loro** forms. The same is true of other verbs made up of a prefix plus **-porre**. Study the following forms:

Infinitive:	**porre**	**comporre**
Root:	**pon-**	**compon-**
Root for **io** *and* **loro**:	**pong-**	**compong-**
io	pongo	compongo
tu	poni	componi
lui, lei, Lei	pone	compone
noi	poniamo	componiamo
voi	ponete	componete
loro, Loro	pongono	compongono

Below is a list of commonly used verbs ending in **-porre**.

disporre	*to dispose, to provide*	**posporre**	*to postpone*
esporre	*to expose, to show, to expound*	**proporre**	*to propose*
imporre	*to impose*	**riporre**	*to put back*
opporre	*to oppose*	**supporre**	*to suppose*

26. Complete the following sentences with the appropriate present indicative forms of the indicated verbs:
    1. I signori_____l'appuntamento.   *posporre*
    2. Voi_____i soldi in banca.   *porre*
    3. Lo scienziato_____una nuova teoria.   *esporre*
    4. Noi_____senza sapere.   *supporre*
    5. Tu_____una poesia.   *comporre*

27. Rewrite the following sentences putting the subjects and verbs in the plural:
    1. Lui propone l'appuntamento.
    2. Tu imponi queste regole.
    3. Io propongo una soluzione.
    4. Tu componi il tema.

Rimanere, valere, salire

The verbs **rimanere** (*to stay, to be left*), **valere** (*to be worth*), and **salire** (*to climb*) also have a -g- in the **io** and **loro** forms of the present indicative. All other forms are regular, and the personal endings are either those of **-ere** or **-ire** verbs, depending upon the conjugation to which the verb belongs.

Infinitive	**rimanere**	**valere**	**salire**
Root:	**riman-**	**val-**	**sal-**
Root for **io/loro**:	**rimang-**	**valg-**	**salg-**
io	rimango	valgo	salgo
tu	rimani	vali	sali
lui, lei, Lei	rimane	vale	sale
noi	rimaniamo	valiamo	saliamo
voi	rimanete	valete	salite
loro, Loro	rimangono	valgono	salgono

28. Complete the following with the appropriate forms of the present indicative of the indicated verbs:

1. Quest'anello _____molto.   *valere*
2. Io _____lí solamente due giorni.   *rimanere*
3. Quanto tempo _____ tu?   *rimanere*
4. Io _____ le scale in fretta.   *salire*
5. Voi _____ sul treno.   *salire*

29. Answer the following with full sentences as indicated.

1. Ragazze, rimanete qui molti giorni?   *No, pochi*
2. Chi sale le scale in fretta?   *Noi*
3. Marco, vali molto alla tua famiglia?   *Sí*
4. Luisa, è vero che posponi le tue vacanze?   *No*
5. Professore, Lei impone molte regole in classe?   *No*
6. Ragazzi, voi valete molto alla vostra squadra di calcio?   *Sí*

Trarre and verbs ending in -trarre

The verb **trarre** (*to pull, to extract, to draw*) and all verbs formed by **-trarre** with a prefix have a double **g** in the **io** and **loro** forms. All other forms come from the original Latin infinitive *trahěre*. Study the following forms of **trarre** and **attrarre** (*to attract, to draw*):

Infinitive:	**trarre**	**attrarre**
Root:	**tra-**	**attra-**
Root for **lo/loro**:	**tragg-**	**attragg-**
io	traggo	attraggo
tu	trai	attrai
lui, lei, Lei	trae	attrae
noi	traiamo	attraiamo
voi	traete	attraete
loro, Loro	traggono	attraggono

The following are some verbs with **-trarre** as suffix:

distrarre	*to distract*
contrarre	*to contract*
estrarre	*to extract*
sottrarre	*to subtract*

30. Complete the following with the appropriate present indicative forms of the indicated verbs:

1. Il circo _____ molta gente.   *attrarre*
2. I giocattoli _____ i bambini.   *distrarre*
3. Tu _____molta attenzione.   *attrarre*
4. Noi_____una conclusione dalla storia.   *trarre*
5. I ragazzi _____un raffreddore.   *contrarre*
6. Io_____ispirazione dalle tue parole.   *trarre*

31. Rewrite the following in the plural:
  1. Il gioco distrae il ragazzo.
  2. Lo studente trae le conclusioni.
  3. Io contraggo la febbre.
  4. Tu attrai la mia simpatia.

32. Answer the following questions in full as indicated.
  1. Signorina, Lei attrae molti amici?   *Sí*
  2. Traete molte lezioni dalle vostre esperienze?   *Sí; quasi sempre*
  3. Come distraete i bambini?   *con i giocattoli*
  4. Signor dentista, Lei estrae sempre i denti con facilità?   *No, non sempre*
  5. -Stefano, contrai molti raffreddori d'inverno? -E voi, ragazzi?   *Sí; Anche noi*
  6. Signori, Loro salgono le scale in fretta?   *No*

Verbs ending in -gliere

All verbs ending in **-gliere**, such as **cogliere** (*to pick, to gather, to seize* [an opportunity, etc.]), change to **-olgo** and **-olgono** in the **io** and **loro** forms respectively. Study the following:

Infinitive:	**cogliere**
io	colgo
tu	cogli
lui, lei, Lei	coglie
noi	cogliamo
voi	cogliete
loro, Loro	colgono

Below is a list of commonly used verbs ending in **-gliere**.

accogliere	*to welcome, to receive*
raccogliere	*to collect, to gather, to pick up*
togliere	*to remove, to take away, to deduct*

33. Complete the following with the appropriate forms of the present indicative of the indicated verbs:
  1. Maria_____gli ospiti.   *accogliere*
  2. I bambini_____i giocattoli.   *raccogliere*
  3. Noi_____l'occasione.   *cogliere*
  4. Io_____i fiori nel giardino.   *raccogliere*
  5. Voi_____il tappeto.   *togliere*
  6. Tu_____i tuoi parenti a braccia aperte.   *accogliere*
  7. Antonio_____i regali.   *raccogliere*

34. Answer the following questions in full as indicated.
  1. Marisa, tu accogli bene i tuoi amici?   *Sí*
  2. Cosa raccogli tu dal tuo giardino?   *Un mazzo di fiori*
  3. Ragazzi, cogliete la frutta dagli alberi?   *Sí*
  4. Chi toglie la spazzatura ogni settimana?   *loro*
  5. Signora, Lei dove accoglie le Sue amiche?   *Nel salotto*
  6. Renzo e Marisa, togliete la polvere ogni giorno? *No*

Tenere and venire

The verbs **tenere** (*to have, to keep*) and **venire** (*to come*) (and any verbs made up of a prefix plus **-tenere** or **-venire**) have a **g** in the **io** and **loro** forms. In addition, the vowel of the root changes to **-ie-** in the **tu** and **lui/lei** forms.

Study the following:

Infinitive:	**tenere**	**venire**
io	tengo	vengo
tu	tieni	vieni
lui, lei, Lei	tiene	viene
noi	teniamo	veniamo
voi	tenete	venite
loro, Loro	tengono	vengono

The following is a list of useful verbs with a prefix plus **-tenere** or **-venire**:

appartenere	*to belong*	**avvenire**	*to happen, to occur*
contenere	*to contain*	**contravvenire**	*to contravene*
intrattenere	*to entertain*	**convenire**	*to convene*
mantenere	*to maintain*	**divenire**	*to become*
ottenere	*to obtain*	**intervenire**	*to intervene*
ritenere	*to retain*	**provenire**	*to come from, to proceed*
sostenere	*to sustain, to support*	**sovvenire**	*to help*
trattenere	*to withhold, to detain*	**svenire**	*to faint*

35. Complete the following with the appropriate forms of the present indicative of the indicated verbs:
1. Queste scatole_____esplosivi.   *contenere*
2. I miei amici_____alle nove.   *venire*
3. Luigi_____un favore da suo zio.   *ottenere*
4. Voi_____una tesi falsa.   *sostenere*
5. Noi_____ il comitato martedí.   *riconvenire*

36. Answer each question in the affirmative with a complete sentence.
1. Luigi, vieni a scuola oggi?
2. Signora, viene domani Sua figlia?
3. Ragazzi, provenite da Nuova York?
4. Olga, vengono con noi le tue amiche?
5. Roberto, appartieni al Club italiano?
6. Chi intrattiene gli ospiti? (*voi*)

37. Rewrite each sentence, putting the subject and the verb in the singular.
1. Mantenete bene i giardini?
2. Queste riviste contengono poco.
3. Ottengono i biglietti Loro?
4. Intratteniamo gli amici.
5. Le studentesse appartengono a quella classe.

38. Answer the following questions in full as indicated.
1. Ragazzi, appartenete a un club sportivo?   *Sí*
2. Perché parete un po' confusi?   *Because we are confused*
3. Chi mantiene i giardini della città?   *Il giardiniere*
4. Signorina, come ottiene Lei buoni risultati a scuola?   *Studiando*
5. Signore, oggi Lei viene solo al ristorante?   *No; with a friend (f.)*
6. Signori, Loro appartengono al nostro gruppo?   *Sí*

Verbs with -io

Parere

The verb **parere** (*to seem*), interchangeable with the regular verb **sembrare** (*to seem*), takes an **i** with **io** and **loro**, and with the alternate **noi** form (in parentheses). Study the following:

Infinitive:	**parere**
io	paio
tu	pari
lui, lei, Lei	pare
noi	paiamo (pariamo)
voi	parete
loro, Loro	paiono

39. Complete the following with the appropriate form of the present indicative of the verb parere:

1. Oggi io_____ molto stanco.
2. Quel signore_____triste.
3. Gli studenti_____preparati per l'esame.
4. Noi_____riposati.
5. Tu_____arrabbiato oggi.
6. Voi_____ stanchi.
7. _____stanco Marcello?
8. _____riposati i signori?

Morire

The verb **morire** (*to die*) also takes an **i** in the **io** and **loro** forms. In addition, the vowel **o** changes to **uo** in all forms except **noi** and **voi**. Study the following:

Infinitive:	**morire**
io	muoio
tu	muori
lui, lei, Lei	muore
noi	moriamo
voi	morite
loro, Loro	muoiono

40. Complete the following with the appropriate form of the present indicative of the verb morire:

1. Loro_____dalle risa.
2. Io_____dal caldo.
3. Voi_____dalla noia (*boredom*).
4. Tu_____dal sonno.
5. Noi_____dalla vergogna (*shame*).
6. Lui_____dalla paura.

41. Supply the appropriate subject pronouns and verb forms as indicated.

1. Signora, anche_____dalle risa?   *you; morire*
2. Ragazzi, anche_____dal caldo?   *you; morire*
3. Guardate la signorina; anche_____stanca.   *she; parere*
4. Abbiamo lavorato tanto! Anche_____stanchi.   *we; parere*
5. Signori,_____sono stanchi oppure_____dalla noia. *you; morire*

Other Verbs with a Vowel Change in the Root

Sedere

The verb **sedere** (*to sit down*) changes the vowel **e** to **ie** in all forms except **noi** and **voi**. Note also the less frequently used alternate forms for **io** and **loro** in parentheses.

Infinitive:	**sedere**
Root:	**sied-**
Root for **noi** *and* **voi**:	**sed-**
io	siẹdo (seggo)
tu	siẹdi
lui, lei, Lei	siẹde
noi	sediạmo
voi	sedete
loro, Loro	siẹdono (sẹggono)

42. Complete the following with the correct form of the present indicative of the verb sedere:

1. Io _____ qui e tu_____ lí.
2. Marịa e Carlo_____in prima fila (*row*).
3. Dove_____voi?
4. Signora Monti, Lei_____ qui o lí?
5. Noi _____ sempre in fondo.
6. Carlo, perché_____lontano da tutti?

Udire

The vowel **u** in **udire** (*to hear*) changes to **o** in all forms except **noi** and **voi**.

Infinitive:	**udire**
Root:	**ud-**
Root for **noi** *and* **voi**:	**od-**
io	odo
tu	odi
lui, lei, Lei	ode
noi	udiạmo
voi	udite
loro, Loro	ọdono

43. Complete the following with the appropriate present indicative forms of udire:

1. Gli studenti_____parlare la maẹstra.
2. Io _____la rạdio.
3. Ragazzi, _____il suọno del campanello?
4. Signorina, _____la mịa voce?
5. Noi_____il telegiornale.
6. Carlo, _____quella bella canzone?

Uscire

The vowel **u** of the verb **uscire** (*to go out*) changes to **e** in all forms of the present indicative except **noi** and **voi**. Note that the verb **riuscire** (*to succeed*) is conjugated like **uscire**. Observe the following:

Infinitive:	**uscire**	**riuscire**
Root for **noi** *and* **voi**:	**usc-**	**riusc-**
irregular Root:	**esc-**	**riesc-**

io	esco	riesco
tu	esci	riesci
lui, lei, Lei	esce	riesce
noi	usciamo	riusciamo
voi	uscite	riuscite
loro, Loro	escono	riescono

44. Complete the following with the appropriate present indicative forms of the indicated verbs:

1. Luisa e Pietro _____ insieme il sabato.   *uscire*
2. Olga _____ molto bene a scuola.   *riuscire*
3. I miei nonni _____ soltanto la domenica.   *uscire*
4. Voi _____ di casa alle otto di mattina.   *uscire*
5. Signori, _____ a trovare l'orario?   *riuscire*
6. Tu _____ sempre con gli stessi amici.   *uscire*
7. Io non _____ bene in matematica.   *riuscire*

Fare

Study the following forms of the irregular verb **fare** (*to do, to make*). You will note that the **io** and **noi** forms return to the original Latin infinitive *facĕre*. Also, the two-syllable third-person plural **fanno** doubles the -**n**- as do **dare** (**danno**), **stare** (**stanno**), and **sapere** (**sanno**).

Infinitive:	**fare**
io	faccio (fo)
tu	fai
lui, lei, Lei	fa
noi	facciamo
voi	fate
loro, Loro	fanno

45. Complete the following with the appropriate present indicative forms of the verb fare:

1. Il cuoco_____tutto a perfezione.
2. Noi _____i buoni.
3. Tu_____il meccanico.
4. Cosa_____Lei?
5. Dove_____le vacanze voi?
6. I giovani_____una gita in campagna.
7. Oggi io non_____niente.
8. Cosa_____tuo padre?

Sapere

Study the following forms of the irregular verb **sapere** (*to know, to know how to*). Note the similarity of the forms **so**, **sai**, **sa**, and **sanno** with the same present indicative forms of **dare** (*to give*), **fare** (*to do, to make*), and **stare** (*to stay, to be*).

Infinitive:	**sapere**
io	so
tu	sai
lui, lei, Lei	sa
noi	sappiamo
voi	sapete
loro, Loro	sanno

46. Complete the following with the appropriate present indicative forms of sapere:

1. Quei giovani_____sciare molto bene.
2. Antonio_____suonare il violino.

3. Noi_____dove abitate.
4. Io non_____cosa fare.
5. La bambina_____contare fino a cento.
6. Tu non_____il nome del maestro.
7. _____ guidare Loro?
8. Voi _____ molte cose.

Modal verbs (Verbi modali)

Dovere (*to have to, to must*), **potere** (*to be able to, to can*), and **volere** (*to want, to wish*) are known as *modal verbs*: when they are conjugated, they may be followed by an infinitive. For example:

> **Voglio partecipare**, ma non **posso venire** perché **devo stare** a casa.
> *I want to participate, but I cannot come because I must stay home.*

In compound tenses, *modal verbs* are conjugated with the auxiliary verbs (helping verbs) **avere** and **essere**. For details, see the section on the *present perfect* (*passato prossimo*) in this chapter.

Dovere
Dovere (*to have to, must*) is irregular in all forms except the **voi** form (**dovete**). Note that **io** and **loro** have two forms each (**io devo** or **debbo**; **loro devono** or **debbono**). Observe the following:

Infinitive:	**dovere**
io	devo (debbo)
tu	devi
lui, lei, Lei	deve
noi	dobbiamo
voi	dovete
loro, Loro	devono (debbono)

47. *Complete the following with the appropriate present indicative forms of dovere:*
1. Noi _____ studiare di piú.
2. Io _____ finire questo lavoro.
3. Loro _____ arrivare alle tre.
4. Tu _____ dormire di meno.
5. Voi _____ parlare ad alta voce.
6. Luigi _____ tornare a casa.
7. Io non _____ scrivere molte lettere.
8. Noi _____ cercare gli amici.

Potere
All present indicative forms of **potere** (*to be able to, can*) are irregular except **voi** (**potete**). Observe the following:

Infinitive:	**potere**
io	posso
tu	puoi
lui, lei, Lei	può
noi	possiamo
voi	potete
loro, Loro	possono

48. *Complete the following with the appropriate present indicative forms of potere:*
1. Luisa _____ andare a teatro con noi.
2. Noi _____ guardare la televisione fino a tardi.

3. Piẹtro e Olga _____ suonare il pianoforte.
4. Cosa _____ fare Lei?
5. Adesso voi non _____ fare niẹnte.
6. Io _____ giocare fino alle quạttro.
7. Carlo, _____ prestarmi (*lend me*) la bicicletta?
8. Con tutta quẹsta neve, il signor Martini non _____ andare in uffịcio.

Volere

The present indicative forms of **volere** (*to want*, *to desire*) are all irregular except for the **voi** form (**volete**). Observe the following:

Infinitive:	**volere**
io	vọglio
tu	vuọi
lui, lei, Lei	vuọle
noi	vogliạmo
voi	volete
loro, Loro	vọgliono

49. Complete the following with the appropriate present indicative forms of volere:
1. Quẹst'estate io_____andare in Europa.
2. I ragazzi _____ giocare tutto il giọrno.
3. (Tu) _____ andare al cịnema stasera (*tonight*)?
4. Signore, _____ comprare qualcosa?
5. Noi _____ vedere i nonni.
6. Adesso cosa (voi) _____ fare?
7. I signori _____ viaggiạre in aẹreo.
8. Io _____ imparare a sciạre (*to ski*).

Avere

In the present tense, **avere** (*to have*, *to hold*) is irregular in all forms except **voi (avete)**. Note that most forms of **avere** begin with **h-** (never pronounced) in order to distinguish the verb's personal forms from other words with similar spellings but different meanings. Observe the following:

Infinitive:	**avere**
io	ho
tu	hại
lui, lei, Lei	ha
noi	abbiạmo
voi	avete
loro, Loro	hanno

50. Complete the following with the appropriate present indicative form of avere:
1. Luịgi _____ la penna in mano.
2. Io _____ dụe fratelli e tre sorelle.
3. Le studentesse _____ molti cọmpiti da fare.
4. Tu _____ una bella voce.
5. Voi _____ degli ọttimi amici.
6. Il padre di Roberto _____ un negọzio nel centro della città.
7. Oggi noi _____ ọspiti in casa.
8. Stẹfano _____ una motocicletta giapponese.

Ęssere

In the present tense, ęssere (*to be*) is irregular in all of its forms. (Note that the **io** and **loro** forms have the same spelling, **sono**. This is seldom confusing since the correct meaning is evident from the context.) Observe the following:

Infinitive:	ęssere
io	sono
tu	sęi
lui, lei, Lei	è
noi	siamo
voi	sięte
loro, Loro	sono

51. Complete the following with the appropriate present indicative forms of ęssere:

1. Quęsti signori _____ americani.
2. La madre di Olga _____ greca.
3. Dove _____ i bambini?
4. Noi _____ pronti a giocare.
5. Ragazzi, _____ a scuǫla alle dųe?
6. La domęnica io _____ sempre a casa.
7. _____ in Italia i tuǫi genitori?
8. Marcello non _____ qui, _____ da sųo zio.

52. Answer the following questions in the affirmative with a complete sentence. Use the cues, when given.

1. Carlo, sęi italiano?
2. Signora, è a casa Sųa figlia?
3. Ragazzi, sięte pronti adesso?
4. Sono nello stadio i giocatori?
5. Luisa, sei l'amica di Giovanni?
6. Siamo bravi o cattivi? *bravi*
7. Antonio, dove sono i tuǫi genitori? *al cinema*
8. Silvia, sono io il tuo compagno di scuǫla?

Special Use of the Present Indicative and the Preposition *da*

The present indicative, together with the preposition **da**, may be used to describe an action which began in the past and is still going on in the present. Note that in English, as shown below, a past tense, the present perfect, is used to convey the same concept. Observe the following:

Da quanto tempo Lei stųdia l'italiano?
How long have you been studying Italian?

Stųdio l'italiano da due anni. (*or:* Sono due anni che stųdio l'italiano.)
I have been studying Italian for two years.

53. Complete the following with the appropriate present indicative forms of the indicated verbs:

1. Noi _____ negli Stati Uniti da tre anni.	*vivere*
2. Da quanti anni Lei _____ qui?	*lavorare*
3. Tu _____ Stęfano da sęi anni.	*conoscere*
4. Mio zio _____ il dottore da quindici anni.	*fare*
5. Da quanto tempo (voi) _____ l'inglese?	*studiare*

54. Answer the following questions in complete sentences, according to the cues:

1. Da quanto tempo frequenti questa scuola?			*due anni*
2. Da quanto tempo studi l'italiano?				*un anno*
3. Da quanto tempo vivi in questa città?			*cinque anni*
4. Da quanto tempo conosci il tuo migliore amico?		*molti anni*
5. Da quanto tempo non vedi i tuoi nonni?			*tre mesi*
6. Da quanto tempo non vai a teatro?				*sei mesi*

REVIEW

55. Complete the following with the appropriate present indicative forms of the indicated verbs:

1. Noi _____ fino a tardi.				*ballare*
2. Mio fratello _____ in un ospedale.			*lavorare*
3. Cosa _____ i signori?				*preferire*
4. Carlo, dove _____ con i tuoi amici?			*giocare*
5. Alcune persone _____ presto.			*invecchiare*
6. Voi _____ il caffè agli amici.			*offrire*
7. Che rivista _____ Lei?				*leggere*
8. Tu _____ in Italia in aereo.				*andare*
9. I nostri amici _____ canadesi.			*essere*
10. Il mio maestro _____ molti esami.			*dare*
11. Gli Stati Uniti _____ molte automobili.		*produrre*
12. Io _____ il libro sul tavolo.			*porre*
13. Loro _____ al circolo italiano.			*appartenere*
14. Voi _____ che io _____ sempre.			*dire, contraddire*
15. Questi giornali _____ ai lettori.			*piacere*

IMPERFECT INDICATIVE TENSE (*IMPERFETTO INDICATIVO*)

Regular -are verbs

The imperfect indicative is used to express a recurrent event in the past, to indicate age, time, size, color, etc., in the past. See pages 106 to 115 for full details (Chapter 6). The imperfect indicative of **-are** verbs is formed by dropping the infinitive ending **-are** and adding the following endings to the root: **-avo, -avi, -ava, -avamo, -avate,** and **-avano.** Observe the following:

Infinitive:	**guardare** *(to look at)*	**parlare** *(to speak)*	**giocare** *(to play)*
Root:	**guard-**	**parl-**	**gioc-**
io	guardavo	parlavo	giocavo
tu	guardavi	parlavi	giocavi
lui, lei, Lei	guardava	parlava	giocava
noi	guardavamo	parlavamo	giocavamo
voi	guardavate	parlavate	giocavate
loro, Loro	guardavano	parlavano	giocavano

56. Complete the following with the appropriate imperfect indicative forms of the indicated verbs:

1. Noi _____ sempre dai nonni.			*andare*
2. Molti anni fa io _____ sempre in autobus.		*viaggiare*
3. Mia sorella _____ ogni giorno.			*cantare*
4. I giovani _____ tutti gl'inverni.			*sciare*
5. Voi _____ spesso i vostri parenti.			*vedere*
6. Tu _____ a tennis con gli amici.			*giocare*
7. Da piccolo io _____, non _____.			*saltare (to jump), camminare*
8. Mio zio mi _____ molti regali.			*portare*

57. Rewrite the following in the imperfect indicative:

1. Antonio parla molto.
2. Voi camminate per le strade.
3. Mia madre compra molte cose.
4. Noi giochiamo nel parco.
5. Le ragazze cantano ad alte voce.
6. Io ascolto i miei maestri con attenzione.
7. Tu guardi la televisione tutte le sere.
8. Vede Lei i Suoi cugini?
9. Viaggiate molto?
10. Studiano con diligenza gli studenti?

Regular -ere Verbs

The imperfect indicative of regular -ere verbs is formed by dropping the infinitive ending -ere and adding the following endings to the root: -evo, -evi, -eva, -evamo, -evate, -evano. Observe the following:

Infinitive:	correre *(to run)*	leggere *(to read)*	mettere *(to place; to put)*
Root:	corr-	legg-	mett-
io	correvo	leggevo	mettevo
tu	correvi	leggevi	mettevi
lui, lei, Lei	correva	leggeva	metteva
noi	correvamo	leggevamo	mettevamo
voi	correvate	leggevate	mettevate
loro, Loro	correvano	leggevano	mettevano

58. Complete the following with the appropriate imperfect indicative forms of the indicated verbs:

1. Anni fa, Pietro _____ molti romanzi.   *leggere*
2. I bambini _____ sempre.   *piangere*
3. Noi _____ ad ogni occasione.   *correre*
4. I gelatai _____ molti gelati durante l'estate.   *vendere*
5. Gli studenti _____ le domande.   *ripetere*
6. Olga e Anna _____ sempre le lezioni.   *sapere*
7. Tu _____ sempre a carte.   *perdere*
8. Le bambine _____ molti giocattoli.   *avere*

59. Rewrite the following in the imperfect indicative:

1. Eleggiamo un nuovo presidente.
2. Descrivete quel paesaggio.
3. Friggo (*I fry*) le uova.
4. Offendi molte persone.
5. Promettete troppe cose.
6. I bambini cadono spesso.
7. Angelo vende biciclette.

Regular -ire Verbs

The imperfect indicative of all -ire verbs is formed by adding the following endings to the root of the verb: -ivo, -ivi, -iva, -ivamo, -ivate, -ivano. Note that there are no irregular -ire verbs in the imperfect. Observe the following verbs:

Infinitive:	capire	salire
Root:	cap-	sal-
io	capivo	salivo
tu	capivi	salivi

lui, lei, Lei	capiva	saliva
noi	capivamo	salivamo
voi	capivate	salivate
loro, Loro	capivano	salivano

60. Complete the following with the appropriate imperfect indicative forms of the indicated verbs:

1. Gli studenti _____ tutto.   *capire*
2. Io _____ le lezioni alle due.   *finire*
3. Voi _____ dei corsi interessanti.   *seguire*
4. Noi _____ la radio tutti i giorni.   *sentire*
5. Loro _____ il mare alla montagna.   *preferire*
6. Voi _____ molte case a due piani.   *costruire*
7. Tu _____ sempre molto stanco.   *apparire*
8. I bambini _____ ai genitori.   *ubbidire*

61. Rewrite the following in the imperfect indicative:

1. Senti il campanello?
2. Vestite i bambini?
3. Preferiamo un gelato.
4. Capiscono bene.
5. Olga soffre molto.
6. Io seguo i tuoi consigli.
7. Offri sempre il tuo aiuto.
8. Apriamo le finestre.
9. Paolo riapre la porta.
10. Ubbidisco alla madre.

62. Answer the following questions in the affirmative with a complete sentence:

1. Aprivi le porte?
2. Servivate il caffè?
3. Vestivamo elegantemente?
4. Capiva bene Lei?
5. Reagivi cautamente?
6. Finivano presto Loro?
7. Soffrivate molto in ospedale?
8. Seguiva molti corsi Luigi?
9. Vestivamo i bambini?
10. Scandivano le parole gli alunni?

Irregular Verbs

The verbs **fare** (*to do, to make*), **dire** (*to say*), **bere** (*to drink*), **produrre** (*to produce*), and **porre** (*to place, to put*) take their roots for the formation of the imperfect indicative from their original Latin infinitives, most of which are shown in parentheses below. In all other respects they are regular. Note that all verbs ending in -**fare**, -**dire**, -**durre**, and -**porre** follow this same pattern. Study the following:

Infinitive:	**fare**	**dire**	**bere**	**produrre**	**porre**
	(*facĕre*)	(*dicĕre*)	(*bevere*)[6]	(*producĕre*)	(*ponĕre*)
Root:	**fac-**	**dic-**	**bev-**	**produc-**	**pon-**
io	facevo	dicevo	bevevo	producevo	ponevo

---

[6] *Bevere* is actually not the Latin infinitive but an old Italian infinitive no longer in use except in some dialects. It comes from the Latin infinitive *bibĕre*. See p. 94.

tu	facevi	dicevi	bevevi	producevi	ponevi
lui, lei, Lei	faceva	diceva	beveva	preduceva	poneva
noi	facevamo	dicevamo	bevevamo	producevamo	ponevamo
voi	facevate	dicevate	bevevate	producevate	ponevate
loro, Loro	facevano	dicevano	bevevano	producevano	ponevano

63. Rewrite the following sentences in the imperfect indicative:
1. Stefano dice la verità.
2. Queste fabbriche producono pantaloni.
3. Il signor Martini fa il dottore.
4. Io non dico niente.
5. Dove fate le vacanze?
6. Questo terreno (*land*) produce molti legumi.
7. Tu non dici la verità.

64. Complete the following with the appropriate imperfect indicative forms of the indicated verbs:
1. Cosa _____ i tuoi amici?   *dire*
2. Chi _____ il cattivo, Stefano o Luigi?   *fare*
3. L'Italia _____ molti legumi.   *produrre*
4. Io non _____ niente.   *dire*
5. Tu non _____ nessuno.   *contraddire*
6. I miei fratelli _____ i soldati.   *fare*
7. Mio zio _____ un treno.   *condurre*

65. Complete the following with the appropriate imperfect forms of bere:
1. Noi _____ molto latte.
2. Roberto non _____ vino.
3. Voi _____ poco.
4. Tu _____ acqua minerale.
5. Io _____ un tè freddo.
6. _____ qualcosa Loro?
7. Mario _____ mentre pranzava.
8. I ragazzi _____ molte aranciate.

66. Complete the following with the appropriate imperfect indicative forms of the indicated verbs:
1. Il filosofo _____ la sua teoria.   *esporre*
2. Io _____ i libri sul tavolo.   *porre*
3. Tu _____ un'ottima soluzione.   *proporre*
4. I musicisti _____ molte sonate.   *comporre*
5. Noi _____ sempre i nostri appuntamenti.   *posporre*
6. Voi _____ le valige nell'attico.   *porre*
7. _____ molto Lei?   *supporre*
8. Mio nonno _____ molte regole.   *imporre*

Trarre

The irregular root for the imperfect indicative of **trarre** (to *extract*, *to pull*, *to draw*) is **tra-**. This root comes from the original Latin infinitive *trahĕre*. To this root are added the regular -**ere** imperfect indicative endings: -**evo**, -**evi**, etc. Note that all verbs ending in -**trarre**, such as **attrarre** (*to attract*), follow **trarre** as a model.

Infinitive:	**trarre**	**attrarre**
Irregular Root:	**tra-**	**attra-**
io	traevo	attraevo
tu	traevi	attraevi

lui, lei, Lei	traeva	attraeva
noi	traevamo	attraevamo
voi	traevate	attraevate
loro, Loro	traevano	attraevano

67. Complete the following with the appropriate imperfect indicative forms of the indicated verbs:

1. Quella commedia _____ molta gente.	*attrarre*
2. Il poeta _____ ispirazione dalla natura.	*trarre*
3. Tu _____ i bambini.	*distrarre*
4. Voi _____ molte persone.	*ritrarre*
5. Io _____ le conclusioni.	*trarre*
6. Noi _____ i numeri a scuola.	*sottrarre*

Essere

The verb **essere** is irregular in all forms of the imperfect indicative. The imperfect indicative forms come from the original Latin forms: *eram*, etc. Study the following:

Infinitive:	essere
io	ero
tu	eri
lui, lei, Lei	era
noi	eravamo
voi	eravate
loro, Loro	erano

68. Complete the following with the appropriate imperfect indicative forms of essere:

1. Teresa _____ amica di Rosa.
2. Noi _____ a scuola.
3. Dove _____ i tuoi amici?
4. Dove _____ tu?
5. L'argento _____ molto in richiesta. (*in demand*)
6. Voi _____ molto bravi a scuola.
7. Signori, dove _____ Loro?
8. Cosa _____ Lei?

69. Answer the following questions, according to the cues, with complete sentences:

1. Cosa eri?	*studente (-essa)*
2. Dov'erano Maria e Carlo?	*al teatro Verdi*
3. Era pronto quello studente?	*Sí*
4. Chi era quel signore?	*mio zio*
5. Eravamo bravi?	*Sí*
6. Eri a casa spesso?	*Sí*
7. Eravate malati?	*Sí*
8. Dov'era tuo padre?	*in Italia*

Uses of the Imperfect Indicative Tense

Continuing action

The imperfect indicative tense is much less commonly used in English than in Italian. Since the word *imperfect* means *not perfected* or *not completed*, the imperfect indicative is used to express continuance, to express actions in the past which are either customary or habitual. Some common adverbial expressions which would indicate continuance and thus demand the use of the imperfect are

a volte	*at times*
certe volte	*sometimes*
come d'uso	*usually*
con frequenza	*frequently*
continuamente	*continuously*
di quando in quando	*from time to time*
di solito	*usually*
di tanto in tanto	*from time to time*
frequentemente	*frequently*
giorno dopo giorno	*day in and day out*
ininterrottamente	*without interruption*
la domenica (il lunedí, etc.)	*on Sundays (on Mondays, etc.)*
mentre	*while*
ogni giorno (ogni settimana, ogni mese, ogni anno, etc.)	*every day (every week, every month, every year, etc.)*
ogni tanto	*once in a while*
quotidianamente	*daily*
ripetutamente	*repeatedly*
sempre	*always*
senza sosta	*without stopping*
spesso	*often*
spesso spesso	*again and again*
tutti i giorni	*every day*

Study the following examples:

Andavano alla spiaggia ogni giorno.
They would (used to) go to the beach every day.

Quando ero piccolo, vedevo i miei nonni frequentemente.
When I was little, I used to see my grandparents frequently.

Mio zio parlava sempre in inglese.
My uncle always spoke (used to speak) English.

I miei amici e io giocavamo spesso tutto il pomeriggio.
My friends and I would (used to) play often the entire afternoon.

70. ***Rewrite the following sentences in the imperfect indicative:***
1. Mio fratello arriva sempre in ritardo.
2. Tu parli ininterrottamente.
3. Le studentesse vanno spesso in biblioteca.
4. Di solito Olga cena presto.
5. La domenica andiamo al parco.
6. Di quando in quando vedo un bel film.
7. Le mie sorelle vengono a casa tutti i giorni.
8. A volte nevica senza sosta.
9. I bambini piangono frequentemente.
10. Mio cugino scrive ogni mese.

Parallel actions

When two or more descriptive actions occur at the same time, the imperfect indicative must be used. Study the following examples:

Io dormivo e Luigi studiava.
I was sleeping and Louis was studying.

Mentre noi cantavạmo, voi giocavạte.
While we were singing, you were playing.

Tu dormivi, Anna studiạva, e io cucinavo.
You were sleeping, Ann was studying, and I was cooking.

71. Complete the following with the appropriate imperfect indicative forms of the indicated verbs:

1. Antọnio _____ il piạno e tu _____.   *suonare, cantare*
2. Noi _____ i piạtti e voi _____ le camịcie. *lavare, lavare*
3. Mentre io _____, loro _____.   *lavorare, giocare*
4. Stẹfano _____ e noi _____.   *dormire, studiạre*
5. Tu _____ e lui _____ la televisiọne.   *telefonare, guardare*
6. Noi _____ e voi _____.   *scrịvere, parlare*
7. Io _____ e tu _____.   *lẹggere, scrịvere*
8. Luịsa _____ la verità e voi _____.   *dire, mentire*
9. Antọnio _____ e Stẹfano _____.   *gridare (to shout). piạngere*
10. Loro _____ e noi _____ a casa.   *viaggiạre, stare*

Mental activity

In order to express duration of mental activity in the past, the imperfect indicative is used. The following is a partial list of verbs denoting mental activity:

amare	*to love*
capire	*to understand*
crẹdere	*to believe*
decịdere	*to decide*
dedurre	*to deduce*
desiderare	*to desire, to want*
intuịre	*to sense*
odiạre	*to hate*
pensare	*to think*
potere	*to be able, can*
preferire	*to prefer*
ragionare	*to reason*
riflẹttere	*to reflect*
sapere	*to know*
sospettare	*to suspect*
sperare	*to hope*
temere	*to fear*
volere	*to want*

Observe the following examples:

Sempre credẹvano tutto.
They always believed everything.

Volevạmo andare in Itạlia.
We wanted to go to Italy.

Anni fa preferivo il mare alla montagna.
Years ago I preferred the sea to the mountains.

I nostri nonni sapẹvano sempre ciò che pensavạmo.
Our grandparents always knew what we thought (were thinking).

72. Complete the following with the appropriate imperfect indicative forms of the indicated verbs:

1. Mịa madre _____ il caffè al tè.   *preferire*
2. Tu _____ sempre la situazịone.   *capire*
3. Loro _____ spesso il freddo dell'inverno.   *temere*
4. Io non _____ mai al mịo amico Pạolo.   *crẹdere*
5. Mịo nonno _____ senza sosta.   *riflẹttere*
6. Voi non _____ viaggịare in ạereo.   *volere*
7. Anni fa io _____ giocare quando _____.   *potere, desiderare*
8. Tu _____ guidare l'automọbile.   *odiạre*
9. Pịetro _____ ogni perịcolo facilmente.   *intuịre*
10. Noi _____ sempre ai genitori.   *crẹdere*

Description in the past: color, size, inner qualities

The imperfect indicative is often used to describe people or things in the past using color, size, and inner qualities. Observe the following:

Il cịelo era sempre blu.	*The sky was always blue.*
Le strade erano larghe.	*The streets were wide.*
Tua nonna era generosa.	*Your grandmother was generous.*

73. Rewrite the following in the imperfect indicative:

1. La casa è grande.
2. Gli edifici sono rossi.
3. Olga è brava.
4. Gli studenti sono intelligenti.
5. La copertina (*cover*) del libro è verde.
6. I genitori sono pazịenti.
7. Noi siạmo alti.
8. Voi siẹte cattivi.
9. Le camịcie sono biạnche.
10. Tu sẹi basso.

Description in the past: age, time, weather

Descriptions in the past concerning age, time, and weather are usually expressed with the imperfect indicative tense. Observe the following examples:

Quạnti anni aveva tụo nonno?	*How old was your grandfather?*
Aveva ottantacinque anni.	*He was eighty-five years old.*
Che ora era? (*or:* **Che ore ẹrano?**)	*What time was it?*
Era l'una in punto.	*It was one o'clock sharp.*
Ẹrano le nove e mezza.	*It was nine thirty.*
Che tempo faceva?	*How was the weather?*
Faceva bel tempo.	*The weather was good.*
Faceva cattivo tempo.	*The weather was bad.*
Pioveva.	*It was raining.*
Nevicava.	*It was snowing.*
Tirava vento.	*It was windy.*

74. Rewrite the following in the imperfect indicative.

1. Che tempo fa?
2. Quạnti anni hai?
3. Che ora è?

4. Nevica?
5. Sono le quattro e un quarto.
6. Abbiamo sedici anni.
7. Tira vento.
8. Pietro ha diciannove anni.
9. È mezzanotte.
10. Piove.

Special use of the imperfect indicative with the preposition da

You have already studied the special use of **da** with the present indicative (see page 90). In Italian, the preposition **da** is also used with the imperfect indicative to describe an action in the remote past. In English, this is done with the pluperfect tense (past perfect or progressive past perfect). Observe the following examples:

Vincenzo era alla spiaggia da due settimane.
Vincent had been at the beach for two weeks.

Pioveva da tre giorni.
It had been raining for three days.

Lavoravo in quell'edificio da molti anni.
I had been working in that building for many years.

Non mangiavo da due giorni.
I hadn't eaten for two days.

Caterina era a Nuova York da quattro mesi.
Catherine had been in New York for four months.

75. Complete the following with the appropriate imperfect indicative forms of the indicated verbs:

1. Da quanto tempo (voi) _____ in Italia?	*essere*
2. Noi non _____ i nonni da sei mesi.	*visitare*
3. _____ da due giorni.	*nevicare*
4. Il giocatore _____ in quella squadra da sette anni.	*giocare*
5. Loro _____ da molto tempo.	*fumare* (to smoke)
6. Tu _____ lí da tre mesi.	*lavorare*
7. I turisti _____ a Roma da una settimana.	*essere*
8. Io lo _____ da molti anni.	*sapere*

76. Complete the following with the appropriate imperfect indicative forms of the indicated verbs:

1. Maria e Olga _____ sempre insieme.	*giocare*
2. Noi _____ a casa dei nonni ogni giorno.	*andare*
3. Pietro _____ sempre con attenzione.	*ascoltare*
4. Voi _____ per le strade senza sosta.	*correre*
5. Io _____ sempre con gli amici.	*essere*
6. Chi _____ quei signori?	*essere*
7. Quando Gino _____ piccolo, _____ molti giocattoli.	*essere, avere*
8. Quelle miniere _____ molto oro.	*produrre*

77. Answer the following questions in the affirmative, or using the cues, with complete sentences:

1. Dormivi sempre fino a tardi?
2. Andavate in chiesa la domenica?
3. Uscivi frequentemente?
4. Pioveva spesso?
5. Andavate alla spiaggia tutti i giorni?

6. Arrivava sempre tardi Luigi?
7. Piangevano spesso i bambini?
8. Viaggiava ogni estate Lei?
9. Signori, Loro preferivano il mare o la montagna?
10. Era verde la casa di Maria?

PRETERITE TENSE (PASSATO REMOTO)

The *preterite* (also called the *past definite* and the *past absolute*) expresses the completion of an action or a state of being in the past without relation to the present. For example

Federico II morí nel 1250.	*Frederick II died in 1250.*
Dante nacque nel 1265.	*Dante was born in 1265.*
Machiavelli scrisse *Il principe* nel 1513.	*Machiavelli wrote* The Prince *in 1513.*
Mio nonno arrivò in America nel 1898.	*My grandfather arrived in America in 1898.*

For details about its uses, see (pp. 127 to 129). The *preterite* can be understood better when contrasted with other tenses. On p. 128 can be observed the differences between the preterite and the *imperfect indicative* (*Imperfetto indicativo*). For the uses of the *preterite* and the *present perfect (Passato prossimo)* see p. 150. The *preterite* tense is very rich in both regular and irregular verbs. In addition to many verbs that belong to the regular three conjugations, **-are -ere**, and **-ire**, the Preterite has countless irregular verbs. Observe this tense in its many forms and details in the following pages.

Regular -are Verbs

The preterite of regular **-are** verbs is formed by dropping the infinitive ending **-are** and adding to the root the following personal endings: **-ai, -asti, -ò, -ammo, -aste, -arono**. Study the following:

Infinitive:	**parlare** *(to speak)*	**andare** *(to go)*	**camminare** *(to walk)*
Root:	**parl-**	**and-**	**cammin-**
io	parlai	andai	camminai
tu	parlasti	andasti	camminasti
lui, lei, Lei	parlò	andò	camminò
noi	parlammo	andammo	camminammo
voi	parlaste	andaste	camminaste
loro, Loro	parlarono	andarono	camminarono

78. Complete the following with the appropriate preterite endings:

1. I giovani arriv _____ tardi.
2. Io parl _____ troppo.
3. Il dottore cur _____ il malato.
4. Voi gioc _____ tutto il giorno.
5. Tu cammin _____ con gli amici.
6. Le ragazze and _____ a scuola.
7. Noi cant _____ molte canzoni.
8. Antonio studi _____ tutta la notte.
9. I cuochi prepar _____ un'ottima cena.
10. Io lavor _____ fino a tardi.

79. Complete the following with the appropriate preterite forms of the indicated verbs:

1. Gli studenti _____ il conferenziere.	*ascoltare*
2. Maria _____ le sue amiche.	*invitare*
3. Noi _____ lentamente.	*camminare*
4. Tu _____ una bella bicicletta.	*comprare*
5. Voi _____ in quel ristorante.	*pranzare*

80. Rewrite the following sentences in the preterite:

1. Noi visitiamo i nonni.
2. Aspetto mio cugino.
3. Loro comprano alcuni libri.
4. Angela lava l'automobile.
5. Tu porti i regali.
6. Voi mangiate da Carlo.
7. Gli studenti passano gli esami.
8. Tu viaggi solo.
9. Io pago il biglietto.
10. Andiamo a teatro a piedi.

Regular -ere Verbs

The preterite of regular **-ere** verbs is formed by dropping the infinitive ending **-ere** and adding to the root the follow-ing personal endings: **-ei, -esti, -é, -emmo, -este, -erono**. Note that the majority of regular **-ere** verbs have alternate endings in the **io, lui,** and **loro** forms (these alternate endings will appear in parentheses below). Study the following:

Infinitive:	**credere** *(to believe)*	**ricevere** *(to receive)*	**sedere** *(to sit)*
Root:	**cred-**	**ricev-**	**sed-**
io	credei (credetti)	ricevei (ricevetti)	sedei (sedetti)
tu	credesti	ricevesti	sedesti
lui, lei, Lei	credé (credette)	ricevé (ricevette)	sedé (sedette)
noi	credemmo	ricevemmo	sedemmo
voi	credeste	riceveste	sedeste
loro, Loro	crederono (credettero)	riceverono (ricevettero)	sederono (sedettero)

81. Complete the following with the appropriate preterite forms of the indicated verbs:

1. Il malato _____ per molte ore.   *gemere (to shiver, to tremble)*
2. Gli studenti _____ le frasi.   *ripetere*
3. Noi _____ ai nostri amici.   *credere*
4. Voi _____ vicino alla porta.   *sedere*
5. Tu _____ il pacco.   *ricevere*
6. Io _____ l'automobile.   *vendere*

82. Rewrite the following in the preterite tense:

1. Tu ricevi una bella notizia.
2. Mario ripete il corso di geografia.
3. Loro vendono molte cose.
4. Noi sediamo soli.
5. Io credo a tutto.
6. Voi potete venire presto.
7. Tu abbatti la parete.
8. Luisa batte sul banco.

Regular -ire Verbs

The preterite of regular **-ire** verbs is formed by dropping the infinitive ending **-ire** and adding to the root the following personal endings: **-ii, -isti, -í, -immo, -iste, -irono**. Study the following:

Infinitive:	**capire**	**finire**	**preferire**
Root:	**cap-**	**fin-**	**prefer-**

io	capii	finii	preferii
tu	capisti	finisti	preferisti
lui, lei, Lei	capí	finí	preferí
noi	capimmo	finimmo	preferimmo
voi	capiste	finiste	preferiste
loro, Loro	capirono	finirono	preferirono

83. Complete the following with the appropriate preterite endings:
1. Io fin _____ di studiare alle tre.
2. Voi costru _____ dei begli scaffali.
3. Tu rifer _____ il messaggio.
4. Giorgio cap _____ la domanda.
5. Maria e Teresa prefer _____ un tè freddo.
6. Noi reag _____ cautamente. (reagire, *to react*)
7. Antonio non proffer _____ una parola.
8. I ragazzi pul _____ la rimessa (*garage*). [Also: *garage, box per le macchine*]
9. Io part _____ alle sette e mezza.
10. Voi dorm _____ fino a tardi.

84. Complete the following with the appropriate preterite forms of the indicated verbs:
1. I bambini _____ ai genitori. *ubbidire*
2. Voi _____ il significato del libro. *capire*
3. Io _____ dormire fino a tardi. *preferire*
4. Il signor Martini _____ molto. *dimagrire*
5. Tu _____ alle cinque. *finire*
6. Noi _____ una bella casa. *costruire*
7. I lavoratori _____ il parco. *ingrandire*
8. Io _____ quelle poesie. *capire*

85. Rewrite the following in the preterite tense:
1. Gl'impiegati seguono le istruzioni.
2. Il cuoco bolle la carne.
3. Loro sentono il campanello.
4. Il cameriere serve le bevande.
5. Io apro tutte le finestre.
6. Voi offrite un caffè agli amici.
7. I malati soffrono molto.

Irregular Verbs in the Preterite

Many Italian verbs are irregular in the preterite. Most, but not all, of these irregular verbs have infinitives ending in **-ere**.

Many irregular verbs in the preterite can be grouped together since they share common irregularities.

You will note in your study of the irregular preterites that in three forms, namely **tu**, **noi**, and **voi**, these verbs are completely regular in that the infinitive ending is dropped to form the root and the appropriate personal endings are added to this root. In the **io**, **lui/lei/Lei**, and **loro/Loro** forms, however, the root is shortened as are the personal endings.

Let us take the verb **chiudere** (*to close*) as an example of an irregular verb in the preterite. The infinitive ending **-ere** is dropped to form the root **chiud-**. For **tu**, **noi**, and **voi**, we add the regular personal endings to this regular root:

Infinitive: **chiudere**
Root: **chiud-**
——   ——

tu	chiudesti
—	—
noi	chiudemmo
voi	chiudeste
—	—

For the other three forms **io**, **lui/lei/Lei**, and **loro/Loro**, the root is not formed from the infinitive but is changed to **chius-**. To this irregular root we add the personal endings **-i** for **io**, **-e** for **lui/lei/Lei** and **-ero** for **loro/Loro**.

Irregular Root:	**chius-**
io	chiusi
—	—
lui, lei, Lei	chiuse
—	—
—	—
loro, Loro	chiusero

Now let us look at the complete conjugation of this irregular verb:

Infinitive:	**chiudere**
Root:	**chiud-**
Irregular Root:	**chius-**
io	chiusi
tu	chiudesti
lui, lei, Lei	chiuse
noi	chiudemmo
voi	chiudeste
loro, Loro	chiusero

In the remainder of our study of irregular preterites, verbs will be grouped according to their common irregularities in the formation of the root for the **io**, **lui/lei/Lei** and **loro/Loro** forms in order to facilitate the learning of these verbs.

Verbs with a single -s-

Many verbs function the same as **chiudere** and have a second, irregular root with a single **-s-** in the **io**, **iui/lei/Lei**, and **loro/Loro** forms of the preterite. Study the following forms of **ridere** (*to laugh*) and **rimanere** (*to stay*) as models for verbs with a single **-s-**:

Infinitive:	**ridere**	**rimanere**
io	risi	rimasi
tu	ridesti	rimanesti
lui, lei, Lei	rise	rimase
noi	ridemmo	rimanemmo
voi	rideste	rimaneste
loro, Loro	risero	rimasero

Other verbs that function the same as **ridere**[7] and **rimanere** in the preterite are:

chiedere	*to ask*	chiesi, chiedesti, …
chiudere	*to close*	chiusi, chiudesti, …
concludere[8]	*to conclude*	conclusi, concludesti, …
decidere[9]	*to decide*	decisi, decidesti, …

---

[7] Another verb conjugated like **ridere** is **sorridere** (*to smile*).

[8] Other verbs conjugated like **concludere** are **accludere** (*to enclose, to inclose*), **escludere** (*to exclude*), **includere** (*to include*).

[9] Other verbs conjugated like **decidere** are: **coincidere** (*to coincide*), **uccidere** (*to kill*).

dividere	*to divide*	divisi, dividesti, …
prendere[10]	*to take*	presi, prendesti, …
rispondere	*to answer*	risposi, rispondesti, …
mettere[11]	*to put*	misi, mettesti, … (note also the vowel change)

The verb **porre**[12] functions the same as the above **-s-** verbs. The root, however, for the **tu**, **noi**, and **voi** forms is derived from the original Latin infinitive *ponĕre*. Study the following:

Infinitive:	**porre**
Root for **tu**, **noi**, *and* **voi**:	**pon-**
Root:	**pos-**
io	posi
tu	ponesti
lui, lei, Lei	pose
noi	ponemmo
voi	poneste
loro, Loro	posero

You will note that the single **-s-** in all of the above verbs when preceded and followed by a vowel is pronounced like a **z**. The verbs **correre**[13] (*to run*), **scegliere**[14] (*to choose*), and **volgere**[15] (*to turn*) also have a single **-s-** in the preterite. Since this single **-s-** is preceded by a consonant, it is pronounced like an **s**. Study the following:

Infinitive:	**correre**	**scegliere**	**volgere**
io	corsi	scelsi	volsi
tu	corresti	scegliesti	volgesti
lui, lei, Lei	corse	scelse	volse
noi	corremmo	scegliemmo	volgemmo
voi	correste	sceglieste	volgeste
loro, Loro	corsero	scelsero	volsero

86. Complete the following with the appropriate preterite forms of the indicated verbs:

1. Perché _____ (tu) tanti favori?   *chiedere*
2. Noi _____ la porta.   *chiudere*
3. Noi _____ con Angelo.   *rimanere*
4. Voi _____ molto.   *ridere*
5. Voi _____ bene.   *rispondere*
6. Dove _____ (tu) i libri?   *porre*
7. Noi _____ i passaporti sul tavolo.   *porre*
8. Voi non _____ niente.   *concludere*
9. Perché _____ tu?   *correre*
10. _____ (voi) il vostro regalo.   *scegliere*

87. Complete the following with the appropriate preterite forms of the indicated verbs:

1. Io _____ le finestre.   *chiudere*
2. Io _____ di studiare a Roma.   *decidere*

---

[10] Other verbs conjugated like **prendere** are: **accendere** (*to light, to turn on*), **apprendere** (*to learn*), **attendere** (*to wait*), **difendere** (*to defend*), **offendere** (*to offend*), **scendere** (*to descend*), **sorprendere** (*to surprise*), **spendere** (*to spend, to extinguish*), **stendere** (*to extend, to offer*).

[11] Other verbs conjugated like **mettere** are: **ammettere**, **commettere**, **permettere**, **promettere**, **rimettere**, **smettere**, **trasmettere**.

[12] Other verbs conjugated like **porre** are: **comporre**, **disporre**, **opporre**, **preporre**, **proporre**.

[13] Other verbs conjugated like **correre** are: **occorrere**, **incorrere**, **precorrere**, **rincorrere**, **scorrere**, **trascorrere**.

[14] Other verbs conjugated like **scegliere** are: **accogliere**, **cogliere**, **raccogliere**, **togliere**.

[15] Other verbs conjugated like **volgere** are: **dipingere**, **fingere**, **giungere**, **piangere**, **scorgere**, **sorgere**, **spingere**, **svolgere**.

   3. Io non _____ niente.   *prom̧ettere*
   4. Rosa _____ i passaporti coi biglietti.   *porre*
   5. Teresa _____ le valige in macchina.   *m̧ettere*
   6. Il mio amico _____ tutto il denaro.   *sp̧endere*
   7. Le mie amiche _____ poesie.   *comporre*
   8. Loro _____ dei bei regali.   *sçegliere*
   9. Loro _____ a tutte le domande.   *risp̧ondere*
  10. I bambini _____ molto.   *piangere*

88. Answer the following questions in the affirmative with complete sentences:
   1. Chiedesti molte informazioni?
   2. Chiudesti la porta?
   3. Decidesti di rimanere qui?
   4. Rispondesti alle sue domande?
   5. Prendesti il denaro?
   6. Mettesti il libro sul tavolo?
   7. Volgesti le spalle?
   8. Scegliesti un vestito?

89. Answer the following questions in the affirmative with complete sentences:
   1. Divisero (Loro) il premio in due?
   2. Risposero (Loro)?
   3. Decisero (Loro) immediatamente?
   4. Chiusero (Loro) le finestre?
   5. Presero (Loro) i passaporti?
   6. Misero (Loro) i fiori nel vaso?
   7. Scelsero (Loro) dei bei regali?
   8. Corsero (Loro)?

90. Complete the following with the correct preterite forms of the indicated verbs:
   1. Marco _____ molti favori.   *chiedere*
   2. Noi _____ un aumento (*increase*) di salario.   *chiedere*
   3. Finalmente i giocatori _____ la partita.   *concludere*
   4. L'oste _____ la porta della taverna.   *chiudere*
   5. Io _____ le finestre.   *richiudere*
   6. Voi _____ i nomi dei vicini.   *includere*
   7. I turisti _____ molte informazioni.   *chiedere*
   8. Tu _____ alcuni ragazzi dalla gita.   *escludere*
   9. Le date _____ molto bene.   *coincidere*
  10. Giovanni _____ a crepapelle (*ridere* ..., to roar with laughter).   *ridere*
  11. Voi _____ di tornare in Italia.   *decidere*
  12. Noi _____ agli amici.   *sorridere*
  13. La giuria _____ il primo premio in due.   *dividere*
  14. Noi _____ senza sosta.   *ridere*
  15. Luisa _____ di studiare a Londra.   *decidere*

91. Complete the following with the appropriate preterite forms of the indicated verbs:
   1. L'atleta _____ velocemente.   *correre*
   2. Noi _____ le vacanze in montagna.   *trascorrere*
   3. Noi _____ gli ospiti.   *accogliere*
   4. I giovani _____ dei vestiti blu.   *scegliere*
   5. Io _____ una cravatta rossa.   *scegliere*

6. Il bambino _____ i giocạttoli.   *raccọgliere*
7. Noi _____ un bel regalo.   *scẹgliere*
8. Mạrio _____ le spalle agli amici.   *vọlgere*

Verbs with a double s (-ss-)

The verbs **lẹggere**[16] (*to read*), **scrịvere**[17] (*to write*), and **vịvere** (*to live*) have a double s (-ss-) in the **io**, **lui/lei/Lei** and **loro/Loro** forms of the preterite. Since the **-s-** is preceded by a vowel, it must be doubled to maintain the s sound. Study the following forms:

Infinitive:	**lẹggere**	**scrịvere**	**vịvere**
io	lessi	scrissi	vissi
tu	leggesti	scrivesti	vivesti
lui, lei, Lei	lesse	scrisse	visse
noi	leggemmo	scrivemmo	vivemmo
voi	leggeste	scriveste	viveste
loro, Loro	lẹssero	scrịssero	vịssero

All verbs ending in **-durre**, such as **produrre**[18] (*to produce*), and the verb **dire**[19] (*to say*, *to tell*) also have a double **s** in the **io**, **lui/lei/Lei** and **loro/Loro** forms of the preterite. The root for the **tu**, **noi**, and **voi** forms comes from the original Latin infinitives *prodŭcĕre* and *dịcĕre*. Study the following forms:

	produrre	**dire**
	(*prodŭcĕre*)	(*dịcĕre*)
io	produssi	dissi
tu	producesti	dicesti
lui, lei, Lei	produsse	disse
noi	producemmo	dicemmo
voi	produceste	diceste
loro, Loro	produssero	dịssero

Note that the verb **trarre**[20] (*to pull*, *to extract*, *to draw*), which also has a double **s**, adds an **e** in the **tu**, **noi**, and **voi** forms since the root is derived from the original Latin infinitive *trahĕre*. **Sottrarre** (*to subtract*) is also conjugated below.

Infinitive:	**trarre**	**sottrarre**
io	trassi	sottrassi
tu	traẹsti	sottraẹsti
lui, lei, Lei	trasse	sottrasse
noi	traẹmmo	sottraẹmmo
voi	traẹste	sottraẹste
loro, Loro	trạssero	sottrạssero

92. Complete the following with the appropriate preterite forms of the indicated verbs:

1. Teresa _____ il giornale.   *lẹggere*
2. Noi _____ il presidente.   *elẹggere*
3. Io _____ la rivista.   *rilẹggere*
4. Tu _____ i cọmpiti.   *corrẹggere*
5. Le studentesse _____ il romanzo.   *lẹggere*

---

[16] Other verbs conjugated like **lẹggere** are: **corrẹggere, elẹgger, protẹggere, rẹggere**.
[17] Other verbs conjugated like **scrịvere** are: **descrịvere, iscrịvere, prescrịvere, trascrịvere**.
[18] Other verbs conjugated like **produrre** are: **addurre, condurre, indurre, introdurre, ridurre, tradurre**.
[19] Other verbs conjugated like **dire** are: **contraddire, disdire, indire, maledire, predire, ridịre**.
[20] Other verbs conjugated like **trarre** are: **attrarre, contrarre, detrarre, distrarre, ritrarre**.

6. Stefano _____ un bel riassunto.   *scrivere*

7. Tu _____ il tuo viaggio agli amici.   *descrivere*

8. Io _____ mio fratello all'università.   *iscrivere (to register)*

93. *Complete the following with the appropriate preterite forms of the indicated verbs:*

1. La casa editrice (publishing company) _____ un gran numero di libri.   *produrre*

2. Tu _____ l'ospite d'onore.   *introdurre*

3. Io _____ molte lettere in inglese.   *tradurre*

4. Noi _____ gli amici a cantare.   *indurre*

5. Gino _____ la verità.   *dire*

6. Noi _____ la sfortuna.   *maledire*

94. *Complete the following with the appropriate preterite forms of the indicated verbs:*

1. Loro _____ una certa soddisfazione.   *trarre*

2. Il circo _____ molti spettatori.   *attrarre*

3. Voi _____ molta gente.   *attrarre*

4. Noi _____ molte conclusioni.   *trarre*

5. Io _____ i numeri.   *sottrarre*

6. Tu _____ un raffreddore.   *contrarre*

Verbs with a double consonant other than s

The verbs **cadere**[21] (*to fall*), **tenere**[22] (*to have, to keep*), and **volere** (*to want*) double the consonant of the infinitive root in the **io**, **lui/lei/Lei** and **loro/Loro** forms of the preterite. Study the following:

Infinitive:	**cadere**	**tenere**	**volere**
io	caddi	tenni	volli
tu	cadesti	tenesti	volesti
lui, lei, Lei	cadde	tenne	volle
noi	cademmo	tenemmo	volemmo
voi	cadeste	teneste	voleste
loro, Loro	caddero	tennero	vollero

The preterite root for the verb **bere** comes from its original Italian infinitive *bevere*, and the **v** of the irregular root is doubled in the **io**, **lui/lei/Lei** and **loro/Loro** forms of the preterite:

Infinitive:	**bere**
io	bevvi
tu	bevesti
lui, lei, Lei	bevve
noi	bevemmo
voi	beveste
loro, Loro	bevvero

The verb **venire**[23] (*to come*) doubles the **n** of the infinitive in the **io**, **lui/lei/Lei**, and **loro/Loro** forms of the preterite. As with the other irregular verbs in the preterite, the personal endings are **-i** for **io**, **-e** for **lui/lei/Lei** and **-ero** for **loro/Loro**. Since **venire** is an **-ire** or third-conjugation verb, the endings for the regular **tu**, **noi**, and **voi** forms conform to those of an **-ire** verb: **isti**, **immo**, and **iste**, respectively. Observe the verb **venire** and **divenire** (*to become*):

Infinitive:	**venire**	**divenire**
io	venni	divenne
tu	venisti	divenisti

---

[21] Other verbs conjugated like **cadere** include **decadere** and **ricadere**.

[22] Other verbs conjugated like **tenere** are **appartenere, contenere, mantenere, sostenere**.

[23] Other verbs conjugated like **venire** are **avvenire, convenire, intervenire, pervenire, rivenire, sopravvenire, sovvenire, and svenire**.

lui, lei, Lei	venne	divenne
noi	venimmo	divenimmo
voi	veniste	diveniste
loro, Loro	vennero	divennero

Study the following forms of the verbs **conoscere**[24] (*to know*, *to be acquainted with*), **rompere** (*to break*), and **sapere** (*to know*, *to know about*), which also have a double consonant in the **io**, **lui/lei/Lei** and **loro/Loro** forms of the preterite. In the cases of **rompere** and **sapere**, note also the vowel change.

Infinitive:	**conoscere**	**rompere**	**sapere**
io	conobbi	ruppi	seppi
tu	conoscesti	rompesti	sapesti
lui, lei, Lei	conobbe	ruppe	seppe
noi	conoscemmo	rompemmo	sapemmo
voi	conosceste	rompeste	sapeste
loro. Loro	conobbero	ruppero	seppero

95. Complete the following with the appropriate preterite forms of the indicated verbs:

1. I bambini _____ a terra. *cadere*
2. L'impero romano _____ dopo molti secoli di gloria. *decadere*
3. Io _____ nella stessa situazione. *ricadere*
4. Noi _____ improvvisamente. *cadere*
5. Teresa _____ a memoria l'intera poesia. *tenere*
6. Quegli studenti _____ al circolo italiano. *appartenere*
7. Tu _____ l'amicizia con Antonio. *mantenere*
8. Voi _____ un'attitudine positiva. *sostenere*

96. Complete the following with the appropriate preterite forms of the verb bere:

1. Noi _____ troppo vino.
2. Mario _____ soltanto birra.
3. Loro _____ senza sosta.
4. Io _____ un po' di grappa (*brandy*).
5. Voi _____ tutto il latte.

97. Complete the following with the correct preterite forms of the indicated verbs:

1. Angela _____ con i suoi amici. *venire*
2. Noi _____ alla discussione. *intervenire*
3. La zia di Maria _____ dal calore. *svenire*
4. Tu _____ dopo poche ore. *rivenire*
5. Stefano e Luisa _____ che hai ragione. *convenire*
6. Noi _____ i loro cugini. *sovvenire*
7. Il fratello di Marco _____ campione olimpico. *divenire*

98. Complete the following with the appropriate preterite forms of the indicated verbs:

1. Io _____ Francesco a casa di Giuseppe. *conoscere*
2. Tu _____ la fotografia di Silvana. *riconoscere*
3. Noi _____ la materia dopo molto studio. *conoscere*
4. Loro _____ Maria dalla voce. *riconoscere*
5. Io _____ i bicchieri di cristallo. *rompere*
6. I bambini _____ i giocattoli. *rompere*
7. Voi _____ il nostro gioco. *interrompere*

---

[24] Another verb conjugated like **conoscere** is **riconoscere**.

Verbs with -qu-

The verbs **nạscere** (*to be born*) and **piacere**[25] (*to please, to like*) have a **-qu-** in the **io**, **lui/lei/Lei** and **loro/Loro** forms of the preterite. Note that **nạscere** drops the **-s-** in these forms. Study the following:

Infinitive:	**nạscere**	**piacere**
io	nacqui	piạcqui
tu	nascesti	piacesti
lui, lei, Lei	nạcque	piạcque
noi	nascemmo	piacemmo
voi	nasceste	piaceste
loro, Loro	nạcquero	piạcquero

99. Complete the following with the appropriate preterite forms of the indicated verbs:

1. Dante _____ nel 1265.   *nạscere*
2. Noi _____ ai tuọi genitori.   *piacere*
3. Io _____ in Itạlia.   *nạscere*
4. Anche voi _____ in Itạlia.   *nạscere*
5. La nostra attitụdine _____ a quẹi signori.   *dispiacere*
6. Tu non _____ a nessuno.   *piacere*
7. Quạndo _____ Stẹfano io avevo cinque anni.   *nạscere*
8. Le mịe fịglie _____ di notte.   *nạscere*

Vedere

Study the following irregular preterite forms of the verb **vedere**[26] (*to see*):

Infinitive:	**vedere**
io	vidi
tu	vedesti
lui, lei, Lei	vide
noi	vedemmo
voi	vedeste
loro, Loro	vịdero

100. Complete the following with the appropriate preterite forms of the indicated verbs:

1. I turisti _____ i monumenti antichi.   *vedere*
2. Voi _____ molti vecchi amici.   *rivedere*
3. Lui _____ il disastro.   *prevedere*
4. Marco e Anna _____ le bevande.   *provvedere*
5. Io _____ un inganno.   *intravedere*
6. Noi _____ un bel film.   *vedere*
7. Silvana _____ sua zịa.   *rivedere*
8. Giọrgio e Olga _____ il vostro successo. *prevedere*

Fare

Study the following irregular preterite forms of the verb **fare**[27] (*to do, to make*). You will note that the **tu**, **noi**, and **voi** forms are based on the original Latin infinitive *fạcĕre*. Observe also **Soddisfare** (*to satisfy*).

Infinitive:	**fare**	**soddisfare**
io	feci	soddisfeci
tu	facesti	soddisfacesti

---

[25] Other verbs conjugated like **piacẹre** are **compiacẹre**, **dispiacẹre**, and **giacẹre**.

[26] Other verbs conjugated like **vedere** are: **intravedere**, **prevedere**, **provvedere**, **rivedere**.

[27] Other verbs conjugated like **fare** are: **contraffare**, **disfare**, **rifare**, **sopraffare**.

lui, lei, Lei	fece	soddisfece
noi	facemmo	soddisfacemmo
voi	faceste	soddisfaceste
loro, Loro	fecero	soddisfecero

101. Complete the following with the appropriate preterite forms of the indicated verbs:

1. Giorgio _____ i compiti in poche ore.   *fare*
2. Noi _____ i bravi.   *fare*
3. Quelle letture _____ la nostra curiosità.   *soddisfare*
4. Voi _____ il letto.   *disfare*
5. Io _____ le nostre difficoltà.   *sopraffare*
6. Dopo tanti sbagli, loro _____ tutto.   *rifare*
7. Tu _____ tutti quei bei piani.   *disfare*
8. Vi preparaste ma non _____ niente.   *fare*

Avere

Study the following irregular forms of the verb **avere** (*to have*) in the preterite:

Infinitive:	**avere**
io	ebbi
tu	avesti
lui, lei, Lei	ebbe
noi	avemmo
voi	aveste
loro, Loro	ebbero

102. Complete the following with the appropriate preterite forms of the verb avere:

1. Finalmente tuo zio _____ ragione.
2. Al mercato io _____ una grande occasione.
3. Loro _____ molti problemi.
4. Noi _____ buoni amici.
5. Tu _____ molta fortuna.
6. Voi _____ una lunga vacanza.

Essere

Study the following preterite forms of the irregular verb **essere** (*to be*):

Infinitive:	**essere**
io	fui
tu	fosti
lui, lei, Lei	fu
noi	fummo
voi	foste
loro. Loro	furono

103. Complete the following with the appropriate preterite forms of essere:

1. Dante _____ un gran poeta.
2. I Romani _____ un popolo illustre.
3. Tu _____ in Italia molti anni fa.
4. Noi _____ felici.
5. Io _____ a casa di Carlo.
6. Voi _____ ottimi studenti.

7. Michelangelo e Da Vinci _____ dei geni (*genius*).

8. Pio II _____ un papa del Rinascimento.

Dare, stare

Study the following preterite forms of the irregular verbs **dare** (*to give*) and **stare** (*to stay, to be*). Note the alternate forms (in parentheses) given for the verb **dare**.

Infinitive:	**dare**	**stare**
io	diędi (detti)	stetti
tu	desti	stesti
lui, lei, Lei	dięde (dette)	stette
noi	demmo	stemmo
voi	deste	steste
loro, Loro	diędero (dęttero)	stęttero

104. Rewrite the following in the preterite:

1. Loro stanno al bar fino a tardi.
2. Io do un regalo a Luigi.
3. Voi state qui per poche ore.
4. Mario dà il biglietto a Luisa.
5. Noi stiamo a casa con i bambini.
6. Voi date i libri alle studentesse.
7. Io sto con mio zio.
8. Tu dai l'indirizzo al cliente.
9. Olga sta con sua cugina.
10. Tu stai in ufficio.
11. Gli studenti danno gli esami.

REVIEW

105. Complete the following with the appropriate preterite forms of the indicated verbs.

1. I ragazzi_____lungo la spiaggia.
2. La signora Martini_____una collana di perle.
3. Voi_____i panini.
4. Tu_____un regalo dall'Italia.
5. Stefano_____accanto alla finestra.
6. Noi_____giornali e riviste.
7. I turisti_____restare in albergo.
8. Tu non_____niente.
9. Mario_____di lavorare alle quattro.
10. Voi_____a casa tutto il giorno.
11. Io_____il mio biglietto a Carlo.
12. Noi_____dallo zio per poche ore.
13. I nostri amici_____ragione.
14. Tu_____troppa birra.
15. Loro_____un tè caldo.

camminare
comprare
portare
ricęvere
sedere
vęndere
preferire
capire
finire
stare
dare
ęssere
avere
bere
bere

106. Rewrite the following sentences in the preterite:

1. Tu rispondi alle domande di Mario.
2. Loro rispondono bene agli esami.
3. Noi rompiamo un piatto e due bicchieri.
4. Gli studenti sanno la lezione.
5. Io scelgo un paio di pantaloni marrone.
6. Voi accogliete gli ospiti stranieri (*foreign*).
7. Teresa scrive a tutti i parenti.
8. Loro sostengono un'opinione ottimista.
9. Il circo attrae una grande folla.
10. Io rivedo i miei vecchi amici.

Uses of the Preterite

Completed past action

The preterite expresses the completion of an action or a state of being in the past without any relation to the present. The following are some common expressions that usually complement the preterite:

iẹri	*yesterday*
iẹri pomeriggio	*yesterday afternoon*
iẹri sera	*last night*
l'altro iẹri	*two days ago, the day before yesterday*
l'altro giọrno	*the other day*
due giọrni fa	*two days ago*
la settimana scorsa	*last week*
il mese scorso	*last month*
l'anno scorso	*last year*
stamani	*this morning*
di colpo	*suddenly*
per molto tempo	*for a long time*
l'estate (inverno, etc.) scorsa	*last summer (winter, etc.)*
poco fa	*a little while ago*
per poco tempo	*for a little while*

107. Complete the following with the appropriate forms of the preterite of the indicated verbs:

1. Iẹri _____ i miẹi cugini dall'Italia.   *arrivare*
2. Dante _____ nel 1321.   *morire*
3. L'anno scorso i miẹi genitori _____ in Europa.   *andare*
4. L'altro giọrno io _____ un ọttimo libro.   *lẹggere*
5. Mio zịo _____ ammalato per molto tempo.   *ẹssere*
6. I miẹi amici _____ di partire.   *decịdere*
7. Carlo, dove _____ l'estate scorsa?   *passare*
8. Noi _____ i cọmpiti iẹri sera.   *finire*
9. Due anni fa io _____ una bella sorpresa.   *avere*
10. Il mese scorso voi non _____ alla riuniọne.   *venire*
11. La settimana scorsa Antọnio _____ il mịo invito.   *rifiutare*
12. L'altro iẹri voi _____ i libri.   *restituịre*

Verbs with special meaning in the preterite

Some verbs acquire special meaning when used in the preterite. To express actions or emotions in the past, verbs dealing with mental activity are usually conjugated in the imperfect indicative (see page 112); their meanings change considerably when they are conjugated in the preterite. Observe the following:

Gli studenti non vọllero studiare.	*The students* refused *to study.*
Luịgi poté arrivare in tempo.	*Louis* managed *to arrive on time.*
Voi non poteste finire.	*You* couldn't *finish* (but you tried).
Noi lo sapemmo stamani.	*We* found it out *this morning.*
Io conobbi il nuọvo mẹdico.	*I* met *the new doctor.*

108. Translate the following sentences:

1. They refused to participate.
2. We couldn't find the address (*indirizzo*).
3. I managed to leave early.
4. He met my brother last summer.
5. They found it out a little while ago.

Differences between Preterite and Imperfect Indicative

Completed versus continuing action

In general terms, the imperfect describes a continuing or recurring action in the past (review pages 111-112); the preterite is used to express an action begun and completed in the past regardless of its duration (review page 115). Observe the following:

> **Arrivai ięri sera alle nove.**
> *I arrived last night at nine.*

> **Sempre arrivavo alle nove**.
> *They always arrive at nine.*

> **Vedemmo i nonni dụe giọrni fa.**
> *We saw our grandparents two days ago.*

> **Vedevamo i nonni tutti i giọrni**.
> *We used to see our grandparents every day.*

> **Andại solamente una volta in montagna**.
> *I went to the mountains only once.*

> **Andavo spesso in montagna**.
> *I used to go to the mountains often.*

> **Antọnio fu in Itạlia**.
> *Anthony was in Italy.* (He is no longer there.)

> **Gli studenti ẹrano in Europa**.
> *The students were in Europe.* (It is not stated whether they are still there.)

109. *Rewrite the following, changing l'altro giọrno to spesso. Make all necessary changes.*
1. Lui venne qui l'altro giorno.
2. Io lo vidi l'altro giorno.
3. Carlo me lo ripeté l'altro giorno.
4. Ricevemmo una lęttera da lui l'altro giorno.
5. Lui mi chiamò l'altro giorno.

110. *Rewrite the following, changing ripetutamente to due giọrni fa. Make all necessary changes.*
1. Lui ci visitava ripetutamente.
2. Lei mi aiutava ripetutamente.
3. Io andavo lí ripetutamente.
4. Loro me lo dicẹvano ripetutamente.
5. Tu mangiạvi in quẹl ristorante ripetutamente.

111. *Rewrite each of the following in the appropriate tense (preterite or imperfect indicative) according to the given time expression:*
1. L'altro giọrno andại a Chicago.
   _____ ogni mese.
2. Marịa partí stamani per Brooklyn.
   Anche due mesi fa _____.
3. Mia zịa era sempre malata.
   _____ per dụe anni.
4. Visitavo i miẹi cugini di quạndo in quạndo.
   _____ frequentemente.
5. L'anno scorso incontrammo dei vecchi amici.
   Ogni tanto _____.

6. Viaggiaste in Francia il mese scorso.

_____ spesso spesso (very often).

112. Answer the following questions in the preterite or imperfect according to the model as indicated by the expressions:

Leggere la rivista? Sí, l'altro giorno.

Sí, lui lesse la rivista l'altro giorno.

Comprare il giornale? Sí, ogni giorno.

Sí, lui comprava il giornale ogni giorno.

1. Visitare l'Europa?   Sí, l'estate scorsa.
2. Andare al cinema?   Sí, ogni domenica.
3. Scalare un monte?   Sí, nel 1965.
4. Vedere i nonni?   Sí, tutti i giorni.
5. Fare i bagni?   Sí, sempre.
6. Ricevere la patente di guida?   Sí, ieri.
7. Viaggiare con gli amici?   Sí, frequentemente.
8. Essere malato?   Sí, per poco tempo.

Two actions in one sentence

When two or more *continuing* actions are expressed in the past, the imperfect indicative is used:

Mentre Luigi studiava, Antonio dormiva.
While Louis was studying, Anthony was sleeping.

Noi parlavamo, Luigi dormiva, e tu guardavi la televisione.
We were talking, Louis was sleeping, and you were watching television.

When two or more actions in the past are described as *completed*, the preterite is used:

Mario andò a teatro, e io rimasi a casa.
Mario went to the theater, and I stayed home.

Ieri sera io vidi i miei parenti, Antonio andò al cinema, e Luigi rimase a casa.
Last night I saw my relatives, Anthony went to the movies, and Louis stayed home.

When a continuing action in the past is interrupted by another, the former is conjugated in the imperfect indicative, and the latter in the preterite:

Mentre Luigi Studiava, arrivò Antonio. *While Louis was studying, Anthony arrived.*
Io dormivo, quando squillò il telefono. *I was sleeping, when the telephone rang.*

113. Complete the following with the appropriate forms of the preterite or imperfect indicative (as needed) of the indicated verbs:

1. I ragazzi _____ mentre noi _____.   *giocare, studiare*
2. Pietro _____ il violino, quando _____ i suoi amici.   *suonare, entrare*
3. Noi _____ i compiti, quando qualcuno _____ alla porta.   *discutere, bussare*
                                                                                       (to knock)
4. Mia zia _____ la cena, quando _____ gl'invitati.   *preparare, arrivare*
5. Stamani io _____ alle sette, e Pietro _____ alle nove.   *cominciare, comindare*
6. Mentre _____ in Italia, di colpo mio fratello _____ ammalato.   *essere, ammalarsi*
7. Le mie sorelle _____ la radio mentre io _____.   *ascoltare, studiare*
8. Quando noi _____ alla stazione, _____ cattivo tempo.   *arrivare, fare*
9. Alcuni giovani _____ mentre gli altri _____.   *ballare, cantare*

10. Mentre voi _____ la televisione, una notizia
speciale _____ il programma.   *guardare, interrompere*

114. Complete the following as if you were telling someone what happened:
1. I giocatori _____, e gli spettatori _____.   *giocare, applaudire*
2. Mio padre _____, e io _____ la mappa.   *guidare, guardare*
3. Luigi _____ i panini, e noi _____ fuori.   *comprare, aspettare* (to wait)
4. Maria _____ la lezione, e Carlo _____ la rivista.   *studiare, leggere*
5. Io _____ le finestre, e mia madre _____ la mobilia. *chiudere, spolverare*

115. Rewrite the sentences of the previous exercise as if you were describing what was happening:
1. _____
2. _____
3. _____
4. _____
5. _____

THE FUTURE TENSE (IL FUTURO SEMPLICE)

As in English, in Italian the *future* tense expresses an action that will definitely happen in the future. Whereas in English the future is formed by using the auxiliaries *shall* or *will* before the infinitive form of the verb (leaving out, of course, the word *to* as in *to meet*), in Italian the future consists of a single word formed by adding an appropriate future ending to the root of an infinitive after dropping the infinitive ending. Observe the following examples from each of the three regular conjugations ending in **-are**, **-ere**, and **-ire**.

A) First conjugation: **-are**.

Infinitive: **incontrare**, *Root:* **incontr-**,   *Future endings:* -erò, -erai, -erà, -eremo, -erete, -eranno.
Domani (io) incontrerò i miei amici   *Tomorrow I will (shall) meet my friends.*
Domani (tu) incontrerai tuo zio.   *Tomorrow you will (shall) meet your uncle.*
Domani (lui, lei) incontrerà me.   *Tomorrow he/she will (shall) meet me.*
Domani Lei incontrerà la maestra.   *Tomorrow you (formal s.) will (shall) meet the teacher (f.).*

Domani (noi) incontreremo i vicini.   *Tomorrow we will (shall) meet our neighbors.*
Domani (voi) incontrerete Paolo e Isa.   *Tomorrow you will (shall) meet Paul and Isa.*
Domani (loro) incontreranno voi e noi.   *Tomorrow they will (shall) meet you and us.*
Domani (Loro) incontreranno un attore.   *Tomorrow you (formal pl.) will (shall) meet an actor.*

B) Second conjugation: **-ere**.

Infinitive: **leggere**, *Root:* **legg-**, *Future endings:* same as 1st conjugation above.

(io) leggerò, (tu) leggerai, (lui, lei, Lei) leggerà, (noi) leggeremo, (voi) leggerete, (loro, Loro) leggeranno
I will (shall) read, etc.

C) Third conjugation: **-ire**.

Infinitive: **partire**, *Root:* **part-**, *Future endings:* -irò, -irai, -irà, -iremo, -irete, -iranno
(io) partirò, (tu) partirai, (lui, lei. Lei) partirà, (noi) partiremo, (voi) partirete, (loro, Loro) partiranno
I will (shall) leave, etc.

Regular Verbs Ending in -are

The future tense of first-conjugation regular verbs (**-are**) is formed by changing the infinitive ending **-are** into **-er** to obtain the root for the future tense (this is done by changing the initial **-a-** to **-e-** and by dropping the final **-e**).

The following future endings are then added to the root: **-ò**, **-ai**, **-à**, **-emo**, **-ete**, **-anno**. Observe the following:

Infinitive:	**cantare**	**portare**	**tirare**
Root for Future:	**canter-**	**porter-**	**tirer-**
io	canterò	porterò	tirerò
tu	canterai	porterai	tirerai
lui, lei, Lei	canterà	porterà	tirerà
noi	canteremo	porteremo	tireremo
voi	canterete	porterete	tirerete
loro, Loro	canteranno	porteranno	tireranno

116. ***Complete the following with the appropriate forms of the future of the indicated regular -are verbs:***

1. Domani Luigi e Antonio _____ il giradischi.   *portare*
2. L'anno prossimo noi _____ l'università.   *frequentare*
3. I nonni _____ la settimana prossima.   *arrivare*
4. Il coro degli Alpini _____ al teatro Verdi.   *cantare*
5. Io _____ al nuovo concorso.   *partecipare*
6. Tu e Mario _____ di politica.   *parlare*
7. Gli studenti _____ una seconda lingua.   *imparare*

Regular Verbs Ending in *-ere* and *-ire*

The future tense of most (regular) second- and third-conjugation verbs (**-ere** and **-ire**) is formed by simply dropping the final **-e** of the infinitive ending to obtain the root and adding to the root the following future end ings: **-ò**, **-ai**, **-à**, **-emo**, **-ete**, **-anno**. Observe the following:

Infinitive:	**credere**	**partire**
Root for Future:	**creder-**	**partir-**
io	crederò	partirò
tu	crederai	partirai
lui, lei, Lei	crederà	partirà
noi	crederemo	partiremo
voi	crederete	partirete
loro, Loro	crederanno	partiranno

117. ***Complete the following with the appropriate forms of the future of the indicated regular -ere and -ire verbs.***

1. Noi _____ per l'Italia il mese prossimo.   *partire*
2. Gli studenti _____ molti libri.   *leggere*
3. Tu e Carlo _____ la lezione.   *ripetere*
4. Il negoziante _____ tutta la merce.   *vendere*
5. Noi _____ le nuove regole.   *capire*
6. Gli atleti _____ per un'ora.   *correre*
7. Il bambino _____ la mancanza dei genitori.   *sentire*

Note the spelling of verbs with infinitives ending in **-ciare** and **-giare**. These verbs drop the **i** before adding the future endings to the root:

Infinitive:	**cominciare**	**viaggiare**
Root for Future:	**comincer-**	**viagger-**
io	comincerò	viaggerò
tu	comincerai	viaggerai

lui, lei, Lei	comincerà	viaggerà
noi	cominceremo	viaggeremo
voi	comincerete	viaggerete
loro, Loro	cominceranno	viaggeranno

Note that verbs with infinitives ending in **-care** and **-gare** add an **h** to the root for the future to preserve the hard sound of the **c** or **g** of the infinitive.

Infinitive:	**cercare**	**pagare**
Root for Future:	**cercher-**	**pagher-**
io	cercherò	pagherò
tu	cercherai	pagherai
lui, lei, Lei	cercherà	pagherà
noi	cercheremo	pagheremo
voi	cercherete	pagherete
loro, Loro	cercheranno	pagheranno

118. Complete the following with the appropriate future forms of the indicated verbs:

1. Noi _____ a casa dei nonni.   *mangiare*
2. Le studentesse _____ la lezione alle nove.   *cominciare*
3. Io _____ la macchina qui vicino.   *parcheggiare* (to park)
4. I soldati _____ tutto il pomeriggio.   *marciare*
5. Tu _____ una macchina nuova.   *noleggiare*
6. Voi _____ in autobus.   *viaggiare*

119. Complete the following with the appropriate future forms of the indicated verbs:

1. Noi _____ un altro albergo.   *cercare*
2. Loro _____ il conto con un assegno.   *pagare*
3. Il turista _____ a Genova.   *sbarcare*
4. Gli scienziati _____ questa teoria.   *attaccare*
5. Io _____ all'appello.   *mancare*
6. Voi _____ il salotto.   *allargare*
7. L'impiegato _____ i regali.   *impaccare*
8. Noi _____ i bambini.   *divagare*

Irregular Verbs

Dare, stare, fare

In the future, **dare**, **stare**, and **fare** simply drop the final **-e** of their infinitives and form the roots **dar-**, **star-**, and **far-**, respectively; to these roots are added the future endings. Observe the following:

Infinitive:	**dare**	**stare**	**fare**
Root for Future:	**dar-**	**star-**	**far-**
io	darò	starò	farò
tu	darai	starai	farai
lui, lei, Lei	darà	starà	farà
noi	daremo	staremo	faremo
voi	darete	starete	farete
loro, Loro	daranno	staranno	faranno

120. Complete the following with the appropriate forms of the future of the indicated verbs:

1. Io _____ gli esami finali lunedí prossimo.   *dare*
2. Noi _____ il viaggio insieme.   *fare*

3. Mio fratello _____ a casa mia per due mesi.　　　*stare*
4. Il maestro ci _____ i voti alla fine del corso.　　　*dare*
5. Domani tu mi _____ l'indirizzo di Carlo.　　　*dare*
6. Lui non _____ quel lavoro.　　　*fare*
7. I bambini _____ a casa tutto il giorno.　　　*stare*
8. Voi _____ i regali alle bambine.　　　*dare*
9. Cosa _____ loro?　　　*fare*
10. Noi _____ in albergo per poco tempo.　　　*stare*

Essere

All forms of **essere** are irregular in the future. The root is **sar-** and to this root are added the future endings. Observe the following:

Infinitive:	**essere**
Root for Future:	**sar-**
io	sarò
tu	sarai
lui, lei, Lei	sarà
noi	saremo
voi	sarete
loro, Loro	saranno

121. *Complete the following with the appropriate future forms of essere:*
1. Carlo, _____ a casa domani?
2. Stasera noi _____ in ritardo.
3. Domani _____ la seconda volta che andiamo al cinema insieme.
4. Voi _____ in Italia per due anni.
5. Io _____ in compagnia di alcuni amici.
6. Tu _____ la nostra salvezza.
7. Noi _____ lieti di conoscere le tue cugine.
8. Gl'invitati _____ qui alle cinque e mezza.

Andare, avere, cadere, dovere, potere, sapere, vedere, vivere

The verbs **andare** (*to go*), **avere** (*to have*), **cadere** (*to fall*), **dovere** (*to have to*), **potere** (*to be able to*), **sapere** (*to know*), **vedere** (*to see*), and **vivere** (*to live*) have a shortened root for the formation of the future in that the vowel **a** or **e** is dropped from the infinitive. Study the following:

Infinitive:	**andare**	**avere**	**cadere**	**dovere**
Root for Future:	**andr-**	**avr-**	**cadr-**	**dovr-**
io	andrò	avrò	cadrò	dovrò
tu	andrai	avrai	cadrai	dovrai
lui, lei, Lei	andrà	avrà	cadrà	dovrà
noi	andremo	avremo	cadremo	dovremo
voi	andrete	avrete	cadrete	dovrete
loro, Loro	andranno	avranno	cadranno	dovranno

Infinitive:	**potere**	**sapere**	**vedere**	**vivere**
Root for Future:	**potr-**	**sapr-**	**vedr-**	**vivr-**
io	potrò	saprò	vedrò	vivrò
tu	potrai	saprai	vedrai	vivrai
lui, lei, Lei	potrà	saprà	vedrà	vivrà
noi	potremo	sapremo	vedremo	vivremo
voi	potrete	saprete	vedrete	vivrete
loro. Loro	potranno	sapranno	vedranno	vivranno

The verb **udire** (*to hear*) can be conjugated two ways in the future: as a regular verb or in a shortened form. These forms are used interchangeably. Observe the following:

Infinitive:	**udire**	
io	udirò	udrò
tu	udirai	udrai
lui, lei, Lei	udirà	udrà
noi	udiremo	udremo
voi	udirete	udrete
loro, Loro	udiranno	udranno

122. Complete the following with the appropriate forms of the future of the indicated verbs:

1. Domani noi _____ a visitare gli zii.   *andare*
2. Domani voi _____ una risposta.   *avere*
3. Io _____ aspettare fino a tardi.   *potere*
4. Luisa _____ parlare inglese.   *sapere*
5. L'anno prossimo i miei genitori _____ in Italia.   *andare*
6. Tu _____ un posto importante.   *avere*
7. Carlo e io _____ telefonare agli amici.   *dovere*
8. Il bambino _____.   *cadere*

Bere, volere, valere, tenere, rimanere, parere, morire, venire

The verbs **bere** (*to drink*), **volere** (*to want*), **valere** (*to be worth*), **tenere** (*to have*), **rimanere** (*to stay*), **parere** (*to seem*), **morire** (*to die*), and **venire** (*to come*) have a double **r** (**-rr-**) in the future. Study the following:

Infinitive:	**bere**	**volere**	**tenere**	**rimanere**	**parere**	**morire**	**venire**
Root for Future:	**berr-**	**vorr-**	**terr-**	**rimarr-**	**parr-**	**morr-**	**verr-**
io	berrò	vorrò	terrò	rimarrò	parrò	morrò	verrò
tu	berrai	vorrai	terrai	rimarrai	parrai	morrai	verrai
lui, lei, Lei	berrà	vorrà	terrà	rimarrà	parrà	morrà	verrà
noi	berremo	vorremo	terremo	rimarremo	parremo	morremo	verremo
voi	berrete	vorrete	terrete	rimarrete	parrete	morrete	verrete
loro, Loro	berranno	vorranno	terranno	rimarranno	parranno	morranno	verranno

123. Complete the following with the appropriate future forms of the indicated verbs:

1. I ragazzi _____ molte aranciate.   *bere*
2. La tua opinione _____ molto.   *valere*
3. I miei amici _____ ballare.   *volere*
4. Francesco _____ i suoi libri a nostra disposizione.   *tenere*
5. Io _____ partecipare alla discussione.   *volere*
6. Noi _____ un po' di vino.   *bere*
7. Gli studenti _____ preparati.   *parere*
8. L'amore non _____ mai.   *morire*

Special Uses of the Future

The future to express probability

The future tense in Italian may be used to express probability or possibility in the present. Observe the following:

Dove sarà Pietro?
Where can Peter be?

Sarà a casa.
He is probably at home.

Che ora sarà?
What time can it be?

Saranno le quattro.
It is probably four o'clock.

Quanti anni avrà Luigi?
How old can Louis be?

Avrà ventitré anni.
He is probably twenty-three.

124. Answer the following questions, according to the cues, using the future to express probability:

1. Dove sono i ragazzi?	*a casa*	
2. Quanti anni ha Maria?	*sedici*	
3. Che ore sono?	*10:30* A.M.	
4. Costa molto quest'orologio?	*no*	
5. Quando arrivano gli ospiti?	*alle 7:00* A.M.	
6. È a casa o a scuola Antonio?	*scuola*	
7. Quanti libri hai?	*un centinaio*	
8. A che ora parte il treno?	*alle due*	
9. Chi è, Pietro o Antonio?	*Pietro*	
10. È americano o italiano?	*italiano*	

The future after **quando** *and* **se**
If **quando** (*when*) and **se** (*if*) imply a future action, the verb that follows is in the future. Observe the following:

Quando arriveranno, discuteremo il problema.
When they arrive, we'll discuss the problem.

Quando verrà Pietro, andremo a teatro.
When Peter comes, we'll go to the theater.

Se faranno domande, risponderemo.
If they ask questions, we'll answer.

Se farà cattivo tempo, resteremo a casa.
If the weather is bad, we'll stay home.

125. Complete each sentence with the appropriate form of the indicated verb:

1. Se io _____ in Italia, vedrò molti musei.   *andare*
2. Quando i turisti _____, andranno in albergo.   *arrivare*
3. Se (tu) _____ tua zia, lei sarà molto contenta.   *vedere*
4. Se _____, non potremo uscire.   *nevicare*
5. Se _____ bel tempo, giocheremo a tennis.   *fare*
6. Quando (io) _____ a casa, guarderò la televisione.   *arrivare*
7. Quando _____ i nostri amici, parleremo del problema.   *vedere*
8. Se _____ abbastanza denaro, faremo il viaggio.   *avere*

126. Review all the examples of the special uses of the future, then translate the following:

1. The boys are probably at the movies.
2. What time can it be?
3. When are you (*tu*) going to study?
4. If I go to Italy, I'll see many museums.
5. When the tourists arrive, they'll go to the hotel.
6. If you (*voi*) visit your aunt, she'll be very happy.

CONDITIONAL TENSE (CONDIZIONALE)

First-Conjugation (-are) Verbs

In Italian, the conditional tense is used in much the same way that it is used in English. The root for the conditional is the same as the future root. The infinitive ending **-are** changes to **-er**, and to this root the following conditional endings are added: **-ęi, -esti, -ebbe, -emmo, -este, -ębbero**. Observe the following:

Infinitive:	**parlare**	**cantare**	**ballare**
Root for Conditional:	**parler-**	**canter-**	**baller-**
io	parlerei	canterei	ballerei
tu	parleresti	canteresti	balleresti
lui, lei, Lei	parlerebbe	canterebbe	ballerebbe
noi	parleremmo	canteremmo	balleremmo
voi	parlereste	cantereste	ballereste
loro, Loro	parlerębbero	canterębbero	ballerębbero

Remember that verbs ending in **-ciare** and **-giare** drop the i and have **-ce** and **-ge** in the conditional root, and verbs ending in **-care** and **-gare** add an **h** to keep the hard sound of the **c** and **g**, and thus have **-che** and **-ghe**.

127. Complete the following with the appropriate conditional forms of the indicated verbs.

1. I ragazzi _____, ma non ricordano le parole.	*cantare*
2. Luigi _____, ma è troppo stanco.	*camminare*
3. Loro _____ i nonni, ma non ci sono.	*vedere*
4. Tu _____ una macchina, ma non hai soldi.	*comprare*
5. Io _____ in tempo, ma non posso.	*arrivare*
6. Voi _____ volentieri, ma non sapete ballare.	*ballare*
7. Teresa _____ i compiti, ma non ha voglia.	*completare*
8. Noi _____ la cena, ma non sappiamo cucinare.	*preparare*

Second- and Third-Conjugation (-ere and -ire) Verbs

In the conditional, **-ere** and **-ire** verbs have the same root as their future counterparts (for full details, see page 131). The root is obtained by simply dropping the final **-e** of the infinitive ending and adding the conditional endings: **-ęi, -esti, -ebbe, -emmo, -este, -ębbero**. Observe the following:

Infinitive:	**leggere**	**aprire**
Root for Conditional:	**lęgger-**	**aprir-**
io	leggerei	aprirei
tu	leggeresti	apriresti
lui, lei, Lei	leggerebbe	aprirebbe
noi	leggeremmo	apriremmo
voi	leggereste	aprireste
loro, Loro	leggerębbero	aprirębbero

128. Complete the following with the appropriate conditional forms of the indicated verbs:

1. Noi _____, ma siamo stanchi.	*correre*
2. Tu _____, ma sei rauco.	*leggere*
3. Io _____ la porta, ma fa freddo.	*aprire*
4. Luisa _____ il corso, ma non può.	*seguire*
5. Loro _____ il pesce, ma non c'è olio.	*friggere*
6. Voi _____ il segreto, ma non sapete come.	*scoprire*
7. Noi _____ la casa, ma nessuno vuole comprarla.	*vendere*
8. Tu _____ il tè, ma non è pronto.	*servire*

Irregular Verbs

The same verbs that are irregular in the future are irregular in the conditional, and the same root is used for the formation of both the future and conditional. Study the following conditional forms of some irregular verbs:

Infinitive:	**dare**	**stare**	**fare**	
Root:	**dar-**	**star-**	**far-**	
io	darei	starei	farei	
tu	daresti	staresti	faresti	
lui, lei, Lei	darebbe	starebbe	farebbe	
noi	daremmo	staremmo	faremmo	
voi	dareste	stareste	fareste	
loro, Loro	darebbero	starebbero	farebbero	

Infinitive:	**essere**
Root:	**sar-**
io	sarei
tu	saresti
lui, lei, Lei	sarebbe
noi	saremmo
voi	sareste
loro, Loro	sarebbero

Infinitive:	**andare**	**avere**	**cadere**	**dovere**
Root:	**andr-**	**avr-**	**cadr-**	**dovr-**
io	andrei	avrei	cadrei	dovrei
tu	andresti	avresti	cadresti	dovresti
lui, lei, Lei	andrebbe	avrebbe	cadrebbe	dovrebbe
noi	andremmo	avremmo	cadremmo	dovremmo
voi	andreste	avreste	cadreste	dovreste
loro, Loro	andrebbero	avrebbero	cadrebbero	dovrebbero

Infinitive:	**potere**	**sapere**	**vedere**	**vivere**
Root:	**potr-**	**sapr-**	**vedr-**	**vivr-**
io	potrei	saprei	vedrei	vivrei
tu	potresti	sapresti	vedresti	vivresti
lui, lei, Lei	potrebbe	saprebbe	vedrebbe	vivrebbe
noi	potremmo	sapremmo	vedremmo	vivremmo
voi	potreste	sapreste	vedreste	vivreste
loro, Loro	potrebbero	saprebbero	vedrebbero	vivrebbero

Infinitive:	**bere**	**morire**	**parere**	**rimanere**
Root:	**berr-**	**morr-**	**parr-**	**rimarr-**
io	berrei	morrei	parrei	rimarrei
tu	berresti	morresti	parresti	rimarresti
lui, lei, Lei	berrebbe	morrebbe	parrebbe	rimarrebbe
noi	berremmo	morremmo	parremmo	rimarremmo
voi	berreste	morreste	parreste	rimarreste
loro, Loro	berrebbero	morrebbero	parrebbero	rimarrebbero

Infinitive:	**tenere**	**valere**	**venire**	**volere**
Root:	**terr-**	**varr-**	**verr-**	**vorr-**
io	terrei	varrei	verrei	vorrei
tu	terresti	varresti	verresti	vorresti
lui, lei, Lei	terrebbe	varrebbe	verrebbe	vorrebbe
noi	terremmo	varremmo	verremmo	vorremmo
voi	terreste	varreste	verreste	vorreste
loro, Loro	terrebbero	varrebbero	verrebbero	vorrebbero

129. *Complete the following with the appropriate conditional forms of the indicated verbs:*

1. Noi _____ adesso, ma è troppo presto.   *cominciare*
2. Io _____ molta paura, ma ci sei tu.   *avere*
3. Mario _____ un po' di vino, ma non gli piace.   *bere*
4. Voi _____ partire, ma l'autobus è in ritardo.   *dovere*
5. Da vicino tu _____ molto meglio.   *udire*
6. Questo vaso _____ di piú altrove.   *valere*
7. Antonio e Teresa _____ subito, ma non sanno l'indirizzo.   *venire*
8. Io _____ il conto, ma non ho denaro.   *pagare*
9. Noi _____ volentieri in quel ristorante.   *mangiare*
10. Forse Pietro _____ disposto a viaggiare con noi.   *essere*

THE PRESENT PERFECT OR CONVERSATIONAL PAST (IL PASSATO PROSSIMO)

The **passato prossimo** (*present perfect, conversational past*) is a compound indicative tense that expresses an action or a fact completed in the past. It is formed by using the conjugated present indicative forms of the *auxiliary verbs* (*helping verbs*) **avere** and **essere** and the past participle of the acting verb. **Avere** helps transitive verbs, and essere helps intransitive verbs. (See the first page of Chapter 6 for details on transitive and intransitive verbs.)

The regular past participle is formed by dropping the infinitive ending of the verb and by adding the endings **-ato**, for -are verbs, **-uto** for -ere verbs, and **-ito** for -ire verbs. (Note that **venire** (*to come*), though an **-ire** verb, takes **-uto** in the past participle: **venuto**.)

Past Participles Conjugated with *Avere*

Infinitive:	**cantare**	>	Root: **cant-**	+	Ending:	**-ato**	=	**cantato**
Infinitive:	**vendere**	>	Root: **vend-**	+	Ending:	**-uto**	=	**venduto**
Infinitive:	**sentire**	>	Root: **sent-**	+	Ending:	**-ito**	=	**sentito**

The following is a partial list of regular past partciples:

ballare	→	**ballato**	**avere**	→	**avuto**	**capire**	→	**capito**
cantare	→	**cantato**	**cadere**	→	**caduto**	**finire**	→	**finito**
giocare	→	**giocato**	**sapete**	→	**saputo**	**servire**	→	**servito**
parlare	→	**parlato**	**vendere**	→	**venduto**	**vestire**	→	**vestito**

Irregular Past Participles

Many verbs in Italian have irregular past participles. Below is a list of some of the most common infinitives, along with an example compound infinitive.

Infinitive		Past Participle	Compound Infinitive		Compound Past Participle
reggere	→	**retto**	**correggere**	→	**corretto**
cuocere	→	**cotto**	**stracuocere**	→	**stracotto**

dire	→	detto	predire	→	predetto
fare	→	fatto	strafare	→	strafatto
lęggere	→	letto	rilęggere	→	riletto
rǫmpere	→	rotto	corrǫmpere	→	corrotto
scrivere	→	scritto	riscrivere	→	riscritto
trarre	→	tratto	ritrarre	→	ritratto
			attrarre	→	attratto
			contrarre	→	contratto
chiędere	→	chiesto	richiędere	→	richiesto
rispǫndere	→	risposto	corrispǫndere	→	corrisposto
porre	→	posto	suppǫrre	→	supposto
			compǫrre	→	composto
			frappǫrre	→	frapposto
mettere	→	messo	commęttere	→	commesso
			rimęttere	→	rimesso
			ammęttere	→	ammesso
cǫgliere	→	colto	raccǫgliere	→	raccolto
scęgliere	→	scelto	prescęgliere	→	prescelto
vǫlgere	→	volto	rivǫlgere	→	rivolto
rimanere	→	rimasto			
piạngere	→	piạnto			
vincere	→	vinto	convincere	→	convinto
accęndere	→	acceso	riaccęndere	→	riacceso
chiụdere	→	chiụso	racchiụdere	→	racchiụso
difęndere	→	difeso			
dividere	→	diviso	condividere	→	condiviso
inclụdere	→	incluso			
pręndere	→	preso	compręndere	→	compreso
ridere	→	riso	irridere	→	irriso
uccidere	→	ucciso			
assistere	→	assistito			
bere	→	bevuto			
venire	→	venuto	convenire	→	convenuto
vivere	→	vissuto	rivivere	→	rivissuto
aprire	→	aperto	riaprire	→	riaperto
coprire	→	coperto	scoprire	→	scoperto
morire	→	morto			
offrire	→	offerto			
soffrire	→	sofferto			
apparire	→	apparso	riapparire	→	riapparso
cǫrrere	→	corso	rincǫrrere	→	rincorso
			precǫrrere	→	precorso
pęrdere	→	perso (perduto)			

Study the following forms of regular verbs in the **passato prǫssimo**, or conversational past.

Infinitive:	**parlare**	**vęndere**	**finire**
io	ho parl<u>ato</u>	ho vend<u>uto</u>	ho fin<u>ito</u>
tu	hai parl<u>ato</u>	hai vend<u>uto</u>	hai fin<u>ito</u>
lui, lei, Lei	ha parl<u>ato</u>	ha vend<u>uto</u>	ha fin<u>ito</u>
noi	abbiamo parl<u>ato</u>	abbiamo vend<u>uto</u>	abbiamo fin<u>ito</u>
voi	avete parl<u>ato</u>	avete vend<u>uto</u>	avete fin<u>ito</u>
loro, Loro	hanno parl<u>ato</u>	hanno vend<u>uto</u>	hanno fin<u>ito</u>

Observe the following full sentences as examples:

Ięri sera a teạtro, Pavarotti ha cantato come un gran tenore.
Last night at the theater, Pavarotti sang (has sung) like a great tenor.

Domęnica scorsa i calciatori hanno giocato per vịncere.
Last Sunday the soccer players played (have played) to win.

Finalmente gli studenti hanno finito gli esami.
Finally the students finished (have finished) the exams.

Come sempre, la nonna ha preparato un pranzo fantạstico.
As always, our grandmother prepared (has prepared) a fantastic dinner.

130. Complete the following with the appropriate forms of the passato prọssimo of the indicated verbs:

1. Noi _____ con lui ięri sera.   *parlare*
2. Antọnio _____ un buọn pranzo.   *preparare*
3. Lei _____ molto bene.   *cantare*
4. Noi _____ i suọi regali.   *accettare*
5. Tu _____ a casa dei nonni.   *pranzare*
6. Voi _____ molte cose.   *comprare*
7. Io _____ la televisiọne.   *guardare*
8. Il fattorino _____ i bigliẹtti.   *controllare* (to check)
9. I mięi cugini _____ molto.   *viaggiạre*
10. Chi mi _____ ?   *chiamare*

131 Complete the following with the appropriate form of the passato prọssimo of the indicated verbs:

1. Io _____ le chiạvi.   *pẹrdere*
2. Perché non _____ (tu) la domanda?   *ripẹtere*
3. Loro _____ la casa.   *vẹndere*
4. Noi _____ molte lẹttere.   *ricẹvere*
5. Lui _____ molta gente.   *conọscere*

132. Rewrite the following in the passato prọssimo:

1. Loro capịscono tutto.   4. Noi serviạmo il pranzo.
2. Noi finiạmo il lavoro.   5. Marịa finisce il lavoro.
3. Io vesto il bambino.

133. Complete each sentence with the appropriate form of the passato prọssimo of the indicated verb:

1. Noi _____ il giornale.   *lẹggere*
2. Chi _____ il bicchięre?   *rọmpere*
3. Loro non _____ nessun vantạggio.   *trarre*
4. Mia sorella _____ il viạggio.   *fare*
5. Io non _____ nięnte.   *dire*
6. I miei genitori mi _____ due lẹttere.   *scrịvere*
7. Tu non _____ lo sbạglio.   *corrẹggere*
8. Io non _____ .   *rispọndere*
9. Cosa _____ (tu)?   *scẹgliere*
10. I soldati _____ la battạglia.   *vịncere*

134. Complete the following with the appropriate forms of the conversational past, or present perfect tense (passato prọssimo), of the indicated verbs:

1. Noi _____ i suọi regali.   *accettare*

     2. Tu _____ a casa dei nonni.   *pranzare*
     3. Luigi _____ molte persone.   *conoscere*
     4. Loro _____ una bella canzone.   *cantare*
     5. Voi _____ la verità.   *dire*
     6. Maria _____ la lezione.   *finire*
     7. Io _____ parecchi giornali.   *leggere*
     8. Il bambino _____ il bicchiere.   *rompere*
     9. Tu _____ una motocicletta.   *comprare*
    10. Noi _____ molte cose.   *promettere*

135. Rewrite the following in the present perfect, or conversational past:
     1. Luisa canta bene.
     2. Leggiamo la lettera.
     3. Scrivete molte lettere.
     4. Chiudi la porta.
     5. Mangio con gli amici.
     6. Aprono le finestre.
     7. Finiamo il compito.
     8. Aspettate Giovanni.
     9. Lavoro fino a tardi.
    10. Rompi il piatto.

Agreement of the Past Participle with Verbs Conjugated with *Avere* in the Present Perfect (*Passato Prossimo*)

In the conversational past, or present perfect (and other compound tenses), the past participle of the acting verb must agree in gender and number with the direct object pronoun *preceding* the verb form. Observe the following sets of sentences:

Hanno veduto lo zio.	*They have seen their uncle.*
but: **Lo hanno veduto.**	*They have seen him. (Also:* **L'hanno veduto***)*
Ho comprato i libri.	*I have bought the books.*
but: **Li ho comprati.**	*I have bought them.*
Abbiamo veduto Luisa.	*We have seen Louise.*
but: **L'abbiamo veduta.**	*We have seen her.*
Hai ricevuto le lettere.	*You have received the letters.*
but: **Le hai ricevute.**	*You have received them.*

136. Rewrite the following sentences, substituting the underlined words with the appropriate direct object pronouns and making all other necessary changes:
     1. Maria ha conosciuto i miei fratelli ieri.
     2. Ho comprato questa penna in quel negozio.
     3. Non ho salutato le tue zie.
     4. Ho bevuto l'aperitivo in pochi secondi.
     5. Ieri pomeriggio ho dato gli esami di storia.
     6. Abbiamo controllato l'uscita del cinema.
     7. Hai letto quelle riviste?
     8. Avete finito i compiti?
     9. Ho aperto la finestra poco fa.
    10. Hanno scritto le lettere facilmente

PASSATO PRỌSSIMO OF VERBS CONJUGATED WITH ẸSSERE

The auxiliary verb ẹssere plus the past participle is used to form the **passato prọssimo** (*present perfect*) and other compound tenses of almost all intransitive verbs. (Intransitive verbs are those that do not take a direct object. Study the first page of Chapter 6 to refresh your memory on the subject.) These verbs usually express motion or a state of being. Note that ẹssere and **stare** have the same past participle, **stato, -a, -i, -e**. All regular past participles that take ẹssere for the reasons just cited, undergo the same changes from the infinitive as those regular past participles conjugated with **avere** (see p. 138). Study the following three verbs, **andare** (*to go*), **cadere** (*to fall*), and **uscire** (*to go out*), fully conjugated with ẹssere in the **passato prọssimo**:

Study the following forms:

Infinitive:	**andare**	**cadere**	**uscire**
Root for Past Participle:	**and-**	**cad-**	**usc-**
io	sono and<u>ato</u>(<u>-a</u>)	sono cad<u>uto</u>(<u>-a</u>)	sono usc<u>ito</u>(<u>-a</u>)
tu	sei and<u>ato</u>(<u>-a</u>)	sei cad<u>uto</u>(<u>-a</u>)	sei usc<u>ito</u>(<u>-a</u>)
lui, lei, Lei	è and<u>ato</u>(<u>-a</u>)	è cad<u>uto</u>(<u>-a</u>)	è usc<u>ito</u>(<u>-a</u>)
noi	siamo and<u>ati</u>(<u>-e</u>)	siamo cad<u>uti</u>(<u>-e</u>)	siamo usc<u>iti</u>(<u>-e</u>)
voi	siẹte and<u>ati</u>(<u>-e</u>)	siẹte cad<u>uti</u>(<u>-e</u>)	siẹte usc<u>iti</u>(<u>-e</u>)
loro, Loro	sono and<u>ati</u>(<u>-e</u>)	sono cad<u>uti</u>(<u>-e</u>)	sono usc<u>iti</u>(<u>-e</u>)

As you have seen in the conjugated verbs above, all verbs conjugated with ẹssere must reflect in the past partiple the number and gender of the subject. Observe the following full sentences.

L<u>a</u> ragazz<u>a</u> è andat<u>a</u> a scuọla.	*The girl went (has gone) to school.*
L<u>e</u> ragazz<u>e</u> sono andat<u>e</u> a scuọla.	*The girls went (have gone) to school*
Il ragazz<u>o</u> è andat<u>o</u> a scuọla.	*The boy went (has gone) to school.*
I ragazz<u>i</u> sono andat<u>i</u> a scuọla.	*The boys went (have gone) to school.*

If the gender of the subject is *mixed* or *unknown,* the masculine form of the *past participle* is used:

Il ragazzo e la ragazza sono andati a scuọla	*The boy and the girl went (have gone) to school.*
Noi siạmo andati a scuọla.	*We went (have gone) to school.*

As you already know, the formal subject pronouns **Lei** and **Loro** refer to both genders, masculine and feminine. When these subject pronouns are present in the context of the passato prossimo, the ending of the *past participle* must agree in number and gender with the nouns they represent. Observe the following examples:

Lei (*formal m. s.*) **è andato in Itạlia l'anno scorso?**	*Did you (formal m. s.) go to Italy last year?*
Lei (*formal f. s.*) **è andata in Itạlia l'anno scorso?**	*Did you (formal f. s.) go to Italy last year?*
Loro (*formal m. pl.*) **sono andati in Itạlia l'anno scorso?**	*Did you (formal m. pl.) go to Italy last year?*
Loro (*formal f. s.*) **sono andate in Itạlia l'anno scorso?**	*Did you (formal f. pl.) go to Italy last year?*

The same agreement in number and gender would be also necessary, of course, if the nouns appeared instead of the subject pronouns (whose number and gender appeared in parentheses above). Observe the following:

Professor Boni, è andato in Itạlia l'anno scorso?	*Prof. Boni, did you go to Italy last year?*
Dottoressa Boni, è andata in Itạlia l'anno scorso?	*Dr. Boni, did you go to Italy last year?*
Signor Boni e signor Lari, siete andati in Itạlia l'anno scorso?	*Mr. Boni and Mr. Lari, did you go to Italy last year?*
Signora Boni e signora Lari, sono andate in Itạlia l'anno scorso?	*Mrs. Boni and Mrs. Lari, did you go to Italy last year?*

PAST PARTICIPLES CONJUGATED WITH ẸSSERE

Infinitive: **andare** > *Root:* **and-** + *Ending:* **-ato, -a, -i, -e = andato, andata, andati, andate**
Infinitive: **cadere** > *Root:* **cad-** + *Ending:* **-uto, -a, -i, -e = caduto, caduta, caduti, cadute**
Infinitive: **uscire** > *Root:* **usc-** + *Ending:* **-ito, -a, -i, -e = uscito, uscita, usciti, uscite**

The following is a partial list of the most commonly used verbs of this category and their regular past participles. Note how they change from *infinitive* to *past participle* to *fully conjugated form* with **ęssere**:

andare (*to go*) ——————— **andato** (*gone*) **Io** (m.) **sono andato** a Toronto. *I went (have gone) to Toronto.*

bastare (to be enough) ——————— **bastato** (*to have been enough*) **Le bevande sono bastate.** *The drinks were enough (have been enough).*

arrossire (*to blush*) —————— **arrossito** (*blushed*) **Il bambino tịmido è arrossito.** *The timid child blushed (has blushed).*

arrivare (*to arrive*) ——————— **arrivato** (*arrived*) **Tu** (tu) **sei arrivata** tardi. *You arrived (have arrived) late.*

costare (*to cost*) —————— **costato** (*cost*) **Quęl viạggio è costato** troppo. *That trip cost (has cost) too much.*

diventare (*to become*) —————— **diventato** (*become*) **Filippo è diventato** ricco. *Philip became (has become) rich.*

durare (*to last*) ————— **durato** (*lasted*) **La partita è durata** due ore. *The game lasted (has lasted) two hours.*

entrare (*to enter*) —————— **entrato** (*entered*) **Noi** (m.) **siạmo entrati** soli. *We entered (have entered) alone.*

invecchiạre (*to grow old*) ——————— **invecchiạto** (*grown old*) **Voi** (f) **non siẹte invecchiạte** affatto. *You didn't grow old (haven't grown old) at all.*

restare (*to stay*) —————— **restato** (*stayed*) **I ragazzi sono restati** dai nonni. *The boys stayed (have stayed) at their grandparents'.*

ringiovanire (*rejuvenate*) ——————— **ringiovanito** (*rejuvenated*) **Le nonne sono ringiovanite** dopo tanto riposo. *The grandmothers rejuvenated (have rejuvenated) after so much rest.*

ritornare (*to return*) ——————— **ritornato** (*returned*) **L'esploratore** (m.) **è ritornato** dall'Ạfrica. *The explorer returned (has returned) from Africa.*

tornare (*to return*) —————— **tornato** (*returned*) **La dottoressa è tornata** da una conferenza. *The doctor (f.) returned (has returned) from a conference.*

sembrare (*to seem*) —————— **sembrato** (*seemed*) **Le studentesse sono sembrate** preparate. *The students (f.) seemed prepared.*

Observe the following common irregular past participles used with ẹssere in the passato prossimo:

apparire (*to appear*) ————— **apparso** (*appeared*) **Mạrio è apparso senza telefonare.** *Mario appeared (has appeared) without telephoning.*

crẹscere (*to grow*) —————— **cresciụto** (*grown*) **Marịa è cresciụta** molto. *Mary grew (has grown) a lot.*

ẹssere (*to be*) —————— **stato** (*been*) **Ragazze, siẹte state contente?** *Girls, have you been happy?*

morire (*to die*) —————— **morto** (*died*) **I ragazzi sono morti dalle risa.** *The boys died (have died) laughing.*

nạscere (*to be born*) —————— **nato** (*born*) **Le ragazze sono nate fortunate.** *The girls were (have been) born lucky.*

piacere (*to please*) —————— **piaciụto** (*pleased*) **Il cibo è piaciụto a tutti.** *The food pleased (has pleased) everyone.*

rimanere (*to stay*) ————— **rimasto** (*stayed*) **Signori, sono rimasti un'ora?** *Sirs, did you stay (have you stayed) one hour?*

scẹndere (*to descend*) —————— **sceso** (*descended*) **Gli scalatori sono scesi dal monte.** *The climbers descended the mountain. Also:* **Ivo ha sceso le scale.** *Ivo descended the stairs.*

stare (*to stay, to be*) —————— **stato** (*stayed, been*) **Ivo e Isa, dove siẹte stati?** *Ivo and Isa, where have you been?*

venire (*to come*) ————— **venuto** (*come*) **Luịsa, tu sei venuta in aẹreo all'improvviso!** *Louise, you came (have come) by plane suddenly!*

vịvere (*to live*) —————— **vissuto** (*lived*) **Signora, quạnti anni è vissuta in Svịzzera?** *Madame, how many years did you live (have you lived) in Switzerland?*

Note that **vịvere** is also a *transitive verb* (it takes a direct object) and as such it uses **avere** as auxiliary in the **passato prọssimo**: **Giọrgio ha vissuto una vita piẹna di avventure.** *Giorgio lived (has lived) a life full of adventures.*

137. *Complete the following with the appropriate present perfect (passato prọssimo) forms of the indicated verbs.*

    1. Le ragazze _____ a Firenze.   *ẹssere*

    2. Antọnio _____ in ritardo.   *arrivare*

    3. La commẹdia _____ due ore.   *durare*

4. Voi _____ in montagna.   *andare*
5. Quei vini _____ a tutti.   *piacere*
6. I ragazzi _____ alle dięci.   *uscire*
7. Luisa _____ tardi.   *ritornare*
8. Il cibo _____ per tutti.   *bastare*
9. I libri _____ troppo.   *costare*
10. Noi _____ a casa di Mario.   *restare*

138. Rewrite the following in the present perfect (passato prossimo):

1. Marco va al mercato.
2. Luisa esce con Pietro.
3. Giuseppe e Antonio ritornano alle nove.
4. Olga e Maria entrano in un negozio.
5. Mario e Anna partono per l'Italia.
6. Noi siamo dai nonni.
7. Le ragazze arrivano insięme.
8. I ragazzi stanno a casa.

139. Give the Italian equivalents of the following sentences.

1. This car cost thirty thousand euros.
2. Mrs. Cherubini, where have you been lately?
3. Today Marisa and Anthony went to school at 8 A.M.
4. At what time have you (*tu, m.*) arrived today?
5. Girls, did you come by bus or by plane?
6. Mr. and Mrs. Boni, where did you live two years ago?
7. I (*f.*) grew up with my grandparents.
8. Fausto and Anna died from fear!
9. My little sister was born in 2000.
10. The lentils pleased everyone.

Passato Prossimo of Modal Verbs: *Dovere, Potere,* and *Volere.*

In the *present perfect* (**passato prossimo**), **dovere**, **potere**, and **volere** are conjugated with both **avere** and **ęssere**. When used A) without an infinitive (that follows the modal verbs), their *auxiliary* (*helping*) verb must be **avere**. B) With an infinitive that takes **avere**, the modal verbs must also be conjugated with **avere**. C) With an infinitive that takes **ęssere**, the modal verbs take **ęssere**, but D) in colloquial (conversational) Italian, many Italians choose to use **avere** before the modals **dovere**, **potere**, and **volere**. Moreover, there are some people who use exclusively the auxiliary **avere**. E) When *direct object pronouns* (**lo, la, li, le**, and the formal **Lo, La, Li, Le**) are used with modal verbs in the **passato prossimo**, be sure to agree the past participle with the number and gender of the *pronouns* when the latter precede the verb forms; when the pronouns are attached to the infinitive, there is no agreement. Observe the following examples:

A: Without an infinitive:

Q: Perché sei andato dal mędico?   *Why did you go to the doctor?*
A: Perché ho dovuto.   *Because I had to.*

Q: Hanno portato i bambini al parco?   *Did they take the children to the park?*
A: No, non hanno potuto!   *No, they couldn't! (No, they haven't been able to!)*

Q: Sięte tornati presto?   *Did you return (have you returned) early?*
A: No, non abbiamo voluto!   *No, we didn't want to!*

*B: With an infinitive (that takes **avere**):*

Q: Che hai fatto ięri?   *What have you done yesterday?*
A: Ho dovuto pulire la casa.   *I had (have had) to clean the house.*

Q: È andata a teatro Luisa?   *Did Luisa go to the theater?*
A: No, non ha potuto lasciare il lavoro.   *No, she couldn't (wasn't able to) leave work.*

Q: Hanno falciato l'erba i ragazzi?   *Did the boys mow the lawn?*
A: No, non hanno voluto falciare niente!   *No, they refused to mow anything!*

C: With an infinitive (that takes essere):

Q: Dov'è andata Olga?   *Where did Olga go?*
A: Olga è dovuta andare dal dentista.   *Olga had to go to the dentist.*

Q: È arrivata l'avvocatessa?   *Did the attorney (f.) arrive?*
A: No, l'avvocatessa non è potuta venire.   *No, the attorney couldn't come.*

Q: La signora è ancora al quinto piano?   *The lady is still on the fifth floor?*
A: Sí, la signora non è voluta scendere.   *Yes, she didn't want to come down.*

*D: Colloquial use of **avere** with modals that take **essere**:* (All the answers in C, above, can take **avere**).

Al: Olga ha dovuto andare dal dentista.
A2: L'avvocatessa non ha potuto venire.
A3: La signora non ha voluto scendere.

*E: Use of direct object pronouns with modals that take **avere** in the **passato prossimo**:*

Q: Aldo, hai preparato il discorso?   *Aldo, have you prepared the speech?*
A: Sí, l'ho dovuto preparare. [l' = lo].   *Yes, I had (have had) to prepare it.*
(Sí, ho dovuto prepararlo.)

Q: Ragazzi, avete letto i giornali?   *Boys, have you read the newspapers?*
A: Sí, li abbiamo potuti leggere.   *Yes, we were able to read them.*
(Sí, abbiamo potuto leggerli.)

Q: Ha comprato la cena Anna?   *Did Anna buy supper?*
A: Sí, Anna l'ha voluta comprare. [l'= la]   *Yes, Anna did want to buy it.*
(Sí, Anna ha voluto comprarla.)

Q: Signori, hanno portato gli asparagi?   *Sirs, have you brought the asparagus?*
A: No, non li abbiamo voluti portare.   *No, we refused to bring them.*
(No, non abbiamo voluto portarli.)

Note that in the simple tenses, the *direct object pronouns* may precede the conjugated *modal verbs,* and may be attached to the *infinitives* (after dropping the final **-e**). Observe the following examples in the *present indicative*:

Il vestito? Lo devo comprare. Or: Il vestito? Devo comprarlo.   *The suit? I have to buy it.*
La bambina? La posso chiamare. Or: La bambina? Posso chiamarla.   *The child (f)? I can call her.*
Le automobili? Le voglio guidare. Or: Le automobili? Voglio guidarle   *The cars? I want to drive them.*

140. *Rewrite in full the following sentences in the spaces provided. Place the direct object pronouns before the passato prossimo and make all necessary changes throughout.*

1. Gli asparagi? Ho dovuto prepararli.

   _____

2. Teresa? Non abbiamo potuto vederla.

   _____

3. Le scarpe? Hai voluto comprarle.

   _____

4. Il televisore? Avete dovuto portarlo.

   _____

5. I libri? Ha dovuto lęggerli.

_____

141. Give the Italian equivalents; when possible, translate in more than one way.

1. I (f.) couldn't go to the dentist.

_____

2. The boys didn't want to wash the driveway (*il passo carraio*).

_____

3. Mario wasn't able to play outside.

_____

Passato Prọssimo of Reflexive Verbs

All reflexive verbs (**alzarsi**: *to get up*) and reciprocal verbs (**scrịversi**: *to write one another*) are conjugated with the auxiliary **ęssere** in the *conversational past* (**passato prọssimo**). The *reflexive pronoun* **si**, which appears attached to the *infinitive of reflexive verbs*, changes into **mi**, **ti**, **si**, **ci**, **vi**, and **si**; these *pronouns* appear before the **passato prọssimo**: the *past participles* must agree in number and gender with subjects (or subject pronouns) represented by the reflexive pronouns. Note that when the third person reflexive pronoun **si** represents the formal subject pronouns **Lei** (*you* formal s.) and **Loro** (*you* formal pl.), the **si** may be written with a capital **S-** (=**Si**) in order to avoid ambiguity. Study the following conjugated forms of the *reflexive verbs* **alzarsi** and **divertirsi**:

Infinitive:	**alzarsi**	**divertirsi**
Root for past participle:	**alz-**	**divert-**
io	mi sono alz<u>ato</u> (<u>-a</u>)	mi sono divert<u>ito</u> (<u>-a</u>)
tu	ti sei alz<u>ato</u> (<u>-a</u>)	ti sei divert<u>ito</u> (<u>-a</u>)
lui, lei, Lei	si è alz<u>ato</u> (<u>-a</u>)	si è divert<u>ito</u> (<u>-a</u>)
noi	ci sịamo alz<u>ati</u> (<u>-e</u>)	ci sịamo divert<u>iti</u> (<u>-e</u>)
voi	vi sięte alz<u>ati</u> (<u>-e</u>)	vi sięte divert<u>iti</u> (<u>-e</u>)
loro, Loro	si sono alz<u>ati</u> (<u>-e</u>)	si sono divert<u>iti</u> (<u>-e</u>)

Below is a list of some very common Italian reflexive verbs:

alzarsi	*to get up*	**muọversi**	*to move*
annoiạrsi	*to get bored*	**prepararsi**	*to prepare oneself*
arrabbiạrsi	*to get angry*	**riposarsi**	*to relax oneself*
chiamarsi	*to be named*	**sbarbarsi**	*to shave oneself*
coricarsi	*to go to bed*	**scusarsi**	*to excuse oneself*
dimenticarsi	*to forget*	**sedersi**	*to sit down*
divertirsi	*to enjoy oneself*	**sentirsi**	*to feel*
guardarsi	*to look at oneself*	**sentirsi bene**	*to feel well*
lamentarsi	*to complain*	**sentirsi male**	*to feel ill*
laureạrsi	*to graduate (from college)*	**sposarsi**	*to get married*
lavarsi	*to wash oneself*	**svegliạrsi**	*to wake up*
męttersi	*to wear*	**vergognarsi**	*to be ashamed*
męttersi a ...	*to set out to, to start (+ -ing verb form)*	**vestirsi**	*to get dressed*

Some reflexive verbs are called reciprocal reflexive: for example, as a reflexive verb, **guardarsi** means *to look at oneself*; as a reciprocal reflexive, **guardarsi** means *to look at one another*. There are some verbs we don't usually consider reflexive that may become reciprocal reflexive by simply attaching the reflexive pronoun **si** to the infinitive (after dropping the final **-e**): **scrịvere** (*to write*) > **scrịversi** (*to write one another*), **visitare** (*to visit*) > **visitarsi** (*to visit one another*). And there are some very frequently used verbs that fulfill three functions; for example, the verb 1) **lavare** (to *wash*): **Lavo la mạcchina** = *I'm washing the car*; 2) **lavarsi** (*to wash oneself*): **Ci laviạmo spesso** = *We wash ourselves often*; and 3) **lavarsi** (*to wash one another*): **Ci laviạmo** = *We wash one another*. Study the following reciprocal reflexives. Some of them appear as *regular reflexive* verbs on the list above and are repeated here as *reciprocal* *reflexive* verbs:

abbracciarsi	*to hug one another*	**prestarsi**	*to loan (something) one another*
aiutarsi	*to help one another*	**rimproverarsi**	*to reproach one another*
annoiarsi	*to bore one another*	**ringraziarsi**	*to thank one another*
baciarsi	*to kiss one another*	**scherzarsi**	*to kid one another*
chiamarsi	*to call one another*	**scriversi**	*to write one another*
dimenticarsi	*to forget one another*	**sgridarsi**	*to yell at one another*
guardarsi	*to look at one another*	**telefonarsi**	*to telephone one another*
ignorarsi	*to ignore one another*	**vedersi**	*to see one another*
piacersi	*to like one another*		

As with other verbs conjugated with essere in the **passato prossimo** (and other compound tenses), the *past participle* of *reflexive verbs* and *reciprocal reflexive* verbs must agree in number and gender with the subject of the sentence. Observe the following:

Luisa si è svegliata alle sette di mattina.	*Louise woke up at seven A.M.*
Anche i suoi fratelli si sono svegliati alle sette.	*Even her brothers woke up at seven.*
Noi (*unknown gender*) **ci siamo conosciuti cinque anni fa.**	*We met five years ago.*
Le due amiche si sono vedute spesso.	*The two friends (f.) saw one another often.*
Mia madre e io (f.s.) ci siamo telefonate sempre.	*My mother and I always telephoned one another.*
Il bambino si è coricato alle venti.	*The child went to bed at ten P.M.*
E Lei, signorina, quando si è riposata?	*And you, Miss, when did you rest?*
E Lei, dottore, dove si è laureato?	*And you, Doctor, where did you graduate from?*

142. *Rewrite the following sentences in the present perfect (passato prossimo).*

1. Mi alzo di buon'ora.
2. I ragazzi non si sbarbano.
3. Ci sediamo vicino alla finestra.
4. Gli amici si divertono.
5. Lei (*f.*) si laurea quest'anno?
6. Dottoressa, Lei si sente bene?
7. Quelle sorelle si scrivono spesso.
8. Mi compro un paio di scarpe.
9. Quel ragazzo si lamenta sempre.
10. Ragazzi, vi arrabbiate troppo.

Essere versus avere

Many verbs can be used in both a reflexive or reciprocal sense as well as in a nonreflexive or nonreciprocal sense (see page 146). When the latter is the case, they are conjugated with **avere** and are often followed by a direct object. Study the following examples:

La ragazza si è lavata.	*The girl washed (herself).*
Lei ha lavato la sua macchina.	*She washed her car.*
Gli amici si sono scritti.	*The friends wrote one another.*
Gli amici hanno scritto due lettere.	*The friends wrote two letters.*

143. *Complete the following with essere or avere, as needed:*

1. Le amiche si _____ incontrate al ristorante.
2. Le amiche _____ incontrato molti turisti.
3. Quei signori si _____ conosciuti pochi giorni fa.
4. Quei signori _____ conosciuto mio padre.
5. Maria e Carmela si _____ viste al cinema.

6. Maria e Carmela _____ visto alcune amiche al cinema.
7. I giovani si _____ dati la mano.
8. I giovani _____ dato la mano a mio fratello.
9. Le studentesse si _____ aiutate per gli esami.
10. Le studentesse _____ aiutato le loro amiche per gli esami.

Uses of the Passato Prossimo

The **passato prossimo,** or present perfect, is used to express an action that was completed at a definite time in the past:

L'altro giorno Alberto ha visitato il museo.	*The other day Albert visited the museum.*
Loro sono arrivati ieri.	*They arrived yesterday.*
Stamani mi sono alzato(-a) alle sette.	*This morning I got up at seven.*

Some common adverbial expressions that are used with the **passato prossimo** are as follows:

ieri	*yesterday*
ieri pomeriggio	*yesterday afternoon*
ieri sera	*last night*
l'altro giorno	*the other day*
due giorni fa	*two days ago*
l'anno scorso	*last year*
stamani	*this morning*

144. Complete the following with the appropriate form of the passato prossimo of the indicated verb:

1. Lui_____il suo amico l'altro giorno.   *vedere*
2. Voi_____un viaggio in Italia l'anno scorso.   *fare*
3. Noi_____una macchina la settimana scorsa.   *comprare*
4. Loro lo_____ due giorni fa.   *dire*
5. Ieri i miei cugini_____dall'Italia.   *arrivare*
6. L'anno scorso i miei genitori_____in Italia.   *andare*
7. Io_____quel libro l'altro giorno.   *leggere*
8. Noi_____i compiti ieri sera.   *finire*
9. Due anni fa io_____una bella sorpresa.   *avere*
10. Il mese scorso voi non_____alla riunione.   *venire*

Differences between the *Passato Prossimo* and the Imperfect Indicative

Completed versus continuing action

You have already learned the basic uses of the imperfect indicative and the **passato prossimo** (present perfect or conversational past). The imperfect indicative is used to describe a continuing, habitual past action of long duration, whereas the **passato prossimo** is used to express an action which began and was completed at a definite time in the past. Even though the action may have taken place in the past for an extended period of time, the **passato prossimo** is used if the action has been terminated.

L'altro giorno Alberto ha visto i nonni.	*The other day Albert saw his grandparents.*
La domenica Alberto vedeva i nonni.	*On Sundays Albert would see his grandparents.*
L'ho veduto soltanto una volta.	*I saw him only once.*
Lo vedevo spesso.	*I used to see him often.*

145. Rewrite the following, changing l'altro giorno to spesso:

1. L'ho veduto l'altro giorno.
2. Abbiamo parlato con lui l'altro giorno.

3. Carlo mi ha chiamato l'altro giorno.
4. Loro hanno ricevuto una lettera da lui l'altro giorno.
5. Angelina ha veduto i suoi cugini l'altro giorno.

146. Rewrite the following, changing *ripetutamente* to *due giorni fa*:
1. Lui mi visitava ripetutamente.
2. Lei mi aiutava ripetutamente.
3. Andavo lí ripetutamente.
4. Me lo dicevano ripetutamente.
5. Lo facevi ripetutamente.

147. Complete the following, making new sentences in the passato prossimo or in the imperfect indicative according to the indicated time expression:
1. Ieri sono andato a Chicago.
   _____ogni mese.
2. Maria partiva sempre di mattina.
   Ieri_____.
3. Visitavo i miei cugini di quando in quando.
   _____l'anno scorso.
4. Ieri sera abbiamo incontrato dei vecchi amici.
   Ogni tanto_____.
5. Hai viaggiato in Francia il mese scorso?
   _____spesso spesso?
6. Parlavamo sempre di politica.
   Ieri sera_____.
7. Andavamo a teatro ogni domenica.
   _____domenica scorsa.
8. Loro andavano al mercato giorno dopo giorno.
   _____una volta.

148. Answer the following according to the model. Use the passato prossimo or the imperfect indicative as indicated by the expressions:

Leggere il giornale? Sí, ieri.   Comprare la rivista? Sí, sempre.
Sí, ho letto il giornale ieri.   Sí, compravo sempre la rivista.

1. Andare alla spiaggia? Sí, la settimana scorsa.
2. Dormire molto? Sí, ieri sera.
3. Lavorare troppo? Sí, stamani.
4. Andare al cinema? Sí, ogni domenica.
5. Viaggiare con gli amici? Sí, frequentemente.
6. Fare delle spese? Sí, ogni mattina.
7. Parlare con lui? Sí, tre giorni fa.
8. Vedere il film? Sí, venerdí.

Two actions in one sentence
When two or more continuing actions are expressed in the past, the imperfect indicative is used:

Mentre Luigi studiava, Antonio dormiva.
While Louis was studying, Anthony was sleeping.

Noi parlavamo, Luigi dormiva e tu guardavi la televisione.
We were talking, Louis was sleeping, and you were watching television.

When two or more actions in the past are completed, the **passato prossimo** is used:

> **Teresa è andata al cinema, e io sono rimasto(-a) a casa.**
> *Theresa went to the movies, and I stayed home.*

> **Ieri sera io ho visitato il municipio.**
> *Last night I visited city hall.*

> **Teresa è andata al cinema e Luigi è rimasto a casa.**
> *Theresa went to the movies, and Louis stayed home.*

When a continuing action in the past is interrupted by another action, the former is in the imperfect indicative and the latter is in the **passato prossimo**:

> **Maria leggeva il giornale quando io sono arrivato.**
> *Mary was reading the newspaper when I arrived.*

> **Io dormivo quando è suonato il campanello.**
> *I was sleeping when the doorbell rang.*

149. *Complete the following with either the passato prossimo or the imperfect of the indicated verbs:*

1. Alcuni amici_____mentre gli altri_____il sole.   *nuotare, prendere*
2. Maria_____con sua madre quando io_____.   *parlare, arrivare*
3. Tu_____Antonio quando egli_____in Italia.   *conoscere, essere*
4. _____quando noi_____.   *piovere, uscire*
5. Io_____quando_____ il telefono.   *dormire, squillare*
6. Loro_____quando io_____.   *pranzare, telefonare*
7. Quando loro_____all'aeroporto,_____bel tempo.   *arrivare, fare*
8. Alcuni giovani_____mentre gli altri_____.   *ballare, cantare*
9. Stamani io_____alle sette, e Pietro_____alle nove.   *alzarsi, alzarsi*
10. Io non_____perché_____.   *uscire, nevicare*

Uses of the Present Perfect (*Passato Prossimo*) and Preterite (*Passato Remoto*)

You have studied both the **passato prossimo** (pages 138–148) and the **preterite** (pages 115–127). In Italian, the **passato prossimo** is used more often than the preterite in order to describe a completed action; this holds true especially in conversational Italian. However, the preterite **(passato remoto)** is usually preferred as a literary past tense over the present perfect, and it is also used when the past described is quite remote. Observe the following:

> **Dante nacque nel 1265.**   **Federico II regnò nel Duecento.**
> *Dante was born in 1265.*   *Frederick II reigned in the Thirteenth Century.*

> **Boccaccio morí nel 1375.**   **Federico II morí nel 1250.**
> *Boccaccio died in 1375.*   *Frederick II died in 1250.*

150. *Review both past tenses by rewriting the underlined verb in each sentence first in the present perfect and then in the preterite:*

1. Visito lo zoo.
   A: _____
   B: _____
2. Mangio poco ma spesso.
   A: _____
   B: _____
3. Hai un po' di fortuna.
   A: _____
   B: _____
4. Arriva Luisa!
   A: _____
   B: _____

5. Usciamo alle otto.
   A: _____
   B: _____
6. Leggete un dramma.
   A: _____
   B: _____
7. Partono all'alba.
   A: _____
   B: _____

8. Tu e io parliamo molto.
   A: _____
   B: _____
9. Scrivi a tua madre?
   A: _____
   B: _____
10. Ritorno alle due.
   A: _____
   B: _____

PLUPERFECT INDICATIVE TENSE (TRAPASSATO PROSSIMO)

The pluperfect indicative is formed by using the imperfect indicative of the auxiliary verbs **avere** or **essere**, as needed, with the past participle of the acting verb. (For details on when to use **avere** and **essere**, see pages 141 and 142. Review the past participles on pages 138–139 and 143.) Observe the following verbs representing all three conjugations, **-are**, **-ere**, and **-ire**:

Verbs using *avere*

Infinitive:	**parlare**	**credere**	**finire**
io	avevo parlato	avevo creduto	avevo finito
tu	avevi parlato	avevi creduto	avevi finito
lui, lei, Lei	aveva parlato	aveva creduto	aveva finito
noi	avevamo parlato	avevamo creduto	avevamo finito
voi	avevate parlato	avevate creduto	avevate finito
loro, Loro	avevano parlato	avevano creduto	avevano finito

Verbs using *essere*

Infinitive:	**andare**	**cadere**	**uscire**
io	ero andato(-a)	ero caduto(-a)	ero uscito(-a)
tu	eri andato(-a)	eri caduto(-a)	eri uscito(-a)
lui, lei, Lei	era andato(-a)	era caduto(-a)	era uscito(-a)
noi	eravamo andati(-e)	eravamo caduti(-e)	eravamo usciti(-e)
voi	eravate andati(-e)	eravate caduti(-e)	eravate usciti(-e)
loro, Loro	erano andati(-e)	erano caduti(-e)	erano usciti(-e)

The pluperfect indicative is used in Italian the same way it is used in English: to express a past action completed prior to another past action. Study the following:

Già erano partiti quando sono arrivato.
They had already left when I arrived.

Avevo chiuso le finestre quando è cominciato a piovere.
I had shut the windows when it started to rain.

Avevamo paura perché i bambini non erano ritornati.
We were afraid because the children had not returned.

151. Complete the following with the appropriate pluperfect indicative forms of the indicated verbs:
1. Noi_____a lungo.   *parlare*
2. Io_____in ritardo.   *arrivare*

3. Lo studente_____l'esame.   *finire*
4. Voi_____i biglietti.   *comprare*
5. Tu_____in Italia l'anno anteriore.   *stare*
6. Loro_____ai tuoi problemi.   *credere*

152. *Complete the following with the appropriate pluperfect indicative forms of the indicated verbs:*
1. Non siamo partiti perché non_____i bambini.   *vedere*
2. Ho letto i libri che_____ da Roma.   *portare*
3. Noi_____quasi a casa, quando è cominciato a piovere a dirotto.   *arrivare*
4. Loro non sono andati al negozio perché già_____i regali.   *comprare*
5. Adesso so che tu non_____le mie lettere.   *ricevere*
6. Gli studenti erano stanchi perché_____fino a tardi.   *studiare*

PRETERITE PERFECT TENSE (TRAPASSATO REMOTO)

The preterite perfect tense is formed by using the preterite of the auxiliary verbs **avere** or **essere** and the past participle of the acting verb. Study the following:

Infinitive:	**cantare**	**credere**	**arrivare**	**uscire**
io	ebbi cantato	ebbi creduto	fui arrivato(-a)	fui uscito(-a)
tu	avesti cantato	avesti creduto	fosti arrivato(-a)	fosti uscito(-a)
lui, lei, Lei	ebbe cantato	ebbe creduto	fu arrivato(-a)	fu uscito(-a)
noi	avemmo cantato	avemmo creduto	fummo arrivati(-e)	fummo usciti(-e)
voi	aveste cantato	aveste creduto	foste arrivati(-e)	foste usciti(-e)
loro, Loro	ebbero cantato	ebbero creduto	furono arrivati(-e)	furono usciti(-e)

The preterite perfect, used mostly in literary contexts, is always preceded by time expressions such as **appena, non appena** (*scarcely, as soon as*), **dopo che** (*as soon as*), **quando** (*when*), **come** (*as*), or **finché non** (*up until*), and is followed by the preterite (**passato remoto**) in the independent clause. Observe the following:

Appena fu arrivato, si mise a parlare.
As soon as he had arrived, he started to speak.

Dopo che ebbe finito di parlare, cominciò a mangiare.
As soon as he had finished talking, he started to eat.

153. *Complete the following with the appropriate forms of the preterite perfect of the indicated verbs:*
1. Finché non_____Antonio, aspettammo in silenzio.   *arrivare*
2. Appena i signori_____, io me ne andai.   *parlare*
3. Quando noi_____, partimmo.   *cenare*
4. Appena noi_____, voi arrivaste.   *finire*
5. Come lui_____, la conferenza cominciò.   *arrivare*

FUTURE PERFECT TENSE (FUTURO ANTERIORE)

The future perfect tense is formed by using the future of the auxiliary **avere** or **essere** and the past participle of the acting verb:

Infinitive:	**comprare**	**andare**	**dire**	**uscire**
io	avrò comprato	sarò andato(-a)	avrò detto	sarò uscito(-a)
tu	avrai comprato	sarai andato(-a)	avrai detto	sarai uscito(-a)
lui, lei, Lei	avrà comprato	sarà andato(-a)	avrà detto	sarà uscito(-a)

noi	avremo comprato	saremo andati(-e)	avremo detto	saremo usciti(-e)
voi	avrete comprato	sarete andati(-e)	avrete detto	sarete usciti(-e)
loro, Loro	avranno comprato	saranno andati(-e)	avranno detto	saranno usciti(-e)

The future perfect is used to express a future action that will be completed prior to another future action:

Loro avranno cenato prima di partire.
They will have had supper before leaving.

Voi sarete già partiti quando noi arriveremo.
You will have already left when we (shall) arrive.

154. Complete the following with the appropriate future perfect forms of the indicated verbs:

1. Domani pomeriggio noi_____i nonni.	*vedere*
2. Tu_____le informazioni prima di venerdí.	*avere*
3. Loro_____senza dire niente.	*ritornare*
4. Voi_____gli esami prima delle tre.	*dare*
5. Noi_____al padre di Pietro.	*parlare*
6. I ragazzi_____nel parco.	*giocare*
7. Mio fratello_____con gli amici.	*uscire*
8. Domani a quest'ora io_____a Roma.	*arrivare*

CONDITIONAL PERFECT TENSE (CONDIZIONALE PASSATO)

The conditional perfect is formed by using the conditional of the auxiliary verb **avere** or **essere** and the past participle of the acting verb. Study the following:

Infinitive:	**ballare**	**andare**	**credere**	**salire**
io	avrei ballato	sarei andato(-a)	avrei creduto	sarei salito (-a)
tu	avresti ballato	saresti andato(-a)	avresti creduto	saresti salito(-a)
lui, lei, Lei	avrebbe ballato	sarebbe andato(-a)	avrebbe creduto	sarebbe salito(-a)
noi	avremmo ballato	saremmo andati(-e)	avremmo creduto	saremmo saliti(-e)
voi	avreste ballato	sareste andati(-e)	avreste creduto	sareste saliti (-e)
loro, Loro	avrebbero ballato	sarebbero andati(-e)	avrebbero creduto	sarebbero saliti(-e)

The conditional perfect is used to express what would have taken place had something else not interfered:

Loro sarebbero venuti ma non avevano abbastanza tempo.
They would have come but they didn't have enough time.

Avevi promesso che avresti scritto spesso.
You had promised that you would have written often.

155. Complete the following with the appropriate conditional perfect forms of the indicated verbs:

1. Noi_____ma cominciò a piovere.	*uscire*
2. Io_____ma non avevo la macchina.	*venire*
3. Lui aveva detto che_____alle due.	*arrivare*
4. Voi_____telefonare prima di partire.	*potere*
5. Tu_____ma faceva troppo caldo.	*correre*
6. Le ragazze_____al cinema.	*andare*

THE SUBJUNCTIVE (CONGIUNTIVO)

The use of the subjunctive usually appears to be quite difficult for those who speak English. The reason for this is that the subjunctive is seldom used in English, whereas it is widely used in Italian. The use of the subjunctive is, however, most logical once one understands the meaning of the word *subjunctive* as contrasted with the word *indicative*.

Many grammar books categorize the types of verbs or expressions that must be followed by the subjunctive. Categories such as desire, sentiment, volition, cause, demand, request, doubt, necessity, etc., are given. This nearly endless list is quite difficult to remember when attempting to speak the language.

A simpler basic rule for using the subjunctive is as follows: *The subjunctive implies subjectivity. If there exists the possibility that the action about which one is speaking has not taken place or may not take place, it is necessary to use the subjunctive. If, however, it is a realized fact that the action has taken place or definitely will take place, the indicative is used.*

Because of the indefinite nature of the subjunctive, it is found in a dependent clause. It is introduced by some statement that lends subjectivity and vagueness to the definite realization of the action in the dependent clause. Study the following examples:

> *John is going to the store.*
> *John went to the store.*

In these two sentences the speaker is relating an objective fact. Therefore the indicative is used. Study the following examples:

> *I want John to go to the store.*
> *I tell John to go to the store.*
> *I hope John goes to the store.*
> *I prefer that John go to the store.*
> *It is necessary for John to go to the store.*
> *It is possible that John will go to the store.*

In all of the above statements it is not fact that John will actually go to the store. For this reason all of these clauses would be in the subjunctive in Italian. Whereas in English an infinitive construction is often used, in Italian a clause must be used—*I want that John go to the store.*

Note that the subjunctive may also be used in adverbial clauses:

> *I will see John as soon as he arrives.*

Since John has not yet arrived, the subjunctive must be used, because there is no absolute guarantee that he will arrive. However, observe the following example:

> *I saw John as soon as he arrived.*

Since John has in reality arrived, there is no need for the subjunctive. The indicative would be used.

Formation of the Present Subjunctive

The root of the present subjunctive of most verbs, regular and irregular, is formed by dropping the final **-o** of the first-person singular of the present indicative; to this root are added the personal endings of the present subjunctive for each conjugation. You will note that the present subjunctive endings of **-ere** and **-ire** verbs are the same, and that the **noi** and **voi** endings of all three conjugations are the same. The **loro** ending of all verbs in the present subjunctive is formed by adding **-no** to all present subjunctive singular forms.

Regular verbs

	-are[28]	**-ere**	**-ire**
Infinitive:	**parlare**	**credere**	**dormire**
Root:	**parl-**	**cred-**	**dorm-**
che io	parl<u>i</u>	cred<u>a</u>	dorm<u>a</u>

---

[28] Remember the spelling changes of verbs ending in **-care** and **-gare**: **cerchi, cerchi, cerchi, cerchiamo, cerchiate, cerchino; paghi, paghi, paghi, paghiamo, paghiate, paghino**.

Remember the spelling changes of verbs ending in **–ciare** and **-giare**: **baci, baci, baci, baciamo, baciate, bacino; mangi, mangi, mangi, mangiamo, mangiate, mangino**.

Note the spelling of verbs ending in **-ciare** when the **i** is stressed in all forms except **noi** and **voi**: **scii, scii, scii, sciamo, sciate, sciino**.

che tu	parli	creda	dorma
che lui, che lei, che Lei	parli	creda	dorma
che noi	parliamo	crediamo	dormiamo
che voi	parliate	crediate	dormiate
che loro, che Loro	parlino	credano	dormano

The following is a partial list of **-are**, **-ere**, and **-ire** verbs that are regular in the present subjunctive and are conjugated in the same way as **parlare**, **credere**, and **dormire**:

Infinitive		*Root*	*Present Subjunctive*
arrivare	*to arrive*	**arriv-**	**che io arrivi**, etc.
ballare	*to dance*	**ball-**	**che io balli**, etc.
camminare	*to walk*	**cammin-**	**che io cammini**, etc.
cantare	*to sing*	**cant-**	**che io canti**, etc.
chiamare	*to call*	**chiam-**	**che io chiami**, etc.
guardare	*to look*	**guard-**	**che io guardi**, etc.
apprendere	*to learn*	**apprend-**	**che io apprenda**, etc.
cadere	*to fall*	**cad-**	**che io cada**, etc.
descrivere	*to describe*	**descriv-**	**che io descriva**, etc.
scrivere	*to write*	**scriv-**	**che io scriva**, etc.
vivere	*to live*	**viv-**	**che io viva**, etc.
aprire	*to open*	**apr-**	**che io apra**, etc.
coprire	*to cover*	**copr-**	**che io copra**, etc.
offrire	*to offer*	**offr-**	**che io offra**, etc.
seguire	*to follow*	**segu-**	**che io segua**, etc.
sentire	*to hear; feel*	**sent-**	**che io senta**, etc.

156. *Complete the following with the appropriate present subjunctive forms of the indicated verbs:*

1. Roberto vuole che tu_____la finestra.　　　　*aprire*
2. La maestra desidera che gli studenti_____in tempo.　　　*arrivare*
3. È necessario che Loro_____spesso.　　　*scrivere*
4. Ho paura che il bambino_____dalla sedia.　　　*cadere*
5. Mia madre vuole che io_____ogni settimana.　　　*telefonare*
6. Temiamo che voi non_____le istruzioni.　　　*seguire*
7. È possibile che io non_____il campanello da qui.　　　*sentire*
8. Desidero che voi_____la vostra gita.　　　*descrivere*

157. *Complete the following with the appropriate forms of the present subjunctive of the indicated verbs:*

1. Non voglio che i bambini_____i bicchieri di cristallo.　　　*toccare*
2. Il cameriere desidera che voi_____il conto adesso.　　　*pagare*
3. È necessario che io_____le chiavi.　　　*cercare*
4. Dubiti che noi_____bene a carte.　　　*giocare*
5. Suggeriamo che Loro_____poco.　　　*mangiare*
6. La maestra vuole che gli studenti_____a studiare.　　　*cominciare*

Irregular verbs

Since the first-person singular of the present indicative serves as the base for the formation of the present subjunctive, any verb with an irregular first-person present indicative form will have an irregular root for the present subjunctive. Study the following:

Infinitive:	**bere**	**dire**	**fare**	**potere**
Present Indicative (io):	**bevo**	**dico**	**faccio**[29]	**posso**

---

[29] **facci-** drops the **-i-** before the **noi** ending **-iamo**.

Root for Present Subjunctive:	**bev-**	**dic-**	**facci-**	**poss-**
che io	beva	dica	faccia	possa
che tu	beva	dica	faccia	possa
che lui/lei/Lei	beva	dica	faccia	possa
che noi	beviamo	diciamo	facciamo	possiamo
che voi	beviate	diciate	facciate	possiate
che loro/Loro	bevano	dicano	facciano	possano

Infinitive:	**tradurre**	**volere**
Present Indicative (io):	**traduco**	**voglio**[30]
Root for Present Subjunctive:	**traduc-**	**vogli-**
che io	traduca	voglia
che tu	traduca	voglia
che lui/lei/Lei	traduca	voglia
che noi	traduciamo	vogliamo
che voi	traduciate	vogliate
che loro/Loro	traducano	vogliano

Study the following forms of **capire** as a model for those **-ire** verbs that have **-isc-** in all forms of the present indicative except **noi** and **voi**. You will note that the **-isc-** is also used in all forms of the present subjunctive except **noi** and **voi**.

	Present Indicative	*Present Subjunctive*
io	**capisco**	**che io capisca**
tu	**capisci**	**che tu capisca**
lui, lei, Lei	**capisce**	**che lui/lei/Lei capisca**
noi	**capiamo**	**che noi capiamo**
voi	**capite**	**che voi capiate**
loro, Loro	**capiscono**	**che loro/Loro capiscano**

Just as the verb **capire** (*to understand*) and all other third-conjugation verbs with **-isc-** in the present indicative have a different root for the **noi** and **voi** forms, many verbs that are irregular in the present subjunctive form their **io, tu, lui, lei,** and **loro** forms from the **io** form of the present indicative, but return to the **noi** form of the present indicative for the **noi** and **voi** subjunctive forms. Study the verb **dovere** (*to have to, must*) as a model for such verbs:

dovere

Present Indicative	*Present Subjunctive*
devo(debbo)	che io deva (debba)
devi	che tu deva (debba)
deve	che egli deva (debba)
dobbiamo	che noi dobbiamo
dovete	che voi dobbiate
devono(debbono)	che loro devano(debbano)

Below is a list of other verbs that function in the same way as **dovere** in the present subjunctive. Remember that all subject pronouns, when used with the subjunctive forms, are always preceded by **che: che io colga, che tu colga,** etc.

andare	**cogliere**	**scegliere**
vada	colga	scelga
vada	colga	scelga
vada	colga	scelga
andiamo	cogliamo	scegliamo
andiate	cogliate	scegliate
vadano	colgano	scelgano

---

[30] **vogli-** drops the -i- before the **noi** ending **-iamo**.

porre	rimanere	salire	tenere	trarre	valere	venire
ponga	rimanga	salga	tenga	tragga	valga	venga
ponga	rimanga	salga	tenga	tragga	valga	venga
ponga	rimanga	salga	tenga	tragga	valga	venga
poniamo	rimaniamo	saliamo	teniamo	traiamo	valiamo	veniamo
poniate	rimaniate	saliate	teniate	traiate	valiate	veniate
pongano	rimangano	salgano	tengano	traggano	valgano	vengano

apparire	morire	parere
appaia	muoia	paia
appaia	muoia	paia
appaia	muoia	paia
appariamo	moriamo	pariamo
appariate	moriate	pariate
appaiano	muoiano	paiano

cuocere	sedere	sonare	udire	uscire
cuocia	sieda	suoni	oda	esca
cuocia	sieda	suoni	oda	esca
cuocia	sieda	suoni	oda	esca
cociamo	sediamo	soniamo	udiamo	usciamo
cociate	sediate	soniate	udiate	usciate
cuociano	siedano	suonino	odano	escano

158. *Change the following sentences, substituting each underlined subject pronoun with each of the indicated subject pronouns, making all necessary verb changes.*

1. È necessario che <u>io</u> venga subito.　　　　　　*tu, loro, voi, noi*
2. Bisogna che <u>noi</u> diciamo la verità.　　　　　　*tu, lui, voi, loro*
3. Roberto vuole che <u>voi</u> facciate i compiti.　　　*io, tu, lei, loro*
4. È necessario che <u>voi</u> rimaniate qui.　　　　　　*io, tu, lui, loro*
5. Bisogna che <u>tu</u> capisca la lezione.　　　　　　*lui, noi, voi, loro*
6. Noi vogliamo che voi soniate il violino.　　　　　　*tu, lei, loro*
7. È necessario che <u>lui</u> esca subito.　　　　　　　*io, noi, voi, loro*
8. Bisogna che <u>loro</u> scelgano presto.　　　　　　*io, lui, noi, voi*

Avere, essere, sapere, dare, stare

The verbs **sapere**, **avere**, **essere**, **dare**, and **stare** are completely irregular in the formation of the present subjunctive. Study the following forms:

sapere	avere	essere	dare	stare
sappia	abbia	sia	dia	stia
sappia	abbia	sia	dia	stia
sappia	abbia	sia	dia	stia
sappiamo	abbiamo	siamo	diamo	stiamo
sappiate	abbiate	siate	diate	stiate
sappiano	abbiano	siano	diano	stiano

159. *Complete the following with the appropriate forms of the indicated verbs:*

1. Io non voglio che i bambini_____paura.　　　　*avere*
2. Lui teme che i suoi genitori non_____presenti.　　*essere*
3. Perché insisti che io ti_____cento euro?　　　*dare*
4. È possibile che loro non lo_____.　　　　　　　*sapere*
5. Io non voglio che voi mi_____neanche un regalo.　*dare*

6. È necessario che voi_____a casa alle otto.   *essere*
7. Speriamo che voi_____bene.   *stare*

Uses of the Present Subjunctive

Subjunctive in noun clauses

As it has been explained on page 154, the subjunctive is required in clauses following verbs which denote will, desire, fear, doubt, denial, necessity, etc. The subjunctive verb is usually preceded by the conjunction **che**. Some common verbs requiring the subjunctive are as follows:

With verbs of will, desire, preference, suggestion, hope

insistere	*to insist*
volere	*to want*
desiderare	*to wish*
preferire	*to prefer*
suggerire	*to suggest*
sperare	*to hope*

Voglio che tu venga qui.
I want you to come here.

Desiderano che io parli piú spesso.
They want me to speak more often.

Preferisci che io arrivi alle due?
Do you prefer that I arrive at two o'clock?

Suggerisco che voi partiate presto.
I suggest (that) you leave early.

Spero che vengano subito.
I hope they come soon.

With verbs of denial

negare *to deny*

Antonio nega che io sia un suo amico.
Anthony denies that I am a friend of his.

With verbs of emotion

avere paura	*to be afraid*
temere	*to fear*
arrabbiarsi	*to get angry*
essere contento	*to be happy*
essere triste	*to be sad*
essere sorpreso	*to be surprised*
dispiacersi	*to be sorry*

Ho paura che i ragazzi si perdano.
I'm afraid the boys may get lost.

Mi dispiace che Lei parta cosí presto.
I am sorry you are leaving so soon.

Sono sorpreso che ci siano tutti.
I am surprised that everyone is here.

With verbs expressing commands

comandare	*to command, to order*
esigere	*to demand*
ordinare	*to order, to command*
pretendere	*to demand*
richiedere	*to require, to demand*

Pietro esige che tutto sia pronto.
Peter demands that everything be ready.

Il maestro richiede che tutti facciano i compiti.
The teacher requires that all do their homework.

With verbs showing permission or refusal of permission

lasciare	*to let*
consentire	*to allow, to permit*
permettere	*to permit, to allow*
proibire	*to forbid*

Questi genitori lasciano che i bambini giochino fuori.
These parents let their children play outside.

Io proibisco che voi arriviate tardi.
I forbid you to arrive late.

160. *Complete the following with the appropriate subjunctive forms of each of the indicated verbs:*

1. Voglio che voi_____.   *parlare, partire, cenare, dormire, credere, venire, salire, studiare*
2. Preferiscono che tu_____.   *tornare, uscire, venire, scrivere, lavorare, scendere, parlare, dormire*
3. Hai paura che io_____.   *cantare, parlare, dormire, uscire, partire, ridere, credere, avere ragione*
4. Perché ordini che loro_____?   *uscire, tornare, mangiare, salire, partire, cantare, studiare dormire*

161. *Rewrite the following according to the model:*

Voglio che: Tu stai qui. —→ Voglio che ti stia qui.
Voglio che:

1. Loro vengono alle nove.
2. Tu scrivi una lettera.
3. Voi parlate ad alta voce.
4. Pietro dice la verità.
5. Noi partiamo presto.
6. Lui lo sa.

Ordiniamo che:

7. Tu vai in biblioteca.
8. Voi dite la verità.
9. Loro comprano i libri necessari.
10. Luigi rimane a casa.
11. Tu sai la lezione.
12. Voi traducete la lettura.

Mi dispiace che:

13. Voi siete tristi.
14. Pietro non può venire.
15. Tu scrivi cosí male.
16. Loro hanno molti problemi.
17. Nevica molto.
18. Voi partecipate poco.

Tu insisti che:

19. Io parto domani.
20. I bambini dọrmono.
21. Luịsa va a casa.

22. Noi studiạmo
23. Loro ạprono le finestre.
24. Io so la lezịone.

162. *Complete the following sentences with the appropriate forms of the indicated verbs:*

1. Sperịamo che voi _____ quị.   *restare*
2. Ho paụra che Carlo _____ presto.   *partire*
3. Insịstono che tu _____ in uffịcio.   *venire*
4. Proịbisco che i bambini _____ fuọri.   *uscire*
5. Vuọle che noi _____ tutto.   *sapere*
6. Sperịamo che vọi _____ alle otto.   *arrivare*
7. I signori nẹgano che i loro amici _____ l'accaduto.   *sapere*
8. Mi dispịace che Pịetro _____ malato.   *ẹssere*
9. Pạolo consente che tu _____ a vederlo.   *andare*
10. Esigịamo che Loro ci _____ i libri.   *riportare*

Subjunctive with impersonal expressions

The subjunctive is also used after many impersonal expressions that denote an element of subjectivity. Some common impersonal expressions that require use of the subjunctive follow:

è mẹglio che …	*it is better that …*
è necessạrio che …	*it is necessary that …*
bisogna che …	*it is necessary that …*
convịene che …	*it is fitting that …*
basta che …	*it suffices that …*
è giụsto che …	*it is right that …*
è possịbile che …	*it is possible that …*
è impossịbile che …	*it is impossible that …*
è probạbile che …	*it is probable that …*
si dụbita che …	*it is doubtful that …*
importa che …	*it matters that …*
non importa che …	*it doesn't matter that …*
è importante che…	*it is important that …*
è peccato che …	*it is a pity that …*
è raro che …	*it is rare that …*
è fạcile che …	*it is easy that …*
è diffịcile che …	*it is difficult that …*
sorprende che …	*it is surprising that …*
è essenzịale che …	*it is essential that …*
è di prassi che …	*it is pragmatic that …*

Non importa che arrịvino tardi.
It doesn't matter that they arrive late.

È giụsto che voi scrivịate ogni tanto.
It is right that you write once in a while.

È essenzịale che io parta il piú presto possịbile.
It is essential that I leave as soon as possible.

È probạbile che nẹvichi fra non molto.
It's probable that it will snow before long.

È peccato che tu sịa quạsi sempre malato.
It's a pity that you are almost always ill.

163. Complete the following sentences with the appropriate present subjunctive forms of each of the indicated verbs:

1. È possịbile che lui lo_____. *preparare, ricẹvere, lẹggere, scrịvere, finire, cercare, pagare, sapere*

2. È difficile che voi lo_____. *incontrare, conọscere, ricẹvere, trovare, sapere, fare, avere, cercare*

3. È necessạrio che tu lo_____. *fare, portare, descrịvere, dire, sapere, ottenere, preparare, finire*

4. È probạbile che io_____. *venire, salire, partire, uscire, lẹggere, tradurre, sciạre, sbagliạre*

5. È raro che loro lo_____. *preparare, portare, finire, cercare, pagare, crẹdere, dire, mandare*

164. Introduce each of the following with the indicated expression, making all appropriate changes:

1. Io ricevo certe lẹttere.　　*È importante*
2. Pagate il conto.　　　　　 *È giụsto*
3. Ritọrnano tardi.　　　　　 *È probạbile*
4. Riporta i libri.　　　　　　*Bisogna*
5. Uscịamo presto.　　　　　 *È mẹglio*

6. Parto subito.　　　　　　　*È impossịbile*
7. Tu finisci la lẹttura.　　　　*Non importa*
8. Paọlo stụdia molto.　　　　*È necessạrio*
9. Voi potete partecipare.　　 *Sperịamo*
10. Loro fanno i bravi.　　　　 *Convịene*

With expressions of doubt

The present indicative is used with expressions such as the following when they imply certainty:

crẹdere	*to believe*
pensare	*to think*
è certo che …	*it is certain that …*
è sicuro che …	*it is sure that …*
non si dụbita che…	*it is not doubtful that…*
non c' è dụbbio che …	*there is no doubt that …*
si crede che …	*it is believed that …*

The present subjunctive is used in the negative and interrogative forms of the above expressions, however, since uncertainty is implied. Study the following:

Indicative
Credo che loro sono qui.
I believe they are here.

Non dụbito che lo sa.
I don't doubt that he knows

È sicuro che vịene.
He is (It is) sure he is coming.

Tu pensi che arrịvano tardi.
You think they (will) arrive late.

Subjunctive
Non credo che loro sịano qui.
I don't think they are here.

Dụbito che lui lo sạppia.
I doubt that he knows.

Non è sicuro che venga.
He is not sure he is coming.

Pensi che arrịvịno tardi?
Do you think they may arrive late?

165. Complete the following with the appropriate forms of each of the indicated verbs:

1. Credo che loro_____. *ẹssere qui, arrivare presto, uscire insịeme, fare i compiti*
2. Non credo che voi_____. *fare i buọni, portare i libri, finire la lezịone, sapere l'indirizzo, cenare quị, lẹggere molto, avere pazịenza, partire presto*

166. Give the Italian equivalents of the following sentences.
1. They are sure they are coming at three.
2. She is not sure they are coming today.
3. Do you (voi) believe your brother arrives late?
4. We do not doubt that you (Loro) are sincere.
5. Do you (tu) believe that Paolo knows it?

167. Complete the following with the correct form of the indicated verb:
1. È certo che loro_____a casa adesso.   *essere* [There is no doubt]
2. Non è sicuro che voi_____ragione.   *avere*
3. Credo che tu_____sciare.   *sapere* [I actually believe]
4. Non pensi che io_____guidare?   *potere*
5. Dubitiamo che Roberto_____in Italia.   *andare*
6. Credono che noi_____la città.   *conoscere*

With subordinate conjunctions
The following subordinate conjunctions require the present subjunctive:

prima che	*before*
finché (non)	*until*
senza che	*without*
nonostante che	*although, even though*
a patto che	*provided that*
purché	*provided that*
malgrado	*although*
in modo che	*so that*
affinché	*in order that*
cosí che	*so that*
a meno che (non)	*unless*
posto che	*supposing that*
supposto che	*supposing that*
benché	*although*
sebbene	*although*

With indefinite pronouns and adjectives

quantunque	*although*
chiunque	*whoever*
dovunque	*wherever*
ovunque	*wherever*
qualunque	*whatever*

168. Complete the following sentences with the correct forms of the indicated expressions:
1. Sebbene voi_____,   io suono la chitarra. *leggere, studiare, dormire, fare i compiti, scrivere una lettera, avere un mal di testa, essere malati, non ascoltare*
2. Prima che loro _____,   voglio saperlo. *arrivare, finire, telefonare, chiamare, bussare, uscire, salire, dormire*
3. Chiunque_____, non m'interessa.   *scrivere, venire, bussare, parlare, telefonare, cantare, arrivare, uscire*
4. Devo partire nonostante che io_____.   *essere stanco, avere la febbre, non volere, non potere*

169. Complete the following sentences with the correct forms of the indicated verbs:

1. Benché_____tardi, devo uscire.   *essere*
2. Prima che Luisa_____, voglio vederla.   *partire*
3. A meno che non_____bel tempo, non usciamo affatto.   *fare*
4. Roberto vuole comprare un'automobile senza che_____i soldi.   *avere*
5. Venite presto affinché_____finire.   *potere*
6. I turisti vogliono che_____accompagnati da un interprete.   *essere*

As a command

The present subjunctive may function as an indirect command:

Che venga qui immediatamente!
Let him (her) come here immediately!

Che se ne vada in pace!
Let him (her) go away in peace!

Viva il presidente!
Long live the president!

Che sia cosí!
So be it! (Let it be!)

170. Change the sentences according to the model:

Viene alle due. ⟶ Che venga alle due!
He is coming at two o'clock. → He should come (must come) at two o'clock!

1. Parla con me.   5. Legge il romanzo.
2. Partono presto.   6. Scrivono molto.
3. Finisce la lettura.   7. Scia cautamente.
4. Portano i regali.   8. Sanno la domanda.

Present Subjunctive in Relative Clauses

Indefinite antecedent

The present subjunctive is used in relative clauses when the antecedent (the word the clause modifies) is indefinite. If the antecedent is definite, the present indicative is used. Observe the following:

Conosco un dottore che parla italiano.
I know a doctor who speaks Italian.

Ho bisogno di un dottore che parli italiano.
I need a doctor who speaks Italian. (I don't know one yet.)

Conosco una segretaria che sa l'italiano.
I know a secretary who knows Italian.

Cerco una segretaria che sappia l'italiano.
I'm looking for a secretary who knows Italian. (I haven't found one yet.)

171. Complete the following with the appropriate forms of the indicated expressions:

1. Conosco una segretaria che_____.   *parlare italiano, scrivere bene, sapere formattare (to format) i documenti.*

2. Ho bisogno di una segretaria che _____.   *parlare italiano, scrivere bene, sapere usare l'elaboratore (word processor).*

172. Rewrite the following according to the models:

Conosco un giovane. Sa l'inglese. —→ Conosco un giovane che sa l'inglese.
Ho bisogno di una maestra. Sa l'italiano. —→ Ho bisogno di una maestra che sappia l'italiano.

1. Cerco un segretario. Sa creare un sito web (to create a web site).
2. Ho una camicia. Va bene con il vestito.
3. Voglio comprare una cravatta. Va bene con la camicia.
4. Abbiamo bisogno di un dottore. Abita vicino.
5. Hai una macchina. È meravigliosa.
6. Cerco un lavoro. È interessante.

173. Complete the following with the appropriate forms of the indicated verbs:

1. Conosco un ragazzo che_____bene a tennis.   *giocare*
2. Cerchiamo un negozio che_____prodotti italiani.   *avere*
3. Roberto ha bisogno di un tassí che lo_____all'aeroporto.   *portare*
4. Abbiamo una casa che_____due piani.   *avere*
5. Conosco molti studenti che_____sempre.   *studiare*
6. Cerco una persona che_____darmi alcune informazioni.   *potere*
7. Abbiamo bisogno di alcune signorine che_____cantare.   *sapere*
8. Ho un cane che_____di notte.   *abbaiare* (to bark)

With relative superlatives

The present subjunctive is also used in a relative clause that modifies a relative superlative expression since the superlative expression is considered to be an exaggeration. (Review the relative superlative on page 63.)

È la professoressa piú intelligente che io conosca.
She is the most intelligent teacher I know.

È l'orologio piú antico che esista.
It is the oldest watch in existence (that exists).

174. Complete the following with the appropriate forms of the indicated verbs:

1. È il migliore studente che io_____.   *conoscere*
2. Tokyo è la città piú popolata che_____.   *esistere*
3. È il peggiore dizionario che voi_____.   *avere*
4. Paolo è la persona meno simpatica che loro_____. *conoscere*
5. Questo è il piú bel parco che ci_____in questa città. *essere*

With solo and unico

The present subjunctive is used in relative clauses after the expressions **il solo, la sola, i soli**, and **le sole**, and **l'unico, l'unica, gli unici**, and **le uniche**. (Note that when they are used in this context, **solo** and **unico** must be preceded by the appropriate definite article.)

È il solo giocatore brasiliano che abbiano nella squadra.
He is the only Brazilian player they have on the team.

Sono gli unici studenti che partecipino in classe.
They are the only students who participate in class.

175. Complete the following with the appropriate forms of the indicated verbs:

1. Anna è l'unica ragazza che io_____per telefono.   *chiamare*
2. Questa è la sola lezione che tu_____.   *capire*
3. Quelli sono gli unici turisti che_____dall'Italia.   *venire*
4. Questo è il solo dizionario che io_____.   *avere*
5. Questo è l'unico vestito che mi_____.   *piacere*

With negative expressions

The present subjunctive is also used in a clause that modifies a negative word or expression. As with superlatives, the statement is considered to be an unrealistic exaggeration. Observe the following:

> **Non c'è nessuno che lo sappia.**
> *There is no one who knows it.*

> **Non c'è niente che valga qualcosa.**
> *There is nothing worth anything.*

176. Complete the following with the appropriate forms of the indicated verbs:
1. Non c'è nessuno che ci_____.   *aiutare*
2. Non c'è niente che_____disturbare Roberto.   *potere*
3. Non c'è nessun negozio che_____vestiti a buon mercato.   *vendere*
4. Sei pessimista; in questo mondo non c'è niente che ti_____un po' di fiducia. *dare*
5. Non c'è nessun posto che_____a Stefano.   *piacere*

Replacing the Present Subjunctive with an Infinitive Construction

When the subject of the dependent clause is the same as that of the main clause, the infinitive is used. Observe the following:

> **Roberto spera di venire.** *Robert hopes to come.*
> **Siete contenti di poter(e) riposare.** *You are happy about being able to relax.*

The infinitive construction may also be used after verbs denoting command, permission, refusal, and suggestion (see pages 158–163). The subjunctive clause may be replaced by an indirect object preceded by **a** and followed by an infinitive introduced by **di**. Observe the following:

> **Non permetto che mio figlio fumi.**
> **Non permetto a mio figlio di fumare.**
> *I don't allow my son to smoke.*

When the indirect object is replaced by a pronoun, **a** is not used.

> **Vi suggerisco che arriviate presto.**
> **Vi suggerisco di arrivare presto.**
> *I suggest that you arrive early.*

177. Translate the following sentences using the infinitive construction as explained above:
1. They are happy to be here.
2. Antonio hopes to pass the exams.
3. You (tu) suggest that she arrive early?
4. They allow me to play tennis with them.
5. Boys, I suggest that you finish the homework.
6. My father does not allow me to smoke.

PRESENT PERFECT SUBJUNCTIVE (CONGIUNTIVO PASSATO)

The present perfect subjunctive is formed by using the present subjunctive of the auxiliary verbs **avere** or **essere** and the past participle of the acting verb. (Review the past participle on pages 138–143 and the uses of **avere** and **essere** on pages 141 and 142.) Observe the following:

	parlare	**andare**
che io	abbia parlato	sia andato(-a)
che tu	abbia parlato	sia andato(-a)

che lui, lei, Lei	ạbbia parlato	sịa andato(-a)
che noi	abbiạmo parlato	siạmo andati(-e)
che voi	abbiạte parlato	siạte andati(-e)
che loro, Loro	ạbbiano ciarlato	sịano andati(-e)

The present perfect subjunctive is used when a present indicative or future verb in a main clause governs a verb requiring the subjunctive which refers to a past action in a dependent clause:

Main Clause   **Dependent Clause**
Present Indicative   > *Present Perfect Subjunctive*

Non credo che sịano andati in Itạlia.
I don't believe (that) they went to Italy.

Mi dispiạce che lui ạbbia parlato cosí.
I'm sorry (that) he spoke that way.

Speriạmo che ạbbia superato gli esami.
We hope (that) he/she passed the exams.

Dụbiti che io sịa riuscito a vịncere?
Do you doubt (that) I managed to win?

178. *Complete the following with the appropriate forms of the present perfect subjunctive of the indicated verb:*

1. Sono contento che Loro_____.   *arrivare*
2. È possịbile che Pạolo non ti_____la verità.   *dire*
3. Abbiạmo paụra che voi_____il segreto.   *svelare* (to reveal)
4. Non credo che tu_____malato.   *ẹssere*
5. Pensi che io non_____i compiti?   *finire*
6. È impossịbile che loro non_____niẹnte.   *vedere*

179. *Rewrite the following placing the action of the dependent clause from the present subjunctive to the present perfect subjunctive.*

1. Dụbito che voi capiạte. _____
2. Spero che Luịgi arrivi presto. _____
3. È impossibile che tu legga tanto. _____
4. Non crediạmo che loro (f.) vẹngano. _____
5. Ha paụra che io sbagli strada. _____
6. Pensi che Isa sịa ammalata? _____

180. *Rewrite the following placing the action of the dependent clause from the present perfect subjunctive to the present subjunctive.*

1. Abbiạmo paụra che Luịgi non si sịa laureạto. _____
2. È probạbile che Silvana ạbbia smesso d'insegnare. _____
3. Hai paụra che io non mi sịa scusato? _____
4. Hanno l'impressiọne che voi abbiạte giocato troppo. _____
5. Non so se lei sịa tornata oggi. _____
6. Pẹnsano che Lei ạbbia voluto scherzare. _____

IMPERFECT SUBJUNCTIVE (IMPERFETTO DEL CONGIUNTIVO)

The imperfect subjunctive is used in sentences with main-clause verbs requiring the subjunctive mood and when the verb of the main clause is in a past indicative tense or the conditional. Note the following sequence of tenses:

Main clause	Dependent Clause	
Imperfect indicative	Imperfect Subjunctive	**Volevo che tu lo facessi.**
		I wanted you to do it.
Preterite		**Volli che tu lo facessi.**
		I wanted you to do it.
Present Perfect		**Ho voluto che tu lo facessi.**
		I wanted you to do it.
Conditional		**Vorrei che tu lo facessi.**
		I would want you to do it.

Formation of the Imperfect Subjunctive

Regular verbs

The imperfect subjunctive of regular **-are** verbs is formed by dropping the infinitive ending and adding to the root the following personal endings: **-assi, -assi, -asse, -assimo, -aste, -assero.** Observe the following:

Infinitive:	**cantare**	**parlare**	**tornare**
Root:	**cant-**	**parl-**	**torn-**
che io	cantassi	partassi	tornassi
che tu	cantassi	parlassi	tornassi
che lui, lei, Lei	cantasse	parlasse	tornasse
che noi	cantassimo	parlassimo	tornassimo
che voi	cantaste	parlaste	tornaste
che loro, Loro	cantassero	parlassero	tornassero

The imperfect subjunctive of regular **-ere** verbs is formed by dropping the infinitive ending and adding to the root the following personal endings: **-essi, -essi, -esse, -essimo, -este, -essero.** Study the following:

Infinitive:	**credere**	**vedere**	**sapere**
Root:	**cred-**	**ved-**	**sap-**
che io	credessi	vedessi	sapessi
che tu	credessi	vedessi	sapessi
che lui, lei, Lei	credesse	vedesse	sapesse
che noi	credessimo	vedessimo	sapessimo
che voi	credeste	vedeste	sapeste
che loro, Loro	credessero	vedessero	sapessero

The imperfect subjunctive of **-ire** verbs is formed by dropping the infinitive ending and adding to the root the following personal endings: **-issi, -issi, -isse, -issimo, -iste, -issero** Note that there are no irregular **-ire** verbs in the imperfect subjunctive. Observe the following:

Infinitive:	**capire**	**finire**	**venire**
Root:	**cap-**	**fin-**	**ven-**
che io	capissi	finissi	venissi
che tu	capissi	finissi	venissi
che lui, lei	capisse	finisse	venisse
che noi	capissimo	finissimo	venissimo
che voi	capiste	finiste	veniste
che loro, Loro	capissero	finissero	venissero

Irregular verbs

Very few verbs are irregular in the imperfect subjunctive, and most of the verbs that appear to be irregular simply return to their original old Italian or Latin infinitives to form the root for the imperfect subjunctive. Study the following:

Infinitive	Old Form	Root	Imperfect Subjunctive
bere	(*bevere*)	**bev-**	**che io bevessi,** etc.

dire	*(dícĕre)*	dic-	**che io dicessi,** etc.
fare	*(fācĕre)*	fac-	**che io facessi,** etc.
condurre	*(condūcĕre)*	conduc-	**che io conducessi,** etc.
tradurre	*(tradūcĕre)*	traduc-	**che io traducessi,** etc.
trarre	*(trahĕre)*	tra-	**che io traęssi,** etc.

Ẹssere

The verb **ẹssere** is irregular in all forms in the imperfect subjunctive. Study the following:

Infinitive:	**ẹssere**
che io	fossi
che tu	fossi
che lui/lei/Lei	fosse
che noi	fọssimo
che voi	foste
che loro/Loro	fọssero

Dare, stare

The verbs **dare** and **stare** are also irregular in all forms in the imperfect subjunctive. Study the following:

Infinitive:	**dare**	**stare**
che io	dessi	stessi
che tu	dessi	stessi
che lui/lei/Lei	desse	stesse
che noi	dẹssimo	stẹssimo
che voi	deste	steste
che loro/Loro	dẹssero	stẹssero

Uses of the Imperfect Subjunctive

In noun clauses

The same noun clauses that require the present subjunctive (page 154) require the imperfect subjunctive when the verb of the main clause is in the imperfect indicative, preterite, present perfect (conversational past) or conditional.

> **Non volevo che tu lo facessi cosí presto.**
> *I didn't want you to do it so soon.*

> **Luigi suggerí che Olga partisse.**
> *Louis suggested that Olga should leave.*

> **Ho voluto che i bambini dormịssero.**
> *I wanted the children to sleep.*

> **Vorrẹbbero che io raccontassi una stọria.**
> *They would like me to tell a story.*

181. Complete the following with the appropriate forms of each of the indicated verbs:

1. I genitori volẹvano che i figli _____. *studiare, dire la verità, partire, tornare, dormire, fare i compiti*

2. Roberto ha proibito che noi_____. *sciare, tradurre, uscire, cantare, venire, ẹssere in ritardo, ripẹtere la domanda, bere troppo,*

3. Suggerirei che tu_____. *tornare, partire, studiạre, cenare, finire il lavoro, lẹggere, scrịvere, dormire*

4. Era necessario che Luigi lo_____.   *capire, sapere, scrivere, dire, fare*
5. Io preferirei che voi lo_____.   *guardare, spiegare, vendere, finire, dire, fare*

182. Complete the following with the appropriate forms of the indicated verbs:

1. Lui ordinò che io_____immediatamente.   *finire*
2. Tu non volevi che loro_____in Italia.   *andare*
3. Preferirei che voi_____alle sette.   *tornare*
4. Hanno insistito che tu lo_____.   *scrivere*
5. Volevo che Antonio_____la verità.   *dire*
6. Roberto e Carlo speravano che io_____bene. *stare*

183. Introduce the following statements with the indicated expressions:

1. Parliamo italiano.   *Insisteva che*
2. Tu non lo compri.   *Avevano paura che*
3. Voi partite.   *Voleva che*
4. Io lo so.   *Preferivi che*
5. Carlo arriva alle sei.   *Speravamo che*

184. Rewrite the following changing the main verbs to the imperfect indicative. Make all necessary changes:

1. Vogliono che usciamo con loro.
2. Proibiscono che io fumi.
3. Spera che voi finiate il lavoro.
4. Ho paura che tu abbia ragione.
5. Insisti che io lo faccia.

With impersonal expressions

The imperfect subjunctive is used after impersonal expressions that demand the subjunctive when the main verb is in the imperfect indicative, preterite, present perfect (conversational past), or conditional tense.

Era impossibile che io fossi presente.
It was impossible for me to be present.

Fu necessario che tu tornassi presto.
It was necessary for you to return soon.

È stato difficile che loro finissero il lavoro.
It was difficult for them to finish their work.

Sarebbe meglio che io andassi a casa.
It would be better for me to go home.

185. Complete the following with the appropriate forms of the indicated verbs:

1. Era certo che noi_____.   *vincere*
2. È stato impossibile che loro_____. *finire*
3. Sarebbe difficile che tu_____presto. *partire*
4. Fu necessario che lei_____.   *studiare*
5. Era meglio che voi_____ gli zii.   *visitare*
6. Sarebbe piú facile che io_____l'autobus. *prendere*

In relative clauses

The imperfect subjunctive is used in relative clauses modifying an indefinite antecedent when the verb of the main clause is in the imperfect indicative, preterite, conversational past, or conditional tense.

Cercavo una segretaria che parlasse italiano.
I was looking for a secretary who spoke Italian.

Ovunque guardassi, non ho visto ciò che volevo.
Wherever I looked, I didn't see what I wanted.

Preferirei un dottore che fosse anche chirurgo.
I would prefer a doctor who was also a surgeon.

186. *Complete the following with the appropriate forms of the indicated verbs:*

1. Cercavamo un amico che_____a carte.   *giocare*
2. Vorrei un dizionario che_____vocaboli tecnici.   *avere*
3. Cercavo un negozio che_____scarpe italiane.   *vendere*
4. Non avevamo neanche un amico che ci_____aiutare.   *potere*
5. Avevate bisogno di una casa che_____ in campagna.   *essere*
6. Preferiresti un fotografo che_____molta pazienza.   *avere*
7. Volevo una macchina che_____piccola ma comoda.   *essere*
8. Ho avuto bisogno di una cinepresa che_____economica.   *essere*

With expressions contrary to fact or unlikely

The imperfect subjunctive is used in expressions contrary to fact or unlikely to happen. In these cases the imperfect subjunctive is often preceded by the adverbs **magari**, **pure**, **se solo**, etc.

Magari vincessi un milione di dollari!
Would that I could win a million dollars!

Se solo dicessero la verità!
If they would only tell the truth!

Vincessimo pure!
If we would indeed win!

Avessi la tua fortuna!
I wish I had your luck!

187. *Rewrite the following in the appropriate subjunctive forms by using the indicated adverbs, when given:*

1. (noi) arrivare in tempo!   *magari*
2. (loro) continuare a studiare!   *se solo*
3. (io) essere fortunato (-a)!
4. (loro) telefonare!   *pure*
5. venire i nostri amici!   *se solo*
6. smettere di piovere!   *magari*

With adverbial expressions

The imperfect subjunctive is used after adverbial expressions if the main clause is in the imperfect indicative, preterite, conversational past, or conditional tense. (For a list of adverbial expressions, see page 162.)

Ho creduto tutto senza che fosse vero.
I believed everything without its being true.

Benché avessi fretta, restai con gli amici.
Although I was in a hurry, I stayed with my friends.

Lo farei viaggiare da solo a patto che fosse cauto.
I would let him travel alone provided that he were cautious.

188. *Complete the following with the appropriate forms of the indicated verbs:*

1. Malgrado Rosa_____molto, non parlava mai.   *sapere*
2. Gli telefonerei affinché lui_____qui.   *venire*
3. Abbiamo svolto il tema sebbene_____difficile.   *essere*

4. I bambini potẹvano restare purché non_____. *gridare*
5. Fu fạcile riconọscerlo benché_____lontano. *ẹssere*
6. Partiremmo volentiẹri malgrado_____cattivo tempo. *fare*
7. Nonostante che_____, uscịrono senza ombrello. *piọvere*
8. La salutavạmo senza che le_____. *parlare*

To express hypothetical in the past

When speculating *in the present* about whether or not an action happened *in the past,* the imperfect subjunctive is used in the dependent clause even though the main verb of the sentence is in the present indicative.

Crediạmo che vendẹssero scarpe.
We believe (that) they sold shoes.

Dụbito che Roberto fosse cattivo.
I doubt (that) Robert was bad.

Non so se fọssero italiani.
I don't know if they were Italian.

189. *Complete the following with the appropriate forms of the imperfect subjunctive of each of the indicated verb phrases:*

1. Non so se loro_____. *studiạre, partire per l'Itạlia, lẹggere molto, ẹssere bravi, avere soldi, lavorare poco*
2. Dubitiạmo che tu_____. *potere sciạre, sapere guidare, andare a scuọla, avere paziẹnza, stare a casa, giocare a tennis, lavorare, lẹggere*

PLUPERFECT SUBJUNCTIVE (CONGIUNTIVO TRAPASSATO)

The pluperfect subjunctive is formed by using the imperfect subjunctive of the auxiliaries **avere** or **ẹssere** and the past participle of the acting verb. (See pages 138–143 for lists of past participles.)

Formation of the pluperfect subjunctive

With avere

Conjugation:	-are	-ere	-ire
Infinitive:	**comprare**	**ripetere**	**finire**
che io	avessi comprato	avessi ripetuto	avessi finito
che tu	avessi comprato	avessi ripetuto	avessi finito
che lui, lei, Lei	avesse comprato	avesse ripetuto	avesse finito
che noi	avẹssimo comprato	avẹssimo ripetuto	avẹssimo finito
che voi	aveste comprato	aveste ripetuto	aveste finito
che loro, Loro	avẹssero comprato	avẹssero ripetuto	avẹssero finito

With ẹssere

Conjugation:	-are	-ere	-ire
Infinitive:	**andare**	**cadere**	**salire**
che io	fossi andato(-a)	fossi caduto(-a)	fossi salito(-a)
che tu	fossi andato(-a)	fossi caduto(-a)	fossi salito(-a)
che lui, lei, Lei	fosse andato(-a)	fosse caduto(-a)	fosse salito(-a)
che noi	fọssimo andati(-e)	fọssimo caduti(-e)	fọssimo saliti(-e)
che voi	foste andati(-e)	foste caduti(-e)	foste saliti(-e)
che loro, Loro	fọssero andati(-e)	fọssero caduti(-e)	fọssero saliti (-e)

The pluperfect subjunctive is used in clauses which require the subjunctive when the main verb is in a past tense and the action of the verb of the dependent clause was completed prior to that of the governing verb.

Credeva che fọssimo arrivati ieri.
He thought we had arrived yesterday.

Non ho creduto che avẹssero detto tali cose.
I didn't believe they had said such things.

Avrebbe preferito che tu gli avessi scritto prima.
He would have preferred that you had written him before.

190. Complete the following with the appropriate pluperfect subjunctive forms of the indicated verbs:
    1. Avevo preferito che loro_____alle tre.   *arrivare*
    2. Luịgi ha creduto che noi_____i cọmpiti.   *finire*
    3. Tu volevi che io_____il telefonino.   *portare*
    4. Avremmo preferito che voi_____insiẹme.   *partire*
    5. Avrei avuto paụra che tu_____un incidente.   *avere*
    6. Era contento che tutti_____un viạggio in Itạlia. *fare*
    7. Credevo che voi_____la verità.   *dire*
    8. Avrei preferito che lei_____piú presto.   *uscire*

Se clauses

Se (*if*) clauses are usually used to express contrary-to-fact or uncertain conditions. For such clauses there is a specific sequence of tenses to be followed. Observe the following:

Vado in Itạlia se ho il denaro.
I'm going to Italy if I have the money.

Andrò in Itạlia se avrò il denaro.
I'll go to Italy if I have the money.

Andrei in Itạlia se avessi il denaro.
I would go to Italy if I had the money.

Sarei andato in Itạlia se avessi avuto il denaro.
I would have gone to Italy if I had had the money.

The regular sequence of tenses for contrary-to-fact or uncertain statements with **se** is as follows:

Main Clause	*Se Clause*
Present Indicative	⟶ Present Indicative
Future	⟶ Future
Conditional (Present)	⟶ Imperfect Subjunctive
Conditional Perfect	⟶ Pluperfect Subjunctive

Note that the only forms of the subjunctive that may be used after **se** are the imperfect or the pluperfect subjunctive. The present subjunctive is never used after **se**. After **se**, never use the present conditional or past conditional.

191. Complete the following with the appropriate forms of the indicated verbs according to the regular sequence of tenses:
    1. Se_____abbastanza tempo, andranno in Europa. *avere*
    2. Avremmo lavorato fino a tardi se ci_____piú lavoro. *ẹssere*
    3. Se_____bel tempo, andremmo alla spiạggia.   *fare*
    4. Se_____adesso, arriveremo alle cịnque.   *partire*
    5. Se_____ricco, girerẹi il mondo.   *ẹssere*
    6. Li avrebbe salutati se li_____.   *vedere*

REVIEW

192. Complete the following with the appropriate forms of the indicated verbs:

1. Sono contento che voi_____qui.　　　　　　　*essere*
2. Benché Stefano_____, è un bravo studente.　　*sbagliare*
3. Vogliamo che tu_____questo progetto.　　　　*finire*
4. Non c'è niente che ci_____.　　　　　　　　*piacere*
5. Desiderano che noi non_____.　　　　　　　*fumare*
6. Magari _____bel tempo!　　　　　　　　　*fare*
7. Se loro _____adesso, usciremo insieme.　　　*venire*
8. Antonio voleva che io_____alle otto.　　　　*partire*
9. Puoi restare qui purché_____zitto.　　　　　*stare*
10. Preferirei che voi_____in tempo.　　　　　*arrivare*

IMPERATIVE (*IMPERATIVO*)

Formal Commands

The formal commands are formed by using the subjunctive form of the verb. Note that the vowel of the subjunctive ending is **-i** for **-are** verbs and **-a** for -**ere** and -**ire** verbs. Also note that the formal pronouns **Lei** and **Loro** are usually omitted with the commands. An exclamation mark usually follows the command forms.

Infinitive	*Singular* (**Lei**)	*Plural* (**Loro**)
parlare	Parli!	Parlino!
cantare	Canti!	Cantino!
vendere	Venda!	Vendano!
scrivere	Scriva!	Scrivano!
dormire	Dorma!	Dormano!
partire	Parta!	Partano!
finire	Finisca!	Finiscano!
pulire	Pulisca!	Puliscano!

You Formal Singular: Lei

Signora Perrone, per favore, parli Lei!
Maestro Pavarotti, per cortesia, canti Lei!
Professore, scriva la lettera Lei!
Signore (m.), mi venda l'auto Lei!
Signor delegato, finisca Lei il discorso!
Signora Lari, per cortesia, adesso parta Lei!

You Formal Plural: Loro

Signori De Lena, per piacere, parlino Loro!
Signore (f.), per cortesia, cantino Loro!
Professori, scrivano le lettere Loro!
Signori, ci vendano le auto Loro!
Signori delegati, finiscano Loro i discorsi!
Signorine, per piacere, adesso partano Loro!

The first-person singular of the present indicative serves as the root for the formation of the formal commands. The final **-o** is changed to **-i** (**Lei**) and **-ino** (**Loro**) for **-are** verbs and to **-a** (**Lei**) and **-ano** (**Loro**) for -**ere** and -**ire** verbs. Study the following formal command forms of stem-changing and irregular verbs:

Formal Commands

Infinitive	*Present* (**io**)	*Singular* (**Lei**)	*Plural* (**Loro**)
sedere	siedo	Sieda!	Siedano!
sonare	suono	Suoni!	Suonino!
udire	odo	Oda!	Odano!
uscire	esco	Esca!	Escano!
apparire	appaio	Appaia!	Appaiano!
porre	pongo	Ponga!	Pongano!
rimanere	rimango	Rimanga!	Rimangano!
salire	salgo	Salga!	Salgano!
trarre	traggo	Tragga!	Traggano!

venire	vengo	Venga!	Vengano!
cogliere	colgo	Colga!	Colgano!
scegliere	scelgo	Scelga!	Scelgano!
bere	bevo	Beva!	Bevano!
dire	dico	Dica!	Dicano!
tradurre	traduco	Traduca!	Traducano!
fare	faccio	Faccia!	Facciano!
andare	vado	Vada!	Vadano!

The following verbs have completely irregular formal command forms:

Formal Commands

Infinitive	Singular (Lei)	Plural (Loro)
avere	Abbia!	Abbiano!
sapere	Sappia!	Sappiano!
essere	Sia!	Siano!
dare	Dia!	Diano!
stare	Stia!	Stiano!

Note that the same form of the verb is used for the negative formal commands.

Non parli!	Non parlino!
Non scriva!	Non scrivano!
Non parta!	Non partano!
Non finisca!	Non finiscano!
Non cuocia!	Non cuociano!
Non salga!	Non salgano!

193. Answer the following questions according to the model:

> Parlo? —→ Sí, parli!
>   —→ No, non parli!

1. Dormo?
2. Scrivo?
3. Ritorno?
4. Rispondo?
5. Arrivo presto?
6. Credo a tutto?
7. Ballo?
8. Leggo?
9. Guardo la televisione?
10. Vedo il film?

194. Answer the following questions according to the model:

> Dormiamo? —→ Sí, dormano!
>   —→ No, non dormano!

1. Parliamo?
2. Scriviamo le lettere?
3. Leggiamo la rivista?
4. Chiudiamo la finestra?
5. Compriamo i libri?
6. Guardiamo lo spettacolo?
7. Dividiamo i regali?
8. Partiamo alle otto?

9. Mandiamo il pacco?

10. Prepariamo il tè?

Familiar commands

Affirmative of regular verbs

The familiar singular (**tu**) command of regular **-are** verbs is the same as the third-person singular (**Lei**) form of the present indicative. The plural **voi** command is the same as the **voi** form of the present indicative.

Infinitive	Singular (**tu**)	Plural (**voi**)
cantare	Canta!	Cantate!
parlare	Parla!	Parlate!
mangiare	Mangia!	Mangiate!

The familiar commands for regular **-ere** and **-ire** verbs are the same as the **tu** and **voi** forms of the present indicative.

Infinitive	Singular (**tu**)	Plural (**voi**)
vendere	Vendi!	Vendete!
scrivere	Scrivi!	Scrivete!
dormire	Dormi!	Dormite!
salire	Sali!	Salite!
finire	Finisci!	Finite!
pulire	Pulisci!	Pulite!

195. Answer the following in the affirmative with the familiar command according to the model:

Parlo? ⟶ Sí, parla!

1. Canto?
2. Torno?
3. Scio?
4. Cerco?
5. Mangio?

6. Scrivo?
7. Temo?
8. Dormo?
9. Sento?
10. Salgo?

196. Answer the following in the affirmative with the familiar command according to the model:

Parliamo? ⟶ Sí, parlate!

1. Cantiamo?
2. Mangiamo?
3. Torniamo?
4. Sciamo?
5. Pensiamo?

6. Temiamo?
7. Scriviamo?
8. Dormiamo?
9. Sentiamo?
10. Saliamo?

Affirmative of irregular verbs

The following verbs have irregular forms for the familiar commands in the **tu** and **voi** forms:

Infinitive	Familiar Singular (**tu**)	Familiar Plural (**voi**)
andare	Va'! (Vai!)	Andate!
dare	Da'! (Dai!)	Date!
stare	Sta'! (Stai!)	State!
avere	Abbi!	Abbiate!
essere	Sii!	Siate!
dire	Di'!	Dite!
fare	Fa'! (Fai!)	Fate!
sapere	Sappi!	Sappiate!

197. *Answer the following according to the model:*

Andare in fretta? ⟶ **Va' in fretta!**

1. Dare i saluti?
2. Stare attento?
3. Dire la verità?
4. Sapere la risposta?
5. Essere in tempo?
6. Fare i compiti?
7. Avere pronta la lezione?

198. *Answer the following according to the model:*

Essere bravi? ⟶ **Siate bravi!**

1. Fare bene il lavoro?
2. Dire tutto?
3. Sapere i dettagli?
4. Dare il benvenuto?
5. Stare a casa?
6. Avere pazienza?
7. Andare a studiare?

Negative forms

The negative **tu** command forms of all verbs are formed by the infinitive of the verb preceded by **non**. Observe the following:

Infinitive	Affirmative (**tu**)	Negative (**tu**)
cantare	Canta!	Non cantare!
mangiare	Mangia!	Non mangiare!
andare	Va'!	Non andare!
avere	Abbi!	Non avere!
credere	Credi!	Non credere!
dire	Di'!	Non dire!
essere	Sii!	Non essere!
fare	Fa'!	Non fare!
sapere	Sappi !	Non sapere !
dormire	Dormi!	Non dormire!
finire	Finisci!	Non finire!

The negative **voi** command forms of all verbs are formed simply by placing **non** before the affirmative **voi** form. Study the following:

Infinitive	Affirmative (**voi**)	Negative (**voi**)
parlare	parlate!	non parlate!
fare	fate!	non fate!
credere	credete!	non credete!
dormire	dormite!	non dormite!
finire	finite!	non finite!

199. *Answer the following questions with commands according to the model:*

Vado? ⟶ **Sí, va'!**
        No, non andare!

1. Parlo ad alta voce?
2. Preparo il caffè?

3. Rispondo al telefono?
4. Dormo fino a tardi?

5. Suono il piano?   8. Dico la verità?
6. Vengo da solo?   9. Sto a casa?
7. Ho vergogna?   10. Scrivo una lettera?

200. Answer the following questions with commands according to the model:

Andiamo al cinema? ⟶ **Sí, andate al cinema!**
                      ⟶ **No, non andate al cinema!**

1. Torniamo tardi?
2. Ceniamo insieme?
3. Diamo i libri a Mario?
4. Stiamo a casa?
5. Crediamo a tutto?
6. Siamo cattivi?
7. Abbiamo pazienza?
8. Vediamo il film?

201. Change the following familiar commands into formal commands:

1. Canta bene!   6. Credete tutto!
2. Vieni qui!   7. Mangia di meno!
3. Sii buono!   8. Cercate i bambini!
4. Scrivi la lettera!   9. Restituisci i libri!
5. Lavorate di piú!   10. Rimanete qui!

202. Rewrite the following commands in the negative:

1. Venga qui!
2. Vieni qui!
3. Venite qui!
4. Vengano qui!
5. Parla molto!
6. Parli molto!
7. Parlate molto!
8. Parlino molto!
9. Sii buono!
10. Abbia pazienza!

203. Rewrite the following negative commands in the affirmative:

1. Non gridare!
2. Non tagliate il foglio!
3. Non essere pronto!
4. Non vengano insieme!
5. Non dica tutto!
6. Non avere pazienza!

First-Person Commands (let's and let's not)

In order to express the idea *let's,* the first-person plural form (**noi**) of the present indicative is used. Note that, in order to distinguish between the present indicative and the command, an exclamation mark is placed next to the latter.

Let's not is expressed by placing **non** before the command. Observe the following:

Infinitive	Present Indicative		First-Person (noi) Command	
mangiare	mangiamo	*we eat*	Mangiamo!	*Let's eat!*
cantare	non cantiamo	*we don't sing*	Non cantiamo!	*Let's not sing!*
credere	crediamo	*we believe*	Crediamo!	*Let's believe!*
dormire	non dormiamo	*we do not sleep*	Non dormiamo!	*Let's not sleep!*
andare	andiamo	*we go*	Andiamo!	*Let's go!*
stare	stiamo	*we stay*	Stiamo!	*Let's stay!*

204. Follow the model:

Andare in Europa.⟶ **Andiamo in Europa!**
Non tornare a casa.⟶ **Non torniamo a casa!**

1. Cenare in quel ristorante.
2. Non ballare molto.
3. Telefonare a Stefano.
4. Dire la verità.
5. Non uscire tardi.
6. Preparare la valigia.

GERUND (GERUNDIO)

Present Gerund

In Italian, the present gerund of regular **-are** verbs consists of the infinitive verb root plus **-ando**:

Infinitive	Root	Gerund
parlare	**parl-**	parlando
cantare	**cant-**	cantando
mangiare	**mangi-**	mangiando
cominciare	**cominci-**	cominciando
sbagliare	**sbagli-**	sbagliando

The present gerund of regular **-ere** and **-ire** verbs consists of the infinitive verb root plus **-endo**:

Infinitive	Root	Gerund
credere	**cred-**	credendo
leggere	**legg-**	leggendo
scrivere	**scriv-**	scrivendo
capire	**cap-**	capendo
partire	**part-**	partendo
uscire	**usc-**	uscendo

Note that most verbs with irregular gerunds form the latter with the root of the present indicative **io** form. Study the following list:

Infinitive	Root	Gerund
bere	**bev-**	bevendo
dire	**dic-**	dicendo
fare	**fac-**[31]	facendo
tradurre	**traduc-**	traducendo
trarre	**tra-**[31]	traendo

---

[31] **Fare** and **trarre** do not use the present indicative **io** form.

Observe the following use of the present gerund:

Camminando, ho incontrato Carlo.
While walking, I met Charles.

Studiando, Paolo impara molto.
While studying, Paul learns a lot.

Traducendo, ho fatto molti errori.
While translating, I made many errors.

Essendo amici, abbiamo parlato a lungo.
Being friends, we spoke at length.

Ci guardavamo sorridendo.
We were looking at one another smiling.

Il bambino si lamentava piangendo.
The child (m.) was complaining crying.

Mi divertivo leggendo.
I was enjoying myself reading.

È uscita di casa cantando.
She left the house singing.

205. Complete the following sentences with the present gerund of the infinitive in parentheses.
1. Spesso si impara_____. (sbagliare)
2. Gli amici sono partiti_____. (salutare)
3. La maestra insegna_____. (spiegare)
4. Ascoltavamo Paolo_____. (sorridere)
5. Il bambino gridava_____. (piangere)
6. Tu sempre parli _____. (lavorare)

Note that the conjunctive pronouns are often attached to the present gerund. Observe the following:

Reflexive pronouns:
vestirsi (to dress) > vestendomi; vestendosi
lavarsi (to wash) > lavandosi; lavandoci

Direct and Indirect Objects:
parlare (to speak) > parlandogli; parlandoti; parlandole; parlandovi
Note that the *present gerund* is used extensively in the *progressive tenses*, explained in the next few pages.

Past Gerund

The past gerund is formed with the present gerund of the auxiliaries **avere (avendo)** and **essere (essendo)** plus the past participle of the acting verb. Remember mat verbs requiring **avere** have invariable past participles, whereas verbs requiring **essere** must have past participles that agree in gender and in number with the subject. (However, also remember that if a pronoun precedes **avere**, the past participle must agree in gender and number with the pronoun. For more details, see page 141.)

Infinitive	*Past Gerund*	
cantare	avendo cantato	*having sung*
finire	avendo finito	*having finished*
parlare	avendo parlato	*having spoken*

| arrivare | essendo arrivato (a, -i, -e) | *having arrived* |
| venire | essendo venuto (-a, -i, -e) | *having come* |

Avendo pranzato, Pietro andò al cinema.
Having dined, Peter went to the movies.

Essendo arrivati in ritardo, ci siamo scusati.
Having arrived late, we excused ourselves.

but: **Ci siamo scusati essendo arrivati in ritardo.**
   We excused ourselves for having arrived late.

Avendola veduta (vista), l'abbiamo salutata.
Having seen her, we greeted her.

but: **L'abbiamo salutata avendola veduta (vista).**
We greeted her after having seen her.

Essendo venuta presto, Luisa ha dovuto aspettare.
Having come early, Louise had to wait.

but: **Luisa ha dovuto aspettare essendo venuta presto.**
   Louise had to wait after having come early.

206. *Complete the following sentences with the past gerund of the verbs in parentheses. Use the appropriate auxiliary verb, avere or essere, as needed.*

1. _____, i ragazzi hanno guardato la televisione. (cenare)
2. _____ tardi, Isa non è arrivata in tempo. (partire)
3. _____ molto, ci siamo riposati. (studiare)
4. _____ di casa, dove sono andati Loro? (uscire)
5. _____, ci siamo stancati. (aspettare)
6. _____ lo zoo, ci siamo divertiti. (visitare)

Note that in the *past gerund* the conjunctive pronouns are attached to the present gerund of the auxiliary verbs, as above.

PROGRESSIVE TENSES (FORMA DURATIVA)

The progressive tenses in Italian are very graphic, pictorial tenses. When used, they show that the action of the verb is in the process of taking place. The progressive forms are most commonly used with the present indicative and the imperfect indicative, and sometimes with the future, the conditional, the present subjunctive, and the imperfect subjunctive. The progressive tense is composed of the conjugated forms of the verb **stare** plus the present gerund (*-ing*) of the acting verb. (Although verbs such as **seguire** and **venire** may also be used as auxiliaries in a progressive sense, **stare** is the most commonly used.) Remember that, for **-are** verbs, the present gerund suffix is **-ando**; for **-ere** and **-ire** verbs the suffix is **-endo**. Study the formation of the present gerund on p. and p. Study the following:

Present Indicative	>	*Present Progressive*
Faccio la spesa.	>	**Sto facendo la spesa.**
I shop, I am shopping for food.	>	*I am shopping for food*
(It is not specified that the action is	>	*(The action is unfolding at this moment.)*
unfolding at this moment.)		
Il meccanico aggiusta il motore.	>	**Il meccanico sta aggiustando il motore.**
The mechanic fixes (is fixing) the	>	*(The mechanic is fixing the motor at this moment.)*
motor. (We don't know exactly when.)		

Imperfect Indicative	>	*Imperfect Progressive*
I bambini giocạvano.	>	**I bambini stạvano giocando.**
The children were playing. (It's not specified when.)	>	*The children were playing. (They were in the act of playing.)*
Io scrivevo una lẹttera.	>	**Io stavo scrivendo una lẹttera.**
I was writing a letter. (Not specified when.)	>	*I was writing a letter. (I was writing a letter at that specific moment.)*

As was mentioned above, although the indicative present and imperfect progressives are the most commonly used in Italian (and not as often as in English), other progressive tenses may be used in special contexts and especially in fiction in order to capture certain nuances. Observe the following examples:

Present Indicative Progressive	>	*Present Subjunctive Progressive*
Mạrio sta scrivendo.	>	**Credo che Mạrio stịa scrivendo.**
Mạrio is writing.	>	*I think (that) Mạrio is writing.*
Ivo e Isa stanno studiạndo.	>	**È probabile che Ivo e Isa stiạno studiạndo.**
Ivo and Isa are studying.	>	*It's probable (that) Ivo and Isa are studying.*
Imperfect Indicative Progressive	>	*Imperfect Subjunctive Progressive*
Pạolo stava preparando la merenda.	>	**Dubitavo che Pạolo stesse preparando la merenda.**
Paolo was preparing the snack.	>	*I doubted (that) Paolo was preparing the snack.*
I ragazzi stạvano dormendo.	>	**Pensavo che i ragazzi stẹssero dormendo.**
The boys were sleeping.	>	*I thought (that) the boys were sleeping.*
Simple Future (of Probability)	>	*Future Progressive*

Cosa fa Riccardo?

Riccardo studierà.	>	**Riccardo starà studiạndo.**
Riccardo is probably studying.	>	*Riccardo is probably studying. (Riccardo is in the act of studying.)*
Imperfect Subjunctive	>	*Present Conditional Progressive*
Se potessi..., adesso starei sciạndo.		
If I could.., now I would be skiing.		
Se fosse possịbile.., quẹgli studenti starẹbbero studiạndo in Eurọpa.		
If it were possible..., those students would be studying in Europe.		

Present Progressive

Infinitive:	**cantare**	**scrịvere**	**dormire**
io	sto cantando	sto scrivendo	sto dormendo
tu	stai cantando	stai scrivendo	stai dormendo
lui, lei, Lei	sta cantando	sta scrivendo	sta dormendo
noi	stiạmo cantando	stiạmo scrivendo	stiạmo dormendo
voi	state cantando	state scrivendo	state dormendo
loro, Loro	stanno cantando	stanno scrivendo	stanno dormendo

Imperfect Progressive

Infinitive:	**parlare**	**vịvere**	**salire**
io	stavo parlando	stavo vivendo	stavo salendo
tu	stavi parlando	stavi vivendo	stavi salendo

lui, lei, Lei	stava parlando	stava vivendo	stava salendo
noi	stavamo parlando	stavamo vivendo	stavamo salendo
voi	stavate parlando	stavate vivendo	stavate salendo
loro, Loro	stavano parlando	stavano vivendo	stavano salendo

207. Rewrite the following supplying the present gerund of each indicated verb:

1. I ragazzi stanno giocando.   *parlare, scrivere, gridare, salire, scendere*
2. Io sto uscendo.   *mangiare, ascoltare, discutere, sentire, venire*
3. Tu stai partendo.   *contare, piangere, servire il tè, leggere, cantare*

208. Rewrite the following using the present progressive:

1. Tu suoni e Pietro canta.
2. Io dormo e voi studiate.
3. Loro parlano e noi guardiamo la televisione.
4. Loro arrivano e noi partiamo.
5. Voi uscite e loro entrano.
6. Noi leggiamo e tu ascolti la radio.
7. Io scrivo e Anna lavora.

209. Rewrite the following using the imperfect progressive:

1. Io giocavo a carte.
2. Voi tornavate dal centro.
3. Tu leggevi alcune riviste.
4. Loro salivano rapidamente.
5. Olga studiava la lezione.
6. Io giravo l'Europa.
7. Voi mangiavate in fretta.
8. Noi vedevamo un film.

REFLEXIVE VERBS (VERBI RIFLESSIVI)

A reflexive verb expresses an action performed and received by the same subject. Not all verbs can become reflexive. Those that do drop the **-e** of the infinitive ending and add the pronoun **si**. For example, the verb **lavare** (*to wash*) becomes **lavarsi** (*to wash oneself*) in the reflexive infinitive. Since the subject also receives the action, an additional pronoun is needed when conjugating a reflexive verb. This is called the reflexive pronoun. There is a different reflexive pronoun for almost every personal form. Study the following forms for the verbs **alzarsi** (*to get oneself up*), **mettersi** (*to put [something] on*), and **coprirsi** (*to cover oneself*):

Infinitive:	**alzarsi**	**mettersi**	**coprirsi**
(io) mi	mi alzo	mi metto	mi copro
(tu) ti	ti alzi	ti metti	ti copri
(lui, lei, Lei) si	si alza	si mette	si copre
(noi) ci	ci alziamo	ci mettiamo	ci copriamo
(voi) vi	vi alzate	vi mettete	vi coprite
(loro, Loro) si	si alzano	si mettono	si coprono

The following is a list of common Italian reflexive verbs:

accorgersi (di)	*to notice*
addormentarsi	*to fall asleep*
alzarsi	*to get up*
arrabbiarsi	*to get angry*
chiamarsi	*to be named*
coprirsi	*to cover oneself*
coricarsi	*to lie down, to go to bed*
diplomarsi	*to get a diploma*
divertirsi	*to have fun, to enjoy oneself*
farsi il bagno	*to bathe oneself*

farsi la doccia	to take a shower
farsi male	to get hurt, hurt oneself
ferirsi	to wound oneself
fidanzarsi (con)	to get engaged to
fidarsi (di)	to trust
innamorarsi (di)	to fall in love with
lamentarsi (di)	to complain about
lavarsi	to wash oneself
laurearsi	to graduate
mettersi	to put on (clothing, etc.)
pentirsi (di)	to repent of
pettinarsi	to comb one's hair
prepararsi (per)	to get ready
pulirsi	to clean oneself
radersi	to shave
ricordarsi (di)	to remember
sbarbarsi	to shave
sedersi	to sit down
sentirsi	to feel
spogliarsi	to undress
sposarsi (con)	to get married
svegliarsi	to wake up
vestirsi	to get dressed
voltarsi	to turn

210. Complete the following with the appropriate present indicative reflexive forms of the indicated verbs:

1. Quei ragazzi _____ alle otto.　　　　　　　*alzarsi*
2. D'inverno voi _____ sempre il cappotto.　　*mettersi*
3. I bambini _____ facilmente.　　　　　　　　*addormentarsi*
4. Io _____ Roberto.　　　　　　　　　　　　　*chiamarsi*
5. Noi _____ rapidamente.　　　　　　　　　　*vestirsi*
6. La signorina Martini _____ in medicina.　　*laurearsi*

211. Complete the following with the appropriate reflexive pronouns:

1. Io _____ alzo alle sette e mezzo.
2. Noi _____ addormentiamo facilmente.
3. Voi _____ pettinate con cura.
4. Luigi _____ veste lentamente.
5. I signori _____ mettono la cravatta ogni giorno.
6. Tu _____ svegli sempre alla stessa ora.
7. Gli studenti _____ laureano quest'anno.
8. Noi _____ laviamo le mani spesso.

Compound Tenses

All reflexive verbs form their compound tenses with the appropriate conjugated tenses of **essere** and with the past participles of the acting verbs. Remember that the past participle of reflexive verbs must agree in gender and number with the subject.

Stamani Carlo si è alzato alle sette in punto.
This morning Charles got up at seven o' clock sharp.

Le signorine si sono sedute vicino alla finestra.
The young ladies sat near the window.

Domani a quest'ora Pietro e Anna si saranno già sposati.
Tomorrow at this time Peter and Ann will have gotten married.

212. *Rewrite the following in the present perfect (passato prossimo):*
1. Io (*m.*) mi siedo vicino alla porta.
2. Luigi si sbarba con difficoltà.
3. I ragazzi si alzano alle sette.
4. Voi (*m.*) vi arrabbiate facilmente.
5. Ragazze, a che ora vi svegliate?
6. Signori, a che ora si alzano Loro?

Reciprocal Reflexives

Reciprocal reflexive verbs express a reciprocal action which involves, of course, more than one person. The following is a partial list of common reciprocal reflexives:

abbracciarsi	*to embrace each other (one another), to hug (one another)*
aiutarsi	*to help each other (one another)*
amarsi	*to love each other (one another)*
ammirarsi	*to admire each other (one another)*
baciarsi	*to kiss each other (one another)*
conoscersi	*to know each other* (also: *to meet*)
consolarsi	*to comfort each other (one another)*
incontrarsi	*to meet (each other)*
innamorarsi	*to fall in love (with each other)*
insultarsi	*to insult each other (one another)*
piacersi	*to like each other (one another)*
riconoscersi	*to recognize each other (one another)*
rispettarsi	*to respect each other (one another)*
rivedersi	*to see each other again (one another)*
salutarsi	*to greet each other (one another)*
scriversi	*to write to each other (one another)*
sposarsi	*to get married (to each other)*
vedersi	*to see each other (one another)*
volersi bene	*to like each other, to love each other (one another)*

Giovanni e Anna si vedono spesso.
John and Ann see each other often.

Alberto e Luigi si sono conosciuti allo stadio.
Albert and Louis met at the stadium.

Gli amici si aiutano a vicenda. (a vicenda emphasizes reciprocity)
Friends help one another.

Si sono piaciuti appena si sono incontrati.
They liked each other as soon as they met.

213. *Complete the following sentences with the present indicative of the indicated verbs:*

1. Noi _____ sempre.   *salutarsi*
2. Giorgio e Teresa _____.   *sposarsi*
3. I signori _____ molto.   *rispettarsi*
4. Carlo e Giovanna _____ ogni mese.   *scriversi*
5. Maria e Olga _____ da brave amiche.   *aiutarsi*
6. Voi _____ ogni giorno.   *salutarsi*

Reflexive versus Nonreflexive

Reflexive verbs express an action performed and received by the same subject (review pages 182–184). When many of these verbs are used nonreflexively (that is, without the reflexive pronouns), their meaning changes. Observe the following sentences:

Reflexive	*Nonreflexive*
Roberto si lava.	**Roberto lava la macchina.**
Robert washes (himself).	*Robert washes the car.*
Io mi alzo.	**Io alzo il ricevitore.**
I get up.	*I lift the receiver.*
Tu ti chiami Maria.	**Tu chiami i bambini.**
Your name is Mary.	*You call the children.*

Note the difference in meaning between the reflexive and nonreflexive forms of the following verbs. The nonreflexive forms below are transitive (they take a direct object).

Reflexive		*Nonreflexive*	
addormentarsi	*to fall asleep*	**addormentare**	*to put to sleep*
aiutarsi	*to help oneself, each other, etc.*	**aiutare**	*to help (someone)*
alzarsi	*to get up*	**alzare**	*to raise, to lift*
chiamarsi	*to be named*	**chiamare**	*to call (someone)*
divertirsi	*to have fun*	**divertire**	*to amuse (someone)*
farsi il bagno	*to bathe oneself*	**fare il bagno (a)**	*to bathe (someone)*
farsi male	*to hurt oneself*	**fare male (a)**	*to hurt (someone)*
lavarsi	*to wash oneself*	**lavare**	*to wash (someone or something)*
mettersi	*to put on (clothing, etc.)*	**mettere**	*to place (someone or something)*
pettinarsi	*to comb oneself*	**pettinare**	*to comb (someone or something)*
prepararsi	*to get ready*	**preparare**	*to prepare (someone or something)*
pulirsi	*to clean oneself*	**pulire**	*to clean (someone or something)*
ricordarsi (di)	*to remember*	**ricordare**	*to remember, to remind (someone or something)*
sentirsi	*to feel*	**sentire**	*to feel, to hear (someone or something), to listen to (someone), to smell*
svegliarsi	*to wake up*	**svegliare**	*to wake (someone) up*
vestirsi	*to get dressed*	**vestire**	*to dress (someone), to wear (something)*

214. *Complete the following sentences with the reflexive pronoun when it is necessary:*

1. Noi _____ vestiamo i bambini.
2. Carlo _____ sveglia alle otto e mezza.
3. Teresa e Gino _____ lavano i piatti.
4. Voi _____ divertite molto.
5. Io _____ chiamo gli amici.

6. Tu _____ chiami Ernesto.
7. Marco _____ aiuta suo padre.
8. Noi _____ laviamo le mani.

USES OF THE INFINITIVE (USI DELL'INFINITO)

The Infinitive after Prepositions

The infinitive is used after most prepositions, such as **per**, **prima di**, **senza**, etc. In English, the equivalent of the Italian infinitive often appears as a present gerund (the *-ing* form of the verb).

Siamo pronti per uscire.	*We are ready to go out.*
Gli ho parlato prima di partire.	*I spoke to him before leaving.*
Se ne sono andati senza dire niente.	*They went away without saying anything.*

The past infinitive may also be used after **senza**. The past infinitive is formed with the auxiliaries **essere** or **avere** plus the past participle of the acting verb: **essere venuto**, **avere cenato**. Note that it is common to drop the final **-e** of the auxiliary verb in the past infinitive: **esser venuto**, **aver cenato**.

Sono venuti senza aver telefonato.
They came without having telephoned.

Sono ritornati dall'Italia senza esser stati a Venezia.
They returned from Italy without having been in Venice.

Dopo is always followed by the past infinitive.

È ritornata dopo aver comprato i biglietti.
She returned after having bought the tickets.

215. Substitute each indicated infinitive in the following sentences:
   1. Gli ho parlato prima di <u>uscire</u>. *studiare, finire, mangiare, giocare, ballare, cantare, lavorare*
   2. Sono entrati senza *dire* <u>niente</u>. *parlare, salutare, sorridere, dare il buongiorno*

216. Complete the following with the correct past form of the indicated infinitive:

1. È ritornato dopo _____ il film.	*vedere*
2. Siete arrivati senza _____.	*telefonare*
3. Sono partiti senza _____ niente a nessuno.	*dire*
4. È ritornata dopo _____ l'Italia.	*visitare*
5. Dopo _____ lui è venuto trovarmi.	*arrivare*

The Infinitive as a Noun

In Italian the infinitive may also function as a noun.

Dormire poco non è giudizioso.
To sleep little is not wise.

Viaggiare stanca.
Traveling is tiring.

217. Answer the following questions according to the model:

Dormi poco? $\longrightarrow$ **No, dormire poco non è giudizioso.**
   1. Lavori troppo?
   2. Mangi molto?
   3. Parli sempre?
   4. Viaggi ogni giorno?

5. Studi continuamente?
6. Balli senza sosta?

The Infinitive as an Indirect Command

The infinitive is used to give instructions in the affirmative in a variety of situations.

Entrare!	Enter! (noun: **entrata**)
Uscire!	Exit! (noun: **uscita**)
Spingere!	Push!
Tirare!	Pull!
Tenere la destra!	Keep right!
Tenere la sinistra!	Keep left!
Tenersi a distanza!	Keep off! Keep away!
Tenersi lontano!	Keep off! Keep away!

When the indirect command is in the negative, the infinitive is usually preceded by the past participle **vietato** (literally: *prohibited*).

Vietato entrare!	No entrance!
Vietato fumare!	No smoking!
Vietato girare a destra!	No right turn!
Vietato girare a sinistra!	No left turn!
Vietato parlare!	No talking!
Vietato sostare!	No parking! or No stopping!
Sosta vietata!	No parking! or No stopping!

218. Rewrite the following instructions in the negative:
1. Entrare!
2. Tirare!
3. Spingere!
4. Fumare!
5. Girare a destra!
6. Uscire!

219. Translate the following:
1. No smoking!
2. No left turn!
3. Keep right!
4. Pull!
5. Push!
6. Keep off!

The Infinitive after *lasciare*, *vedere*, and *sentire*

Letting, seeing, or *hearing* someone do something is expressed by the conjugated forms of **lasciare**, **vedere**, and **sentire**, respectively, plus the infinitive.

Ho lasciato giocare i bambini.
I've let the children play. (or: *I let the children play.*)

Ho sentito cantare Teresa.
I heard Theresa sing.

Ho veduto (visto) dormire i bambini.
I saw the children sleep.

220. Answer the following according to the model:

I bambini saltavano? (vedere) $\longrightarrow$ **Sí, ho visto saltare i bambini.**

1. I ragazzi giocavano?	*lasciare*
2. Le studentesse studiavano?	*vedere*
3. Il tenore cantava?	*sentire*
4. Il ragazzo parlava?	*lasciare*
5. Gli studenti ballavano?	*vedere*
6. La ragazza leggeva?	*sentire*

Fare in Causative Constructions

In causative constructions the verb **fare** is followed by an infinitive and expresses the idea of having someone do something or having something done or made.

Faccio studiare i ragazzi.
I have (make) the boys study.

Ho fatto arrivare a tempo gli studenti.
I had (made) the students arrive on time.

Abbiamo fatto fare quella sedia.
We had that chair made.

Note that if the object is a noun, it always follows the infinitive. If the object is a pronoun, however, it precedes the verb **fare**.

Faccio studiare i ragazzi.
Li faccio studiare.
Ho fatto arrivare a tempo gli studenti.
Li ho fatti arrivare a tempo.

When a causative sentence has two objects, one becomes an indirect object. The indirect object is the person being made to do something. In Italian, the indirect object is introduced by the preposition **a** (alone or in its articulated form, as required). Observe the following:

One object:
Il maestro fa leggere lo studente.
The teacher has (makes) the student read.

Two objects:
Il maestro fa leggere la lettura allo studente.
The teacher has (makes) the student read the passage.

When either one or both of the objects is a pronoun, the object pronouns precede the verb **fare**. Observe the following:

Il maestro fa leggere la lettura allo studente.	*The teacher has the student read the reading.*
Il maestro la **fa leggere allo studente.**	*The teacher has the student read it.*
Il maestro gli **fa leggere la lettura.**	*The teacher has him read the reading.*
Il maestro gliela **fa leggere.**	*The teacher has him read it.*

If, however, the indirect object pronoun is **loro** (see p. 212), the pronoun **loro** follows the infinitive. Observe the following. (Note that **compiti** (m. pl.) in Italian, has a singular equivalent in English, *homework;* hence the direct object pronoun **li** becomes English *it.*)

Io ho fatto scrivere i compiti agli **studenti.**   *I had the students write the homework.*

Io li ho fatti scrivere agli studenti.	*I had the students write it.*
Io ho fatto scrivere loro i compiti.	*I had them write the homework.*
(*Also:* Io gli ho fatto scrivere i compiti.)	*I had them write the homework*
Io li ho fatti scrivere loro.	*I had them write it.*
(*Also:* Io glieli ho fatti scrivere.)	*I had them write it.*

[*Homework* is singular in English but plural (*i compiti*) in Italian. The agreement, in Italian, should be plural (**li**); the same goes for *it* (**li**) because it refers to *homework = i compiti*.]

In order to avoid ambiguity with the indirect object, the preposition **da** instead of **a** can introduce the indirect object. For example, consider this sentence: **Abbiamo fatto mandare il pacco a Maria.** It can mean: (1) *We had (made) Mary send the package;* or (2) *We had the package sent to Mary.* If the first meaning is intended, **da** can replace **a**:

Abbiamo fatto mandare il pacco da Maria.
We had (made) Mary send the package.

The reflexive **farsi** can also be used in a causative construction when one is having something done or made for oneself.

Mi faccio tagliare i capelli.
I have (am having) my hair cut.

Mi farò fare un vestito.
I'll have a suit made (for myself).

If the reflexive verb **farsi** is in a compound tense such as the **passato prossimo**, the verb **essere** is used.

Mi son fatto tagliare i capelli.
I had (have had) my hair cut.

Mi son fatto fare un vestito.
I had a suit made (for myself).

Me lo son fatto fare.
I had it made (for myself).

221. Translate the following:

1. I had the boy sing.
2. I had the boy sing the song.
3. I had the boy sing it.
4. I had him sing the song.
5. I had him sing it.
6. I had the boys sing the song.
7. I had the boys sing it.
8. I had them sing the song.
9. I had them sing it.

222. Rewrite the following, replacing the objects with pronouns according to the model:

Roberto fa chiamare gli amici. ⟶ Roberto li fa chiamare.

1. Luisa fa fare il lavoro.
2. Noi facciamo entrare la signora.
3. Il maestro fa recitare le poesie.
4. Tu fai mandare il pacco.
5. Io mi son fatto costruire la casa.
6. Io ho fatto tradurre la lettera a Gina.

PASSIVE VOICE

The passive voice is used frequently in Italian. It is formed with the conjugated forms of the verb **essere** plus the past participle of the verb. The agent or person who performs the action is introduced by the preposition **da** (which when necessary is contracted with the appropriate definite article. See page 240.) Note that the past participle agrees in gender and number with the subject. Observe the following:

Passive Voice:	**Le lęttere sono state distribuịte dal postino.**
	The letters were delivered by the letter carrier.
Active Voice:	**Il postino ha distribuịto le lęttere.**
	The letter carrier delivered the letters.
Passive Voice:	**I pacchi sono stati mandati da Teresa.**
	The packages were sent by Theresa.
Active Voice:	**Teresa ha mandato i pacchi.**
	Theresa sent the packages.
Passive Voice:	**Il bigliętto sarà comprato dalla signorina.**
	The ticket will be bought by the young lady.
Active Voice:	**La signorina comprerà il bigliętto.**
	The young lady will buy the ticket.
Passive Voice:	**La bicicletta gli è stata regalata dagli zịi.**
	The bicycle was given to him as a gift by his uncles (or: *his uncle and aunt).*
Active Voice:	**Gli zịi gli hanno regalato la bicicletta.**
	His uncles (or: *uncle and aunt) gave him the bicycle as a gift.*

223. *Rewrite the following sentences in the active voice according to the model:*
I libri sono stati comprati da Arturo.   *The books were bought by Arthur.*
Arturo ha comprato i libri.   *Arthur bought the books.*

1. Quẹl pạẹse è stato distrutto da un terremoto.
2. Quẹste poesịe sono state composte da Olga.
3. Quẹlla casa è stata costruịta da noi.
4. Gli scaffali sono stati fatti dagli studenti.
5. La lettera è stata inviạta da mia zịa.
6. Il pacco è stato portato da Giovanni.

Note: Newspaper headlines often make use of an abbreviated form of the passive voice:

Giọvane di ventidụe anni ucciso da un cạmion.
Young man of twenty-two killed by a truck.

Città distrutta da un terremoto.
City destroyed by an earthquake.

Passive Voice with *si*

A common way to form the passive voice in Italian is by using the reflexive pronoun **si** with the third-person singular or plural form of the verb. This construction is most common when the person by whom the action is carried out (the agent) is unimportant, or when the action is habitual or normal.

Quị si parla italiạno.
Italian is spoken here.

In quel negọzio si vẹndono camịcie e cravatte.
Shirts and neckties are sold in that store.

This construction is also used to convey an indefinite subject:

Si dice che Roberto è tornato in Italia.
It is said (They say) that Robert went back to Italy.

Ancora si parla della seconda guerra mondiale.
People (They) still talk about World War II.

224. Complete the following sentences with the appropriate forms of the indicated verbs:
1. Da quel ponte_____un panorama magnifico.   *vedersi*
2. _____inglese qui?   *parlarsi*
3. Come_____"pencil" in italiano?   *dirsi*
4. In questo negozio_____scarpe.   *vendersi*
5. In Sicilia vi_____un clima meraviglioso.   *trovarsi*

225. Complete the following with the appropriate forms of the imperative of the indicated verbs:
1. Roberto,_____una bella canzone!   *cantare*
2. Ragazzi,_____la casa!   *pulire*
3. Signora,_____ad alta voce!   *parlare*
4. Signori,_____ una birra!   *bere*
5. Ragazzo,_____pazienza!   *avere*
6. Antonio e Teresa,_____bravi!   *essere*
7. Professore,_____questa lettura!   *tradurre*
8. Olga,_____qui!   *venire*

226. Supply the progressive forms of the italicized verbs:
1. Paolo *parla* con suo zio.
2. *Cantavano* quando arrivò Carlo.
3. Chi *arriva* ora?
4. I ragazzi *scrivono* agli amici.
5. Cosa *fai*? —*Leggo* un romanzo.
6. Cosa *facevate* quando vi abbiamo chiamati.

227. Supply the passato prossimo forms of the italicized verbs:
1. *Si siedono* in prima fila.
2. *Ci divertiamo* molto con gli amici.
3. Luisa *si addormenta* alle dieci.
4. Ragazze, a che ora *vi alzate?*
5. La studentessa *si prepara* per l'esame.

228. Translate the following into Italian:
1. Traveling is interesting.
2. Keep right!
3. No smoking!
4. No parking!
5. Pull!
6. We saw the children play.

Negative Words and Constructions

MAKING A SENTENCE NEGATIVE

The most common way to make a sentence negative in Italian is to place the word **non** before the verbal expression. Observe the following:

Affirmative

Voglio dormire.
I want to sleep.

Andremo a Venezia insieme.
We shall go to Venice together.

Carlo e Maria parlavano italiano.
Charles and Mary spoke Italian.

Ho finito il mio lavoro.
I finished my work.

Negative

Non voglio dormire.
I don't want to sleep.

Non andremo a Venezia insieme.
We shall not go to Venice together.

Carlo e Maria non parlavano italiano.
Charles and Mary did not speak Italian.

Non ho finito il mio lavoro.
I did not finish my work.

If an object pronoun (see Chapter 9) precedes the verb, the negative word **non** precedes the object pronoun. Study the following:

Affirmative

Lo conosco.
I know him.

Lo abbiamo fatto. (L'…)
We did it.

Ci alziamo.
We get up.

Si telefonano.
They telephone one another.

Negative

Non lo conosco.
I don't know him.

Non lo abbiamo fatto. (l'…)
We didn't do it.

Non ci alziamo.
We don't get up.

Non si telefonano.
They don't telephone one another.

193

1. Rewrite the following sentences in the negative:

1. Vogliamo andare a teatro. 1. _____.
2. Io conosco quei ragazzi. 2. _____.
3. Luisa vuole venire adesso. 3. _____.
4. Andavate alia spiaggia ogni estate. 4. _____.
5. Si sveglieranno alle quattro. 5. _____.
6. Gli amici portano i regali. 6. _____.
7. Tu mangi troppo. 7. _____.
8. Lo hanno dimenticato. 8. _____.
9. Ho visto Roberto ieri sera. 9. _____.
10. I miei amici visitano il museo 10. _____.

COMMON NEGATIVE EXPRESSIONS

Some very commonly used negative expressions are:

nessuno	*no one, nobody*
niente (nulla)	*nothing*
né … né	*neither … nor*
nessun, nessuno, nessuna	*no, not … any*

(When used as an adjective, it must agree in gender and number with the noun it modifies.)

neanche, nemmeno, neppure	*not even*
non … affatto	*not at all*
non … ancora	*not yet*
non … mai	*never*
non … né … né	*neither … nor*
non … neanche (nemmeno, neppure)	*not even*
non … niente (nulla)	*nothing*
non … nessuno	*no one*

Study the following:

Affirmative	*Negative*
Qualcuno parla.	**Non parla nessuno.**
Someone speaks.	or **Nessuno parla.**
	No one speaks.
Vedo qualcuno.	**Non vedo nessuno.**
I see someone.	*I don't see anyone.*
Voglio qualcosa (qualche cosa).	**Non voglio niente.**
I want something.	*I don't want anything.*
Tutto mi piace.	**Non mi piace niente.**
I like everything.	or **Niente mi piace.**
	I don't like anything. I like nothing.
Lui sempre va al cinema.	**Lui non va mai al cinema.**
He always goes to the movies.	or **Lui mai va al cinema.**
	He never goes to the movies.

Ho ricchezza e fortuna.	**Non ho né ricchezza né fortuna.**
I have riches and fortune.	*I have neither riches nor fortune.*
Paolo e Iva parlano cinese.	**Né Paolo né Isa parlano cinese.**
Paul and Isa speak Chinese.	*Neither Paul nor Isa speaks Chinese.*

*(With **né … né**, in Italian the plural form of the verb is used: **parlano**; in English, with **neither … nor**, the singular form is used: **speaks**, even though the subject, **Paul and Isa**, is plural.)*

Compro qualche libro.	**Non compro nessun libro.**
I buy some books.	*I don't buy any books.*
Ho ricevuto qualche lettera.	**Non ho ricevuto nessuna lettera.**
I have received some letters.	*I haven't received any letters.*
Anch'io lo farò.	**Neanch'io (Nemmeno io, Neppure io) lo farò.**
I too will do it.	*Not even I will do it. (or I won't do it either.)*

Note that the placement of the negative word (or words) in the sentence can vary. When the negative word precedes the verb, **non** is omitted.

Mai viaggiamo in aereo.	*We never travel by plane (ever).*
Non viaggiamo mai in aereo.	*We never travel by plane.*

Nessun and **niente** almost always follow the verb when they function as the object. When they are the subject of the sentence, their position can vary.

Nessuno parla.	*(Absolutely) No one speaks.*
Niente mi piace.	*I like nothing (at all).*
Non parla nessuno.	*No one speaks.*
Non mi piace niente.	*I don't like anything.*

Unlike English, more than one negative word can be used in the same sentence in Italian.

Carlo non dice mai niente a nessuno.
Charles never says anything to anybody.

2. Rewrite the following sentences in the negative:
1. C'è qualcosa sul tavolo.
2. Qualcuno ti ha telefonato.
3. Vedo qualcuno nella stanza.
4. Sempre andiamo alla spiaggia.
5. Lei ha penna e carta?
6. Luigi sempre dice la stessa cosa.
7. C'è qualcuno in cucina.
8. Vuole qualche cosa?
9. Carlo sempre parla con qualcuno.
10. Sempre leggo qualche giornale italiano.

NEGATION OF COMPOUND TENSES

Verbs in compound tenses are also made negative by placing **non** before the auxiliary verb. Some words that are combined with **non** may take different positions in the sentence. Study the following combinations:

non … nessuno	*no one, nobody*
non … niente	*nothing*

non ... nulla	*nothing*
non ... né ... né	*neither ... nor*
non ... mai	*never*
non ... ancora	*not yet*
non ... più	*no longer*
non ... affatto	*not at all*
non ... mica	*not at all (in the least)*
non ... neanche	*not even*
non ... nemmeno	*not even*
non ... neppure	*not even*
non ... che	*only*

When they are used with **non,** the negative expressions **nessuno**, **niente**, **né ... né**, and **che** always follow the past participle. Observe the following:

<u>Non</u> hanno trovato <u>nessuno</u>.	*They haven't found anyone.*
<u>Non</u> abbiamo visto <u>nessun</u> ragazzo.	*We haven't seen any boys.*
<u>Non</u> abbiamo visto <u>nessuna</u> ragazza.	*We haven't said anything.*
<u>Non</u> hanno detto <u>niente</u>.	*They haven't said anything.*
<u>Non</u> ho trovato <u>né</u> il passaporto <u>né</u> il biglietto.	*I found neither the passport nor the ticket.*
<u>Non</u> ho letto <u>che</u> due libri.	*I have read only two books.*

With the combinations **non ... mica** and **non ... punto**, **mica** and **punto** always come between the auxiliary verb and the past participle.

<u>Non</u> ha <u>mica</u> parlato.	*He hasn't spoken at all.*
<u>Non</u> è <u>affatto</u> arrivato.	*He hasn't arrived at all.*

Affatto, ancora, mai, neanche (nemmeno, neppure) and **piú,** when used with **non,** can be placed either between the auxiliary verb and the past participle or after the past participle.

Luigi <u>non</u> è tornato <u>affatto</u>.	*Louis hasn't returned at all.*
Luigi <u>non</u> è <u>affatto</u> tornato.	
<u>Non</u> si sono svegliati <u>ancora</u>.	*They haven't awakened yet.*
<u>Non</u> si sono <u>ancora</u> svegliati.	
<u>Non</u> ha viaggiato <u>mai</u>.	*He has never traveled.*
<u>Non</u> ha <u>mai</u> viaggiato.	
<u>Non</u> sei tornato <u>piú</u>.	*You haven't returned anymore.*
<u>Non</u> sei <u>piú</u> tornato.	
<u>Non</u> mi ha salutato <u>neanche</u>.	*He didn't even greet me.*
<u>Non</u> mi ha <u>neanche</u> salutato.	

3. Rewrite the following sentences, adding the Italian equivalent of the English words:

1. Siamo andati a sciare.   *never*
2. Ha chiamato.   *not at all*
3. Sono arrivati.   *not yet*
4. Tu sei entrato.   *not even*
5. Loro hanno visto uno spettacolo. *not any*
6. Il cane è tornato.   *never*
7. Abbiamo visto.   *no one*
8. Si sono svegliati.   *not yet*

9. Ho visto quel film.   *never*
10. Noi abbiamo cantato.   *not at all*
11. Ha scritto poesie.   *only*

4. Answer the following questions using the cues provided:

1. Chi ti ha telefonato ieri sera?   *non ... nessuno*
2. Cosa hai detto?   *non ... niente*
3. Quando sono arrivati i tuoi amici?   *non ... ancora*
4. Quanti libri hai letto?   *non ... che due*
5. Cosa hai fatto ieri sera?   *non ... niente*
6. Hai comprato dischi o riviste?   *non ... né ... né*
7. Quando lo hai visto?   *non ... piú*
8. Quando sei andato(-a) in Italia?   *non ... mai*
9. Cosa ha detto quando è arrivato?   *non ... neanche buon giorno*
10. Cosa ha cantato?   *non ... mica*

Neanche, nemmeno, neppure

Neanche, **nemmeno**, or **neppure** are the negative words used to replace **anche**. These three words can be used inter-changeably. Observe the following:

Lui lo sa.	**Anch'io lo so.**
He knows it.	*I know it too (also).*
Lui non lo sa.	**Neanch'io (Nemmeno io, Neppure io) lo so.**
He doesn't know it.	*I don't know it either.*

5. Replace anche with neanche, nemmeno, or neppure in the following sentences and make the necessary changes:

1. Anche lui è ricco.
2. Anche le sue cugine hanno molto denaro.
3. Maria lo sa e anch'io lo so.
4. Anche Giovanni viene.
5. Anche lui lo ha fatto.

Negative Infinitive Construction.

In order to form a *negative infinitive* within a full sentence, place the negative **non** between the preposition **di** and the *infinitive*. The beginning of each sentence may be quite varied in the uses of tenses, and the possibilities are many. Note that it's possible to attach object pronouns to the infinitive. The following suggestions are just a few examples of what can be done:

I miei genitori mi dicono **di non fumare**.	I miei genitori mi hanno detto **di non fumare**.
My parents tell me **not to smoke**.	*My parents told me* **not to smoke**.
Mio zio mi dice **di non sciare**.	Mio zio mi suggerisce **di non sciare**.
My uncle tells me **not to ski**.	*My uncle suggests* **that I not ski**.
Tu mi raccomandi **di non comprarla**.	Loro ci suggeriscono **di calmarci**.
You recommend **that I not buy it**.	*They suggest* **that we calm down**.
Chi ti ha detto **di non cantare**?	Chi vi dice di **non giocare**?
Who told you **not to sing**?	*Who is telling you* **not to play**?
Ragazzi, cercherete **di non gridare**?	Mario, cerca **di non fumare**!
Boys, will you try **not to yell**?	*Mario, try* **not to smoke**!

6. Complete the following sentences with the Italian equivalents of the phrases in parentheses.

1. Roberto ci dice_____.   *not to play here*
2. Mio nonno sempre ci diceva_____.   *not to smoke*
3. Gli amici ci diranno_____.   *not to run*
4. Il maestro ci ha imposto_____in classe.   *not to yell*
5. Tua madre ti ordina_____la porta.   *not to slam*
6. Marisa ci raccomanda_____a lungo la televisione.   *not to watch*
7. Signorina, Le suggerisco_____.   *not to get angry*
8. Signore (m. s.), Le raccomando_____.   *not to drink a lot*

REVIEW

7. Rewrite the following sentences in the negative:

1. Marco vuole andare a sciare.
2. Siamo sempre andati in montagna.
3. Ho libri e penne.
4. Loro ci dicono tutto.
5. Anche voi andate in Italia.
6. Qualcuno mi ha telefonato.
7. Tu leggi qualche rivista moderna.
8. Voi giocate sempre.

8. Rewrite each of the following sentences, using the Italian equivalent of the English cues:

1. Abbiamo giocato a tennis.   *never*
2. Hanno lavorato.   *not at all*
3. Hai veduto.   *no one*
4. Avete finito.   *not yet*
5. Ho fatto una telefonata.   *not any*
6. Ha salutato.   *not even*

9. Give the Italian equivalents of the following sentences.

1. Not even you (tu) can yell here._____.
2. They don't speak German, they speak Spanish._____.
3. My aunt Paolina tells us not to smoke._____.
4. She never returned anymore._____.
5. He hasn't telephoned at all._____.
6. The children haven't awakened yet._____.

CHAPTER 8

Interrogative Words and Constructions

FORMING QUESTIONS IN ITALIAN

In Italian a statement may be changed into a question by placing a question mark at the end of it. In spoken Italian the question is conveyed to the listener by using a *high → low → high* intonation extended throughout the sentence. This works well with reasonably short sentences.

Statement	Question
Sẹrgio compra i libri. *Sergio buys the books.*	**Sẹrgio compra i libri?** *Does Sergio buy the books?*
Hai molto tempo lịbero. *You have a lot of free time.*	**Hai molto tempo lịbero?** *Do you have a lot of free time?*
Avete dụe figli. *You (voi) have two children.*	**Avete dụe figli?** *Do you have two children?*
Signora, Lei ha una fịglia. *Madame, you have a daughter.*	**Signora, ha una fịglia Lei?** *Madame, do you have a daughter?*

Statements can also be changed into questions by placing the subject either at the end of the sentence or after the verb. Note that subject pronouns are often omitted; they are usually included only for contrast or emphasis (except in the case of the formal forms, when they are used for clarity):

Statement	Question
Marịa viẹne a casa. *Mary comes home.*	**Viẹne a casa Marịa?** or **Viẹne Marịa a casa?** *Does Mary come home?*
Tu parli bene. *You speak well.*	**Parli bene tu?** *Do you speak well?*

199

Lei scrive ai ragazzi.
You (formal singular) write to the boys.

Scrive ai ragazzi Lei?
Do you (formal singular) write to the boys?

Roberto ha due figli.
Robert has two children.

Ha due figli Roberto?
Does Robert have two children?

Loro vanno a Torino.
You (formal pl.) go to Turin.

Vanno a Torino Loro?
Do you go to Turin?

A statement can be changed into a question by adding the expression **no?**, **non è vero?**, **è vero?**, or **vero?** to the end of a statement. Observe the following:

Arriverete stasera alle otto, vero?
You'll arrive tonight at eight, right?

Tuo zio ha avuto un incidente, è vero?
Your uncle had an accident, didn't he?

È il padrone, non è vero?
He is the owner, isn't he?

Domani cominceranno le nostre vacanze, no?
Our vacation will begin tomorrow, right?

1. Rewrite the following statements, using the same words, changing them into questions:
1. Luigi è arrivato alle cinque.
2. Noi ci sediamo qui.
3. Tu hai paura.
4. Loro (formal) portano il vino.
5. Voi siete andati a teatro.
6. Lei (formal) ha giocato a carte.
7. I giovani ballano molto.
8. Lui ha tradotto quel libro.

2. Rewrite the following questions as statements. Note that answers may vary.
1. Vanno a casa i ragazzi?
2. Sono tornate le studentesse?
3. Hai perduto (perso) la partita tu?
4. Vi siete alzati presto voi?
5. Escono alle sei Loro?
6. Abbiamo ballato molto noi?

3. Change the following statements into questions by using expressions such as no?, vero?, etc. Note that answers may vary.
1. Nostro fratello tornerà domani.
2. Quel vestito non costa molto.
3. Ci siamo incontrati per caso (by chance).
4. Mi riporterete il mio dizionario.
5. Sei stato malato fino a ieri.
6. Andremo in Italia insieme.

INTERROGATIVE ADVERBS AND ADVERBIAL EXPRESSIONS

The following interrogative words are the most commonly used to introduce a question:

A che ora?	*At what time?*
Come?	*How?*
Come mai?	*How come? Why (on earth)? Why ever?*
Dove?	*Where?*
Perché?	*Why?*
Quando?	*When?*
Quanto?	*How much?*

Note that in Italian the subject and verb are often inverted in interrogative sentences:

A che ora partono i tuoi amici?
At what time are your friends leaving?

Come sta Luigi?
How is Louis?

Dove sono i bambini?
Where are the children?

Dov'é il bambino?
Where is the child?

Perché fumi tanto?
Why do you smoke so much?

Quando usciamo?
When do we go out?

Quanto fa due piú tre?
How much is two plus three?

Note that the subject and verb are not inverted with **come mai**:

Come mai Mario non è qui?
How come Mario is not here? or *Why ever isn't Mario here?*

4. Complete the following with the appropriate question words, using the italicized words as hints:
   1. Paolo mangia *poco*._____ mangia Paolo?
   2. Voi arrivate *tardi*._____arrivate voi?
   3. I signori sono stati *al centro*._____ sono stati i signori?
   4. Ci siamo alzate *alle otto*._____ci siamo alzate?
   5. Roberto sta *molto male*._____sta Roberto?
   6. Le scarpe sono costate *cento euro*. _____sono costate le scarpe?
   7 Dieci meno otto fa *due*_____fa dieci meno otto?
   8. Maria corre *perché ha fretta*._____corre Maria?
   9. Sono partiti *presto*._____sono partiti?
   10. Arriva a scuola *correndo*._____ arriva a scuola?

5. Give the Italian equivalents.
   1. Where is your little brother? _____
   2. How are you (*tu*) today? _____
   3. How come they (*f.*) haven't arrived?_____
   4. Why don't you (*Lei*) stop smoking? _____
   5. How much is seven plus four?_____
   6. At what time will he arrive? _____

INTERROGATIVE PRONOUNS *che, chi*

The interrogative pronouns **che** (*what*) and **chi** (*who, whom*) can be used as subjects, direct objects, or objects of a preposition. Observe the following examples:

Che (cosa, che cosa) succede? Che sta succedendo?   *What is happening?*
Che vuoi?   *What do you want?*
Di che parlano?   *What are they talking about?*

Chi è lui?	*Who is he?*
Chi cerchi?	*Whom are you looking for?*
Di chi parlano?	*Whom are they talking about?*
Di chi è?	*Whose is it?*
Di chi sono?	*Whose are they?*

Note that **che** can also be expressed by **che cosa** and **cosa**:

Che fai?	
Che cosa fai?	*What are you doing?*
Cosa fai?	

6. Complete the following with chi or che (cosa, che cosa) based on the cue given.

1. _____vedi?   *Antonio*
2. _____vedi?   *I francobolli*
3. Di_____parlano?   *Di politica*
4. Di_____parlano?   *Di Angelina*
5. _____fate, siete matti?   *What*

7. Complete the following with the appropriate interrogative words:

1. Giovanni scrive molto._____scrive molto?
2. Scrive un romanzo._____scrive?
3. Diamo i fiori agli amici._____diamo agli amici?
4. Diamo i fiori agli amici._____diamo i fiori?
5. Hai ricevuto un regalo da me._____hai ricevuto un regalo?
6. Hai ricevuto un regalo da me._____hai ricevuto da me?
7. Parlate di tutto._____parlate?
8. Voteranno per Anna._____voteranno?
9. Parlano della situazione politica._____parlano?
10. S'incontra con Giorgio._____s'incontra?

8. Give the Italian equivalents.

1. Boys, what are you doing? _____.
2. What is happening at this moment? _____.
3. Who are those gentlemen? _____.
4. Whose are these toys? _____.
5. What did they talk about? _____.
6. Who is she? Do we know her? _____.

INTERROGATIVE PRONOUNS *quale, quali*

Quale or **quali** is the interrogative pronoun that corresponds to the English *which* or *which one* or *ones*. **Quale** is both masculine and feminine singular, and **quali** is both masculine and feminine plural.

Quale dei libri preferisci?
Which one of the books do you prefer?

Di questi due libri, quale preferisci leggere?
Of these two books, which one do you prefer to read?

Note that **quale** drops the final **-e** before **è** or **era**, and that an apostrophe is not used:
Qual era il libro che leggevi?
Qual è il tuo film favorito?

9. Complete the following with either quale or quali:

1. Delle due case,_____preferisce Lei?
2. _____dei quattro figli sono nati in Italia?
3. _____delle due figlie è nata in Italia?
4. _____è la piú intelligente delle due?
5. _____sono le tue poesie favorite?

INTERROGATIVE ADJECTIVES *quale(-i), quanto(-a, -i, -e)*

The interrogative adjective **quale** (*which*) must agree in number and gender with the noun it modifies. **Quale** has only two forms, **quale** and **quali**.

Quale ragazzo parla?   **Quale ragazza parla?**
Which boy is speaking?   *Which girl is speaking?*

Quali ragazzi parlano?   **Quali ragazze parlano?**
Which boys are speaking?   *Which girls are speaking?*

Note that there is a difference in meaning between **che** and **quale**. In the question **Quali dischi preferisci comprare?**, the meaning is *Of the records you are looking at, which records do you prefer to buy?* In the question **Che dischi preferisci comprare?**, the message is *What type of records do you prefer to buy (for example, classical or popular)?*

The interrogative adjective **quanto** (*how many, how much*) must also agree in number and gender with the noun it modifies. Note that **quanto** has four forms:

Quanto denaro ha Lei?   *How much money do you have?*
Quanti libri ha letto Lei?   *How many books have you read?*
Quanta farina c'è?   *How much flour is there?*
Quante studentesse ci sono?   *How many students (f.) are there?*

10. Complete each sentence with the correct form of quale:

1. _____case sono bianche, queste o quelle?
2. _____libri legge Lei?
3. _____film hanno visto ieri sera?
4. In_____ristorante vogliono mangiare stasera?
5. _____è il fiume piú lungo?

11. Complete each sentence with the correct form of quanto:

1. _____anni ha Lei?
2. _____melanzane (*eggplants*) devo preparare?
3. _____lettere ha scritto Lei?
4. _____sale devo mettere nella salsa?
5. _____gente (f. s.) c'è!

REVIEW

12. Rewrite the following sentences, changing them from statements to questions. Note that answers may vary.

1. Marco compra molti libri.
2. Tuo fratello è il padrone (*owner*) di quella casa.
3. I ragazzi arrivano sempre in ritardo.
4. Teresa va al cinema stasera.
5. Voi andate a scuola in macchina.
6. Il biglietto costa cinque dollari.

    7. Marco compra molti libri.
    8. I signori Porta hanno tre figli.
    9. Marisa lavora in una banca.
  10. Tu le insegni a sciare.

13. *Complete each of the following questions with the appropriate interrogative word:*
    1. Ti sei alzato presto._____ti sei alzato?
    2. Mio padre sta bene._____sta bene?
    3. Cinque piú due fa sette._____fa cinque piú due?
    4. I bambini giocano gridando._____ giocano i bambini?
    5. Mangiamo perché abbiamo fame._____mangiamo?
    6. Di_____è quel dizionario?
    7. _____ chi sono questi quaderni?
    8. _____ora arriva l'autobus?
    9. _____è la città piú popolata del mondo?
  10. Che _____stai facendo, Enzo?

14. *Give the Italian equivalents.*
    1. Whose is this suitcase? _____
    2. Which computer have you (*tu*) bought? _____
    3. How much money have you (*voi*) brought? _____
    4. How many euros do you (*tu*) pay for an ice cream?_____
    5. Whose e-mail is this (*f.*)?_____
    6. Which boy is playing today?_____
    7. What is happening at home?_____
    8. At what time can you (*Lei*) come out? _____

CHAPTER 9

Pronouns

SUBJECT PRONOUNS

Note that in Italian there are basically four ways to say *you*. The familiar pronouns **tu** (singular, s.) and **voi** (plural, pl.) are used to address relatives, friends, fellow students, children, and people whom one knows very well. The formal pronouns **Lei** (singular) and **Loro** (plural) are used to address strangers, superiors, people one does not know very well, those to whom one wishes to show particular respect, and those older than oneself. It is important to note the distinction between the capitalized **Lei** and **Loro**, which mean *you*, and **lei** (*she*) and **loro** (*they*): this distinction prevents ambiguity and fosters clarity. The pronoun **Loro** is considered very formal and is sometimes replaced with the **voi** form. **Voi** may also be used when addressing a single person one knows or even a stranger (see Chapter 6 for further comments, especially the section on formal versus familiar forms, p. 85). This type of **voi** has always been and still is in use in Tuscany and other central Italian regions, and generally throughout southern Italy. Note also that **Voi** (with a capital **V**) is widely used in business correspondence. In this context, **Voi** is used to address formally a single person or persons.

In modern spoken Italian, **lui**, **lei**, and **loro** are used much more frequently for *he*, *she*, and *they* than the other third-person forms. **Egli** and **ella** are still sometimes used to express **he** and **she**. They do appear in the latest best Italian grammars published in Italy. Although in this book **lui** is used instead of **egli** and **esso** for *he*, and **lei** instead of **ella** and **essa** for *she*, it is not meant to imply that these pronouns have disappeared entirely from usage; in fact, they are still widely used, especially in formal contexts, in literature, and in business language.

Observe the following list of subject pronouns with appropriate explanatory examples. Note that the formal singular *you*, **Lei**, and the formal plural *you*, **Loro**, take the third-person verb endings, singular and plural, respectively.

Singular Forms

io *(I, first-person singular; it shows no gender)*

Io parlo italiano.	*I speak Italian.*
Io sono italiano.	*I am Italian* (m. s.).
Io sono Italiana.	*I am Italian* (f. s.).

tu *(you, second-person familiar singular; it shows no gender)*

Tu sei americano.	*You are American* (m. s.).
Tu sei americana.	*You are American* (f. s.).
Olga, tu sei romana?	*Olga, are you Roman?*

Roberto, tu sei toscano?	*Robert, are you Tuscan (m. s.)?*
Bambino, tu come ti chiami?	*Little boy, what is your name?*

lui *(he, third-person singular masculine)*

Lui lavora in centro.	*He works downtown.*
Chi è lui? Lui è Mario.	*Who is he? He is Mario.*
È bravo lui? Sí, lui è bravo.	*Is he smart? Yes, he is smart.*

lei *(she, third-person feminine singular)*

Lei è la figlia maggiore.	*She is the oldest daughter.*
Chi è lei? Lei è Olga.	*Who is she? She is Olga.*
È brava lei? Sí, lei è brava.	*Is she smart? Yes, she is smart.*

Lei (you, second-person formal singular; it shows no gender)

Come sta Lei, Signora Torre?	*How are you, Mrs. Torre?*
Signorina, Lei è dottoressa?	*Miss, are you a doctor?*
Signor Bianchi, Lei è avvocato?	*Mr. Bianchi, are you a lawyer?*

Plural Forms

noi (we, first-person plural)
Noi shows no gender. Also, **noi** can be substituted for **tu e (ed) io**, **lui e io**, **lei e io**, **Lei e io**, **voi e io**, **loro e io**, and **Loro e io**.

Noi siamo italiani.	*We are Italian (m. pl.).*
Noi siamo italiane.	*We are Italian (f. pl.).*

Voi (you, second-person familiar plural)
Voi shows no gender. Also, **voi** can mean **tu e lui**, **tu e lei**, **tu e Lei**, **tu e tu** [pointing at two different people in the **tu** form], **tu e loro**, and **tu e Loro**.

Voi siete americani.	*You are American (m. pl.).*
Voi siete americane.	*You are American (f. pl.).*
Tu e Mario siete studenti.	*You and Mario are students (m. pl.).*
Tu e Maria siete studentesse.	*You and Maria are students (f. pl.).*
Tu e tu, venite qua!	*You and you, come here!*

As is explained in the introduction to this Chapter, **voi** may be used to address one single person, as has been generally the usage in central and southern Italy. Of course, the formal **Lei** may also be used in the examples below with the appropriate verb forms. Note the following examples:

Buon giorno, zio; come state voi?	*Good morning uncle; how are you?*
E voi, signor Marino, come state?	*And you, Mr. Marino, how are you?*
Ciao, nonna Maria! E voi come vi sentite oggi?	*Hello, grandma Maria! And how are you feeling today?*

loro (they, third-person plural)
Loro shows no gender. Also, **loro** can substitute for **lui e lei**, **lui e lui**, **lei e lei**.

Loro sono spagnoli.	*They are Spanish (m. pl.).*
Loro sono spagnole.	*They are Spanish (f. pl.).*
Lui e lei sono cugini.	*He and she are cousins.*

Loro (you, second-person formal plural)
Loro shows no gender. Also, **Loro** can mean **Lei e lui**, **Lei e lei**, **Lei e Lei** (pointing at two different people in the **Lei** form).

Signori, dove vanno Loro?
Gentlemen, where are you going?

Signore, vanno a teạtro Loro?
Ladies, are you going to the theatre?

Signore e signori, che desịderano Loro dalla cucina?
Ladies and gentlemen, what are you having (what do you wish) from the kitchen?

Lei e Lei, vẹngano con me!
You (Sir) and you (Madam), come with me!

1. Complete the following with the appropriate subject pronouns.

1. E _____, Carlo, quạndo sei nato?
2. Signorina, _____ di dov'è?
3. Signori, dove ạbitano _____?
4. Zịo Pạolo, quạndo dormite _____?
5. E _____, signor Torre, quando venite a trovarci?
6. Signori, _____ sono inglesi o scozzesi?
7. Ragazzini, quạndo giocate _____?
8. Signora Teresa, con chi stavate parlando _____?
9. Signore, _____ è svevo o danese?
10. _____ siạmo studenti universitari.
11. Marịa? _____ è mia cugina.
12. I ragazzi? _____ sono i nipoti del dottor Blasi.
13. Le bambine? _____ ạbitano quị vicino.
14. Vittọrio? _____ insegna in un licẹo.
15. Chi è _____? Olga è la mịa amica favorita.
16. Bambina, _____ come ti chiạmi?
17. Professore, _____ torna la settimana prọssima?
18. Dottore e ingegnere, da quạndo si conọscono _____?
19. _____ sono italiạna e mi chiạmo Rosetta.
20. Pạola e Rosa? _____ hanno pochi amici.

Use or Omission of Subject Pronouns

In English, subject pronouns are always used. In Italian, since the verb ending indicates the subject, it is very common to omit the subject pronoun.

Oggi andiạmo al cịnema.
Today we are going to the movies.

Vọglio andare alla spiạggia.
I want to go to the beach.

Subject pronouns are used in Italian, however, in the following instances:

For emphasis

Lo facciạmo noi.
<u>We'll</u> do it.

I libri li compro io.
<u>I'll</u> buy the books.

For contrast

> **Io lavoro, ma tu canti.**
> *I'm working, but you're singing.*

> **Noi studiamo e voi vi divertite.**
> *We study and you amuse yourselves.*

After **almeno**, **anche**, **magari**, **neanche**, **nemmeno**, **neppure**

> **Almeno (magari) lo facesse lui!**
> *If he would only do it!*

> **Anche noi parliamo francese.**
> *We too speak French.*

> **Nemmeno io vado al cinema.**
> *I won't go to the movies either.*

Note: **almeno** and **magari** require the subjunctive (see Chapter 6).

When the subject pronouns stand alone

> **Chi ha gridato?**   **Lui!**
> *Who yelled?*   *He did!*

> **Chi vuole farlo?**   **Noi!**
> *Who wants to do it?*   *We do!*

2. Rewrite the following sentences, substituting the appropriate subject pronouns for the italicized nouns:

1. *Mario* compra due libri.
2. *I bambini* vogliono molte caramelle.
3. *Teresa* scrive l'esercizio.
4. *Carlo e Giuseppe* lavorano qui vicino.
5. *Le studentesse* studiano molto.
6. *Maria e Luisa* vanno in Italia.

3. Give the correct subject pronoun for each of the following nouns or pronouns:

1. Maria
2. Le ragazze
3. Luigi
4. Elena e Filippo
5. Tu e io
6. Tu e lui

4. Translate the following sentences into Italian:

1. We sing, but she studies.
2. Not even they want to eat.
3. Who wants to play? I do!
4. They too go to Italy.

DIRECT OBJECT PRONOUNS: *lo (l'), la (l') li, le*

The third-person direct object pronouns in Italian are **lo**, **l'**: *him, it*; **la**, **l'**: *her, it*; **li**: *them* (m. pl.); **le**: *them* (f. pl.). **Lo** and **li** are masculine pronouns. **La** and **le** are feminine pronouns. Note that **lo** and **la** are contracted to **l'** before verbs beginning with a vowel or silent **h**. **Li** and **le** are never contracted. These pronouns can refer to either persons or things, and they precede the conjugated form of the verb. Observe the following:

> **Laura legge <u>il giornale</u>.**   *Laura reads the newspaper.*
> **Laura <u>lo</u> legge.**   *Laura reads it.*
> **Io porto <u>i libri</u>.**   *I bring the books.*

Io **li** porto.	*I bring them.*
Loro vẹdono <u>il ragazzo</u>.	*They see the boy.*
Loro **lo** vedono.	*They see him.*
Angelo vede <u>i nonni</u>.	*Angelo sees his grandparents.*
Ạngelo **li** vede.	*Angelo sees them.*
Giọrgio usa la scheda telefọnica	
(carta telefọnica, scheda magnẹtica).	*Giorgio uses the telephone card.*
Giọrgio **la** usa.	*George uses it.*
Teresa chiụde <u>le finestre</u>.	*Theresa closes the windows.*
Teresa **le** chiụde.	*Theresa closes them.*
Noi visitiamo <u>Marịa</u>.	*We visit Mary.*
Noi **la** visitiạmo.	*We visit her.*

5. Complete the following sentences with the appropriate direct object pronouns:

1. Teresa vede Giọrgio. Teresa_____vede.
2. Stẹfano guạrda i regali. Stẹfano_____guạrda.
3. Io chiạmo Gina. Io_____chiạmo.
4. Noi compriạmo le bịbite. Noi_____compriạmo.
5. Marco ha visto la signora Torre. Marco_____ha vista.
6. Noi abbiạmo chiamato lo zịo. Noi_____abbiạmo visitato.
7. Voi leggete i libri. Voi_____leggete.
8. Il postino porta le lẹttere. Il postino_____porta.
9. Antọnio chiụde la porta. Antọnio_____chiụde.
10. Tu prendi il caffè. Tu_____prendi.
11. Loro preparano i panini. Loro_____preparano.
12. Io apro le buste. Io_____apro.

6. Rewrite the following sentences, substituting each italicized object noun with the appropriate pronoun:

1. Mạrio rẹcita *le poesịe*.
2. Noi salutiamo *la nonna*.
3. Teresa sfọglia *i libri*.
4. Il cameriẹre serve *il caffè*.
5. Arturo porta *le sẹdie*.
6. Tu chiami *Olga*.
7. Stẹfano saluta *gli amici*.
8. Tu mandi *il pacco*.
9. Voi aspettate *le zịe*.
10. Loro lẹggono *la lettura*.
11. Io compro *i regali*.
12. Noi invitiạmo *lo zịo*.
13. Usiạmo *i computer* spesso.
14. Ecco il *telecomando!* (*remote control*)

Formal You: *La, Li, Le*

There are four forms of direct-object pronouns expressing the formal *you* in Italian: **La**, **L'**, **Li**, and **Le**. The Italian singular formal direct-object pronoun is **La**. Note that it is always capitalized and is considered both masculine and feminine singular. **La** is contracted to **L'** before verbs beginning with a vowel or silent **h**.

Li and **Le** are the plural masculine and feminine formal direct object pronouns, respectively. They too are always capitalized but are never contracted.

Emphatic Position (after the verb)

Signor Martini, conosco <u>Lei</u>?
Mr. Martini, do I know you?

Signora Martini, conosco <u>Lei</u>?
Mrs. Martini, do I know you?

Weak Position (before the verb)

Signor Martini, <u>La</u> conosco?
Mr. Martini, do 1 know you?

Signora Martini, <u>La</u> conosco?
Mrs. Martini, do I know you?

Signori, conosco Loro?	**Signori, Li conosco?**
Gentlemen, do I know you?	*Gentlemen, do I know you?*
Signora Torre e signorina Pirri, conosco Loro?	**Signora Torre e signorina Pirri, Le conosco?**
Mrs. Torre and Ms. Pirri, do I know you?	*Mrs. Torre and Ms. Pirri, do I know you?*
Signor Martini, ho conosciuto Lei?	**Signor Martini, L'ho conosciuto?** (-a: very formal)
Mr. Martini, have I met you?	*Mr. Martini, have I met you?*
Signora Torre, ho conosciuto Lei?	**Signora Torre, L'ho conosciuta?**
Mrs. Torre, have I met you?	*Mrs. Torre, have I met you?*

7. Complete the following sentences with the appropriate direct object pronouns:

1. Signor Corso, conosco *Lei?* Signor Corso, _____ conosco?
2. Signorine, conosco *Loro?* Signorine, _____ conosco?
3. Signori, conosco *Loro?* Signori, _____ conosco?
4. Dottore, ho conosciuto *Lei?* Dottore, _____ ho conosciuto?
5. Signora, aspetto *Lei?* Signora, _____ aspetto?
6. Ingegnere, aspetto *Lei?* Ingegnere, _____ aspetto?

8. Rewrite the following sentences, substituting each italicized object with the appropriate pronoun:

1. Signori, aiuto *Loro*.
2. Signore, chiamiamo *Loro*.
3. Signora, chiamiamo *Lei*.
4. Signorina, aspettiamo *Lei*.
5. Dottore, aiutiamo *Lei*.
6. Signor Pirri e signora Torre, aspettiamo *Loro*.
7. Dottoressa Merini, chiamo *Lei* domani?
8. Professor Carli, chiamo *Lei* stasera?

Special Use of the Pronoun *lo*

The object pronoun **lo** (generally, *it*) can replace an entire idea. Observe the following examples:

Credi che Giovanni farà bene agli esami?	*Do you believe John will do well in his exams?*
Sí, lo credo.	*Yes, I believe so.*
No, non lo credo.	*No, I don't believe so.*
Dubitate che loro arrivino domani?	*Do you doubt they will arrive tomorrow?*
Sí, lo dubitiamo.	*Yes, we doubt it.*
No, non lo dubitiamo.	*No, we don't doubt it.*
Sei sicuro che andrai in Italia l'anno prossimo?	*Are you sure you will go to Italy next year?*
Sí, lo sono.	*Yes, I am.*
No, non lo sono.	*No, I am not.*
Io sono stanco e lo è anche Teresa.	*I am tired and so is Theresa.*
Noi siamo contenti ma Pietro non lo è.	*We are happy, but Peter is not.*

9. Answer the following questions according to the indicated cues. Use the pronoun lo.

1. Sei sicuro che domani nevicherà?   *Sí*
2. Credi che io possa finire stasera?   *No*
3. Dubitate che loro vengano a cenare con noi?   *Sí*
4. Signora, Lei dubita che Olga sia studiosa?   *No*
5. Ragazzi, credete che pioverà domani?   *Sí*

10. Complete the following sentences with the appropriate object pronouns:

1. Mario è stanco e_____è anche Stefano.
2. Io sono contento e_____siete anche voi.
3. Luigi è pessimista e_____siamo anche noi.
4. Voi siete ottimisti ma io non_____sono.
5. Quegli studenti sono pigri (lazy) ma tu non_____sei.
6. Paola è triste ma Francesca non_____è.

DIRECT AND INDIRECT OBJECT PRONOUNS: *mi, ti, ci, vi*

The pronouns **mi**, **ti**, **ci**, and **vi** function as either direct objects or indirect objects. **Mi**, **ti**, and **vi** can be contracted (**m'**, **t'**, **v'**) before verbs beginning with a vowel or silent **h**. **Ci** contracts (**c'**) only when it precedes a verb beginning with i. These contractions, however, are much more common in spoken Italian than in written Italian.

Maria mi chiama.	*Mary calls me.*
Pietro mi parla.	*Peter talks to me.*
Loro t'invitano.	*They invite you.*
Io ti rispondo.	*I answer you.*
Lei ci vede.	*She sees us.*
Lei ci dice tutto.	*She tells us everything.*
Carlo vi saluta.	*Charles greets you.*
Carlo vi telefona.	*Charles telephones you.*

11. Answer the following questions according to the cues:

1. Ti chiamano i ragazzi?   *Sí*
2. Vi vede Carlo?   *No*
3. Ci sentono Mario e Teresa?   *Sí*
4. Ti parlano quei signori?   *No*
5. Vi telefona Olga?   *Sí*
6. Ti vede Arturo?   *No*
7. Ci salutano gli amici?   *Sí*
8. Ti dicono tutto?   *No*
9. Vi risponde Stefano?   *Sí*
10. Ci parlano quelle signorine?   *No*

12. Rewrite the following sentences, changing the object pronoun to the plural:

1. Carlo mi parla.
2. Maria ti vede.
3. Lui m'insegna la lezione.
4. Io ti saluto.
5. Loro mi guardano.
6. Lei ti risponde.

Personal Direct Object Pronouns in Emphatic Position

Direct personal object pronouns are placed after the verb for emphasis. Observe the following:

Weak Position (before the verb)		*Emphatic Position (after the verb)*	
Carlo mi guarda.	$\longrightarrow$	**Carlo guarda me.**	*Charles watches me.*
Io ti chiamo.	$\longrightarrow$	**Io chiamo te.**	*I call you.*
Tu lo inviti.	$\longrightarrow$	**Tu inviti lui.**	*You invite him.*
Noi la chiamiamo.	$\longrightarrow$	**Noi chiamiamo lei.**	*We call her.*
Io La cerco.	$\longrightarrow$	**Io cerco Lei.**	*I am looking for you.*
Loro ci vogliono.	$\longrightarrow$	**Loro vogliono noi.**	*They want us.*
Lui vi saluta.	$\longrightarrow$	**Lui saluta voi.**	*He greets you.*
Tu li accompagni.	$\longrightarrow$	**Tu accompagni loro.**	*You accompany them.*
Io le invito.	$\longrightarrow$	**Io invito loro.**	*I invite them.*
Noi Li chiamiamo.	$\longrightarrow$	**Noi chiamiamo Loro.**	*We call you.*
Io Le saluto.	$\longrightarrow$	**Io saluto Loro.**	*I greet you.*

13. Rewrite the following sentences in their emphatic forms:

1. Luisa mi saluta.
2. I miei amici ci cercano.
3. Noi ti vogliamo vedere.
4. Lui vi chiama.
5. Io La saluto.

6. Tu la saluti.
7. Loro lo cercano.
8. Noi le invitiamo.
9. Voi li chiamate.
10. Io Le saluto.

INDIRECT OBJECT PRONOUNS: *gli, le, loro*

The third-person indirect object pronouns are **gli** (*to him*) and **le** (*to her*) in the singular, and **loro** (*to them*) in the plural. Note that, in the third person, there is a definite difference between the direct and indirect object pronouns. Note that **gli** and **le** immediately precede the conjugated form of the verb, whereas **loro** immediately follows the conjugated form of the verb. Also, with **loro** there is no gender differentiation. **Gli**, **le**, and **loro** can refer to either persons or things. **Gli** may become **gl'** before verb forms beginning with **i-**, whereas **le** and **loro** never contract.

In colloquial Italian **loro** (*to them*, both m. and f.) is usually replaced with **gli**. **Gli**, which used to mean only *to him* (third-person singular indirect m. pronoun), is now colloquially used also for *to them* (third-person plural indirect object pronoun, m. and f.). This is quite common nowadays: The sentences, **Parlo** *ai ragazzi* and **Parlo** *alle ragazze* is colloquially substituted with, **Gli parlo** (in both cases, m. and f.), instead of **Parlo loro**. In formal Italian, **loro** is preferred. Still, many see **loro** and **gli** as having become interchangeable. The question is not yet fully resolved.

Observe the following examples:

Emphatic Position (after verb)	*Weak Position (before verb)*
Io scrivo a Carlo.	**Io gli scrivo.**
I write to Charles.	*I write him (to him).*
Io insegno la lezione a Carlo.	**Io (gli) gl'insegno la lezione.**
I teach Charles the lesson.	*I teach him the lesson.*
Tu parli a Teresa.	**Tu le parli.**
You speak to Teresa.	*You speak to her.*
Lui parla ai ragazzi.	**Lui parla loro,** or **Lui gli parla.**
He speaks to the boys.	*He speaks to them.*
Rispondo a Maria e a Paolo.	**Rispondo loro,** or **Gli rispondo.**
I answer Mary and Paul.	*I answer them.*
Telefoniamo alle signorine.	**Telefoniamo loro,** and **Gli telefoniamo.**
We telephone the young ladies.	*We telephone them.*

14. Complete the following sentences with the appropriate indirect object pronouns as suggested by the italicized cues:

1. Maria_____scrive.   *a Paolo*
2. Noi_____parliamo.   *a Olga*
3. Tu scrivi_____.   *agli amici*
4. _____posso rispondere?   *alla signorina*
5. Signori, possiamo parlare_____?   *agli studenti*
6. Scriviamo_____.   *a Stefano e a Maria*
7. _____rispondo.   *alla mia amica*
8. _____parliamo.   *a Giuseppe*

15. Rewrite the following sentences, replacing each italicized indirect object noun with the appropriate pronoun:

1. Mando un regalo *a mia madre*.
2. Scriviamo molte lettere *al ragazzo*.
3. Do l'indirizzo *agli amici*.
4. Telefono *alla zia*.
5. Inviamo un telegramma *ai genitori*.
6. Rispondo *a Umberto*.
7. Scrivo *a Luisa*.
8. Diamo il benvenuto *alle signorine*.

16. Complete each sentence with the appropriate direct or indirect object pronoun:

1. Luigi scrive ai suoi fratelli. Luigi scrive_____.
2. Maria telefona a sua zia. Maria_____telefona.
3. Noi salutiamo gli amici. Noi_____salutiamo.
4. Loro guardano il grattacielo (*skyscraper*). Loro_____guardano.
5. Noi inviamo i regali. Noi_____inviamo.
6. Mario invita Giorgio. Mario_____invita.
7. Io telefono a Teresa. Io_____telefono.
8. Do il libro a Mario._____do il libro.
9. Diamo il pacco ai signori. Diamo_____il pacco.
10. Noi riceviamo le lettere. Noi_____riceviamo.

FORMAL INDIRECT OBJECT PRONOUNS: *Le, Loro*

The Italian formal indirect object pronouns are: **Le** (*to you*), formal singular, and **Loro** (*to you*), formal **plural**. Note that with **Le** and **Loro** there is no gender differentiation. Also, they never contract, and they refer only to persons.

As explained in the introduction to this chapter, **voi** may be used to address one single person. See the examples right after the introduction.

In colloquial Italian, **Gli** has replaced the use of **Loro** (*to you*, formal pl.). **Gli** used to mean only to him, nowadays it also means to *you* (formal pl.). The **G-** of **Gli** is capitalized by many in order to avoid confusion with **gli** = *to him*, but it's not required.

Note that **Le** and **Gli** precede the verb and **Loro** always follows the verb. Observe the following:

Signora, parlo a Lei?   ⟶**Signora, Le parlo?**
Madame, do I speak to you?   *Madame, do I speak to you?*

Signor Rossi, parlo a Lei?   ⟶**Signor Rossi, Le parlo?**
Mr. Rossi, do I speak to you?   *Mr. Rossi, do I speak to you?*

Signorine, parlo a Loro?   ⟶**Signorine, parlo Loro?** and **Signorine, Gli parlo?**
Young ladies, do I speak to you?   *Young ladies, do I speak to you?*

Signori, parlo a Loro?   ⟶**Signori, parlo Loro?** and **Signori, Gli parlo?**
Gentlemen, do I speak to you?   *Gentlemen, do I speak to you?*

17. Complete each sentence with the appropriate indirect object pronoun:

1. Signor Pirri, parlo *a Lei?* Signor Pirri, _____ parlo?
2. Signori, mando i pacchi *a Loro?* Signori, _____ mando i pacchi?
3. Signorine, telefono *a Loro?* Signorine, _____ telefono?
4. Signora, mando l'orologio *a Lei?* Signora, _____ mando l'orologio?
5. Dottore, scrivo *a Lei?* Dottore, _____ scrivo?

6. Professoresse, rispondiạmo *a Loro?* Professoresse, _____ rispondiạmo?

7. Dottoressa, parlo *a Lei?* Dottoressa,_____ parlo?

8. Don Pasquạle, telẹfono *a Lei?* Don Pasquạle,_____ telẹfono?

18. Answer the following with complete sentences using the formal indirect object pronouns *Le* and *Loro*:

1. Signor Torre, ci scrive?   5. Professoressa, mi dà un bel voto?

2. Signora, mi parla?   6. Don Carlo, ci manda l'assegno?

3. Dottore, ci dà la ricetta?   7. Signore, mi scrive presto?

4. Signorina, ci manda la lẹttera?   8. Ingegnere, mi restituịsce i libri?

Ci as an Adverb of Place

The pronoun **ci** can be used to replace prepositional phrases beginning with the words **a**, **in**, or **su**. When **ci** is substituted for such phrases, it functions as an adverb of place. **Ci** can also be substituted for such adverbs of place as **dentro** (*inside*), **fuọri** (*outside*), **lí** (*there*), and **quị** (*here*), and it can be substituted for the proper name of a place, in which case it means *there*. Observe the following:

Replacing a, in, su, or a named place

Gino va a Bologna.	**Gino ci va.**
Gino goes to Bologna.	*Gino goes there.*
Vivo in Amẹrica.	**Ci vivo.**
I live in America.	*I live there.*
Salgo sul treno.	**Ci salgo.**
I get on the train.	*I get on it.*

Replacing dentro, fuọri, lí, qui

Luịsa va dentro.	**Luịsa ci va.**	**Luịsa non ci va.**
Louise goes inside.	*Louise goes there.*	*Louise doesn't go there.*
Vai fuọri?	**Ci vai?**	**Non ci vai?**
Are you going outside?	*Are you going there?*	*Are you (tu) going there?*
Vado lí.	**Ci vado.**	**Non ci vado.**
I go there.	*I go there.*	*I don't go there.*
Sto quị.	**Ci sto.**	**Non ci sto.**
I stay here.	*I stay here.*	*I'm not staying here (there).*

19. Rewrite the following, replacing the italicized words with a pronoun:

1. Noi andiạmo *alla spiạggia.*   4. Io resto *qui.*

2. Piẹtro va *fuọri.*   5. Loro vanno *a Palẹrmo.*

3. Luịsa sale *sul tetto.*   6. Maria vive *in Itạlia.*

20. Rewrite ex. 19 above in the negative replacing the italicized words with a pronoun.

1. _____ .   4. _____ .

2. _____ .   5. _____ .

3. _____ .   6. _____ .

21. Answer the following questions in the affirmative with complete sentences, replacing the italicized words with a pronoun:

1. Ragazzi, andate *in campagna?*
2. Luisa, vai *a teatro?*
3. Pietro, resti *a casa?*
4. Signora, va *lí?*
5. Professoressa, va *in biblioteca?*
6. Mario, ritorni *qui?*

22. Answer the questions in ex. 21 above in the negative.

1. _____.
2. _____.
3. _____.
4. _____.
5. _____.
6. _____.

Special Meanings with *ci*

When **ci** is used with certain verbs, the verb can acquire a somewhat different meaning. Study the following:

capirci   *to understand something about it*
> **Io non ci capisco niente.**
> *I don't understand a thing (about it).*

crederci   *to believe in something*
> **Credevano nell'amicizia, e ancora ci credono.**
> *They believed in friendship, and they still believe in it.*

entrarci   *to have something to do with*
> **Una volta m'interessavo molto; adesso non c'entro piú.**
> *Once I was very involved; now I have nothing to do with it.*

metterci   *to take (time)*
> **Anni fa ero a scuola in dieci minuti; adesso ci metto mezz'ora.**
> *Years ago I'd reach school in ten minutes; now it takes me half an hour.*

mettercisi   *to become involved (in it)*
> **In questo affare non mi ci metto.**
> *I'm not becoming involved in this affair.*

pensarci   *to think about it (of it)*
> **Pensi ancora alla gioventú? Non ci pensare piú!**
> *You're still thinking about youth? Don't think about it anymore!*

rifletterci   *to think something over*
> **A volte agivo automaticamente; adesso ci rifletto.**
> *At times I acted automatically; now I think it over.*

sentirci   *to be able to hear*
> **Adesso sto meglio; ci sento.**
> *Now I feel better; I'm able to hear.*

starci   *to agree; to go along with it*
> **Va bene, ci sto!**
> *All right, count me in! (I agree!)*

tenerci   *to care (for it)*
> **Loro ci tengono assai.**
> *They care (for it) a lot.*

> **Noi non ci teniamo affatto.**
> *We don't care at all.*

vederci   *to be able to see*
> **Accendete le luci; non ci vedo.**
> *Turn on the lights; I'm not able to see.*

volerci   *to take (time, space, etc.)*
> **Ci vọgliono mille metri per fare un chilọmetro.**
> *It takes one thousand meters to make one kilometer.*

23. Rewrite the following sentences, replacing the italicized words with a pronoun:
1. Credo *in ciò che tu dici*.
2. Non vede *niẹnte*.
3. Vogliamo riflẹttere *su quẹste cose*.
4. Non sẹntono *niẹnte*.
5. Non credo *in quẹste superstizịọni*.

24. Translate the following sentences into Italian:
1. Do you (*tu*) believe in it?
2. It takes too much time.
3. They are not able to see.
4. I assure (*assicurare*) you (*tu*) that I have nothing to do with it.
5. What are you thinking about?
6. It's necessary to think it over.
7. It takes us ten minutes to get home.
8. Are you (*tu*) able to see?
9. You (*tu*) don't care (for it).
10. I like it because I care (for it).
11. I spoke with Mạrio and he goes along with it.
12. Do you (*tu*) want to become involved in it?
13. You (*voi*) always go there.
14. She doesn't think about it anymore.
15. Sir, you may go there, but 1 don't agree.

THE PRONOUN: *ne*

The pronoun **ne** replaces a prepositional phrase introduced by **da** or **di**. It means *some, any, about, of it, of them, from it, from them,* or *from there.* It is used in the following cases:

In place of a prepositional phrase

Tọrnano da Siẹna.	**Ne tọrnano.**
They return from Sieña	*They return from there.*
Vado a casa e torno tra un'ora.	**Vado a casa e ne torno tra un'ora.**
I'm going home and I'll return in an hour.	*Vado a casa e ne torno tra un'ora.*

To replace the partitive

Ho del tempo.	**Ne ho.**
I have some time.	*I have some.*

With expressions followed by di

Parla di Giọrgio.	**Ne parla.**
He talks about George.	*He speaks about him.*

Ho bisogno (di) tre francobolli.
I need three stamps.

Ne ho bisogno (di) tre.
I need three of them.

With expressions of quantity

Ha molti amici.
He has many friends.

Ne ha molti.
He has many of them.

Ho quattro sorelle.
I have four sisters.

Ne ho quattro.
I have four of them.

Ho alcuni libri.
I have some books.

Ne ho alcuni.
I have some.

Voglio una tazza di caffè.
I want a cup of coffee.

Ne voglio una tazza.
I want a cup of it.

To replace di plus an infinitive

Ho il desiderio di viaggiare.
I feel like traveling.

Ne ho il desiderio.
I feel like it.

25. Rewrite the following sentences, replacing the italicized words with an appropriate pronoun:

1. Parliamo *di Luigi*.
2. Vengono *dal museo*.
3. Comprano tre *biglietti*.
4. Abbiamo voglia *di dormire*.
5. Ha molte *camicie*.
6. È contento *del suo posto*.
7. Mangia *della carne*.
8. Compra una dozzina *di pere*.
9. Non ho voglia *di cenare*.
10. Hai due *fratellini*.
11. Abbiamo bisogno *di una macchina*.
12. Hanno *comprato* solo *dieci libri*.

26. Rewrite the following sentences, replacing the italicized words with ci, ne, gli, le, or loro as needed.

1. Ritorniamo *dallo stadio*.
2. Do *del denaro* a Gino.
3. Offriamo il biglietto *all'amico*.
4. Telefono *a Olga*.
5. Invia il pacco *ai ragazzi*.
6. Tu vai *in Francia*.
7. Restano *qui*.
8. Ricevono pochi *fiori*.
9. Parliamo *alla signorina Bianchi*.
10. Torneranno *da Roma* domani.

Double Object Pronouns

me lo, te lo, ce lo, ve lo

In many cases both a direct and indirect object pronoun will appear in the same sentence. When such occurs, the indirect object pronoun almost always precedes the direct object pronoun. Note that **mi, ti, ci,** and **vi** change to **me, te, ce,** and **ve** when followed by a direct object pronoun. Study the following chart and the examples below:

Double Object Pronouns

Indirect \ Direct	lo	la	l'	li	le	ne
mi → me	me lo	me la	me l'	me li	me le	me ne
ti → te	te lo	te la	te l'	te li	te le	te ne
ci → ce	ce lo	ce la	ce l'	ce li	ce le	ce ne
vi → ve	ve lo	ve la	ve l'	ve li	ve le	ve ne

Lui me lo da.	*He gives it* (m. s.) *to me.*
Lui te la dice.	*He tells it* (f. s.) *to you.*
Loro ce ne portano.	*They bring us some* (*of it, of them*).
Io ve ne do.	*I give you some* (*of it, of them*).
Io ve l'insegno.	*I teach it to you.*
Tu me ne compri.	*You buy me some* (*of it, of them*).
Lui ce le regala.	*He gives them to us as gifts* (*as a gift*).

27. Rewrite the following sentences, replacing the direct and indirect objects with the appropriate pronouns:

1. Maria manda la cartolina a noi.
2. Giovanni dà le lettere a voi.
3. Lui dice i segreti a te.
4. Loro insegnano le lezioni a me.
5. Tu porti il pacco a noi.
6. Antonio presta la penna a voi.
7. Io do il dizionario a te.

28. Complete the following sentences, substituting the italicized direct object nouns with their appropriate direct object pronouns. Make all other necessary changes.

1. Lui mi dà *l'indirizzo*. Lui_____dà.
2. Tu ci porti *il caffè*. Tu_____porti.
3. Roberto ci scrive *molte lettere*. Roberto_____scrive.
4. Vostra (*your*) nonna vi manda *i regali*. Vostra nonna _____ manda.
5. Io ti presto *la macchina*. Io_____presto.
6. Loro mi restituiscono *le penne*. Loro_____restituiscono.
7. Luisa ci mostra *i suoi dipinti* (paintings). Luisa_____mostra.
8. Voi mi ridate *la patente* (license). Voi _____ ridate.

glielo, gliela, glieli, gliele

The indirect object pronouns **gli** (*to him*), **le** (*to her*), and **Le** (*to you*, formal), when followed by the direct object pronouns **lo, la, li, le**, form one word: **glielo** (**gliela, glieli, gliele**). Very often, the capital letter **G-** is used to indicate the formal **Le** (**Glielo, -a, -i, -e**). Observe the following chart and examples:

Indirect Object Pronouns With Direct Object Pronouns

Direct ⟍ Indirect	lo	la	l'	li	le	ne
gli + e	glielo	gliela	gliel'	glieli	gliele	gliene
le → gli + e	glielo	gliela	gliel'	glieli	gliele	gliene
Le → Gli + e	**Glielo**	**Gliela**	**Gliel'**	**Glieli**	**Gliele**	**Gliene**

Do il libro a Paolo.	**Glielo do.**
I give the book to Paul.	*I give it to him.*
Ho dato il libro a Paolo.	**Gliel'ho dato.**
I gave the book to Paul.	*I gave it to him.*
Do la penna a Maria.	**Gliela do.**
Ho dato la penna a Maria.	**Gliel'ho data.**
I gave the pen to Mary.	*I gave it to her.*

Signorina, do i quaderni a Lei.

Miss, I give the notebooks to you.

Signorina, ho dato il libro a Lei.

Miss, I gave the book to you.

Sí, do le lettere al postino.

Yes, I give the letters to the mail carrier.

Sí, ho dato la lettera al postino.

Yes, I gave the letter to the mail carrier.

Do alcune caramelle al bambino.

I give some candies to the child.

Ho dato delle caramelle al bambino.

I gave some candies to the child.

Signora, Le do tre idee.

Madame, I give you three ideas.

Signora, Le ho dato due libri.

Madame, I gave you two books.

Signorina, Glieli do.

Miss, I give them to you.

Signorina, Gliel'ho dato.

Miss, I gave it to you.

Sí, gliele do.

Yes, I give them to him.

Sí, gliel'ho data.

Yes, I gave it to him.

Gliene do alcune.

I give him some (of them).

Gliene ho date.

I gave them to him.

Signora, Gliene do tre.

Madame, I give you three (of them).

Signora, Gliene ho dati due.

Madame, I gave you two (of them).

29. Complete the following sentences replacing the italicized direct object nouns with the appropriate pronouns, and replace the italicized verb forms when needed.

1. Prestiamo *la macchina* a Paolo. _____ prestiamo.
2. Hai *mandato* i *regali* alla bambina. _____ hai _____.
3. Ho *inviato delle caramelle* a Pierino. _____ ho _____.
4. Signora, Le ho *dato* due *libri*. Signora, _____ ho _____ due.
5. Spedisci *le lettere* a tuo padre. _____ spedisci.
6. Professore, Le riporto *il libro*. Professore, _____ riporto.
7. Ho *regalato la penna* a Olga. _____ ho _____.
8. Ho *spiegato la lezione* a Roberto. _____ ho _____.
9. Dottore, Le ho *confermato la ricetta*. Dottore, _____ ho _____.
10. Pierino ha *causato* tanti *problemi* alla madre. _____ ha _____ tanti.

loro, Loro with lo, la, ti, le, ne

The indirect object pronouns **loro** (*to them*, both m. and f.), and **Loro** (*to you*, formal plural, both m. and f.) follow the verbs at all times. In colloquial Italian, **gli** substitutes **loro** (*gli = loro, to them*, both m. and f.) and also **Loro** (*Gli = Loro, to you*, formal plural, both m. and f.). When it replaces **Loro**, **Gli** is often capitalized for clarity (study the formal indirect object pronouns in this chapter). Observe the following chart and examples:

*Indirect Object Pronouns **loro** and **Loro** with Direct Object Pronouns*

Indirect \ Direct	lo	la	l'	li	le	ne
loro	lo + verb + loro	la v. loro	l'* v. loro	li v. loro	le v. loro	ne v. loro
gli + e +	glielo v.	gliela v.	gliel' v.	glieli v.	gliele v.	gliene v.
Loro	lo v. Loro	la v. Loro	l' v. Loro	li v. Loro	le v. Loro	ne v. Loro
Gli + e +	Glielo v.	Gliela v	Gliel' v.	Glieli v.	Gliele v.	Gliene v.

*Verbs beginning with a vowel or *h-* (*present indicative of* **avere**).

Do il libro agli studenti.	**Lo do loro.**
I give the book to the students.	*I give it to them.*
„ „ „ „	**Glielo do.**
„ „ „ „	*I give it to them.*
Ho dato la penna alle studentesse.	**L'ho data loro.**
I gave the pen to the students (f.).	*I gave it to them.*
„ „ „ „	**Gliel'ho data.**
„ „ „ „	*I gave it to them.*
Signori, do i libri a Loro.	**Signori, li do Loro.**
Gentlemen, I give you the books.	*Gentlemen, I give them to you.*
„ „ „ „	**Signori, Glieli do.**
Signore (f. pl.), do le penne a Loro.	**Signore (f. pl.), le do Loro.**
Ladies, I give the pens to you.	*Ladies, I give them to you.*
„ „ „ „	**Signore (f. pl.) Gliele do.**
Signore e Signori, ho dato i regali a Loro.	**Signore e signori, li ho dati Loro.**
Ladies and Gentlemen, I gave you the gifts.	*Ladies and Gentlemen, I gave them to you.*
„ „ „ „	**Signore e signori, Glieli ho dati.**
„ „ „ „	*Ladies and gentlemen, I gave them to you.*
Do dello zucchero ai bambini.	**Ne do loro.**
I give the children some sugar.	*I give them some (of it).*
Ho dato della marmellata ai bambini.	**Gliene ho data.**
I gave the children some marmelade.	*I gave them some (of it).*
Ho dato tre caramelle ai ragazzi.	**Ne ho date loro tre.** (*Also*: **Gliene ho date tre.**)
I gave the boys three candies.	*I gave them three (of them).*
Signori, do Loro dello zucchero.	**Signori, ne do Loro.** (*Also*: **Signori, Gliene do.**)
Sirs, I give you some sugar.	*Sirs, I give you some (of it).*

30. *Rewrite the following replacing the italicized direct and indirect object nouns with the appropriate pronouns. Have certain verb forms agree in gender and number with the nouns or pronouns as needed.*
  1. Mandiamo *i regali ai bambini.* _____.
  2. Ho regalato *questi libri a Loro.* _____.
  3. Tu darai *i biglietti a loro.* _____.
  4. Il maestro dà *il diploma alle studentesse.* _____.
  5. Lo zio ha portato *i documenti ai signori.* _____.
  6. Diamo *la palla ai ragazzi.* _____.
  7. Compro *la merenda alle bambine.* _____.
  8. Signora, *Le* ho dato *troppa marmellata.* _____.
  9. Signore (f. pl.), darò *Loro* alcune *cartoline.* _____.
  10. Ho dato *dello zucchero ai bambini.* _____.
  11. Ieri ho mandato *la e-mail alle signorine.* _____.
  12. Signori, abbiamo spedito *questi libri a Loro.* _____.

31. *Give the Italian equivalents.*
  1. Uncle Tommaso, how are you today? _____.
  2. Mrs. Lari, did you wake up late this morning? _____.
  3. Miss Giardino, are you going to the restaurant today? _____.

4. Boys, you yell when you play! _____.
5. Gentlemen, where do you work? _____.
6. They went on vacation a month ago. _____.
7. Little boy, what's your name? _____.
8. He was reading while she was writing. _____.
9. Whose are these novels, F. Lentricchia's or G. Sorrentino's? _____.
10. Who wants to do it ? It's easy! _____.
11. If they would only study more! _____.
12. We too went to the movies last night. _____.

32. Rewrite the following sentences replacing the italicized direct objects with the appropriate pronouns.

1. Giorgio, perché non chiudi *le finestre?* _____.
2. Abbiamo veduto *la nonna.* _____.
3. Non vediamo *gli zii* da molti anni. _____.
4. Ho mandato *la e-mail* a Teresa. _____.
5. Adesso compro *il gelato.* _____.
6. Tu saluti *Olga e Paolo.* _____.

33. Answer the following questions with full sentences. (Answers may vary.)

1. Giovanna, sei sicura che Paola verrà domani? _____.
2. Tito, credi che Marcello abiti in Svizzera? _____.
3. Ragazzi, dubitate che io vi paghi il pranzo? _____.
4. Io sono stanchissino, e tu? _____.
5. Signora, possiamo aiutarLa? _____.
6. Signori, Li ho riconosciuti? _____.
7. Paolo e Sandra, vi scrivete? _____.
8. Maria, chi ti telefona spesso? _____.
9. Mario e Luisa, ci state? _____.
10. Ragazzi, andate fuori soli? _____.
11. Signora, è mai andata in campagna? _____.
12. È strano! Puoi crederci? _____.
13. Quante ore ci metti in auto da qui a casa? _____.
14. Hai molti euro in tasca? _____.
15. Hai bisogno di molto zucchero? _____.
16. Gli euro chi te li dà? _____.

REVIEW

34. Rewrite the following sentences, replacing the direct and indirect object nouns with the appropriate double object pronouns:

1. Luigi dà *il pallone a me.*
2. Maria manda *la lettera ai suoi genitori.*
3. Il maestro insegna *le lezioni allo studente.*
4. Presto *la chiave a Mario.*
5. Luisa presta *i quaderni a noi.*
6. Antonio regala *la penna a voi.*
7. Do *questo dizionario a Loro.*
8. Inviano *i pacchi a te.*
9. Compriamo *i giocattoli ai bambini.*
10. Mando *gli auguri a tua madre.*
11. Prestano *la radio a Lei.*
12. Il mio amico manda *molte cartoline a me.*

13. Io do *del denaro a te.*
14. Loro comprano *le buste a loro.*
15. Voi date *le informazioni a noi.*
16. Signore (m. s.), il vicino ha prestato *il martello a Lei.*
17. Signorina, io regalo *queste cartoline a Lei.*
18. Signori, Lui manda *quei pacchi a Loro.*
19. Giovanotti, quando ridate *il denaro a me?*
20. Signore (m. s.), io ho portato *la lettera a Lei.*

Position of Object Pronouns

With conjugated verbs, simple and compound.

All object pronouns with the exception of **loro** and **Loro** always precede the conjugated form of the verb. If a sentence is negative, the negative word precedes the object pronouns. With compound tenses, the object pronouns precede the auxiliary verb, and the past participle agrees with the subject in gender and number.

Affirmative	*Negative*
Io glielo do.	**Io non glielo do.**
I give it to him/her.	*I don't give it to him/her.*
Noi l'ascoltiamo.	**Noi non l'ascoltiamo.**
We listen to him/her.	*We don't listen to him/her.*
Le mandiamo loro.	**Non le mandiamo loro.**
Gliele mandiamo.	**Non gliele mandiamo.**
We send them to them.	*We don't send them to them.*
Signora, la spediamo a Lei.	**Signora, non la spediamo a Lei.**
Signora, Gliela spediamo.	**Signora, non Gliela spediamo.**
Madame, we mail it to you.	*Madame, we don't mail it to you.*
Signori, li mostriamo Loro.	**Signori, non li mostriamo Loro.**
Signori, Glieli mostriamo.	**Signori, non Glieli mostriamo.**
Sirs, we show them to you.	*Sirs, we don't show them to you.*
Signore (m. s.), noi seguiamo Lei.	**Signore, noi non seguiamo Lei.**
Signore (m. s.), noi La seguiamo.	**Signore, noi non La seguiamo.**
Sir, we follow you.	*Sir, we don't follow you.*
Signora, noi seguiamo Lei.	**Signora, noi non seguiamo Lei.**
Signora, noi La seguiamo.	**Signora, noi non La seguiamo.**
Madame, we follow you.	*Madame, we don't follow you.*
Ne vendiamo a lui.	**Non ne vendiamo a lui.**
Gliene vendiamo.	**Non gliene vendiamo.**
We sell him some.	*We don't sell him any.*
Signora, ne portiamo a Lei.	**Signora, non ne portiamo a Lei.**
Signora, Gliene portiamo.	**Signora, non Gliene portiamo.**
Madame, we bring you some.	*Madame, we don't bring you any.*
Signori, ne portiamo Loro.	**Signori, non ne portiamo Loro.**
Signori, Gliene portiamo.	**Signori, non Gliene portiamo.**
Gentlemen, we bring you some.	*Gentlemen, we don't bring you any.*

35. Rewrite the following sentences, replacing the direct and indirect object nouns with the appropriate pronouns.

1. Roberto porterà le carte. _____.
2. Rosa ci mandò la radio. _____.
3. Ho dato il dizionario a Olga. _____.
4. Rispondiamo ai cugini. _____.
5. Loro mi spiegarono il diagramma. _____.
6. Stefano ci dà i biglietti. _____.
7. Darò il calendario a Lei. _____.
8. Hai portato la camicia a me. _____.
9. Noi ascoltiamo te. _____.
10. Ne hai portati due a Teresa. _____.
11. Signori, Carlo porterà Loro le lettere. _____.
12. Professore, non abbiamo finito i compiti. _____.
13. Dottore, ha mandato le ricette ai miei nonni? _____.
14. Ragazzi, portate le caramelle a noi! _____.
15. Signore (m. s.), regali i giocattoli ai bimbi. _____.
16. Ascoltiamo i signori! _____.
17. Diamo del cibo ai ragazzi! _____.
18. Diamo del cibo alle ragazze! _____.
19. Professoressa, non dia troppi compiti agli studenti! _____.
20. Maria, per piacere, porta gli esami alla segretaria. _____.
21. Il presidente confessa molte cose al segretario di stato. _____.
22. Ragazzi, ieri ho dato i regali a voi. _____.
23. Quante cose hanno regalato ai nipoti i nonni. _____.
24. Arturo ha raccontato tante storie a noi. _____.
25. Avremmo dovuto fare molte domande! _____.

With infinitives

The object pronouns may either precede the verb that accompanies the infinitive or they may be attached to the infinitive. Note that when the pronoun is attached to the infinitive, the final -e of the infinitive is dropped. Observe the following:

Lui me lo vuole dare.	*He wants to give it to me.*
Lui vuole darmelo.	*He wants to give it to me.*
Io te lo voglio chiedere.	*I want to ask it to you.*
Io voglio chiedertelo.	*I want to ask it to you.*
Signora, lo voglio chiedere a Lei.	*Madame, I want to ask it to you.*
Signora, Glielo voglio chiedere.	*" " " "*
Signora, voglio chiederGlielo.	*" " " "*
Signori, lo possiamo dare Loro.	*Gentlemen, we can give it to you.*
Signori, possiamo darlo Loro.	*" " " "*
Signori, Glielo possiamo dare.	*" " " "*
Noi ve ne vogliamo dare.	*We want to give you some (of it, of them).*
Noi vogliamo darvene.	*We want to give you some (of it, of them).*
Ve la preferiamo inviare.	*We prefer sending it to you.*
Preferiamo inviarvela.	*We prefer sending it to you.*
Glielo posso dare.	*I can give it to him.*
Posso darglielo.	*I can give it to him.*

36. Rewrite the following another way:

1. Possono darmelo.
2. Voglio comprarteli.
3. Preferiscono insegnarceli.
4. Desideriamo regalarvele.

5. Volevo dargliela.
6. Volevano vendermelo.
7. Signore (m. s.), preferisco dirlo a Lei.
8. Signorine, vogliamo inviarle Loro.

37. Rewrite the following, adding the pronouns to the infinitive:

1. Luisa mi può aiutare.
2. Roberto ti deve parlare.
3. Io ve la voglio vendere.
4. Loro ce li possono regalare.

5. Tu gliele puoi mostrare.
6. Noi te ne desideriamo dare.
7. Signori, Glieli vogliamo regalare.
8. Signora, Glielo posso prestare.

38. Rewrite the following according to the model:

Lui vuole dare i fiori a Teresa. →Lui glieli vuole dare.
→Lui vuole darglieli.

1. Voglio regalare i libri a Giovanni.
2. Vogliamo mostrare la macchina a voi.
3. Posso portare il biglietto a te.
4. Preferisco inviare le cartoline a Rosa.
5. Maria vuole regalare qualcosa a me.

6. Voleva cantare una canzone a noi.
7. Signora, io voglio regalare queste riviste a Lei.
8. Signori, noi possiamo riportare il computer a Loro.
9. Signorina, Maria deve comunicare la risposta a Loro.
10. Signore (m. s.), Paolo desidera dare le notizie a Loro.

With progressive tenses

With progressive tenses, the pronouns can either precede the auxiliary verb **stare** or be attached to the present gerund:

Sto leggendo la lettera.	*I am reading the letter.*
La sto leggendo.	*I am reading it.*
Sto leggendola.	*I am reading it.*
Stavamo comprando i libri.	*We were buying the books.*
Li stavamo comprando.	*We were buying them.*
Stavamo comprandoli.	*We were buying them.*

39. Rewrite the following, placing the pronouns before the auxiliary:

1. Roberto stava parlandoci.
2. Lui sta portandole.
3. Voi stavate leggendolo.

4. Tu stai preparandola.
5. Noi stavamo scrivendoti.
6. Loro stanno telefonandogli.

40. Rewrite the following, attaching the pronouns to the gerund:

1. Mi sta invitando.
2. Vi stavano scrivendo.
3. Ce la stanno mandando.

4. Glielo stavano leggendo.
5. Te le stanno offrendo.

41. Rewrite the following sentences according to the model:
Maria canta la canzone. →Maria sta cantandola.
→Maria la sta cantando.

1. Antonio compra i dischi.
2. Io scrivo la lettera.
3. Loro preparano il pacco.
4. Noi portiamo le penne.
5. Tu leggi la lettura.

6. Voi riportate i libri.
7. Luisa prende il treno.
8. Io lavo le camicie.
9. Pietro saluta l'amico.
10. Il sarto cuce (*sews*) i vestiti.

With informal commands

The object pronouns are always attached to the affirmative familiar commands (**tu, voi**) and always precede the negative familiar commands (**tu, voi**). If the command form is monosyllabic, pronouns double their first letter if they begin with **m**, **l**, or **c**. Observe the following examples:

Affirmative		*Negative*	
Fallo!	*Do it!*	**Non lo fare!**	*Don't do it!*
Fammelo!	*Do it for me!*	**Non me lo fare!**	*Don't do it to me (or: for me)!*
Dillo!	*Say it!*	**Non lo dire!**	*Don't say it!*
Dimmelo!	*Say it to me!*	**Non me lo dire!**	*Don't say it to me!*
Dagliela!	*Give it to him!*	**Non gliela dare!**	*Don't give it (m. s.) to him!*
Dammela!	*Give it to me!*	**Non me la dare!**	*Don't give it (f. s.) to me!*
Daccela!	*Give it to us!*	**Non ce la dare!**	*Don't give it (f. s.) to us!*
Fatelo!	*Do it!*	**Non lo fate!**	*Don't do it (m. s.) to us (or: for us)!*
Datelo!	*Give it!*	**Non lo date!**	*Don't give it!*

42. Rewrite the following commands in the negative:

1. Dammelo!
2. Fatele!
3. Portatela!
4. Prestaceli!
5. Mostraglielo!

6. Compraglielе!
7. Mandatemela!
8. Diccelo!
9. Dimmela!
10. Ditegliele!

43. Rewrite the following commands in the affirmative:

1. Non me la mandare!
2. Non gliele scrivete!
3. Non me lo prestare!
4. Non ce li dite!
5. Non me la comprate!

6. Non ce lo fare!
7. Non me le portare!
8. Non ce le insegnare!
9. Non me lo vendete!
10. Non gliela mostrate!

With formal commands

The object pronouns always precede the formal commands (**Lei, Loro**) both in the affirmative and in the negative. Observe the following:

Affirmative		*Negative*	
Me lo dica!	*Say it to me!*	**Non me lo dica!**	*Don't say it to me!*
Lo faccia!	*Do it!*	**Non lo faccia!**	*Don't do it to me (or: for me)!*
La facciano!	*Do it!*	**Non la facciano!**	*Don't do it!*
Gliele diano!	*Give them to him!*	**Non gliele diano!**	*Don't give them to him!*
Me li mandi!	*Send them to me!*	**Non me li mandi!**	*Don't send them to me!*

44. Rewrite the following commands in the negative:

1. Me lo dia!
2. Ce le diano!
3. Me la portino!
4. Ce li scriva!

5. Glielo presti!
6. Gliele mostrino!
7. Lo faccia!
8. Le facciano!

45. Rewrite the following commands in the affirmative:

1. Non me li prestino!
2. Non gliela mostri!
3. Non me le diano!
4. Non ce lo dica!
5. Non gliele insegnino!
6. Non me la scriva!
7. Non glielo mandino!
8. Non ce li legga!

First-person plural: Let's

Object pronouns are attached to the first-person plural command form (**noi**) in the affirmative. They precede the verb in the negative. Observe the following:

Affirmative		*Negative*	
Compriamoli!	*Let's buy them!*	**Non li compriamo!**	*Let's not buy them!*
Alziamoci!	*Let's get up!*	**Non ci alziamo!**	*Let's not get up!*
Facciamolo!	*Let's do it!*	**Non lo facciamo!**	*Let's not do it!*
Sediamoci!	*Let's sit down!*	**Non ci sediamo!**	*Let's not sit down!*
Mandiamole!	*Let's send them!*	**Non le mandiamo!**	*Let's not send them!*
Scriviamola!	*Let's write it!*	**Non la scriviamo!**	*Let's not write it!*

46. Rewrite the following in the affirmative:

1. Non la compriamo!
2. Non ci alziamo!
3. Non lo facciamo!
4. Non le diciamo!
5. Non ci sediamo!
6. Non li mandiamo!

47. Follow the model:

Addormentarci?   →Sí, addormentiamoci!
Shall we go to sleep?   Yes, let's go to sleep!

→No, non ci addormentiamo!
No, let's not go to sleep!

1. Sederci?
2. Vestirci?
3. Metterci il cappello?
4. Prepararci?
5. Lavarci le mani?
6. Alzarci?

Special Verbs with Indirect Objects

The following verbs take the indirect object pronoun and, when used in the third-person singular or plural, they have special meanings; also, note that many of them have the subject appear at the end of the sentence. When the subject is singular, the third-person singular form of the verb is used; when the subject is plural, the third-person plural form of the verb is used.

bastare   *to be enough, to suffice*
Mi basta un po' di pace.   *A little peace is enough for me.*
Ci bastano queste sedie.   *These chairs are enough for us.*

parere   *to seem*   **sembrare**   *to appear*
Ci pare strano vivere qui.   *It seems strange to us living here.*
A me mi sembrano buoni.   *To me they seem to be good.*

occorrere   *to be necessary, to be lacking*
Mi occorre una motocicletta.   *I need a motorcycle.*
Ci occorrono certi libri.   *We need certain books.*

piacere *to like, to be pleasing*

Mi piace sciare.	*I like to ski.*
A lui gli piacciono le città europëë.*	*He likes European cities.*
Ci piace la città di Nuova York.	*We like the city of New York.*
Ti piacciono i panini?	*Do you like the sandwiches?*
Le piace la musica moderna.	*She likes modern music.*
Vi piacciono gli scrittori italiani?	*Do you like Italian writers?*

dolere *to hurt* **fare male** *to hurt*

Mi fa male la testa.	*My head hurts.*
Ci fanno male le gambe.	*Our legs hurt.*
A te ti duole il dente?	*Your tooth hurts?*
Gli dolgono i denti.	*His teeth hurt.*

interessarsi *to be interested in*

Mi interessa la politica.	*I am interested in politics.*
Non mi interessano gli sport invernali.	*I am not interested in winter sports.*

48. Complete the following with the appropriate indirect object pronoun and verb ending:

1. A me_____piac_____quell'orchestra.
2. A me_____piacci_____quei negozi.
3. A te_____occorr_____un mese di riposo.
4. A te_____occorr_____degli spiccioli.
5. A lui_____f_____male la mano.
6. A lui_____f_____male le gambe.
7. A lei_____par_____ottimo dormire sempre.
8. A noi_____sembr_____interessanti questi vasi.
9. A noi_____sembr_____buono quel vino.
10. A voi_____duol_____la testa.
11. A voi_____dolg_____le braccia.
12. A Lei_____bast_____stare sola?

49. Answer the following questions in the affirmative:

1. Vi piace ballare?
2. Ti occorre la macchina?
3. Occorrono Loro quei libri?
4. A Maria le fa male il ginocchio?
5. A noi ci bastano questi soldi?
6. Gli duole la spalla a Sandro?
7. Ci sembrano tristi quei ragazzi?
8. Ti pare nuovo questo vestito?
9. Vi fanno male i denti?
10. Signora, Le occorre qualcosa?

50. Rewrite the following according to the model:

A me / il pesce⟶Mi piace il pesce.

1. A noi / la musica
2. A Paolo / le lingue
3. A loro / il progetto
4. A te / i programmi
5. A Elena / l'arte moderna
6. A Loro / i concerti
7. A noi / l'opera
8. A me / viaggiare

REFLEXIVE PRONOUNS

Reflexive pronouns are used when the action in the sentence is both executed and received by the subject. (For a complete review of reflexive verbs see Chapter 6.) The reflexive pronouns are

io	⟶**mi**	noi	⟶**ci**
tu	⟶**ti**	voi	⟶**vi**
lui, lei, Lei	⟶**si**	loro, Loro	⟶**si**

* The dieresis (¨) indicates the phonological separation of vowels; it is rarely used and always optional.

Io mi pẹttino.	*I comb my hair.*
Noi ci alziạmo.	*We get up.*
Loro si siędono.	*They sit down.*
Tu ti vesti.	*You get dressed.*

51. *Complete the following with the appropriate reflexive pronoun:*

1. Io_____chiạmo Arturo.
2. _____laviạmo le mani.
3. A che ora_____alzi?
4. Perché non_____sedete?
5. Marco_____mette la cravatta blu.
6. Loro_____fanno la dọccia.
7. Tu_____addormenti.
8. Teresa_____cọrica tardi.
9. Io non_____sento bene.
10. Il bambino_____tọglie (*takes off*) la camịcia.

DISJUNCTIVE PRONOUNS

The disjunctive pronouns (pronouns which follow a preposition or a verb) are the same as the subject pronouns with the exception of **io** (**me**) and **tu** (**te**).

Subject Pronouns   *Disjunctive Pronouns*

		← →		
(io)	chiạmo Roberto	io→me	Roberto chiạma	me
(tu)	chiạmi Luịsa	tu→te	Luịsa chiạma	te
(lui)	chiạma Mạrio	lui = lui	Mạrio chiạma	lui
(lei)	chiạma Stẹfano	lei = lei	Stẹfano chiạma	lei
(Lei)	chiạma Carlo	Lei = Lei	Carlo chiạma	Lei
(noi)	chiamiạmo Guịdo	noi = noi	Guịdo chiạma	noi
(voi)	chiạmate Olga	voi = voi	Olga chiạma	voi
(loro)	chiạmano Piero	loro = loro	Pięro chiạma	loro
(Loro)	chiạmano Marịa	Loro = Loro	Marịa chiạma	Loro

52. *Complete the following by changing the italicized words to the appropriate disjunctive pronouns:*

1. Lo facciạmo per_____.   *Gino*
2. Andiạmo a scuọla con_____.   *Teresa e Carlo*
3. Voi cominciạte dopo di_____.   *Marịa*
4. Loro ạbitano sotto di_____.   *io*
5. Sai che Giovanni vive presso di_____.   *tu*
6. Tutti vanno al cịnema tranne (*except*)_____.   *voi*
7. Ci sediạmo dịetro di_____.   *lui*
8. Tutti stụdiano tranne _____.   *noi*
9. Siạmo venuti per_____.   *lei*
10. Siạmo qui per_____.   *Loro*

Disjunctive Pronouns after Comparatives

The disjunctive pronouns **me**, **te**, **lui**, **lei**, **Lei**, **noi**, **voi**, **loro**, **Loro** are preceded by the preposition **di** after comparatives. Study the following:

Teresa stụdia piú di noi.	*Teresa studies more than us.*
Carlo canta mẹglio di me.	*Charles sings better than me.*

Io pạttino pęggio di loro.	*I skate worse than them.*
Tu leggi mẹglio di lui.	*You read better than him.*
Loro suọnano (cosí) bene come lei.	*They play as well as she does.*
Lei lavora (tanto) quạnto te.	*She works as much as you.*
Noi viaggiạmo piú di voi.	*We travel more than you.*
Io dormo meno di Lei.	*I sleep less than you (formal s.).*
Noi studiạmo piú di Loro.	*We study more than you (formal pl.).*

53. Supply the correct disjunctive pronouns according to the cues provided:

1. Quẹi giọvani bạllano piú di_____. *io*
2. Io scrivo piú lẹttere di_____. *Carlo*
3. Noi beviạmo meno latte di_____. *Carlo e Marịa*
4. Loro cạntano mẹglio di_____. *tu e io*
5. Io guịdo pęggio di_____. *tu e lui*
6. Tu hai meno libri di_____. *Luịsa*
7. Mịa sorella legge piú di_____. *mịo fratello*
8. Noi abbiạmo meno esperiẹnza di_____. *quẹi signori*

INDEFINITE ADJECTIVES AND PRONOUNS

The following indefinite adjectives are invariable: **ogni** (*each, every*), **quạlche** (*some, any*) and **qualụnque** (**qualsịasi**) (*all, any kind, whatever*). These adjectives do not have plural forms, and each is used for both masculine and feminine singular nouns. Study the following:

Mi lavo i denti ogni giọrno.
I brush my teeth every day.

Ogni tanto scrivo quạlche lẹttera.
Once in a while I write some letters.

Ci piạce qualụnque (qualsịasi) cibo.
We like all kinds (any kind) of food.

Chiụnque sịa, io non ci sono.
Whoever he/she is, I'm not in.

Note that **quạlche**, though singular in Italian, is translated as a plural in English: **quạlche lẹttera** means *some letters*, and **quạlche libro** means *some books*.

Indefinite Adjectives and Pronouns in the Singular

The following indefinite adjectives are singular: **alcuno (-a)**, **ciascuno (-a)**, (**ciascheduno, -a**), **nessuno (-a)**. Their meanings are *any* (*anyone*), *each* (*ach one*), and *any* (*anyone*), respectively. Note that **alcuno (-a)** is used only in a negative sentence. **Ciascuno** drops the **-o** (**ciascun**) before a noun; **nessuno** also drops the **-o** (**nessun**). Study the following:

Adjectives		*Pronouns*
Non ho alcun parente.	⟶	**Non ho alcuno.**
I don't have any relatives.		*I don't have anyone.*
Non visitiạmo alcuna zịa.	⟶	**Non visitiạmo alcuna.**
We do not visit any aunts.		*We don't visit anyone.*
Diạmo un regalo a ciascụn (ciaschedụn) bambino.	⟶	**Diạmo un regalo a ciascuno (ciascheduno).**
We give a gift to each little boy.		*We give a gift to each one.*

Diamo un regalo a ciascuna (ciascheduna) bambina. *We give a gift to each little girl.*	⟶ **Diamo un regalo a ciascuna (ciascheduna).** *We give a gift to each one.*
Che ognun uomo badi ai propri affari! *Let every man mind his own business!*	⟶ **Che ognuno badi ai propri affari!** *Let everyone (m.) mind his own business.*
Che ognuna donna badi ai propri affari! *Let every woman mind her own business!*	⟶ **Che ognuna badi ai propri affari!** *Let everyone (f.) mind her own business!*
Non vedo nessun amico. *I don't see any friends.*	⟶ **Non vedo nessuno.** *I don't see anyone.*
Non vedo nessuna amica. *I don't see any friends (f.).*	⟶ **Non vedo nessuna.** *I don't see anyone (f.).*

Indefinite Adjectives and Pronouns in the Plural

The following indefinite adjectives, which have the meaning *some*, are plural: **alcuni** (-e), **certuni** (-e), and **taluni** (-e). Study the following:

Adjectives	*Pronouns*
Alcuni esami sono difficili. *Some exams are difficult.*	⟶ **Alcuni sono difficili.** *Some are difficult.*
Alcune vacanze sono bellissime. *Some vacations are very beautiful.*	⟶ **Alcune sono bellissime.** *Some (vacations) are very beautiful.*
Certuni uomini sono ambiziosi. *Some men are ambitious.*	⟶ **Certuni sono ambiziosi.** *Some (men) are ambitious.*
Talune penne non scrivono bene. *Some pens don't write well.*	⟶ **Talune non scrivono bene.** *Some (pens) don't write well.*

Note that **alcuni** (-e), **certuni** (-e), and **taluni** (-e) are often interchangeable.

54. Complete the following sentences by translating the italicized English words:
1. Non abbiamo_____successo.   *any*
2. Luigi si sbarba_____giorno.   *every*
3. Ogni tanto leggo_____rivista.   *some*
4. A me piace_____tipo di pesce.   *any*
5. Loro non hanno_____amico.   *any*
6. _____studente deve studiare.   *each*
7. _____giornali sono noiosi.   *some*
8. _____fotografie sono lucide.   *some*

POSSESSIVE PRONOUNS

In Chapter 3 there is a section on possessive adjectives; review it carefully. Possessive pronouns are used to replace a noun modified by a possessive adjective. A possessive pronoun must agree with the noun it replaces in gender and number and is accompanied by the appropriate definite article or its contracted forms: **al**, **ai**, **allo**, etc. (see contractions on page 33–35.) Observe the difference between the possessive adjectives and the possessive pronouns:

Possessive Adjectives	*Possessive Pronouns*
il mio libro, la mia penna ⟶	**il mio, la mia**
i miei libri, le mie penne ⟶	**i miei, le mie**

il tụo libro, la tụa penna   ⟶ il <u>tụo</u>, la <u>tụa</u>

i tuọi libri, le tụe penne   ⟶ i <u>tuọi</u>, le <u>tụe</u>

il sụo libro, la sụa penna   ⟶ il <u>sụo</u>, la <u>sụa</u>

il Sụo libro, la Sụa penna   ⟶ il <u>Sụa</u>, la <u>Sụa</u>

i Suọi libri, le Sụe penne   ⟶ i <u>Suọi</u>, le <u>Sụe</u>

il <u>nostro</u> libro, la <u>nostra</u> penna   ⟶ il <u>nostro</u>, la <u>nostra</u>

i <u>nostri</u> libri, le <u>nostre</u> penne   ⟶ i <u>nostri</u>, le <u>nostre</u>

il <u>vostro</u> libro, la <u>vostra</u> penna   ⟶ il <u>vostro</u>, la <u>vostra</u>

i <u>vostri</u> libri, le <u>vostre</u> penne   ⟶ i <u>vostri</u>, le <u>vostre</u>

il <u>loro</u> libro, la <u>loro</u> penna   ⟶ il <u>loro</u>, la <u>loro</u>

i <u>loro</u> libri, le <u>loro</u> penne   ⟶ i <u>loro</u> le <u>loro</u>

il <u>Loro</u> libro, la <u>Loro</u> penna   ⟶ il <u>Loro</u>, la <u>Loro</u>

i <u>Loro</u> libri, le <u>Loro</u> penne   ⟶ i <u>Loro</u>, le <u>Loro</u>

Study the following examples:

Ho la mịa bicicletta, non la tụa.
Abbiạmo i nostri libri, non i vostri.
Scrive alle sụe amiche, non alle tụe.
Loro vanno dai loro nonni, non dai nostri.

Note that after the verb **ẹssere**, the definite article is usually omitted in the following construction:

Quẹsta casa è mia. *This house is mine.*

55. Rewrite the following, replacing the italicized phrase with the appropriate possessive pronoun:

1. Quẹsta è *la mịa mạcchina.*
2. *La tụa motocicletta* è piú veloce.
3. Abbiạmo comprato *i nostri bigliẹtti.*
4. Hanno ricevuto *il loro regalo.*
5. Quẹsti sono *i miẹi libri.*
6. *Le nostre amiche* vịvono presso di te.
7. Sto preparando *la mịa valịgia.*
8. Dammi *il tụo passaporto!*
9. *I miẹi zịi* vịvono in Itạlia.
10. Hai portato *i tuọi libri* e *i suọi libri.*
11. *Il nostro amico* aspetta quị vicino.
12. *La vostra piscịna* (swimming pool) è molto grande.
13. Ci piạcciono *il Sụo ufficio* e *i Suọi libri.*
14. *Le mịe cugine* arrịvano domani.
15. Non voglio né la tụa bicicletta né la sụa motocicletta.

DEMONSTRATIVE PRONOUNS

Quẹsto and quẹllo

The demonstrative pronouns are basically the same as the demonstrative adjectives (see Chapter 3). They can refer to either people or things. **Quẹsto** (*this, this one*) and **quẹllo** (*that, that one*) must agree in gender and in number with the noun they substitute.

	Questo		**Quello**	
Masculine singular	**questo**	*this one*	**quello**	*that one*
Masculine plural	**questi**	*these*	**quelli**	*those*
Feminine singular	**questa**	*this one*	**quella**	*that one*
Feminine plural	**queste**	*these*	**quelle**	*those*

For emphasis, all forms of **questo** and **quello** may be followed by **qui** (*here*) and **lí** (*there*): **questo qui** (*this one here*); **quello lí** (*that one there*), etc.

Mi piace questo.	*I like this (one).*
Preferisco quello.	*I prefer that (one).*
Queste qui sono le migliori.	*These are the best (ones).*
Quelli lí sono i peggiori.	*Those are the worst (ones).*

56. Complete the following with the appropriate demonstrative pronouns:

1. Questi cappotti sono buoni, ma preferisco_____.   *those*
2. Quella ragazza è italiana,_____è americana.   *this one*
3. Questo romanzo è noioso,_____è interessante.   *that one*
4. Quelle sedie sono comode,_____sono troppo piccole.   *these*
5. Quelli sono molto costosi,_____vanno a buon mercato.   *these*

RELATIVE PRONOUNS

Che

A relative pronoun is used to introduce a clause that modifies a noun. **Che** (*that, which, who, whom*) can be used to replace either a person or a thing and can function as either the subject or the object of a clause. **Che** does not have gender differentiation.

La ragazza che vedi è la sorella di Pietro.
The girl (whom) you see is Peter's sister.

Il giovane che scrive è molto intelligente.
The young man who is writing is very intelligent.

Ti piacciono i libri che sto comprando?
Do you like the books (that) I am buying?

Ecco i libri che costano poco!
Here are the books that cost little!

57. Complete the following with the relative pronoun.

1. Le cravatte_____vendono in quel negozio sono belle.
2. Il problema_____stiamo discutendo è serio.
3. Le ragazze_____arrivano adesso sono italiane.
4. Il romanzo_____hai comprato è lungo.
5. I giovani_____parlano sono studenti.
6. Le ragazze_____sono invitate da Olga sono brave.
7. La materia_____studia Mario è molto difficile.
8. I signori_____vogliono parlarti sono lí.

Cui

Cui (*[to] whom, [of] whom; [to] which, [of] which,* etc.) is used instead of **che** when it is preceded by a preposition. Note that **cui** can refer to a person or a thing. Note also that the preposition **a** is often omitted with **cui** because **cui** = **a cui**. All other prepositions must be expressed.

cui   *to whom, to which*
a cui   *to whom, to which*
con cui   *with whom, with which*
di cui   *of whom, of which*
da cui   *from whom, from which*
in cui   *in whom, in which*
per cui   *for whom, for which*
su cui   *on whom, on which*

La signora a cui (or; **cui**) **parlavi è dottoressa.**
The lady to whom you were talking is a doctor.

Gli amici di cui parliamo sono in Italia.
The friends of whom we're talking are in Italy.

L'albergo in cui starai è molto buono.
The hotel in which you'll stay is very good.

58. *Complete the following sentences by translating the English pronouns into Italian:*

1. Il sofà_____ci sediamo è molto comodo.   *on which*
2. I giovani_____ti ho parlato sono gentili.   *of whom*
3. La ditta_____lavori è molto grande.   *for which*
4. Gli amici_____scrivo sono in vacanza.   *to whom*
5. I turisti_____viaggiamo sono francesi.   *with whom*
6. Quello è l'edificio_____uscirà mio fratello.   *from which*
7. Questo è l'ufficio_____lavoro.   *in which*

Il quale, la quale, i quali, le quali

The pronoun **il quale** (*the one who, the ones who, the one which, the ones which*) must agree in number and gender with the noun it replaces. **Il quale** has four forms:

il quale (m. s.)   la quale (f. s.)
i quali (m. pl.)   le quali (f. pl.)

Il quale is sometimes used to replace **che** or **cui** either to lend emphasis or to avoid ambiguity. **Che** and **cui**, however, are much more commonly used. Observe the following:

La professoressa che dà le conferenze il venerdí parla molto bene.
The professor, who gives the lectures on Fridays, speaks very well.

La professoressa la quale dà le conferenze il venerdí parla molto bene.
The professor, the one who gives the lectures on Fridays, speaks very well.

Il libro di cui ti parlavo era molto interessante.
The book I was talking to you about was very interesting.

Il libro del quale ti parlavo era molto interessante.
The book, the one I was speaking to you about, was very interesting.

Chi (colui che, colei che, coloro che)

Chi can also be used as a relative pronoun meaning *one who*. Note that it is always followed by a singular verb. Observe the following:

Chi studia, impara.
One who studies learns.

Chi ha visto l'Italia, non la dimenticherà mai.
One who has seen Italy will never forget it.

Alternate forms of **chi** are **colui che** (*he who*), **colei che** (*she who*) and **coloro che** (*those who*). **Coloro che** takes a plural verb:

Colui che studia, impara.
He who studies learns.

Colei che studia, impara.
She who studies learns.

Coloro che studiano, imparano.
Those who study learn.

Colui che, colei che and **coloro che** can also be used to express *the one (ones) who*:

Colui che entra è mio fratello.
The one who is entering is my brother.

Colei che entra è mia sorella.
The one who is entering is my sister.

Coloro che entrano sono i miei fratelli.
The ones who are entering are my brothers.

59. Rewrite the following sentences according to the model:

Arriva mia sorella.→Colei che arriva è mia sorella.

1. Arrivano i miei amici.
2. Parla mio zio.
3. Qualcuno arriva e qualcuno parte.
4. Ascoltano i miei studenti.
5. Si siede Antonio e si alza Marco.
6. Canta la mia amica.

Quello che, quel che, ciò che

The neuter relative pronouns, **quello che**, **quel che**, **ciò che**, are used to replace a general or abstract idea rather than a specific antecedent. They are similar to the English *what* and *that which*. All three of them are interchangeable.

Ciò che dici non è vero.	*What you say is not true.*
Quel che ti consiglio è di studiare.	*What I suggest to you is to study.*
Non capisco quello che dice.	*I don't understand what he/she says..*

60. Rewrite the following by introducing each statement with quello che, quel che, or ciò che.

1. Dice la verità.
2. Vogliamo più tempo.
3. Leggi un ottimo romanzo.
4. Desidera comprare un'automobile.
5. Mi fa paura l'ignoranza.
6. Vogliono fare un lungo viaggio.
7. Suggerite un'ottima idea.
8. Vorrei avere un po'di pace.

Special use of cui

When **cui** is preceded by a definite article, its English equivalent is *whose*. The definite article must agree with the noun following **cui**.

Ecco la signora il cui fratello è psicologo.
Here is the lady whose brother is a psychologist.

Ecco il signore la cui sorella è psicologa.
Here is the man whose sister is a psychologist.

61. *Complete the following sentences:*

1. Ecco le studentesse_____amiche sono italiane.   *whose*
2. Ti presento il giovane_____padre è governatore.   *whose*
3. Voglio conoscere la signorina_____madre è dottoressa.   *whose*
4. Ecco i ragazzi_____zii sono industriali.   *whose*

ECCO WITH PRONOUNS

Direct and indirect object pronouns can be attached to **ecco**. The pronoun **ne** can also be attached to **ecco**. Observe the following; note that **ecco** is used only in the affirmative.

With a direct object pronoun

Eccomi!	*Here I am! [io]*
Eccolo!	*Here (There) he is! (it: m.) [lui]*
Eccola!	*Here (There) she is! (it: f.) [lei]*
EccoLa!	*Here (There) you are! [Lei:* Formal s, m. & f.]*
[EccoLa, professore (m.)! EccoLa, signora!]	
Eccoci!	*Here we are! [noi]*
Eccovi!	*Here (There) you are! [voi]*
EccoLi!	*Here (There) you are! [Loro:* Formal m. pl.]*
EccoLe!	*Here (There) you are! [Loro:* Formal f. pl.]*
Eccoli!	*Here (There) they are! [loro: m. pl.]*
Eccole!	*Here (There) they are! [loro: f. pl.]*

With an indirect object pronoun

Eccoti il libro!	*Here is the book (for you)! [a te]*
Eccovi la bicicletta!	*Here is the bicycle (for you)! [a voi]*
EccoLe la posta!	*Here is the mail (for you)! [a Lei:* Formal s., m. & f.]*
[EccoLe la posta, professore (m.)! EccoLe la posta, signora!]	

Note that formal indirect object pronoun Loro (to you: m. & f. pl.) is not attached.

Ecco Loro i biglietti! *Here are the tickets (for you)! [a Loro]*

With an indirect object pronoun and a direct object pronoun.

Note that, for formal pronouns (a lei & a loro), the -G- is often capitalized for clarity; however, this is not required.

Eccotelo!	*Here it (m.) is for you! [a te]*
Eccoglieli!	*Here they (m. pl.) are for him/her! [a lui; a lei]*
Eccocela!	*Here it (f.) is for us! [a noi]*
Eccovele!	*Here they (f. pl.) are for you! [a voi]*
EccoGlielo!	*Here it is for you! [a Lei:* formal s., m. & f.]*
EccoGlielo!	*Here it is for you! [a Loro:* formal pl., m. & f.]*

but:

Eccolo Loro!	*Here it is for you! [a Loro:* formal s., m. & f.]*

With ne

Eccone!	*Here is some (of it, of them)!*
Eccotene!	*Here is some for you! [a te]*
Eccogliene!	*Here is some for him/her/them! [a lui; a lei; a loro]*

| EccoGliene! | *Here is some for you!* [**a Lei**: formal s., m. & f.] |
| EccoGliene! | *Here is some for you!* [**a Loro**: formal pl., m. & f.] |

But:

| Eccone Loro! | *Here is some for you!* [**a Loro**: formal pl., m. & f.] |

62. Rewrite the following sentences, replacing the italicized words with the appropriate pronouns.
1. Ecco *i libri a voi!*
2. Ecco *Giovanni!*
3. Ecco *le penne a Loro!*
4. Ecco *un poco a te!*
5. Ecco *me!*
6. Ecco *le signorine!*
7. Ecco *i signori!*
8. Ecco *la rivista a Lei!*
9. Ecco *noi!*
10. Ecco *un poco!*
11. Ecco *un poco a Loro!*
12. Ecco *il regalo a Lei!*
13. Ecco *i biglietti a voi!*
14. Ecco *un poco a me.*
15. Ecco *le riviste a noi!*

63. Give the Italian equivalents (Use Ecco in all sentences).
1. Sir, here is the mail for you!
2. Madame, here they (m.) are for you!
3. Rosetta, here it (m.) is for you!
4. Tito and Marcello, here they (f.) are for you!
5. Here they (m.) are for her!
6. Sirs, here it (f.) is for you!

REVIEW

64. Rewrite each sentence, replacing the italicized word with the appropriate pronoun:
1. *I ragazzi* studiano ogni giorno.
2. Tu leggi *le riviste.*
3. Diamo il regalo *a Luisa.*
4. Loro scrivono *a noi.*
5. Saliamo *sul treno.*
6. Comprate *del pane.*
7. Ha due *fratelli.*
8. *A te* piacciono gli sport.

65. Complete the following sentences by translating the words in parentheses:
1. I libri (*that*)_____stai leggendo sono importanti.
2. Quello è il giovane (*of whom*)_____ti ho parlato.
3. (*He who*)_____studia, impara.
4. (*That which*)_____dici, è vero.
5. Sono arrivato, (*here I am*)_____.
6. Non vedo (*anything*)_____.

66. *Choose the correct pronoun to complete each sentence:*

1. Non_____credo in questa superstizione.	(*a*) ne	(*b*) lo	(*c*) ci
2. _____ho due.	(*a*) Gli	(*b*) Ne	(*c*) Le
3. La pago_____, non Lei.	(*a*) lui	(*b*) lei	(*c*) io
4. Teresa chiama me, non_____.	(*a*) te	(*b*) ti	(*c*) tu
5. _____scrivo ogni settimana.	(*a*) Lo	(*b*) Gli	(*c*) Lei
6. Ecco un regalo per_____, signorina.	(*a*)Lei	(*b*) La	(*c*) Le
7. _____mettiamo due ore per arrivare all'ufficio.	(*a*) Noi	(*b*) Ne	(*c*) Ci
8. A me_____fanno male i denti.	(*a*) mi	(*b*) me	(*c*) ci
9. Perché non_____sedete qui?	(*a*) voi	(*b*) vi	(*c*) ti
10. Loro sanno piú di_____.	(*a*) io	(*b*) mi	(*c*) me

CHAPTER 10

Prepositions

Prepositions are used in Italian to indicate a variety of concepts such as possession, distance, origin, intention, purpose, etc. The prepositions **a**, **da**, **in**, **da**, and **di**, however, have some rather specific uses. They acquire different meanings in different contexts and therefore pose many problems. A list of verbs that require **a** and **di** before an infinitive is provided in this chapter.

Most prepositions contract when followed by a definite article. One may contract **con** with **l'**, **il**, and **i**, but it is not required; **fra**, **tra**, **per**, **sopra** and **sotto** do not contract. Prepositions rarely contract before an indefinite article: *Ho bisogno di un [d'un] martello*, etc. Modal verbs **dovere**, **potere**, and **volere** do not require a preposition when followed by an infinitive: *devo partire*; *non posso dormire*; *voglio riposare*; there are many other verbs followed directly by an infinitive, such as *amare, ascoltare, desiderare, guardare, sentire*, etc. (see the list at the end of this chapter).

For an exhaustive list of articulated prepositions, see Chapter 2. For convenience, a simple chart of articulated prepositions is included in this chapter. Observe the many examples given below:

a

The preposition **a** usually means *to* or *at* in English. However, when it is used before the name of a town, city, or small island, it can mean *in* in English.

Note the differences in the following sentences:

Vado a Milano ogni anno.
I go <u>to</u> Milan every year.

Sono a Milano per una settimana.
I am <u>in</u> Milan for a week.

Andiamo a New York.
We are going <u>to</u> New York.

Abitiamo a New York.
We live <u>in</u> New York.

Giovanni studiava a Bologna ogni estate.
John used to study <u>in</u> Bologna every summer.

È nata a Firenze ma abita a Roma.
She was born <u>in</u> Florence but she lives <u>in</u> Rome.

The preposition **a** expresses distance in Italian and conveys the idea of being a certain distance (away) from a specific place. Note the following:

La casa è <u>a</u> due chilometri da qui.
The house is two kilometers (away) from here.

I miei nonni abitano a due miglia da noi.
My grandparents live two miles (away) from us.

I nonni di Gino abitano a 5 Km. da casa sua.
Gino's grandparents live five km. from his house.

L'università è a poche miglia dal centro.
The University is a few miles from downtown.

With Prepositions: Contractions

Italian prepositions and definite articles are almost always contracted. These contractions are listed in the table that follows. The prepositions **a** (*at, to*), **di** (*of, belonging to*), **da** (*from, by, at*), **in** (*in, to*) and **su** (*on*) always contract when they precede the definite article.

	Masculine Singular			Masculine Plural			Feminine Singular		Feminine Singular
	il	lo	l'	i	gli	gl'	la	l'	le
a	al	allo	all'	ai	agli	agl'	alla	all'	alle
da	dal	dallo	dall'	dai	dagli	dagl'	dalla	dall'	dalle
su	sul	sullo	sull'	sui	sugli	sugl'	sulla	sull'	sulle
di (de)	del	dello	dell'	dei	degli	degl'	della	dell'	delle
in (ne)	nel	nello	nell'	nei	negli	negl'	nella	nell'	nelle
con	col	—	—	coi	—	—	—	coll'	—

Andiamo al palazzo delle poste.
L'automobile è dal meccanico.
Le penne sono sulla scrivania.
Il ragazzo è sull'albero.
Il libro è nel cassetto.
I giocatori sono nello stadio.
Ecco i libri degli studenti.

1. *Complete the following by supplying the contracted form of the italicized preposition.*

  1. Ritorniamo _____ montagna.   *da*
  2. L'avvocato è _____ studio.   *in*
  3. Ecco i quaderni _____ studentesse.   *di*
  4. I vestiti sono _____ armadio.   *in*
  5. Gli uccellini sono _____ alberi.   *su*
  6. Camminano _____ sentieri di campagna.   *per*
  7. Vieni _____ tuoi amici.   *con*
  8. Luigi è _____ dentista.   *da*
  9. I turisti ritornano _____ monti.   *da*
  10. I treni vengono _____ città.   *da*
  11. I mesi _____ estate sono piacevoli.   *di*
  12. _____ negozi ci sono tante belle cose.   *in*
  13. Il dono è _____ ragazzo.   *per*
  14. I libri _____ studente sono _____ tavolo.   *di, su*
  15. La studentessa cancella gli sbagli _____ spugna.   *con*
  16. Sono andati _____ tabaccheria Roma per comprare _____ francobolli.   *a, di*

in

The Italian preposition **in** often means *in* in English.

  Roma è in Italia.
  Rome is in Italy.

Abitiạmo negli Stati Uniti.
We live in the United States.

The preposition **in** is used before the names of regions, countries, continents, or large islands to express the English preposition *to*.

L'anno prọssimo andremo in Eurọpa.
Next year we are going to Europe.

Mi piace andare in Sicịlia per le festẹ.
I like to go to Sicily for the holidays.

Andiạmo nel Canadà a visitare i nostri cugini.[1] *(in + il = nel)*
We are going to Canada to visit our cousins.

Quạndo andrete negli Stati Uniti? *(in + gli = negli)*
When are you going to the United States?

In is used to express means of transportation in Italian and is equivalent to the preposition *by* in English.

Study the following common expressions:

in mạcchina (automọbile)	*by car*
in treno	*by train*
in aẹreo	*by plane*
in ạutobus	*by bus*
in bicicletta	*by bicycle*

Note that the preposition **a**, not **in**, is used in the following expressions: **a piẹdi** (*on* [*by*] *foot*) and **a cavallo** (*on horseback*).

Oggigiọrno tutti viạggiano in aẹreo.
Nowadays everyone travels by plane.

Vado a scuọla in bicicletta.
I go to school by bicycle.

The preposition **in** is used *without* the definite article in Italian to express *in, into,* or *to* in English with expressions referring to certain places, rooms of a house, shops, etc. Note the following:

in città	*in (into) the city*
in montagna	*in the mountains*
in campagna	*in (into) the country*
in salotto	*in the living room*
in cucina	*in the kitchen*
in giardino	*in the garden*
in biblioteca	*in the library*
in chiẹsa	*in church*

I miẹi genitori sono in campagna.
My parents are in the country.

Domani mattina andremo in città.
Tomorrow morning we are going to (into) the city.

2. Complete the following sentences with the appropriate form of the preposition a or in as necessary:

1. L'anno scorso sono andato _____ Frạncia.
2. Andiạmo _____ casa di Marịa _____ mạcchina.

---

[1] Note that with masculine countries, the preposition **in** is commonly articulated, **nel**. You will, however, in everyday speech sometimes hear **in Canada**, **in Mẹssico**.

3. Sono due settimane che siamo _____ Capri.

4. La chiesa è_____ due passi dalla piazza.

5. Gli zii di Carlo si trovano _____ Chicago.

6. Enzo è_____ Italia questa settimana ma abita _____ Stati Uniti.

7. Mia zia vive_____Sicilia.

8. Vai_____scuola _____ bicicletta o_____ piedi?

9. Rosella è andata _____ città stamani.

10. Voi andate _____ letto a mezzanotte.

3. Form sentences from the following using the appropriate form of the preposition a or in as necessary. Follow the model:

Roberto / essere / Torino
Roberto è a Torino.

1. turisti / essere / Sicilia
2. io / andare / scuola / piedi
3. ragazza / abitare / Firenze
4. studentesse / studiare / biblioteca
5. andare / voi / Spagna / ogni / anno?
6. mio / padre / abitare / Milano
7. Giovanna / andare / città / bicicletta
8. invitati / essere / salotto
9. zia / di / Laura / essere / chiesa
10. giovani / volere / andare / Messico

da

The Italian preposition **da** means *from* in English. (For a special use of **da** with the present indicative and the imperfect indicative, see Chapter 6, pages 105 and 114.)

Il treno viene da Verona.
The train is coming from Verona.

Da dove venite?
Where do you come from?

Da is used before a personal noun or pronoun to mean *at (to, in) the house of* in English. Its meaning has been extended to places of business, shops, offices, etc. Note the following:

Andremo da Maria stasera?
Shall we go to Mary's house tonight?

Mia figlia è dal dottore.
My daughter is at the doctor's (office).

Ogni mese devo andare dal barbiere.
Every month I have to go to the barber shop (barber's).

Da is used with the disjunctive pronouns (**me**, **te**, **sé**, **noi**, **voi**, **sé**) to mean *by myself, by yourself, by himself/herself, by ourselves, by yourselves, by themselves.* Note that the subject of the sentence and the disjunctive pronoun always refer to the same person.

L'ho fatto tutto da me.
I did it all by myself.

Franca ha finito la lezione da sé.
Frances finished the lesson by herself.

Da is used *before an infinitive or a noun* in Italian to describe the purpose, scope, intention, suitability, or use of the preceding dependent noun. It conveys the preposition *for,* but *for* is rarely used in this way in English. A descriptive adjective is used instead. Observe the following:

Ho bisogno della carta da scrivere.
I need some writing paper (paper for writing).

Hai una macchina da cucire?
Do you have a sewing machine (machine for sewing)?

Mangiamo sempre nella sala da pranzo.
We always eat in the dining room (room for dining).

Ho comprato quel costume da bagno.
I bought that bathing suit (suit for bathing).

Da is used *before an infinitive* to convey the idea that something remains *to be done.* It implies that the action of the infinitive has not been realized or carried out. It may also denote a need or obligation, that something *must be done.* Study the following:

Avete due libri da leggere per domani.
You have two books to read (to be read) for tomorrow.

Ci sono tre stanze da affittare.
There are three rooms for rent (to be rented).

La signora Russo ha una casa da vendere.
Mrs. Russo has a house for sale (to be sold).

Da is also used *before an infinitive* and after the indefinite antecedents molto, poco, niente, nulla, troppo, qualcosa (qualche cosa). This construction with **da** also conveys a passive meaning that something still remains *to be done.*

Abbiamo molto da fare.
We have a lot to do (to be done).

Non c'è niente da mangiare.
There is nothing to eat (to be eaten).

Da is used before a noun to describe a person's behavior, manner, style, or comportment. Note the following:

Mi ha sempre parlato da amico.
He has always spoken to me like a friend.

Domani io farò da guida.
Tomorrow I will act as the guide.

Vive da principe.
He lives like a prince.

Da is used after a noun or adjective to describe the physical characteristics or qualities of a person. English makes use of the preposition *with* or the equivalent descriptive adjective.

Chi è il giovanotto dai capelli biondi?
Who is the young man with the blond hair?
Who is the blond-haired young man?

Chi è quella ragazza dagli occhi verdi?
Who is that girl with the green eyes?

Da plus a noun or pronoun means *by* in English when *by* indicates the agent or the doer of the action of a verb that is in the passive voice. Note the following:

> **Da chi fu scritto quel libro?**
> *By whom was the book written?*

> **Il libro fu scritto da Natalia Gịnzburg.**
> *The book was written by Natalia Ginzburg.*

> **La città fu distruttạ da un terremoto.**
> *The city was destroyed by an earthquake.*

Da is used after a noun to describe the value, worth, price, or cost of something in Italian.

> **Vọglio un francobollo da dụe ẹuro.**
> *I want a two-euro stamp.*

> **È una mạcchina da poco prezzo.**
> *It's a cheap (inexpensive) car.*

Da means *as* in English when *as* is equivalent to the adverb *when*. This construction with **da** replaces the adverbial clause with *when* in English. Note the following:

> **Da ragazzo ero molto spiritoso.**
> *As a boy (When I was a boy), I was very lively.*

> **Da bambino avevo moltị giocạttoli.**
> *As a child (When I was a child), I had many toys.*

Da means *since* or *for* in time expressions when the verb of the sentence is in the present indicative or imperfect indicative tense. (See pages 105 and 114 for use of the preposition **da** in time expressions.)

di

The Italian preposition **di** corresponds to the English preposition *of*. It is used before a noun or pronoun to express possession or ownership or to qualify (describe) another noun.

> **È la mạcchina di Giạnni.**
> *It is John's car.*

> **Vorrẹi un bicchiẹre di vino.**
> *I would like a glass of wine.*

> **È d'oro l'orolọgio?**
> *Is the watch gold?*
> *(Is the watch made of gold?)*

> **È una giạcca di lana.**
> *It's a woolen jacket.*

Di is used to indicate a person's place of origin in Italian. It is equivalent to the English preposition *from*.

> **Di dove sẹi?**
> *Where are you from?*
> *(Where do you come from?)*

> **Sono del Canadà.**
> *I am from Canada.*

> **Ạngela è di Bari.**   *but*   **Ạngela è arrivata da Bari stamani.**
> *Angela is from Bari.*   *Angela arrived from Bari this morning.*

Di is used in Italian in comparative and in relative superlative constructions. (See pages 61 to 63 for the use of **di** in the comparative and the relative superlative.)

Di is used *before an adjective after the indefinite pronouns* **qualcosa, niente, nulla**. (Note that only the masculine form of the adjective is used.)

Abbiamo visto qualcosa di bello.
We saw something beautiful.

Non c'è niente di nuovo.
There is nothing new.

Di is used in some common time expressions in Italian and means *in* or *at* in English. Study the following expressions:

di sera	*in the evening*
di notte	*at night*
di mattino	*in the morning*
dl buon'ora	*early*
di giorno	*in the daytime*
d'inverno[2]	*in the winter*
d'estate	*in the summer*
d'autunno	*in the fall*
di primavera	*in the spring*

Non mi piace lavorare di notte.
I don't like to work at night.

Di mattino leggo sempre il giornale.
I always read the newspaper in the morning.

D'estate andiamo sempre al mare.
In the summer we always go to the sea.

The preposition **di** is used in partitive constructions in Italian and means *some* or *any* in English. (See pages 37–39 for the use of **di** plus the definite articles to express the partitive.)

4. *Complete the following with the appropriate forms of the prepositions da or di as necessary.*
   1. _____ inverno sempre fa freddo.
   2. Rosella è _____ Francia.
   3. _____ bambino non mangiavo mai niente.
   4. Compriamo la frutta _____ fruttivendolo.
   5. Possiamo comprare _____ francobolli _____ tabaccaio?
   6. _____ chi fu scritto questo tema?
   7. _____ quanto tempo abita Lei negli Stati Uniti?
   8. Mi dia un bicchiere _____ acqua, per favore.
   9. Tu sei più alta _____ me.
   10. Queste sono lezioni _____ geografia.
   11. La bicicletta rossa è_____ Elena.
   12. Io studio _____ sera.
   13. Non ricevo lettere _____ due mesi.
   14. Stasera andiamo _____ Stefano.
   15. I bambini dormono nella camera _____ letto.
   16. Dov'è la macchina _____ scrivere?
   17. È una commedia _____ far ridere.
   18. Chi è quell' uomo _____ capelli grigi?
   19. Mi dia cinque francobolli _____ un euro.
   20. Sai fare tutto _____ te?

---

[2] Note that with the words **inverno, estate, autunno**, and **primavera**, the Italian preposition **in** can be used interchangeably with **di**: eg., **In inverno, in estate, in autunno, in primavera**.

5. *Rewrite the following sentences according to the model.*

> Dicono molto → Hanno molto da dire.

1. Mangiamo molto.
2. Vendono poco.
3. Non faccio niente.
4. Bevi qualcosa?
5. Non discutete nulla.
6. Leggete troppo.

The Use of the Prepositions *a* and *di* before an Infinitive

The following verbs take the preposition **a** before an infinitive. Note that **a** becomes **ad** before infinitives beginning with **a-**. Before infinitives beginning with other vowels, **a** and **ad** are interchangeable. See the sections on verbs followed directly by an infinitive, pages 253 to 254.

Luigi ci aiuta a fare i compiti.	*Louis helps us to do our homework.*
Pietro si è dedicato a studiare.	*Peter dedicated himself to studying.*
Maria riesce a parlare bene l'inglese.	*Mary manages to speak English well.*
Voi sempre tardate ad arrivare.	*You are always late in arriving.*
Noi vi insegneremo a dipingere.	*We will teach you how to paint.*

abituarsi a   *to get used to*
  Ci siamo abituati a vivere in questo clima.

affrettarsi a   *to hurry to, to hasten to*
  Gli studenti si affrettano a finire gli esami.

aiutare a   *to help*
  Teresa sempre aiuta Pietro a fare i compiti di scuola.

andare a   *to go*
  Domani andremo a vedere un film di Fellini.

apprendere a   *to learn*
  Dobbiamo apprendere a guidare l'automobile.

aspettare a   *to wait*
  Perché non aspettate a inviare quel pacco?

avere da   *to have to, must*
  Ancora ho da imparare molte cose.

badare a   *to take care of*
  Signore, badi ad includere il Suo indirizzo!

cominciare a   *to begin*
  Adesso comincio a capire la trama.

condannare a   *to condemn*
  Alcuni sono condannati a soffrire.

continuare a   *to continue*
  Continuiamo a bussare ancora.

consentire a   *to agree*
  Consentite a venire alle dieci?

correre a   *to run*
  Paola corre a incontrare suo padre.

costringere a
  Abbiamo costretto Mario ad accompagnarci.

to compel

dare a
  Non diamo a intendere ciò che pensiamo!

to give

darsi a
  Luigi si è dato a collezionare francobolli.

to give oneself over to, to dedicate oneself

decidersi a
  Mi sono deciso a viaggiare un po' di piú.

to make up one's mind

dedicarsi a
  Si sono dedicati ad aiutare i poveri.

to devote oneself

divertirsi a
  Mi sono divertito a montare la bicicletta.

to have fun

esitare a
  Ha esitato a darci il suo numero telefonico.

to hesitate

fare bene a
  Fai bene a non fumare.

to do well

fare meglio a
  Fate meglio ad aspettare.

to be better off

fare presto a
  Facciamo presto a partire!

to hurry up

fare in tempo a
  Faremo in tempo a prendere il treno?

to be on time

forzare a
  Non ti ho mai forzato a lavorare fino a tardi.

to force

godere a
  Abbiamo goduto a vedere giocare i bambini.

to enjoy

imparare a
  Avete imparato a leggere quelle parole difficili?

to learn

incoraggiare a
  Ci hanno incoraggiati a studiare.

to encourage

insegnare a
  Mi hai insegnato a giocare a tennis.

to teach

insistere a
  Pietro ha insistito a parlare di sport.

to insist

inviare a
  Ci hanno inviati a portarvi questi pacchi.

to send

invitare a
  Li abbiamo invitati a cenare con noi.

to invite

istruire a
  Marco è stato istruito a fare il meccanico.

to train, to instruct

mandare a
  L'ho mandato a comprare il giornale.

to send

mẹttere a	*to put, to place*
Ho messo le pẹntola a cuọcere lentamente.	
mẹttersi a	*to begin to*
Dobbiạmo mẹtterci a lavorare.	
obbligare a	*to force, to oblige*
Mi hanno obbligato a stare zitto.	
passare a	*to go on*
Passiạmo a fare altre cose!	
pensare a	*to think of*
Pensi a vẹndere la casa?	
persịstere a	*to persist*
Luịsa persiste a lavorare fino a tardi.	
persuạdere a	*to convince*
Mi hanno persuạso a fare un lungo viạggio.	
prẹndere a	*to begin to*
Di solito prẹndono a parlare di polịtica.	
preparare a	*to prepare*
Li abbiạmo preparati a recitare molto bene.	
prepararsi a to	*to get ready*
Si stanno preparando a dare gli esami.	
procẹdere a	*to proceed to*
Procediạmo a discụtere questo tema!	
provare a	*to try to*
Ho provato a convịncerlo, ma è impossịbile.	
restare a	*to stay, to remain*
È restato a finire il lavoro.	
rimanere a	*to remain, to stay*
Sono rimasto a scrịvere una lẹttera.	
rinunciạre a	*to give up*
Avete rinunciạto a partecipare.	
riprẹndere a	*to resume*
Dopo le vacanze, abbiạmo ripreso a lavorare.	
ritornare a	*to come back, to go back*
È ritornato a completare il progetto.	
riuscire a	*to succeed*
Finalmente siạmo riusciti a risọlvere il problema.	
salire a	*to go up, to climb*
È salito ad aggiustare il tetto.	
sbrigarsi a	*to hurry*
Sbrighiạmoci a lẹggere!	
scẹndere a	*to come down, to go down*
Sono scesi a salutarci.	

seguitare a

Quei signori seguitano a insistere.

to keep on

servire a

Queste tavole servono a fare uno scaffale.

to be good for

stare a

Stiamo qui a farvi compagnia.

to stay

tardare a

Tardano a servirci.

to delay, to be late

temere a

Temete a guidare nel traffico?

to be afraid to

tornare a

Son tornati a vivere a Roma.

to come back, to go back, to return

venire a

Stasera vengono a darci il benvenuto.

to come to

The following verbs take the preposition **di** before an infinitive. Note that **di** may become **d'** before infinitives beginning with **i-**.

Ho cercato di telefonarti, ma non ho potuto.
Hanno deciso d'incominciare troppo tardi.
Hai rifiutato di partecipare al convegno.
A volte fingiamo di non capire.
Mi ha chiesto di portargli un dizionario.

accettare di

Ha accettato di fare parte del gruppo.

to accept

accorgersi di

Si è accorto di aver fatto molti sbagli.

to become aware of

ammettere di

Hanno ammesso di aver detto certe cose.

to admit

approvare di

Il senato ha approvato di continuare il programma.

to approve

arrossire di

Luisa arrossisce di parlare in pubblico.

to blush

aspettare di

Aspetto di ricevere quei documenti.

to wait

aspettarsi di

Ci aspettiamo di vederli stasera.

to expect

astenersi di

Si astengono di votare.

to abstain from

augurare di

Ti auguro di riuscire bene agli esami.

to wish

augurarsi di

Mi auguro di potere andare in Europa.

to hope to

avere paura di

Avete paura di viaggiare in aereo.

to be afraid

avvertire di　　　　　　　　　　　　　　　　　　　　*to warn, to caution*
　　Vi avvertiamo di guidare con cautela.

cercare di　　　　　　　　　　　　　　　　　　　　　*to try*
　　Stiamo cercando di essere pazienti.

cessare di　　　　　　　　　　　　　　　　　　　　　*to stop*
　　Cessate di fare i presuntuosi!

chiedere di　　　　　　　　　　　　　　　　　　　　*to ask*
　　Hanno chiesto di parlarci al piú presto.

comandare di　　　　　　　　　　　　　　　　　　　*to order*
　　Ho comandato di chiamare Paolo.

concludere di　　　　　　　　　　　　　　　　　　　*to conclude, to end*
　　Ha concluso di comandare.

consigliare di　　　　　　　　　　　　　　　　　　　*to advise*
　　Mi hanno consigliato di partire subito.

consolarsi di　　　　　　　　　　　　　　　　　　　*to take comfort, to rejoice*
　　Si consolano di aver vinto.

credere di　　　　　　　　　　　　　　　　　　　　　*to believe in*
　　Credono di contribuire continuamente.

decidere di　　　　　　　　　　　　　　　　　　　　*to decide to*
　　Decidiamo di lasciarli in pace!

determinare di　　　　　　　　　　　　　　　　　　*to determine to*
　　Hanno determinato di smettere il programma.

detestare di　　　　　　　　　　　　　　　　　　　　*to hate, to detest*
　　Detestiamo di continuare cosí.

dimenticare di　　　　　　　　　　　　　　　　　　*to forget to*
　　Ho dimenticato di lasciare l'indirizzo.

dire di　　　　　　　　　　　　　　　　　　　　　　*to say, to tell*
　　Ci ha detto di riportare i libri in biblioteca.

dispensare di　　　　　　　　　　　　　　　　　　　*to excuse*
　　Ci dispensano di fare questo lavoro.

domandare di　　　　　　　　　　　　　　　　　　　*to ask*
　　Mi ha domandato d'inviare i documenti.

dubitare di　　　　　　　　　　　　　　　　　　　　*to doubt*
　　Dubiti di poter venire?

fantasticare di　　　　　　　　　　　　　　　　　　*to day-dream, to imagine*
　　Fantastica di essere un grande attore.

fingere di　　　　　　　　　　　　　　　　　　　　　*to pretend*
　　Sempre fingono di essere contenti.

finire di　　　　　　　　　　　　　　　　　　　　　*to end up, to finish*
　　Finite di scherzare.

giurare di　　　　　　　　　　　　　　　　　　　　　*to swear, to pledge*
　　Giurano di vendicarsi.

godere di
Godiamo di vedere gli amici.

to enjoy

impedire di
Quei signori t'impediscono di parlare.

to prevent from

indignarsi di
Si indignano di fare certi lavori.

to be indignant (to)

infischiarsi di
Luigi s'infischia di lavorare.

to not care a hoot about

indovinare di
Ho indovinato di scrivergli.

to guess right (to)

ingannarsi di
S'ingannano di fare bene.

to deceive oneself

lagnarsi di
Ti lagni di dover studiare.

to complain

lamentarsl di
Ci lamentiamo di dover partire.

to complain (to)

mancare di
Mancano di fare il proprio ([*their*] *own*) dovere.

to lack, to fail (to)

meravigliarsi di
Mi meraviglio di vedervi qui.

to be surprised (to)

minacciare di
Ti minaccia di farti del male.

to threaten (to)

occuparsi di
Vi occupate di fare tutto.

to busy oneself with, to attend (to)

offrire di
Offrono di pagare il conto.

to offer (to)

ordinare di
Vi ordino di stare a casa.

to order (to)

pensare di
Pensiamo di leggere quel romanzo.

to think of

pentirsi di
Si son (sono) pentite di non esser venute.

to regret, to repent (to)

permettere di
Vi permetto di uscire per poche ore.

to allow, to permit (to)

persuadere di
Ci persuade di uscire tardi.

to persuade, to convince (to)

pregare di
Ti prego di non bestemmiare.

to beg

privare di
Le regole ci privano di fare certe cose.

to deprive

proibire di
Ti proibisco di uscire.

to prevent, to prohibit (to)

promẹttere di	*to promise (to)*
Mi ha promesso di visitarmi presto.	
proporre di	*to propose (to)*
Hanno proposto di erịgere (*to erect*) un monumento.	
provare di	*to try (to)*
Proveranno di nuotare da una sponda all'altra.	
raccomandare di	*to recommend, to exhort (to)*
Vi raccomando di tornare presto.	
rẹndersi conto di	*to realize*
Si è reso conto di avere pochi amici fedeli (*loyal*).	
ricordare di	*to remember (to)*
Ricorderại d'impostare le lẹttere?	
ricordarsi di	*to remember (to)*
Non mi son ricordato di scrịvere.	
rifiutare di	*to refuse (to)*
Hanno rifiutato di venire con noi.	
ringraziạre di	*to thank*
Ti ringrạzio di avermi aiutato.	
ripẹtere di	*to repeat*
Ripeto d'invitarti.	
risọlvere di	*to resolve (to)*
Abbiạmo risolto di non ritornare.	
sapere di	*to know*
Sanno di dovere scusarsi.	
sbagliạre di	*to miss, to make a mistake (to)*
Avete sbagliạto di votare per il migliọr candidato.	
sbrigarsi di	*to hasten, to hurry*
Si sono sbrigati di terminare quel contratto.	
scommẹttere di	*to bet (on)*
Hai scommesso di finire per primo?	
scrịvere di	*to write (to)*
Gli ho scritto di tornare.	
scusarsi di	*to apologize (for)*
Stẹfano si è scusato di averli burlati.	
smẹttere di	*to stop*
Ha smesso di fare favori a destra e a sinistra.	
sognare di	*to dream about*
Abbiạmo sognato di ẹssere in un film.	
sperare di	*to hope, to expect*
Sperạvano di arrivare presto.	
stabilire di	*to agree (to)*
Ho stabilito di non fumare piú.	

stancarsi di   *to get tired (of)*
   Si è stancata di rispondere alle domande.

stupirsi di   *to be amazed (at)*
   Ci siamo stupiti di vedere Gino lí.

suggerire di   *to suggest (to)*
   Hanno suggerito di rifare il lavoro.

supplicare di   *to beseech, to beg (to)*
   L'avete supplicato d'inviarvi la patente di guida.

temere di   *to fear (to)*
   Temi di perdere la scommessa?

tentare di   *to try, to attempt*
   Molte volte ho tentato di farlo studiare.

terminare di   *to end, to stop (to)*
   Hanno terminato di accettare assegni.

trattare di   *to deal with, to bargain (to)*
   Hai trattato di comprare quel negozio?

vantarsi di   *to brag about, to vaunt*
   Si vantavano di essere i primi in tutto.

vergognarsi di   *to be ashamed of*
   Si è vergognato di vantarsi.

Verbs Followed Directly by an Infinitive

amare   *to love, to like*
   Ama andare a caccia (*hunting*) e a pesca.

ascoltare   *to listen to*
   Ho ascoltato cantare Teresa.

bastare   *to suffice*
   Basta lavorare e tutto va bene.

bisognare   *to be necessary*
   Bisogna partire al piú presto.

desiderare   *to wish, to desire*
   Desidero rivedere i miei amici.

dovere   *to have to, must*
   Devono finire il progetto.

farsi   *to have something done*
   Si son fatti costruire una villa.

gradire   *to appreciate*
   Gradiamo essere invitati.

guardare   *to look at, to watch*
   Guardo passare la gente.

lasciare   *to allow, to let*
   Per favore, ci lasci vivere in pace!

occorrere Occorre lavorare per poter vivere.	*to be necessary*
osare Antonio non osa avvicinarsi (*to come near, to approach*).	*to dare*
osservare Osserviamo volare gli uccelli.	*to observe, to watch*
parere Pare voler piovere.	*to seem*
piacere A tutti piace divertirsi.	*to like, to please*
potere Se vogliamo, possiamo andare al cinema.	*to be able to*
preferire Abbiamo preferito restare a casa.	*to prefer*
sapere Sa guidare.	*to know how*
sembrare Oggi il sole sembra brillare (*to shine*) di piú.	*to seem*
sentire Mi scusino un momento, sento piangere i bambini.	*to hear*
udire Odi cantare le ragazze?	*to hear*
vedere Hanno veduto (visto) giocare quei giovani.	*to see*
volere Voglio passare le vacanze in montagna.	*to want to*

6. *Complete the following sentences with the appropriate prepositions when necessary:*

1. Vogliamo _____ cantare alcune canzoni.
2. Accetto _____ fare parte del vostro circolo.
3. Alberto non riesce _____ studiare.
4. Sembra _____ piovere a dirotto (*in torrents*, or *cats and dogs*).
5. Mi hanno proibito _____ entrare.
6. Corrado ama _____ andare a caccia.
7. Ci prepariamo _____ dare gli esami.
8. Avete imparato _____ guidare?
9. Silvana si è stupita (*dumbfounded*) _____ vedermi qui.
10. Marco e Mario si sono vergognati _____ parlare.
11. Adesso non oso _____ dire una parola.
12. Vi lamentate _____ lavorare troppo.
13. Hai sentito _____ Teresa?
14. Non possiamo _____ capire queste regole.
15. Mi hanno insegnato _____ parlare inglese.
16. I bambini corrono _____ incontrare lo zio.
17. Occorre _____ studiare per fare bene agli esami.
18. Temo _____ non potercela fare.

19. Avete tentato _____ parlare al direttore?

20. Stefano è riuscito _____ vedere il preside (*principal*).

7. Complete the following sentences using the appropriate forms of the prepositions a, in, da, or di and using the cues, as necessary:

1. Mia sorella abita _____ Sardegna.

2. Vado al negozio _____ autobus.

3. Firenze è _____ Toscana.

4. Ritorneranno _____ mezzanotte.

5. L'ufficio è _____ cinque miglia _____ casa nostra.

6. Abito _____ Milano ma sono _____ Roma.   *romano*

7. Il professore sempre arriva _____ classe _____ buon'ora.

8. Rosella è _____ Francia.

9. La ragazza è andata _____ campagna _____ una macchina _____ corsa.

10. Questi libri sono _____ Pietro.

11. Quella statua è _____ marmo.

12. Voi lavorate _____ giorno; io studio _____ notte.

13. I miei zii sono _____ Sicilia; sono siciliani.

14. Maria viene _____ Bologna.

15. Ho lasciato lo spazzolino _____ denti (*toothbrush*) nella valigia.

16. Il ferro _____ stiro non funziona piú.

17. Studio l'italiano _____ due anni.

18. Sono arrivato _____ Torino stamattina alle cinque.

19. Non c'è un minuto _____ perdere.

20. Abbiamo molto _____ fare oggi.

21. Non avete visto niente _____ bello nel negozio?

22. Il ragazzo si allontanò _____ casa.

23. La signora Milano fa _____ madre a questi due bambini.

24. È un dolore _____ morire.

25. Si comportò _____ eroe.

8. Translate the following sentences into Italian:

1. Franco is from the United States.

2. We went to the city by ourselves.

3. We have a lot to do today.

4. I need a new toothbrush.

5. She has a house for sale.

6. Is there anything to eat?

7. As a child, I liked to go to the mountains.

8. There isn't a moment to lose.

9. As a young man, I was very handsome.

10. In the fall, we used to go to the country by train.

9. Complete the following with the appropriate prepositions when necessary:

1. Lui sempre riesce _____ vincere.

2. L'ho persuaso _____ partire ora.

3. Basta _____ studiare per riuscirci.

4. Quando avete imparato _____ guidare?

5. Mi rendo conto _____ non avere tempo.

6. Ti hanno costretto _____ scrivermi.

7. Domani dobbiamo _____ vedere il nonno.

8. Olga, hai pensato _____ fare un viaggio?

  9. Hanno accettato _____ partecipare.
10. Procediamo _____ lavorare!
11. Se vuoi, puoi _____ aiutarmi.
12. Ricordate _____ comprare il pane.
13. Luisa, ammetti _____ avere dormito troppo?
14. Li abbiamo invitati _____ cenare con noi.
15. A me piace _____ giocare a tennis.

CHAPTER 11

Special Uses of Certain Verbs

EXPRESSIONS WITH *avere*

The verb **avere** means *to have* in English. However, with many common expressions referring to physical or mental states, **avere** takes on the meaning *to be*. And with still other idioms it assumes various other meanings. Observe the following:

avere ... anni ...	*to be ... years old*
Mịo nonno ha sessantadụe anni.	
avere bisogno di[1]	*to need*
Chi ha bisogno di un cerotto?	
avere caldo	*to be hot* (said of a person)
In estate abbiạmo caldo.	
avere da	*to have to*
Ho tanto da fare!	
averne fino agli occhi	*to be fed up (with)*
Non ne posso piú, ne ho fino agli occhi.	
avere fretta	*to be in a hurry*
Tu hai sempre fretta, non ti fermi mai.	
avere freddo	*to be cold*
Di notte ho freddo.	
avere fame (appetito)	*to be hungry*
Marco ha una fame da leọne.	
avere l'ạria di	*to seem, to look as if*
Luigi ha l'ạria di aver mentito.	
avere luọgo	*to take place*
Dove avrà luọgo la partita di cạlcio?	

---

[1] The infinitive **avere** is frequently abbreviated to **aver** before a consonant; e.g., **aver bisogno di, aver caldo, aver fame, aver freddo.**

257

avere mal di gola	*to have a sore throat*
Ha cantato troppo e ora ha mal di gola.	
avere mal di pancia	*to have a stomach ache*
Ho un mal di pancia (*stomach*) terribile.	
avere mal di testa	*to have a headache*
Con questo rumore hai sempre mal di testa.	
avere molto da fare	*to be very busy (to have a lot to do)*
Non possono venire perché hanno molto da fare.	
avere paura (di)	*to be afraid (of)*
Di chi hai paura, di me?	
avere sete	*to be thirsty*
Se hai sete, bevi dell'acqua!	
avere sonno	*to be sleepy*
Abbiamo sonno; non dormiamo da molte ore.	
avere ragione	*to be right*
Lui ha sempre ragione!	
avere torto	*to be wrong*
Noi abbiamo sempre torto.	
avere vergogna (di)	*to be ashamed (of)*
Hanno vergogna di arrivare tardi.	
avere voglia (di)	*to feel like (doing something)*
Hai voglia di guardare la televisione?	

1. *Complete the following with the appropriate present indicative forms of avere:*

    1. I bambini _____ fame.
    2. Noi _____ voglia di nuotare.
    3. Olga _____ mal di denti.
    4. Antonia _____ sempre ragione.
    5. Voi _____ sete.
    6. Tu _____ paura di stare solo.
    7. Loro ne _____ fino agli occhi.
    8. Io _____ vergogna di alzare la mano.

2. *Rewrite the following using idiomatic expressions with avere. Follow the model:*

    Vorrei una limonata. → Ho sete.

    1. Vorrei un panino.
    2. Vorresti dormire?
    3. Luisa vorrebbe una coperta.
    4. Noi vorremmo un'aranciata.
    5. I bambini vorrebbero uscire.
    6. Voi vorreste una fetta di torta.
    7. Io non posso parlare; mi vergogno.
    8. La testa gli gira.
    9. Mi fanno male i denti.
    10. Ti fa male la gola?

SPECIAL USES OF *dovere, potere, sapere* AND *volere*

The verbs **dovere** (*to have to, to must*), **potere** (*to be able to, to can*), **sapere** (*to know, to know about*), and **volere** (*to want*) assume different meanings in different tenses. Observe the following special uses of these verbs:

Dovere

In the present tense: to owe

Gli devo la mịa gratitụdine.
I owe him my gratitude.

Ti devo venti dọllari.
I owe you twenty dollars.

Plus an infinitive: to have to, to must

Devo partire alle otto in punto.
I must leave at eight o'clock sharp.

Dovremo tornare stasera.
We shall have to come back tonight.

Loro hanno dovuto aspettare.
They had to wait.

In the present and imperfect indicative tenses: to be supposed to

Devo ẹssere lí alle due.
I'm supposed to be there at two.

Dovevo presentarmi da solo.
I was supposed to show up by myself (all alone).

Plus ẹssere in the present indicative, present perfect (conversational past), and imperfect indicative tenses: must be, must have been, was probably

Dov'è Marịa?
Where is Mary?

Dev'ẹssere a casa.
She must be home (is probably home).

Dove sono stati i ragazzi?
Where have the boys been?

Hanno dovuto ẹssere a scuọla.
They, must have been (were probably) in school.

Non gliẹl'ho chiesto, ma il viạggio doveva ẹssere piacẹvole.
I didn't ask him (her), but the trip had to be (was probably) pleasant.

In the conditional tenses: should, ought to, should have, ought to have

Dovrei finire i cọmpiti di scuọla a tempo.
I should (ought to) finish my homework on time.

Avrei dovuto telefonarle immediatamente.
I should have (ought to have) telephoned her immediately.

3. Complete the following sentences with the appropriate forms of dovere or ẹssere, as indicated.

1. Signora, La ringrạzio; _____ un gran favore.   *(I owe you)*
2. Mi è dispiaciuto tanto! I bambini _____ piú di un'ora.   *(had to wait)*
3. Olga e Stẹfano, dove _____?   *(have you been)*
4. Dove sono I ragazzi? Bene, _____ a scuọla.   *(they must be)*

5. Rosetta, non puọi giocare; prima _____ pulire la tụa stanza da letto.   *(you should finish)*
6. _____ stasera senza problemi.   *(They'll have to arrive)*
7. _____ a casa a mezzogiọrno a tutti i costi!   *(She is supposed to be)*
8. _____ un'esperiẹnza piacẹvole!   *(It was)*

Potere

In the present indicative tense: to be able to, can

> **Posso uscire?**
> *May I go out?*

> **Posso suonare il trombone.**
> *I can (am able to) play the trombone.*

In the present perfect: to be able to, to succeed

> **Ho potuto spedire il pacco.**
> *I was able to mail the package.*
> *(I succeeded in mailing the package.)*

> **Non son (sono) potuti venire piú presto.**
> *They could not come earlier (but they tried).*

In the conditional tenses: could, would be able, could have, could have been able

> **Potrei arrivare alle tre.**
> *I could arrive at three o'clock. (I would be able to arrive at three o'clock.)*

> **Avrei potuto farlo facilmente.**
> *I could have done it easily. (I would have been able to do it easily.)*

Sapere

In the present indicative tense: to know, to be able to, to know how to

> **So la leziọne.**
> *I know the lesson.*

> **So cantare.**
> *1 know how to sing. (I am able to sing.)*

In the present perfect (conversational past): to know, to find out

> **L'ho saputo iẹri.**
> *I knew it yesterday. (I found it out yesterday.)*

In the conditional tenses: to be able to, can, to find out

> **Non saprei trovarlo.**
> *I wouldn't be able to find it.*

Volere

In the present indicative: to want

> **Vọglio quell'automọbile.**
> *I want that car.*

In the present perfect (conversational past): to decide, to refuse to

Ho voluto farlo.
I wanted to do it. (I decided to do it.)

Marco non ha voluto finirlo.
Mark didn't want to do it. (Mark refused to do it.)

In the conditional: would like

Vorrẹi un bicchiẹre di latte.
I would like a glass of milk.

Vorrẹi vedere i nonni.
I would like to see my grandparents.

4. Complete the following sentences with the appropriate forms of potere, sapere, and volere, as indicated.

1. Capisco, Loro _____ farlo.   *(wanted [decided] to do it.)*
2. Ragazzi, _____ falciạre l'erba.   *(you didn't want [refused] to)*
3. Signorina, Lei _____ scusarsi con le Sụe amiche.   *(ought to)*
4. _____ partire come avevạmo promesso.   *(We were unable)*
5. _____ né il violino né il fagotto.   *(I don't know how to play)*
6. _____ alle otto iẹri mattina.   *(I knew it [found out])*
7. Signori, Loro _____ pronti alle tre?   *(could be)*
8. Carla _____ la cena da sola.   *(was supposed to prepare)*

5. Translate the following sentences into Italian using dovere, potere, sapere, or volere:

1. They refused to do it.
2. We found out a few hours ago.
3. She decided to come early.
4. He knows how to play the guitar (*chitarra*).
5. I wouldn't be able to repeat it.
6. They succeeded in convincing me.
7. They could have read it.
8. You (*voi*) should have studied more.
9. He ought to telephone.
10. She was supposed to leave with us.
11. We owe her ten dollars.
12. They had to finish the exams.
13. I could have helped them.
14. You (*Lei*) must return the books to the library.
15. They must be ill.

EXPRESSIONS WITH *fare*

Expressions that describe the weather use the verb **fare**. Observe the following:

Che tempo fa?	*How is the weather?*
Fa caldo.	*It's hot.*
Fa freddo.	*It's cold.*
Fa bel tempo.	*The weather is good.*
Fa cattivo tempo.	*The weather is bad.*

With many other common Italian expressions, **fare** takes on a variety of meanings. Observe the following:

fare attenzione(a)	to pay attention (to)
farsi il bagno	to take a bath, to swim
farsi la barba	to shave
fare la prima colazione	to have breakfast
fare colazione[2]	to have lunch
fare cena	to have supper
fare domanda	to apply
fare una domanda	to ask a question
fare male (a)	to hurt (someone)
farsi male)	to hurt oneself
fare una partita (a)	to play a game (of)
fare una passeggiata	to take a walk
fare paura (a)	to frighten (someone)
fare presto	to hurry up
fare un regalo	to give a gift
fare tardi	to be late
fare torto	to do wrong
fare le valige	to pack (a suitcase, suitcases)
fare un viaggio	to take a trip
fare una visita	to visit

6. Complete the following sentences by using the appropriate form of the verb fare.

1. Oggi _____.   (the weather is good)
2. Domani _____.   (the weather will be bad).
3. Di solito _____ d'inverno.   (it's cold)
4. Quasi sempre _____ d'estate.   (it's hot)
5. Era cosí terribile che ci_____.   (frightened)
6. Luigi? _____ come sempre!   (he'll be late)
7. Adesso è troppo presto; _____ piú in là.   (we'll have supper)
8. Noi _____ a tennis.   (played a game)
9. Bambini, _____, passa il treno!   (pay attention)
10. Tu _____ all'alba.   (had breakfast)

Giocare, suonare (sonare)

The verb **giocare** means *to play*, as in a game or a sport. Note that the verb **giocare** is usually followed by the preposition **a** with sports.

I bambini giocano sulla spiaggia.
The children play on the beach.

Mario e Carlo giocano a carte.
Mario and Charles play cards.

Olga gioca molto bene a tennis.
Olga plays tennis very well.

Giocare d'azzardo means *to gamble*.

Pietro gioca d'azzardo e perde sempre.
Peter gambles and always loses.

---

[2] The infinitive **fare** is frequently abbreviated to **far** before a consonant; e.g., **far colazione, far male, far torto.**

The verb **suonare** means *to play* a musical instrument or *to ring* or *to sound a doorbell*.

Teresa suọna il pianofọrte.
Theresa plays the piano.

7. Complete the following with giocare or suonare:
1. Voi _____ sempre a pallacanẹstro (basketball).
2. Tu _____ molto bene il sassọfono.
3. I bambini _____ con il gattino.
4. Io non so _____ il violịno.
5. Marco non _____ mai d'azzardo.
6. Noi vogliạmo imparare a _____ a carte.
7. Luịsa _____ il violoncẹllo nell'orchẹstra.
8. I giọvani _____ con un'ọttima squạdra.

Pensare a, pensare di

Pensare a and **pensare di** both mean *to think about*. They are used when one expresses an opinion about someone or something. Observe the following:

In quẹsti giọrni penso a mịa nonna perché è malata.
Nowadays I think about my grandmother because she is ill.

Che cosa pensi di quẹlla mạcchina sportiva?
What do you think about that sportscar? (What is your opinion about that sportscar?)

Spesso pensiạmo ai nostri cugini che vịvono in Itạlia.
We often think about our cousins who live in Italy.

Giọrgio, dimmi la verità! Cosa pensi dell'esame?
George, tell me the truth! What do you think about the exam? (What is your opinion?)

8. Complete the following with the preposition a or di, as needed:
1. Ora che sẹi lontano di casa, pensi molto _____ tụa madre?
2. Olga, cosa pensi _____ automọbile di Stẹfano?
3. Marco è triste perché pensa _____ suọi problemi.
4. Ecco cosa penso _____ te e _____ tuọi amici!
5. Stẹfano è innamorato e pensa sempre _____ Gina.
6. Penso _____ mịa famịglia. Specialmente _____ mịe sorelline.

Servire, servirsi da, servirsi di

Servire means *to serve*.

Il cameriẹre serve il caffè ai cliẹnti.
The waiter serves coffee to the customers.

Servirsi da means *to serve (help) oneself*.

Grạzie lo stesso; ci serviạmo da soli.
Thank you anyway; we'll serve (help) ourselves.

Servirsi di means to use, to avail oneself of.

Per adesso mi servo di quẹsti libri.
For now I use these books. (I avail myself of these books.)

Non servire a nulla means *to be of no use.*

> **Quẹste cose non sẹrvono a nulla.**
> *These things are useless.*

9. Complete the following with the appropriate forms of servire, servirsi da, or servirsi di.
1. Fra non molto ia cameriẹra _____ il tè.
2. In quel ristorante i cliẹnti _____ da soli.
3. Se vuọi tradurre, puọi _____ quẹsto dizionạrio.
4. Quest'orolọgio non funziọna; non _____.
5. Pạolo non chiạma mai la cameriẹra perché lui _____ sé.

Tornare, restituịre, riportare

Tornare means *to return* in the sense of coming back from somewhere; it is interchangeable with **ritornare**.

> **Torniạmo dall'Itạlia.**
> *We're returning from Italy.*

> **I ragazzi ritọrnano stasera.**
> *The boys are coming back tonight.*

Restituịre means *to return* in the sense of giving something back.

> **Mi restituí il denaro che mi doveva.**
> *He returned the money he owed me.*

Riportare means *to return* in the sense of bringing back or taking back.

> **Mi hanno riportato i libri.**
> *They returned my books.*

> **Hai riportato i libri in biblioteca?**
> *Did you return the books to the library?*

10. Complete the following with the appropriate forms of tornare (or ritornare), restituịre, or riportare:
1. Loro _____ dalle vacanze estive (summer, adj.) iẹri.
2. Roberto, quạndo _____ il dizionạrio in biblioteca?
3. Ho prestato la mạcchina a Giọrgio e ancora non me l'ha _____.
4. Sono partiti un mese fa e _____ la prọssima settimana.
5. Adesso ti _____ il denaro che mi hai prestato.

REVIEW

11. Complete the following with an idiomatic expression. Use the indicated cues, when given, as a guide:
1. I ragazzi _____. *Vọgliono mangiạre.*
2. Quẹl signore _____. *Non ha mai torto.*
3. _____, *vorrẹi una limonata.*
4. Gino _____. *Vuọle una coperta.*
5. Olga, ti _____ la mia gratitụdine. *Mi hai fatto un favore.*
6. Non vọglio _____ a carte, devo _____ il piạno.
7. Vọglio _____. *Ho qualcosa da chiẹdere.*
8. Per non ẹssere in ritardo, devi _____.

12. *Translate the following sentences into Italian:*

1. Today they cannot go to school because they have sore throats.
2. I am very hungry; I would like to buy a sandwich.
3. George, I owe you my gratitude (*gratitudine*).
4. We should have seen our grandparents last week.
5. They were able to mail the package two hours ago.
6. Mario refused to buy the tickets for the game.
7. I was supposed to play cards with him.
8. We would like to take a walk this evening.
9. Mary plays the piano and the guitar.
10. Now that I am far from my town, I think about my friends.

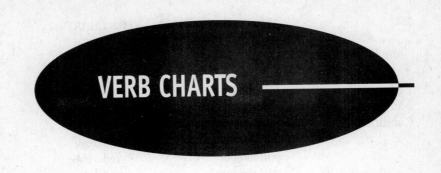

VERB CHARTS

REGULAR VERBS

Present	**parlare**	**crędere**	**dormire**	**finire**
Infinitive	*to speak*	*to believe*	*to sleep*	*to finish*
Present Gerund	parlando	credendo	dormendo	finendo
Past Gerund	avendo parlato	avendo creduto	avendo dormito	avendo finito
Past Participle	parlato	creduto	dormito	finito
Past Infinitive	avere parlato	avere creduto	avere dormito	avere finito

Simple Tenses
INDICATIVE

Present	parlo	credo	dormo	finisco
	parli	credi	dormi	finisci
	parla	crede	dorme	finisce
	parliamo	crediamo	dormiamo	finiamo
	parlate	credete	dormite	finite
	parlano	crędono	dormono	finiscono
Imperfect	parlavo	credevo	dormivo	finivo
	parlavi	credevi	dormivi	finivi
	parlava	credeva	dormiva	finiva
	parlavamo	credevamo	dormivamo	finivamo
	parlavate	credevate	dormivate	finivate
	parlavano	credevano	dormivano	finivano
Preterite	parlai	credei (-etti)	dormii	finii
	parlasti	credesti	dormisti	finisti
	parlò	credé (-ette)	dormí	finí
	parlammo	credemmo	dormimmo	finimmo
	parlaste	credeste	dormiste	finiste
	parlarono	crederono (-ettero)	dormirono	finirono
Future	parlerò	crederò	dormirò	finirò
	parlerai	crederai	dormirai	finirai
	parlerà	crederà	dormirà	finirà

	parleremo	crederemo	dormiremo	finiremo
	parlerete	crederete	dormirete	finirete
	parleranno	crederanno	dormiranno	finiranno
Conditional	parlerei	crederei	dormirei	finirei
	parleresti	crederesti	dormiresti	finiresti
	parlerebbe	crederebbe	dormirebbe	finirebbe
	parleremmo	crederemmo	dormiremmo	finiremmo
	parlereste	credereste	dormireste	finireste
	parlerebbero	crederebbero	dormirebbero	finirebbero

SUBJUNCTIVE

Present	parli	creda	dorma	finisca
	parli	creda	dorma	finisca
	parli	creda	dorma	finisca
	parliamo	crediamo	dormiamo	finiamo
	parliate	crediate	dormiate	finiate
	parlino	credano	dormano	finiscano
Imperfect	parlassi	credessi	dormissi	finissi
	parlassi	credessi	dormissi	finissi
	parlasse	credesse	dormisse	finisse
	parlassimo	credessimo	dormissimo	finissimo
	parlaste	credeste	dormiste	finiste
	parlassero	credessero	dormissero	finissero

Compound Tenses
INDICATIVE

Present Perfect (Conversational Past)	ho hai ha abbiamo avete hanno	parlato	creduto	dormito	finito
Pluperfect	avevo avevi aveva avevamo avevate avevano	parlato	creduto	dormito	finito
Preterite Perfect	ebbi avesti ebbe avemmo aveste ebbero	parlato	creduto	dormito	finito
Future Perfect	avrò avrai avrà avremo avrete avranno	parlato	creduto	dormito	finito

Conditional **Perfect**	avrei avresti avrebbe avremmo avreste avrẹbbero	parlato	creduto	dormito	finito

SUBJUNCTIVE

Present **Perfect**	ạbbia ạbbia ạbbia abbiạmo abbiạte ạbbiano	parlato	creduto	dormito	finito

Pluperfect	avessi avessi avesse avẹssimo aveste avẹssero	parlato	creduto	dormito	finito

Direct Commands

FAMILIAR

Affirmative	**(tu)**	parla!	credi!	dormi!	finisci!
	(voi)	parlate!	credete!	dormite!	finite!
Negative	**(tu)**	non parlare!	non crẹdere!	non dormire!	non finire!

FORMAL

Affirmative	**(Lei)**	parli!	creda!	dorma!	finisca!
	(Loro)	pạrlino!	crẹdano!	dọrmano!	finịscano!

AUXILIARY VERBS

Present Infinitive	**avere** *to have*	**ẹssere** *to be*
Present Gerund	avendo	essendo
Past Gerund	avendo avuto	essendo stato
Past Participle	avuto	stato
Past Infinitive	avere avuto	ẹssere stato

Indicative Tenses

Present	**avere** ho hai ha abbiạmo avete hanno	**ẹssere** sono sei è siạmo siẹte sono	**Present Perfect (Conversational Past)**	**avere** ho hai ha abbiạmo avete hanno	avuto	**ẹssere** sono sei è siạmo siẹte sono	stato(-a) stati(-e)
Imperfect	avevo avevi aveva	ero eri era	**Pluperfect**	avevo avevi aveva	avuto	ero eri era	stato(-a)

	avere	essere		avere	essere
	avevamo	eravamo		avevamo	eravamo } stati(-e)
	avevate	eravate		avevate	eravate
	avevano	erano		avevano	erano
Preterite	ebbi	fui	**Preterite Perfect**	ebbi	fui } stato(-a)
	avesti	fosti		avesti	fosti
	ebbe	fu		ebbe	fu
	avemmo	fummo		avemmo } avuto	fummo
	aveste	foste		aveste	foste } stati(-e)
	ebbero	furono		ebbero	furono
Future	avrò	sarò	**Future Perfect**	avrò	sarò } stato(-a)
	avrai	sarai		avrai	sarai
	avrà	sarà		avrà	sarà
	avremo	saremo		avremo } avuto	saremo
	avrete	sarete		avrete	sarete } stati(-e)
	avranno	saranno		avranno	saranno
Conditional	avrei	sarei	**Conditional Perfect**	avrei	sarei } stato(-a)
	avresti	saresti		avresti	saresti
	avrebbe	sarebbe		avrebbe } avuto	sarebbe
	avremmo	saremmo		avremmo	saremmo
	avreste	sareste		avreste	sareste } stati(-e)
	avrebbero	sarebbero		avrebbero	sarebbero

Subjunctive Tenses

	avere	essere		avere	essere
Present	abbia	sia	**Present Perfect**	abbia	sia } stato(-a)
	abbia	sia		abbia	sia
	abbia	sia		abbia	sia
	abbiamo	siamo		abbiamo } avuto	siamo
	abbiate	siate		abbiate	siate } stati(-e)
	abbiano	siano		abbiano	siano
Imperfect	avessi	fossi	**Pluperfect**	avessi	fossi } stato (-a)
	avessi	fossi		avessi	fossi
	avesse	fosse		avesse	fosse
	avessimo	fossimo		avessimo } avuto	fossimo
	aveste	foste		aveste	foste } stati(-e)
	avessero	fossero		avessero	fossero

Direct Commands
FAMILIAR

		avere	essere
Affirmative	**(tu)**	abbi!	sii!
	(voi)	abbiate!	siate!
Negative	**(tu)**	non avere!	non essere!

FORMAL

		avere	essere
Affirmative	**(Lei)**	abbia!	sia!
	(Loro)	abbiano!	siano!

IRREGULAR VERBS

Note: Only irregular forms are given for the following verbs. An asterisk (*) indicates that the verb is conjugated with **essere** in compound tenses.

andare*   *to go*

Present Indicative	vado, vai, va, andiamo, andate, vanno
Present Subjunctive	vada, vada, vada, andiamo, andiate, vadano
Future	andrò, andrai, andrà, andremo, andrete, andranno
Conditional	andrei, andresti, andrebbe, andremmo, andreste, andrebbero
Imperative (tu)	va' (vai)
(Lei)	vada
(Loro)	vadano

bere   *to drink*

Gerund	bevendo
Past Participle	bevuto
Present Indicative	bevo, bevi, beve, beviamo, bevete, bevono
Present Subjunctive	beva, beva, beva, beviamo, beviate, bevano
Imperfect Indicative	bevevo, bevevi, beveva, bevevamo, bevevate, bevevano
Imperfect Subjunctive	bevessi, bevessi, bevesse, bevessimo, beveste, bevessero
Preterite	bevvi, bevesti, bevve, bevemmo, beveste, bevvero
Future	berrò, berrai, berrà, berremo, berrete, berranno
Conditional	berrei, berresti, berrebbe, berremmo, berreste, berrebbero

cadere*   *to fall*

Preterite	caddi, cadesti, cadde, cademmo, cadeste, caddero
Future	cadrò, cadrai, cadrà, cadremo, cadrete, cadranno
Conditional	cadrei, cadresti, cadrebbe, cadremmo, cadreste, cadrebbero

chiedere   *to ask*

Past Participle	chiesto
Preterite	chiesi, chiedesti, chiese, chiedemmo, chiedeste, chiesero

chiudere   *to close*

Past Participle	chiuso
Preterite	chiusi, chiudesti, chiuse, chiudemmo, chiudeste, chiusero

conoscere   *to know*

Past Participle	conosciuto
Preterite	conobbi, conoscesti, conobbe, conoscemmo, conosceste, conobbero

correre   *to run*

Past Participle	corso
Preterite	corsi, corresti, corse, corremmo, correste, corsero

crescere*   *to grow*

Past Participle	cresciuto
Preterite	crebbi, crescesti, crebbe, crescemmo, cresceste, crebbero

cuocere*   *to cook*

Past Participle	cotto
Present Indicative	cuocio, cuoci, cuoce, cociamo, cocete, cuociono
Present Subjunctive	cuocia, cuocia, cuocia, cociamo, cociate, cuociano
Preterite	cossi, cocesti, cosse, cocemmo, coceste, cossero

dare   *to give*

Present Indicative	do, dai, dà, diamo, date, danno
Present Subjunctive	dia, dia, dia, diamo, diate, diano
Imperfect Subjunctive	dessi, dessi, desse, dessimo, deste, dessero
Preterite	diedi, desti, diede, demmo, deste, diedero
Future	darò, darai, darà, daremo, darete, daranno
Conditional	darei, daresti, darebbe, daremmo, dareste, darebbero

Imperative	**(tu)**	da' (dai)
	(Lei)	dia
	(Loro)	diano

decidere   *to decide*

Past Participle   deciso
Preterite   decisi, decidesti, decise, decidemmo, decideste, decisero

dire   *to say, to tell*

Gerund   dicendo
Past Participle   detto
Present Indicative   dico, dici, dice, diciamo, dite, dicono
Present Subjunctive dica, dica, dica, diciamo, diciate, dicano
Imperfect Indicative dicevo, dicevi, diceva, dicevamo, dicevate, dicevano
Imperfect Subjunctive dicessi, dicessi, dicesse, dicessimo, diceste, dicessero
Preterite   dissi, dicesti, disse, dicemmo, diceste, dissero
Imperative (tu)   di'

dovere   *to have to, must*

Present   devo, devi, deve, dobbiamo, dovete, devono
Present Subjunctive deva, deva, deva, dobbiamo, dobbiate, devano
Future   dovrò, dovrai, dovrà, dovremo, dovrete, dovranno
Conditional   dovrei, dovresti, dovrebbe, dovremmo, dovreste, dovrebbero

fare   *to do, to make*

Gerund   facendo
Past Participle   fatto
Present Indicative   faccio, fai, fa, facciamo, fate, fanno
Present Subjunctive faccia, faccia, faccia, facciamo, facciate, facciano
Imperfect Indicative facevo, facevi, faceva, facevamo, facevate, facevano
Imperfect Subjunctive facessi, facessi, facesse, facessimo, faceste, facessero
Preterite   feci, facesti, fece, facemmo, faceste, fecero
Future   farò, farai, farà, faremo, farete, faranno
Conditional   farei, faresti, farebbe, faremmo, fareste, farebbero

Imperative	**(tu)**	fa' (fai)
	(Lei)	faccia
	(Loro)	facciano

leggere   *to read*

Past Participle   letto
Preterite   lessi, leggesti, lesse, leggemmo, leggeste, lessero

mettere   *to put*

Past Participle   messo
Preterite   misi, mettesti, mise, mettemmo, metteste, misero

morire*   *to die*

Past Participle   morto
Present Indicative   muoio, muori, muore, moriamo, morite, muoiono
Present Subjunctive muoia, muoia, muoia, moriamo, moriate, muoiano

muovere   *to move*

Past Participle   mosso
Preterite   mossi, movesti, mosse, movemmo, moveste, mossero

nascere*   *to be born*

Past Participle   nato
Preterite   nacqui, nascesti, nacque, nascemmo, nasceste, nacquero

parere*   *to seem*

Past Participle	parso
Present Indicative	paio, pari, pare, paiamo (pariamo), parete, paiono
Present Subjunctive	paia, paia, paia, paiamo, paiate, paiano
Preterite	parvi, paresti, parve, paremmo, pareste, parvero
Future	parrò, parrai, parrà, parremo, parrete, parranno
Conditional	parrei, parresti, parrebbe, parremmo, parreste, parrebbero

perdere   *to lose*

Past Participle	perso *or* perduto
Preterite	persi, perdesti, perse, perdemmo, perdeste, persero

piacere*   *to be pleasing*

Past Participle	piaciuto
Present Indicative	piaccio, piaci, piace, piacciamo, piacete, piacciono
Present Subjunctive	piaccia, piaccia, piaccia, piacciamo, piacciate, piacciano
Preterite	piacqui, piacesti, piacque, piacemmo, piaceste, piacquero

piangere   *to cry*

Past Participle	pianto
Preterite	piansi, piangesti, pianse, piangemmo, piangeste, piansero

porre   *to put, to place*

Gerund	ponendo
Past Participle	posto
Present Indicative	pongo, poni, pone, poniamo, ponete, pongono
Present Subjunctive	ponga, ponga, ponga, poniamo, poniate, pongano
Imperfect Indicative	ponevo, ponevi, poneva, ponevamo, ponevate, ponevano
Imperfect Subjunctive	ponessi, ponessi, ponesse, ponessimo, poneste, ponessero
Preterite	posi, ponesti, pose, ponemmo, poneste, posero
Future	porrò, porrai, porrà, porremo, porrete, porranno
Conditional	porrei, porresti, porrebbe, porremmo, poneste, porrebbero

potere   *to be able to, can*

Present Indicative	posso, puoi, può, possiamo, potete, possono
Present Subjunctive	possa, possa, possa, possiamo, possiate, possano
Future	potrò, potrai, potrà, potremo, potrete, potranno
Conditional	potrei, potresti, potrebbe, potremmo, potreste, potrebbero

prendere   *to take*

Past Participle	preso
Preterite	presi, prendesti, prese, prendemmo, prendeste, presero

ridere   *to laugh*

Past Participle	riso
	risi, ridesti, rise, ridemmo, rideste, risero

riempire   *to fill, to stuff*

Gerund	riempiendo
Past Participle	riempito (riempiuto)
Present Indicative	riempio, riempi, riempie, riempiamo, riempite, riempiono
Present Subjunctive	riempia, riempia, riempia, riempiamo, riempiate, riempiano
Preterite	riempiei (riempii), riempiesti (riempisti), riempié (riempí), riempiemmo (riempimmo), riempieste (riempiste), riempierono (riempirono)

rimanere*   *to remain*

Past Participle	rimasto
Present Indicative	rimango, rimani, rimane, rimaniamo, rimanete, rimangono

Present Subjunctive	rimanga, rimanga, rimanga, rimaniamo, rimaniate, rimangono
Preterite	rimasi, rimanesti, rimase, rimanemmo, rimaneste, rimasero
Future	rimarrò, rimarrai, rimarrà, rimarremo, rimarrete, rimarranno
Conditional	rimarrei, rimarresti, rimarrebbe, rimarremmo, rimarreste, rimarrebbero

rispondere   *to answer*

Past Participle	risposto
Preterite	risposi, rispondesti, rispose, rispondemmo, rispondeste, risposero

rompere   *to break*

Past Participle	rotto
Preterite	ruppi, rompesti, ruppe, rompemmo, rompeste, ruppero

salire   *to climb, to go up*

Present Indicative	salgo, sali, sale, saliamo, salite, salgono
Present Subjunctive	salga, salga, salga, saliamo, saliate, salgano

sapere   *to know*

Present Indicative	so, sai, sa, sappiamo, sapete, sanno
Present Subjunctive	sappia, sappia, sappia, sappiamo, sappiate, sappiano
Preterite	seppi, sapesti, seppe, sapemmo, sapeste, seppero
Future	saprò, saprai, saprà, sapremo, saprete, sapranno
Conditional	saprei, sapresti, saprebbe, sapremmo, sapreste, saprebbero
Imperative (tu)	sappi
(Lei)	sappia
(voi)	sappiate
(Loro)	sappiano

scegliere   *to choose*

Past Participle	scelto
Present Indicative	scelgo, scegli, sceglie, scegliamo, scegliete, scelgono
Present Subjunctive	scelga, scelga, scelga, scegliamo, scegliate, scelgano
Preterite	scelsi, scegliesti, scelse, scegliemmo, sceglieste, scelsero

scendere*   *to descend, to go down*

Past Participle	sceso
Preterite	scesi, scendesti, scese, scendemmo, scendeste, scesero

scrivere   *to write*

Past Participle	scritto
Preterite	scrissi, scrivesti, scrisse, scrivemmo, scriveste, scrissero

sedere   *to sit*

Present Indicative	siedo, siedi, siede, sediamo, sedete, siedono
Present Subjunctive	sieda, sieda, sieda, sediamo, sediate, siedano

spendere   *to spend*

Past Participle	speso
Preterite	spesi, spendesti, spese, spendemmo, spendeste, spesero

stare*   *to stay, to be*

Present Indicative	sto, stai, sta, stiamo, state, stanno
Present Subjunctive	stia, stia, stia, stiamo, stiate, stiano
Imperfect Subjunctive	stessi, stessi, stesse, stessimo, steste, stessero
Preterite	stetti, stesti, stette, stemmo, steste, stettero
Future	starò, starai, starà, staremo, starete, staranno
Conditional	starei, staresti, starebbe, staremmo, stareste, starebbero
Imperative (tu)	sta' (stai)
(Lei)	stia
(Loro)	stiano

tenere   *to hold, to keep*

Present Indicative	tengo, tięni, tięne, teniamo, tenete, tęngono
Present Subjunctive	tenga, tenga, tenga, teniamo, teniate, tęngano
Preterite	tenni, tenesti, tenne, tenemmo, teneste, tęnnero
Future	terrò, terrai, terrà, terremo, terrete, terranno
Conditional	terręi, terresti, terrebbe, terremmo, terreste, terrębbero

togliere   *to take away*

Past Participle	tolto
Present Indicative	tolgo, togli, tọglie, togliamo, togliẹte, tọlgono
Present Subjunctive	tolga, tolga, tolga, togliamo, togliate, tọlgano
Preterite	tolsi, togliẹsti, tolse, togliẹmmo, togliẹste, tọlsero

trarre   *to pull, to extract, to draw*

Gerund	traẹndo
Past Participle	tratto
Present Indicative	traggo, trại, trạe, traiamo, traẹte, trạggono
Present Subjunctive	tragga, tragga, tragga, traiamo, traiate, trạggano
Imperfect Indicative	traẹvo, traẹvi, traẹva, traevamo, traevate, traẹvano
Imperfect Subjunctive	traẹssi, traẹssi, traẹsse, traẹssimo, traẹste, traẹssero
Preterite	trassi, traẹsti, trasse, traẹmmo, traẹste, trạssero

udire   *to hear*

Present Indicative	odo, odi, ode, udiamo, udite, ọdono
Present Subjunctive	oda, oda, oda, udiamo, udiate, ọdano

uscire*   *to go out*

Present Indicative	esco, esci, esce, usciamo, uscite, ęscono
Present Subjunctive	esca, esca, esca, usciamo, usciate, ęscano

valere*   *to be worth*

Past Participle	valso
Present Indicative	valgo, vali, vale, valiamo, valete, vạlgono
Present Subjunctive	valga, valga, valga, valiamo, valiate, vạlgano
Preterite	valsi, valesti, valse, valemmo, valeste, vạlsero
Future	varrò, varrai, varrà, varremo, varrete, varranno
Conditional	varręi, varresti, varrebbe, varremmo, varreste, varrębbero

vedere   *to see*

Past Participle	veduto *or* visto
Preterite	vidi, vedesti, vide, vedemmo, vedeste, vịdero
Future	vedrò, vedrai, vedrà, vedremo, vedrete, vedranno
Conditional	vedręi, vedresti, vedrebbe, vedremmo, vedreste, vedrębbero

venire*   *to come*

Past Participle	venuto
Present Indicative	vengo, vięni, vięne, veniamo, venite, vęngono
Present Subjunctive	venga, venga, venga, veniamo, veniate, vęngano
Preterite	venni, venisti, venne, venimmo, veniste, vęnnero
Future	verrò, verrai, verrà, verremo, verrete, verranno
Conditional	verręi, verresti, verrebbe, verremmo, verreste, verrębbero

vịncere   *to win*

Past Participle	vinto
Preterite	vinsi, vincesti, vinse, vincemmo, vinceste, vịnsero

vịvere   *to live*

Past Participle	vissuto
Preterite	vissi, vivesti, visse, vivemmo, viveste, vịssero

Future	vivrò, vivrai, vivrà, vivremo, vivrete, vivranno
Conditional	vivrei, vivresti, vivrebbe, vivremmo, vivreste, vivrebbero
	volere *to want*
Present Indicative	voglio, vuoi, vuole, vogliamo, volete, vogliono
Present Subjunctive	voglia, voglia, voglia, vogliamo, vogliate, vogliano
Preterite	volli, volesti, volle, volemmo, voleste, vollero
Future	vorrò, vorrai, vorrà, vorremo, vorrete, vorranno
Conditional	vorrei, vorresti, vorrebbe, vorremmo, vorreste, vorrebbero
Imperative (voi)	vogliate

VERBS IRREGULAR IN THE PRETERITE AND PAST PARTICIPLE

Note that the following verbs are irregular only in the preterite in the first- and third-person singular and third-person plural and in the past participle:

Verbs with Some Irregular Endings in the Preterite (**-si**) *and Past Participle* (**-so**)

Infinitive	Preterite	Past Participle
accendere	accesi	acceso
alludere	allusi	alluso
appendere	appesi	appeso
ardere	arsi	arso
attendere	attesi	atteso
chiudere	chiusi	chiuso
comprendere	compresi	compreso
concludere	conclusi	concluso
confondere	confusi	confuso
correre	corsi	corso
decidere	decisi	deciso
deludere	delusi	deluso
difendere	difesi	difeso
diffondere	diffusi	diffuso
dipendere	dipesi	dipeso
discendere	discesi	disceso
distendere	distesi	disteso
dividere	divisi	diviso
emergere	emersi	emerso
espellere	espulsi	espulso
esplodere	esplosi	esploso
evadere	evasi	evaso
illudere	illusi	illuso
immergere	immersi	immerso
intrudere	intrusi	intruso
invadere	invasi	invaso
mordere	morsi	morso
occludere	occlusi	occluso
occorrere	occorsi	occorso
offendere	offesi	offeso
perdere	persi	perso
persuadere	persuasi	persuaso
prendere	presi	preso

radere	rasi	raso
rendere	resi	reso
ridere	risi	riso
scendere	scesi	sceso
sommergere	sommersi	sommerso
sorridere	sorrisi	sorriso
spargere	sparsi	sparso
spendere	spesi	speso
tendere	tesi	teso
uccidere	uccisi	ucciso
valere	valsi	valso

Verbs with Some Irregular Endings in the Preterite (**-si**) *and Past Participle* (**-to**)

Infinitive	Preterite	Past Participle
accogliere	accolsi	accolto
accorgersi	mi accorsi	accorto
aggiungere	aggiunsi	aggiunto
aprire	apersi	aperto
assolvere	assolsi (assolvetti)	assolto
assumere	assunsi	assunto
chiedere	chiesi	chiesto
cogliere	colsi	colto
convincere	convinsi	convinto
corrispondere	corrisposi	corrisposto
dipingere	dipinsi	dipinto
distinguere	distinsi	distinto
estinguere	estinsi	estinto
fingere	finsi	finto
giungere	giunsi	giunto
nascondere	nascosi	nascosto
piangere	piansi	pianto
porgere	porsi	porto
porre	posi	posto
presumere	presunsi	presunto
raccogliere	raccolsi	raccolto
rimanere	rimasi	rimasto
risolvere	risolsi (risolvetti)	risolto
rispondere	risposi	risposto
scegliere	scelsi	scelto
sconvolgere	sconvolsi	sconvolto
scoprire	scopersi	scoperto
spegnere	spensi	spento
spingere	spinsi	spinto
tingere	tinsi	tinto
togliere	tolsi	tolto
torcere	torsi	torto
ungere	unsi	unto
vincere	vinsi	vinto
volgere	volsi	volto

Verbs with Some Irregular Endings in the Preterite (**-ssi**) *and Past Participle* (**-sso**)

Infinitive	Preterite	Past Participle
commuovere	commossi	commosso
comprimere	compressi	compresso
concedere	concessi	concesso
deprimere	depressi	depresso
discutere	discussi	discusso
esprimere	espressi	espresso
figgere	fissi	fisso (fitto)
imprimere	impressi	impresso
muovere	mossi	mosso
prefiggere	prefissi	prefisso
reprimere	repressi	represso
riscuotere	riscossi	riscosso
scuotere	scossi	scosso
sopprimere	soppressi	soppresso

Verbs with Some Irregular Endings in the Preterite (**-ssi**) *and Past Participle* (**-tto**)

Infinitive	Preterite	Past Participle
affliggere	afflissi	afflitto
correggere	corressi	corretto
cuocere	cossi	cotto
dire	dissi	detto
dirigere	diressi	diretto
distruggere	distrussi	distrutto
eleggere	elessi	eletto
erigere	eressi	eretto
friggere	frissi	fritto
infliggere	inflissi	inflitto
leggere	lessi	letto
negligere	neglessi	negletto
prediligere	predilessi	prediletto
proteggere	protessi	protetto
scrivere	scrissi	scritto
trarre	trassi	tratto

Verbs with Some Irregular Endings in the Preterite (**-ei**) *and Past Participle* (**-to**)

Infinitive	Preterite	Past Participle
assistere	assistei	assistito
consistere	consistei	consistito
esigere	esigei	esatto
insistere	insistei	insistito
persistere	persistei	persistito
resistere	resistei	resistito

Verbs with Irregular Endings in the Preterite (**-si**) *and Past Participle* (**-sso** *or* **-tto**)

Infinitive	Preterite	Past Participle
mettere	misi	messo
ammettere	ammisi	ammesso

commęttere	commisi	commesso
compromęttere	compromisi	compromesso
dimęttere	dimisi	dimesso
emęttere	emisi	emesso
permęttere	permisi	permesso
promęttere	promisi	promesso
rimęttere	rimisi	rimesso
scommęttere	scommisi	scommesso
smęttere	smisi	smesso
strịngere	strinsi	stretto
costrịngere	costrinsi	costretto
restrịngere	restrinsi	ristretto

More verbs with some irregular endings in the preterite and the past participle follow. These verbs do not have a common irregularity. Note that **piọvere** is conjugated in the third-person singular only. Also note that verbs made by a prefix and one of the following verbs would be conjugated in the same way as the verbs shown below:

Infinitive	Preterite	Past Participle
bere	bevvi	bevuto
conọscere	conobbi	conosciụto
cręscere	crebbi	cresciụto
dare	diędi	dato
fare	feci	fatto
męscere	mescęi	mesciụto
nạscere	nạcqui	nato
parere	parvi	parso
piacęre	piạcqui	piaciụto
piọvere (3rd-person s. only)	piọvve	piovụto
rọmpere	ruppi	rotto
sapere	seppi	saputo
stare	stetti	stato
tenere	tenni	tenuto
vedere	vidi	visto (veduto)
venire	venni	venuto
vịvere	vissi	vissuto
volere	volli	voluto

ANSWERS

Chapter 1

1.
1. ciao
2. ciarlatano
3. ceppo
4. cinico
5. cencio
6. Vincenzo
7. ciò
8. bicicletta
9. cinque
10. baci

2.
1. coppa
2. chiave
3. perché
4. come
5. Corfú
6. chimica
7. parco
8. chiesa
9. credito
10. Chieti

3.
1. vero
2. tenda
3. bella
4. ferro
5. cane
6. neve

4.
1. Gino
2. gente
3. giovane
4. ragione
5. grigi
6. giacca

5.
1. gloria
2. ghiro
3. glicine
4. ghetto
5. gatta
6. laghi
7. ghiaccio
8. gomma
9. gas
10. aghi

6.
1. ragno
2. cognome
3. segno
4. bagnino
5. giugno
6. bagno
7. lavagna
8. disegno
9. lasagne
10. legno

7.
1. ho
2. hai
3. ha
4. hanno
5. ah!
6. eh!
7. oh!

8.
1. luglio
2. meglio
3. sbagli
4. ammiraglio
5. svegliare
6. svogliato

7. maglione
8. figli
9. gli
10. foglie

9. 1. tipo
2. riso
3. zio
4. vino
5. Cina
6. Milano
7. diva
8. farina

10. 1. smaltire
2. sbagli
3. smania
4. sbarbare
5. sgabello
6. svanire

11. 1. cosí
2. cosa
3. girasole.
4. desiderio
5. controsenso
6. preside.
7. autoservizio
8. risentire

12. 1. sci
2. uscita
3. sciopero
4. lasciare
5. scena
6. sciolto
7. scendere
8. sceicco

13. *A*
1. zero
2. zaino
3. zabaione
4. zoo
5. Manzoni
6. ozono
7. zodiaco
8. zelo

B
1. zio
2. zie
3. zucchero
4. terzo
5. grazie

6. calza
7. pazienza
8. Firenze

14. 1. Firenze
2. Zara
3. Domodossola
4. Udine
5. Imola
6. Otranto
7. Cappa
8. York
9. Genova
10. Livorno
11. Empoli
12. Washington
13. Ancona
14. Savona

15. 1. (a) jogurt (b) jolly (c) junior
2. (a) hockey (b) kimono (c) poker
3. (a) Walter (b) watt (c) welter
4. (a) taxi (b) xenofobia (c) box
5. (a) brandy (b) sexy (c) rally

16. 1. cappello
2. nonno
3. tutta
4. cassa
5. canne
6. pappa
7. palla
8. donna
9. coppia
10. soqquadro

17. 1. virtú
2. papà
3. è
4. partí
5. visitò
6. carità
7. cosí
8. perché
9. lunedí
10. città

18. 1. luglio
2. Fiesole
3. scuola
4. iato
5. cuore
6. uomo
7. buoi
8. guai

9. zabaiọne
10. suọi
11. maiụscolo
12. aiuọla
13. paụra
14. aọrta
15. rientrare
16. musẹo
17. poẹta
18. zịo

19. 1. gnu
2. tu
3. sí
4. gru
5. re
6. caffè
7. pẹggio
8. mạncia
9. Rụssia
10. Rẹggio
11. Torino
12. vanịglia
13. Ạngela
14. inverno
15. Firenze
16. parẹntesi
17. mercoledí
18. Inghilterra
19. asterisco
20. apọstrofo

20. 1. ma-gnị-fi-co
2. cu-gi-no
3. mạg-gìo
4. giụ-gno
5. ra-gaz-zi
6. mar-ro-ne
7. Ạn-ge-lo
8. Giu-sep-pe
9. co-nị-glio
10. sem-pli-ce-men-te
11. fiạ-to
12. I-tạ-lia
13. mam-ma
14. pa-dre
15. Fi-ren-ze
16. Do-mo-dọs-so-la
17. Ste-fạ-nia
18. mer-co-le-dí
19. co-sta-re
20. scịm-mia

21. 1. il punto esclamativo
2. le virgolette
3. l'accento grave
4. il punto (punto fermo)
5. la vịrgola
6. la sbarretta
7. i puntini di sospensiọne
8. le parẹntesi quạdre
9. l'accento acuto
10. l'accento circonflesso
11. l'asterisco
12. le parẹntesi tonde
13. la sgraffa
14. il punto interrogativo
15. la diẹresi
16. il punto e vịrgola
17. il trattino
18. i due punti
19. la lineẹtta
20. l'apọstrofo

22. 1. ciạo
2. aceto
3. zịo
4. sbagli
5. caro
6. casa
7. svogliạto
8. chiạvi
9. sci
10. ghiạccio
11. cẹncio
12. scuọla
13. mẹglio
14. perché
15. uscita
16. Gino
17. sbarbo
18. sciọpero
19. prezzo
20. chiẹsa

23. 1. []
2. ´
3. << >>
4. .
5. /
6. *
7. `
8. ?
9. -
10. ()
11. !

12. '
13. ,
14. :
15. ...

24. 1. università
2. comò
3. venerdí
4. servitú
5. affinché
6. purché
7. sí
8. cioè
9. tè
10. karatè

25. 1. cop-pia
2. Ur-bi-no
3. me-ra-vi-glio-so
4. bab-bo
5. Stẹ-fa-no
6. Mar-cel-lo
7. chiẹ-sa
8. Siẹ-na
9. ma-rịt-ti-mo
10. bel-lịs-si-mo
11. caf-fè
12. sbar-ret-ta
13. in-ter-ro-ga-ti-vo
14. uọ-mi-ni

Chapter 2

1. 1. -o
2. -a
3. -o
4. -o
5. -a
6. -o
7. -a
8. -o
9. -a
10. -o
11. -a
12. -o
13. -o
14. -a

2. 1. La; il
2. Lo; il
3. Il; la
4. La; la

5. Lo
6. Il; la
7. Il; la
8. L'; l'
9. Il; il
10. La; il

3. 1. Le signore sono alte.
2. I libri sono pịccoli.
3. Le nonne sono vẹcchie.
4. Le scuọle sono nuọve.
5. I nonni sono bravi.
6. Le ragazze sono alte.
7. Le professoresse sono americane.
8. I quaderni sono giạlli.
9. I maẹstri sono buọni
10. Le cravatte sono rosse.

4. 1. I
2. Le
3. Gli
4. I
5. Le
6. Le; gli
7. Gli
8. I
9. Gli (Gl')
10. Le (L')

5. 1. La
2. Il
3. Il
4. Il
5. Il
6. Lo
7. La
8. Il
9. La
10. La
11. La
12. La
13. Il
14. La

6. 1. Il
2. la
3. Il; il
4. La; la
5. il

7. 1. Le classi sono allegre.
2. Le madri sono generose.
3. I dottori sono famosi.

4. I padri sono generosi.
5. Le canzoni sono melodiose.
6. Le navi sono belle.
7. Gli studenti sono alti.
8. I cantanti sono bravi.
9. Le chiavi sono piccole.

8. 1. Il clima
2. Il programma
3. La violinista
4. Il sistema
5. Il dramma
6. Il poeta

9. 1. i poemi
2. i drammi
3. le dentiste
4. i farmacisti
5. i pianeti
6. i piloti
7. le giornaliste
8. le pianiste
9. i telecronisti
10. i dentisti

10. 1. Le radio sono istruttive.
2. Le dinamo sono utili.
3. Le foto sono belle.
4. I bambini sono carini.
5. Le auto sono rosse.
6. Le moto sono giapponesi.

11. 1. Le colleghe sono americane.
2. Le oche sono grasse.
3. Le pesche sono deliziose.
4. Le formiche sono piccole.
5. Le rughe sono naturali.
6. Le mosche sono seccanti.
7. Le tuniche sono bianche.
8. Le barche sono rosse.

12. 1. I sacchi sono pesanti.
2. I dialoghi sono difficili.
3. I chirurghi sono giovani.
4. I monologhi sono tediosi.
5. I fuochi sono pericolosi.
6. I luoghi sono vicini.
7. I cataloghi sono questi!
8. Gli obblighi sono mutui.

13. 1. I monaci sono religiosi.
2. I teologi sono studiosi.
3. I parroci sono devoti.
4. Gli asparagi sono gustosi.
5. I portici sono alti.

14. 1. Gli uffici sono spaziosi.
2. I dizionari sono grossi.
3. Gli studi sono di Mario.
4. Gli stadi sono immensi.
5. Gli (gl') inizi sono importanti.
6. Gli esempi sono buoni.
7. Gli empori sono ben forniti.
8. Gli armadi sono pieni.
9. Gli usci sono aperti.
10. Gli esercizi sono difficili.

15. 1. A: i muri　　B: le mura
2. A: i gesti　　B: le gesta
3. A: gli anelli　B: le anella
4. A: i cigli　　B: le ciglia
5. A: i risi　　B: le risa
6. A: i lenzuoli　B: le lenzuola
7. A: i diti　　B: le dita
8. A: i gridi　　B: le grida
9. A: i membri　B: le membra
10. A: i fili　　B: le fila

16. 1. Le lenzuola sono bianche.
2. Le uova sono sode.
3. Le braccia sono lunghe.
4. Le dita sono piccoline.
5. Le ginocchia sono dure.
6. Le ciglia sono nere.

17. 1. Le cosce di pollo sono deliziose.
2. Le rocce sono pericolose.
3. Le docce calde sono buone.
4. Le piogge sono piacevoli.
5. Le fasce sono bianche.
6. Le frange sono delicate.

18. 1. Le tribú sono isolate.
2. Le università sono necessarie.
3. I brindisi sono spiritosi.
4. Questi caffè sono forti.
5. Le città sono affollate.
6. Le crisi sono severe.

19. 1. I tè sono deliziosi.
2. I dí sono lunghi.
3. Le gru sono alte.
4. I re sono vecchi.

20. 1. ali
2. buoi
3. dèi
4. mogli
5. uomini
6. templi

21.
1. La studentessa lavora molto.
2. La lavoratrice riceve il denaro.
3. La principessa abita nel castello.
4. L'ostessa parla con gli invitati.
5. L'attrice canta bene.
6. La contessa è ricca.

22.
1. il
2. Il
3. l'
4. Il
5. Il
6. il

23.
1. I capogiri
2. Gli arcobaleni
3. I pescecani
4. I pomodori (I pomidoro)
5. Le banconote
6. I cavolfiori
7. I boccaporti

24.
1. I capifila
2. I capireparto
3. I pianoforti
4. I chiaroscuri
5. I malcontenti
6. I capisquadra
7. Gli altoparlanti
8. Le casseforti
9. I capistazione
10. I palcoscenici

25.
1. cagnolino
2. vecchietta
3. bimbetta
4. gattino
5. raccontino
6. libretto (libriccino)
7. scarpina
8. donnuccia

26.
1. vecchione
2. libroni
3. portone
4. scarpone
5. gattone
6. omone

27.
1. La
2. L'
3. Gli
4. I

28.
1. La
2. L'
3. (none)
4. (none)
5. la
6. (none)
7. il
8. (none)
9. i
10. (none)

29.
1. l'
2. il
3. l'
4. (none)
5. (none)
6. (none)
7. (none)
8. L'
9. Il
10. il

30.
1. L'
2. L'; l'
3. (none)
4. (none)
5. la
6. (none)
7. (none)
8. La
9. (none)
10. La

31.
1. in
2. della
3. nel
4. in
5. nell'
6. del
7. della
8. della

32.
1. (none)
2. I
3. (none)
4. (none)
5. Le
6. (none)
7. i
8. Il

33.
1. (none)
2. La
3. (none)

4. la
5. (none)

34. 1. dalla
2. nello
3. delle
4. nell'
5. sugli
6. per le
7. con i
8. dal; dalla
9. dai
10. dalla

35. 1. Pietro compra un dizionario.
2. Paolo prende un'aranciata.
3. La signora Torelli compra una casa grande.
4. Il signor Marini è uno zio di Stefano.
5. Scriviamo una lettera.
6. Roberto è un amico di Giovanni.
7. Il dottore ha uno studio grande.
8. Vincenzo guida un'ambulanza rossa.
9. Teresa porta un abito bianco.
10. I ragazzi comprano un giocattolo.

36. 1. un'
2. una
3. un
4. una
5. una
6. un
7. una
8. un
9. uno
10. un'

37. 1. un
2. (none)
3. (none)
4. (none)
5. uno
6. (none)
7. (none)
8. (none)
9. una
10. un

38. 1. dell'
2. dei
3. dello
4. delle
5. della
6. degli
7. del

8. delle
9. dell'
10. dei

39. 1. Sí, ci piace il tè e prendiamo del tè.
2. Sí, ci piace la carne e mangiamo della carne.
3. Sí, mi piacciono i legumi e voglio dei legumi.
4. Sí, ci piace lo zucchero e compriamo dello zucchero.
5. Sí, mi piace il latte e bevo del latte.
6. Sí, ci piace la minestra e prendiamo della minestra.
7. Sí, ci piace l'acqua minerale e beviamo dell'acqua minerale.
8. Sí, mi piace il pane e mangio del pane.

40. 1. Lui non compra penne.
2. Io non prendo tè.
3. Noi non mangiamo minestra.
4. Non mangio pane.
5. Non beviamo acqua minerale.
6. Non mandiamo pacchi.

41. 1. del
2. di
3. di
4. dei
5. di
6. di
7. del
8. di
9. di
10. della

42. 1. I
2. L'
3. Gli
4. Le
5. la
6. Le
7. Il
8. Gli
9. Lo
10. La
11. i
12. Le
13. L'
14. I
15. La

43. 1. -ista
2. -essa
3. -hi
4. -i

5. -he
6. -à
7. -io
8. -io
9. -e
10. -i

44. 1. il cappellino
2. la sorellina
3. la vecchietta
4. la donnuccia
5. il libretto (il libriccino)
6. il fratellino
7. il raccontino
8. la casetta (la casuccia)

45. 1. I parchi sono grandi.
2. Le estati (L'estati) sono belle.
3. I film sono buoni.
4. Le formiche sono piccole.
5. I guardasigilli sono vecchi.
6. Gli apriscatole sono rotti.
7. Le pianiste sono brave.
8. Gli sport sono necessari.
9. Le gru sono uccelli grandi.
10. Le università sono utili.
11. Le docce sono fredde.
12. Le fasce sono bianche.
13. Le scie delle navi sono lunghe.
14. I teologi sono studiosi.
15. Le uova sono sode.
16. Le telecroniste parlano bene.
17. I problemi sono risolti.
18. Le dinamo sono utili.
19. Le radio sono tedesche.
20. Le mani sono pulite.

46. 1. La
2. (none)
3. (none)
4. I
5. (none); il
6. I
7. una
8. (none); un
9. Le
10. (none)
11. (none)
12. un
13. La; un'
14. nell'
15. L'
16. (none); un'

17. (none); (none)
18. Le
19. Le
20. Le

47. 1. nel; della
2. dalla; sulla
3. all'; col (con il)
4. dalla; al
5. sul; dello
6. del; nell'; dell'; coi (con i)
7. I; sono; per; a
8. (none); è; è; in
9. I; sono; al; al
10. Il; il; gli; di

48. 1. del
2. (none)
3. dei
4. del
5. delle
6. (none)
7. di
8. di
9. di
10. dei
11. di
12. (none)
13. le
14. Gli
15. Il

49. 1. Il collega dell'ingegnere è intelligente.
2. L'amica di Gina è giovane.
3. Il motore è rumoroso.
4. A volte il dialogo è molto lungo.
5. Il lavoro dell'astrologo è affascinante.
6. Il catalogo è questo!
7. Il medico di questo paese è vecchio.
8. Il dizionario è grosso.
9. Lo studio del professore è pieno di libri.
10. L'uscio è quasi sempre aperto.
11. Il tempio greco è maestoso.
12. Il signore è in ritardo, la signora no.

50. 1. A: I ginocchi   B: Le ginocchia
2. A: Gli anelli   B: Le anella
3. A: I diti   B: Le dita
4. A: I gesti   B: Le gesta
5. A: I muri   B: Le mura
6. A: I fili   B: Le fila
7. A: I risi   B: Le risa
8. A: I cigli   B: Le ciglia
9. A: I gridi   B: Le grida

10. A: I muri B: Le mura
11. A: I lenzuoli B: Le lenzuola
12. A: Gli orecchi B: Le orecchie

Chapter 3

1. 1. vecchia, nuova
2. mature, acerbe
3. avari, generosi
4. deliziose
5. calda, fredda
6. primo
7. alti, basso
8. cattive, buone
9. domestico, selvatico
10. bianca, gialla
11. vuoto, pieno
12. moderni
13. accesa
14. rotonda, quadrata
15. sbagliata, corretta
16. rossi, gialli
17. ampie, strette
18. ricco, generoso
19. melodiose
20. nera, rossa

2. 1. intelligenti
2. importante
3. salubre
4. tristi
5. nobile
6. interessanti
7. forti, agili
8. inutili
9. grandi
10. umile
11. difficili
12. verdi

3. 1. italiana
2. greci
3. inglese
4. messicani
5. svizzeri
6. svedesi
7. francesi
8. spagnola
9. canadesi
10. scandinavi

4. 1. messicani
2. americane
3. portoghesi
4. giapponesi
5. scozzesi
6. greca
7. spagnoli
8. irlandese
9. italiane
10. canadesi

5. 1. Sí, la ragazza è svedese.
2. Sí, il signore è canadese.
3. Sí, i vini sono francesi.
4. Sí, le signore sono portoghesi.
5. Sí, la cantante è inglese.
6. Sí, il mio amico è messicano.
7. Sí, i turisti sono irlandesi.
8. Sí, le chitarre sono spagnole.
9. Sí, l'automobile è italiana.
10. Sí, gli ospiti sono americani.

6. 1. Le storie sono lunghe.
2. Le bambine sono stanche.
3. Sono delle espressioni poetiche.
4. Le camicie sono sporche.
5. Sono delle usanze antiche.
6. Quei discorsi sono lunghi.
7. Le bombe sono atomiche.
8. Queste sono le tariffe turistiche.
9. Sono delle battute comiche.
10. Le auto sono cariche di giocattoli.

7. 1. stanco
2. stanca
3. stanco
4. stanca
5. stanchi
6. stanchi
7. stanche
8. stanchi
9. stanco
10. stanca

8. 1. simpatica
2. simpatici
3. simpatiche
4. simpatici
5. simpatiche
6. simpatici
7. simpatici
8. simpatico
9. simpatiche
10. simpatici

9. 1. I ragazzi sono simpatici.
2. I vini sono bianchi.
3. Gli autobus sono carichi.
4. I monumenti sono antichi.
5. I vestiti sono sporchi.
6. Le vedute sono magnifiche.
7. I signori sono stanchi.
8. I fiumi sono larghi.
9. Gil uomini sono buoni.
10. Le strade sono larghe.
11. Le storie sono lunghe.
12. I romanzi sono lunghi.

10. 1. I disegni sono rosa.
2. Le porte sono marrone.
3. I vestiti sono blu.
4. I quaderni sono arancione.
5. Le poltrone sono viola.
6. Le pareti sono blu.
7. I cappelli sono marrone.
8. Le cravatte sono rosa.
9. Le maglie sono arancione.
10. I gilè sono viola.

11. 1. bel
2. bella
3. begli
4. bello
5. belle
6. bei
7. bel; bei

12. 1. gran
2. grand'
3. grande
4. grande
5. grande

13. 1. Sant'
2. Santo (San)
3. Santa
4. Santo
5. Sant'
6. San
7. San
8. Santo (San)
9. San
10. Santa
11. Sant'
12. San

14. 1. buon
2. nessun
3. nessuna

4. buon'
5. buoni
6. nessun
7. buono
8. buon
9. buona; (buon')
10. Buon

15. 1. dottor
2. professor
3. professor
4. ingegnere
5. signore
6. ingegner
7. signor
8. Dottore
9. ispettor
10. dottor
11. professor
12. ispettore
13. ingegner
14. signore
15. dottor

16. 1. il ricco
2. le giovani
3. i cattivi
4. le americane
5. il povero
6. l'italiana
7. il minore

17. 1. I nostri
2. La mia
3. I tuoi
4. Le tue
5. I suoi
6. La vostra
7. Le loro
8. Le mie
9. I nostri
10. I suoi
11. il Suo, le Sue
12. la Sua, i Suoi
13. i Loro
14. le Loro
15. la Loro
16. i Suoi
17. il Loro
18. La nostra
19. il tuo
20. La sua

18. 1. Mia
  2. Le nostre
  3. Vostra
  4. I tuoi
  5. Suo
  6. I loro
  7. La loro
  8. Suo
  9. Mia
  10. I nostri

19. 1. la tua
  2. i suoi
  3. Mia
  4. i nostri
  5. I tuoi
  6. il Suo
  7. le loro
  8. le Loro
  9. Nostra
  10. i suoi
  11. Suo
  12. Le nostre
  13. i loro
  14. le loro
  15. il Suo
  16. Mia
  17. le sue

20. 1. I suoi amici telefonano spesso.
  2. La loro sorella studia molto.
  3. Suo zio è molto ricco.
  4. Sua madre è giovane.
  5. Le sue amiche sono greche.

21. 1. Quello studente è studioso.
  2. Questa cravatta è blu.
  3. Quella spiaggia è bellissima.
  4. Quel signore è americano.
  5. Quest'amico è generoso.
  6. Quell'amica è italiana.
  7. Questo zio è vecchio.
  8. Quell'albero è alto.
  9. Questa macchina è veloce.
  10. Quel libro è vecchio.
  11. Questo giornale è interessante.
  12. Quello zaino è pieno.
  13. Quest'estate è meravigliosa.
  14. Quello psicologo è giovane.

22. 1. Questi
  2. Quelle
  3. Quell'
  4. Quest'

  5. Quell'
  6. Queste
  7. Quegli
  8. Questa
  9. Quello
  10. Quella
  11. Quello
  12. Quegli
  13. Questo
  14. Quel
  15. Quella

23. 1. Che partita!
  2. Che bei fiori!
  3. Quanti libri!
  4. Quanta gioia!
  5. Che idea fantastica!
  6. Quanti amici!
  7. Che bella giornata!
  8. Che belle città!

24. 1. difficilmente
  2. graziosamente
  3. fortemente
  4. terribilmente
  5. internamente
  6. mirabilmente
  7. caramente
  8. militarmente
  9. urgentemente
  10. velocemente
  11. lealmente
  12. aristocraticamente
  13. liberalmente
  14. pazientemente
  15. magistralmente
  16. facilmente
  17. raramente
  18. brevemente
  19. parzialmente
  20. lentamente
  21. singolarmente
  22. preliminarmente

25. 1. buona
  2. gran
  3. lunghe
  4. bianche
  5. marrone
  6. bell'
  7. viola
  8. intelligenti
  9. facili

10. generosi
11. domęstici
12. francese
13. vęcchie
14. blu
15. tedeschi
16. greche
17. pochi
18. stanchi
19. utili
20. importante
21. Santo
22. Sant'
23. nessun
24. buọn
25. buọna (buọn')

26. 1. Buongiọrno (Buọn giọrno), ispettor Brunetti!
2. Il professor Rossi ạbita a Roma.
3. Che bella veduta!
4. Quẹgli studenti sono da paẹsi stranięri.
5. Gli amici di Pạolo sono inglesi.
6. Quạnta gente!
7. Quẹlla spiạggia è lunga e larga.
8. Quẹl cavallo è un campiọne.
9. Luịsa, dove sono i tuọi libri?
10. Signor Peruzzi, quạndo compra i Suọi vestiti nuọvi?

27. 1. facilmente
2. ferocemente
3. coraggiosamente
4. raramente
5. slealmente
6. tristemente
7. irregolarmente
8. brevemente
9. esternamente
10. flebilmente

28. 1. I corridọi sono lunghi e larghi.
2. Le case sono biạnche e magnịfiche.
3. I miẹi zịi sono simpạtici.
4. I lavoratori sono stanchi.
5. Compro dụe (delle) giạcche blu e dụe (delle) camịcie grige.
6. Quẹgli uọmini sono dei grandi calciatori.
7. I grandi artisti sono sempre originali.
8. I professori italiạni vịsitano l'Itạlia.
9. Gli amici di Mạrio sono islandesi.
10. Le nostre amiche sono simpạtiche e intelligenti.

29. 1. Santo
2. buọni
3. Quẹgli
4. gran
5. Sant'
6. buọn'
7. grande
8. Quẹi
9. santi
10. buọn

Chapter 4

1. 1. come
2. quạnto
3. come
4. come
5. quạnto

2. 1. cosí
2. tanto
3. cosí
4. tanto
5. tanto

3. 1. quạnto
2. come
3. quạnto
4. come
5. quạnto

4. 1. tante ... quạnto
2. tanti ... quạnto
3. tante ... quạnto
4. tanti ... quạnto
5. tante ... quạnti
6. tanti ... quạnto
7. quạnti

5. 1. tanto
2. cosí
3. come (quạnto)
4. quạnto (come)

6. 1. piú ... dei
2. meno di
3. piú di
4. meno ... della
5. piú ... di
6. piú ... che
7. meno ... che
8. piú ... che
9. meno ... di
10. piú ... di

11. piú di
12. meno di
13. piú ... che
14. meno ... che
15. piú di

7.
1. Il mio gattino è piú simpatico del tuo.
2. La sua auto è piú veloce della nostra.
3. Quegli elettrodomestici sono meno moderni di questi.
4. Oggi i bambini si sono sentiti bene e hanno mangiato di piú,
5. Con quel mal di testa, ho dormito di meno.
6. La sorella di Gino è piú atletica di tutti noi.
7. Sono sempre stanco; gioco meno di voi.
8. A Roma ci sono piú automobili (macchine; auto) che autobus.
9. Il professore ha piú libri di noi.
10. A Venezia ci sono piú ponti che canali.
11. Maria è ricca! Ha piú di cento euro!
12. Sono molto povero! Ho meno di dieci euro!

8.
1. Loro sono le studentesse piú brave della classe.
2. Carlo e Pietro sono i ragazzi piú bassi del gruppo.
3. Questa scuola è la piú moderna della città.
4. Il padre di Olga è il dottore piú famoso di Roma.
5. La Sicilia è la piú grande isola del Mediterraneo.
6. Pelé è il calciatore piú famoso del mondo.
7. Questi ragazzi sono i piú atletici della scuola.
8. Maria è la piú atletica di tutte.
9. Quelle studentesse sono le piú intelligenti.
10. Il signor Martini è l'ingegnere piú abile della fabbrica.

9.
1. Il signor Rossi è sensibilissimo.
2. Teresa sta benissimo.
3. La stanza è grandissima.
4. La rivista è utilissima.
5. Gli stadi sono grandissimi.
6. È un lavoro difficilissimo.

10.
1. Il teatro è molto affollato.
2. L'esame è molto facile.
3. Roberto sta molto male.
4. L'appartamento è molto moderno.

11.
1. Maria è maggiore di sua sorella.
2. Questo museo è il maggiore della città.
3. Roberto è piú grande del suo amico.
4. Carlo è piccolissimo.
5. Mio nonno è maggiore di mia nonna.

6. Luisa è minore di sua cugina.
7. Olga è la migliore della classe.
8. Stefano è piú piccolo di suo fratello.

12.
1. Chi è la ragazza minore qui?
2. Io sono maggiore di te, ma Antonio è il maggiore.
3. Loro sono buoni ma noi siamo migliori.
4. Giorgio e Gabriele sono i migliori.
5. Questo libro è migliore di quello.
6. Teresa è la mia sorella minore.
7. Stefano è il nostro cugino migliore.
8. Giuseppe è il suo fratello maggiore.

13.
1. peggio
2. il piú
3. meglio
4. meglio
5. meno
6. malissimo
7. benissimo

14.
1. Siamo (tanto) alte quanto loro. (*Also:* [cosí] alte come loro.)
2. Paolo è (cosí) studioso come Maria. (*Also:* [tanto] studioso quanto.)
3. In questa classe ci sono piú ragazzi che ragazze.
4. Hanno tanti amici quanto noi.
5. Lui ha piú di quarant'anni.
6. Teresa studia (tanto) quanto Mario.
7. Olga e Teresa sono le piú intelligenti della classe.
8. Roberto è il meno studioso della classe.
9. Ho meno amici di te.
10. Corrono piú di noi.
11. Cantiamo (cosí) come lei.
12. Carlo è (tanto) basso come suo cugino.
13. Questo pane è migliore dell'altro.
14. Quelle scarpe sono peggiori di queste.
15. Carmelina è la sorella minore.
16. Pietro è il piú piccolo della classe.
17. Questo formaggio è cattivissimo (molto cattivo).
18. Chi è il ragazzo maggiore?
19. Il suo cappotto è pesantissimo (molto pesante).
20. A Venezia ci sono piú chiese che stadi.

15.
1. Paolo ha piú scarpe che cravatte.
2. Luisa manda piú e-mail di me.
3. Voi scrivete meglio di loro.
4. Ezio è meno alto di te.
5. Questi cani abbaiano (tanto) quanto quelli.

6. Marisa Parla spagnolo (cosí) bene come lui, (also: [tanto] bene quanto lui).
7. Lui ha piú euro di noi.
8. Questi bambini hanno tanti giocattoli quanto quelli.
9. Quelle bambine hanno tanti giocattoli quante scarpe.
10. Noi abbiamo piú euro che dollari.
11. Lei (she) non ha fame; (lei) mangia di meno.
12. Loro non sono stanche; (loro) giocano di piú.
13. Questo gatto è piú grande del suo.
14. Le sue sorelle sono maggiori delle mie.
15. Mario è il (ragazzo) piú bravo della classe.
16. Olga e Maria sono le piú atletiche del gruppo.
17. Quelle signore sono ricchissime; infatti, sono le piú ricche.
18. Mi sento malissimo!
19. Quella statua è bellissima; è la piú bella del museo.
20. È stata una lezione lunghissima (molto lunga).

16.
1. A: il piú bello   B: bellissimo
2. A: la piú intelligente B: intelligentissima
3. A: i piú ricchi   B: ricchissimi
4. A: la piú larga   B: larghissima
5. A: le piú utili   B: utilissime
6. A: le piú stanche   B: stanchissime

Chapter 5

1.
1. cinque
2. tredici
3. diciassette
4. ventuno
5. ventotto
6. trentatré
7. quaranta
8. quarantotto
9. cinquantuno
10. cinquantatré
11. sessantasette
12. settantotto
13. settantanove
14. ottantadue
15. ottantotto
16. novanta
17. novantuno
18. cento
19. trecento
20. mille
21. ottomilacinquecentotrentatré
22. tre milioni

2.
1. cento uomini
2. quattromila libri
3. un milione di persone
4. sei miliardi di dollari
5. novecento euro
6. mille euro
7. duemila euro
8. un milione di euro
9. trecentomila euro
10. milletrecentoquarantacinque euro

3.
1. il Novecento
2. il Duecento
3. il Cinquecento
4. l'Ottocento
5. il Quattrocento

4.
1. terzo
2. sesto
3. Decimo
4. Dodicesimo
5. secondo
6. centesima
7. venticinquesimo
8. Primo
9. Seconda
10. Sedicesimo

5.
1. un ottavo
2. due decimi
3. cinque centesimi
4. tre millesimi
5. nove e mezzo
6. dieci e tre quarti
7. un terzo
8. due quinti
9. un decimo
10. due sesti
11. quattro e un quarto

6.
1. duemila
2. decima
3. ventitré
4. due terzi
5. sedicesimo, Cinquecento
6. Quattordicesimo (XIV)
7. primo
8. due milioni
9. millenovecentosettantotto
10. primi due
11. quarantamila euro
12. primo
13. quindici
14. venticinque

15. sei
16. trecentocinquanta euro
17. due, millenovecentoquarantasei
18. trentatreesimo
19. terzo
20. primi

7.
1. moderni; grandi
2. piccola; veloce
3. caldo; delizioso
4. ricchi; generosi
5. blu
6. timida
7. gran
8. intelligenti; studiosi
9. Quelle; svedesi
10. miei; accesa
11. Mia; italiana
12. Quei; bianchi; dolci
13. Questa; bella; matura; acerba
14. Quegli; migliori
15. minori; simpatiche
16. tuoi; sporchi; puliti
17. San, importante
18. Quel; nessun
19. intelligente; studiosa
20. difficili; facili

8.
1. Il Po è il fiume piú lungo d'Italia.
2. La Sicilia è l'isola piú grande del Mediterraneo.
3. Olga è piú brava di Luisa.
4. Quelli sono i piú alti.
5. I cugini di Mario sono in Italia.
6. Antonio è (cosí) intelligente come Stefano.
7. Roma è la capitale d'Italia.
8. Pelé è il calciatore piú famoso del mondo.
9. Maria è (tanto) brava quanto Silvia.
10. I giocatori sono nello stadio.

9.
1. Oggi è lunedí.
2. Mercoledí è il terzo giorno della settimana.
3. In inverno fa freddo.
4. Questo è il duemilasei.
5. Un anno ha dodici mesi.
6. Dante nacque nel milleduecentosessantacinque
7. Oggi ne abbiamo quindici.
8. Nevica in inverno.
9. Sí, la domenica vado al cinema.
10. Oggi è il primo ottobre, duemilasei.
11. I primi tre giorni della settimana sono lunedí, martedí, e mercoledí.
12. I mesi dell'estate sono giugno, luglio, e agosto.
13. Sí, fa caldo in estate.

14. Piove in autunno.
15. Il sabato studio.
16. Dicembre è l'ultimo mese dell'anno.
17. Luglio viene dopo giugno.
18. Fra gli antichi romani, venerdí era dedicato a Venere.
19. Mercoledí era dedicato a Mercurio.
20. Domenica deriva dalla parola latina *dominus*.

10.
1. Domani è domenica, il diciannove dicembre del duemilasei.
2. Viaggeremo in estate.
3. Marzo è pazzo.
4. Mercoledí mangiamo (la) pizza.
5. Oggi è martedí.
6. Domani ne abbiamo otto, (è l'otto).
7. Ci sono sette giorni in una settimana.
8. Ieri era il primo ottobre.
9. Sono nato (-a) nel millenovecentonovantuno.
10. Lunedí è il primo giorno della settimana.

11.
1. Giugno, anno
2. ne, tre
3. primavera, estate, autunno, inverno
4. dodici
5. inverno
6. Venerdí, giorno
7. il diciassette
8. il duemilasei
9. La
10. stagione

12.
1. Sono le undici in punto di mattina.
2. Sono le tredici.
3. Mi alzo alle sei e un quarto di mattina.
4. Il treno parte alle ventidue meno dieci.
5. Luisa arriva alle undici meno dieci di mattina.
6. Mancano venti minuti alle dieci.
7. Manca un quarto all'una.
8. C'incontriamo a mezzogiorno.
9. Sono le tre del pomeriggio.
10. Sí, sono le ventiquattro.

13.
1. alle otto e un quarto in punto di mattina
2. mezzogiorno; l'una e un quarto del pomeriggio
3. a mezzanotte
4. alle cinque di mattina
5. alle due e mezza (mezzo, trenta) del pomeriggio
6. alle otto meno dieci di mattina
7. alle undici meno un quarto di sera
8. alle sette meno venti di sera
9. le undici e dieci di sera
10. le cinque di sera

14. 1. Antonio arriva alle otto e un quarto in punto.
2. No, non sono le dodici, sono le tredici e un quarto.
3. Partiamo alle ventiquattro.
4. Nessuno si alza alle cinque.
5. Dobbiamo essere all'aeroporto alle quattordici e mezza (mezzo, trenta).
6. Fanno la prima colazione alle otto meno dieci.
7. Sí, Giorgio e Piero ci telefoneranno alle ventitré meno un quarto (ventidue e quarantacinque).
8. La festa comincia alle diciotto e quaranta (diciannove meno venti).
9. Sono le ventitré e dieci.
10. Non so, saranno le diciassette.

15. 1. mille
2. sessantatré
3. due milioni
4. millenovecentonovantaquattro
5. centosette
6. cinquantotto
7. novantuno
8. diciassette
9. undici
10. cento

16. 1. il Novecento
2. il Seicento
3. il secolo diciannovesimo
4. il secolo quattordicesimo
5. il Duecento

17. 1. terzo
2. centesimo
3. millesimo
4. nono
5. ventunesimo
6. quarantatreesimo
7. sedicesimo
8. ottavo

18. 1. due ottavi
2. un decimo
3. otto e mezzo
4. cinque centesimi
5. quattro millesimi
6. un terzo
7. nove e tre quarti
8. cinque e due terzi

19. 1. Marzo è il terzo mese dell'anno.
2. Dopo lunedí viene martedí.
3. Domenica è il settimo giorno della settimana.

4. C'è la neve in inverno.
5. Le quattro stagioni sono la primavera, l'estate, l'autunno, e l'inverno.
6. Dopo giugno viene luglio.
7. La mattina mi alzo alle sette.
8. Il treno parte alle quattordici.

20. 1. le due del pomeriggio.
2. a mezzanotte.
3. le otto e mezza (mezzo; trenta) di sera.
4. alle dieci meno un quarto di mattina.
5. alle sette e dieci di mattina.
6. È l'una in punto.

21. 1. Sono le quindici.
2. Sono le ventiquattro.
3. Sono le undici.
4. Sono le ventuno.
5. Sono le sei.
6. Sono le quindici e un quarto.
7. Sono le tredici e trenta.
8. Sono le ventidue meno cinque.

22. 1 venticinque euro
2. duemila euro
3. un milione di euro
4. due miliardi di euro
5. cinquantatré euro

Chapter 6

1. 1. -a
2. -a
3. -ano
4. -ano
5. -ano
6. -iamo
7. -i
8. -a
9. -ate
10. -a

2. 1. pranziamo
2. porta
3. lavi
4. arrivano
5. invitate
6. lavora
7. telefonano
8. canta
9. nuoto
10. guadagna

3. 1. Il ragazzo guarda la partita.
2. Tu impari la lezione.
3. Lui arriva presto.
4. Io ceno tardi.
5. La studentessa torna a casa.

4. 1. Noi chiamiamo i nostri amici.
2. Loro comprano i biglietti.
3. Voi nuotate molto bene.
4. I camerieri portano le bevande.
5. Le signore comprano i giornali.

5. 1. noleggi
2. racconciamo
3. avvinghiate
4. arrischio
5. parcheggia
6. marciano
7. invecchi
8. assaggiamo

6. 1. indaghi
2. divaghiamo
3. attacchi
4. impacchiamo
5. allarghi

7. 1. allargano
2. indago
3. impacca
4. sbarcano

8. 1. Lei
2. tu
3. voi
4. Loro
5. lui

9. 1. -e
2. -i
3. -e
4. -ono
5. -ete
6. -ono
7. -iamo
8. -e
9. -e
10. -ono

10. 1. vendono
2. piangono
3. promette
4. corrono
5. riceviamo
6. perdi
7. apprendono

8. descrivo
9. leggete
10. cadono

11. 1. piace
2. giace
3. tacciono
4. taci
5. giacete
6. taccio

12. 1. Il ragazzo piace alle ragazze.
2. Giaci sul sofà.
3. Io taccio quasi sempre.
4. Tu piaci a me.

13. 1. -ono
2. -e
3. -iamo
4. -ono
5. -e
6. -ono
7. -ite
8. -iamo
9. -ono
10. -e

14. 1. Sí, io apro la finestra.
2. Sí, voi sfuggite il pericolo.
3. Sí, loro scoprono la verità.
4. Sí, Mario veste bene.
5. Sí, il cuoco bolle le verdure.
6. Sí, i malati soffrono molto.
7. Sí, noi riapriamo il negozio.
8. Sí, io servo le bevande.
9. Sí, lei copre la pentola.
10. Sí, Teresa apre la porta.

15. 1. capiscono
2. costruisce
3. finiamo
4. dimagrisci
5. preferisco
6. capisce
7. ubbidite
8. ingrandisce
9. pulisco
10. preferiscono

16. 1. Voi preferite questo disco.
2. Noi riferiamo il suo messaggio.
3. Gli studenti capiscono la lezione.
4. Voi capite tutto.
5. Noi costruiamo una scatola di legno.
6. I bambini ubbidiscono sempre.

17.
1. Sto bene.
2. Sto qui.
3. Do gli esami.
4. Vado al cinema.
5. Sto per partire.
6. Do i regali.
7. Do il benvenuto.
8. Vado in salotto.

18.
1. va
2. sto
3. stanno
4. dà
5. diamo
6. vado
7. andiamo
8. stanno

19.
1. bevo
2. bevono
3. beve
4. beviamo
5. bevono
6. bevete
7. bevi
8. beve

20.
1. Introduci l'amico.
2. Produce molto.
3. Traduco in inglese.
4. Conduci il treno.
5. Riduce la frase.
6. Produco poco.

21.
1. producono
2. traduce
3. conduce
4. introduco
5. riduciamo
6. traduci

22.
1. Lei, traduce
2. voi, riducete
3. producono
4. tu, disdici
5. Loro, contraddicono

23.
1. Disdicono le promesse.
2. Voi contraddite i vostri amici.
3. Le organizzazioni indicono i concorsi.
4. Non malediciamo nessuno.
5. Dite tutto.
6. Che dite?

24.
1. interdicono
2. contraddici
3. dice
4. maledicono
5. disdite
6. indice
7. diciamo
8. contraddicono

25.
1. No, tu non dici mai la verità.
2. Sí, quest'anno quelle città indicono un nuovo concorso di poesia.
3. Sí, a volte noi contraddiciamo le vostre proposte.
4. No, non contraddico sempre i miei soci.
5. No, noi non malediciamo i nostri nemici.
6. Quando non abbiamo niente da dire, (noi) non diciamo niente.

26.
1. pospongono
2. ponete
3. espone
4. supponiamo
5. componi

27.
1. Loro propongono l'appuntamento.
2. Voi imponete queste regole.
3. Noi proponiamo una soluzione.
4. Voi componete il tema.

28.
1. vale
2. rimango
3. rimani
4. salgo
5. salite

29.
1. No, rimaniamo qui pochi giorni.
2. Noi saliamo le scale in fretta.
3. Sí, valgo molto alla mia famiglia.
4. No, non è vero che pospongo le mie vacanze.
5. No, (io) non impongo molte regole in classe.
6. Sí, (noi) valiamo molto alla nostra squadra di calcio.

30.
1. attrae
2. distraggono
3. attrai
4. traiamo
5. contraggono
6. traggo

31.
1. I giochi distraggono i ragazzi.
2. Gli studenti traggono le conclusioni.
3. Noi contraiamo la febbre.
4. Voi attraete la nostra simpatia.

32. 1. Sí, (io) attraggo molti amici.
2. Sí, quasi sempre (noi) traiamo molte lezioni dalle nostre esperienze.
3. Distraiamo i bambini con i giocattoli.
4. No, non sempre estraggo i denti con facilità.
5. Sí, (io) contraggo molti raffreddori d'inverno. -Anche noi contraiamo molti raffreddori d'inverno.
6. No, noi non saliamo le scale in fretta.

33. 1. accoglie
2. raccolgono
3. cogliamo
4. raccolgo
5. togliete
6. accogli
7. raccoglie

34. 1. Sí, io accolgo bene i miei amici.
2. Io raccolgo un mazzo di fiori dal mio giardino.
3. Sí, (noi) cogliamo la frutta dagli alberi.
4. Loro tolgono la spazzatura ogni settimana.
5. Io accolgo le mie amiche nel salotto.
6. No, (noi) non togliamo la polvere ogni giorno.

35. 1. contengono
2. vengono
3. ottiene
4. sostenete
5. riconveniamo

36. 1. Sí, oggi vengo a scuola.
2. Sí, mia figlia viene domani.
3. Sí, proveniamo da Nuova York.
4. Sí, le mie amiche vengono con noi (voi).
5. Sí, appartengo al Club italiano.
6. Voi intrattenete gli ospiti.

37. 1. Mantieni bene i giardini?
2. Questa rivista contiene poco.
3. Ottiene i biglietti Lei?
4. Intrattengo gli amici.
5. La studentessa appartiene a quella classe.

38. 1. Sí, (noi) apparteniamo a un club sportivo.
2. (Noi) pariamo un po'confusi perché siamo confusi.
3. Il giardiniere mantiene i giardini della città.
4. Io ottengo buoni risultati a scuola studiando.
5. No, oggi vengo al ristorante con un'amica.
6. Sí, noi apparteniamo al (vostro) Loro gruppo.

39. 1. paio
2. pare
3. paiono

4. paiamo
5. pari
6. parete
7. Pare
8. Paiono

40. 1. muoiono
2. muoio
3. morite
4. muori
5. moriamo
6. muore

41. 1. Lei muore
2. voi morite
3. lei pare
4. noi pariamo
5. Loro, muoiono

42. 1. siedo; siedi
2. siedono
3. sedete
4. siede
5. sediamo
6. siedi

43. 1. odono
2. odo
3. udite
4. ode
5. udiamo
6. odi

44. 1. escono
2. riesce
3. escono
4. uscite
5. riescono
6. esci
7. riesco

45. 1. fa
2. facciamo
3. fai
4. fa
5. fate
6. fanno
7. faccio
8. fa

46. 1. sanno
2. sa
3. sappiamo
4. so
5. sa

6. sai
7. Sanno
8. sapete

47. 1. dobbiamo
2. devo
3. devono
4. devi
5. dovete
6. deve
7. devo
8. dobbiamo

48. 1. può
2. possiamo
3. possono
4. può
5. potete
6. posso
7. puoi
8. può

49. 1. voglio
2. vogliono
3. Vuoi
4. vuole
5. vogliamo
6. volete
7. vogliono
8. voglio

50. 1. ha
2. ho
3. hanno
4. hai
5. avete
6. ha
7. abbiamo
8. ha

51. 1. sono
2. è
3. sono
4. siamo
5. siete
6. sono
7. Sono
8. è; è

52. 1. Sí, sono italiano.
2. Sí, mia figlia è a casa.
3. Sí, siamo pronti adesso.
4. Sí, i giocatori sono nello stadio.
5. Sí, sono l'amica di Giovanni.

6. Siamo (Siete) bravi (cattivi).
7. I miei genitori sono al cinema.
8. Sí, tu sei il mio compagno di scuola.

53. 1. viviamo
2. lavora
3. conosci
4. fa
5. studiate

54. 1. Frequento questa scuola da due anni.
2. Studio l'italiano da un anno.
3. Vivo in questa città da cinque anni.
4. Conosco il mio migliore amico da molti anni.
5. Non vedo i miei nonni da tre mesi.
6. Non vado a teatro da sei mesi.

55. 1. balliamo
2. lavora
3. preferiscono
4. giochi
5. invecchiano
6. offrite
7. legge
8. vai
9. sono
10. dà
11. producono
12. pongo
13. appartengono
14. dite; contraddico
15. piacciono

56. 1. andavamo
2. viaggiavo
3. cantava
4. sciavano
5. vedevate
6. giocavi
7. saltavo; camminavo
8. portava

57. 1. Antonio parlava molto.
2. Voi camminavate per le strade.
3. Mia madre comprava molte cose.
4. Noi giocavamo nel parco.
5. Le ragazze cantavano ad alta voce.
6. Io ascoltavo i miei maestri con attenzione.
7. Tu guardavi la televisione tutte le sere.
8. Vedeva Lei i Suoi cugini?
9. Viaggiavate molto?
10. Studiavano con diligenza gli studenti?

58. 1. leggeva
2. piangevano

3. correvamo
4. vendevano
5. ripetevano
6. sapevano
7. perdevi
8. avevano

59. 1. Eleggevamo un nuovo presidente.
2. Descrivevate quel paesaggio.
3. Friggevo le uova.
4. Offendevi molte persone.
5. Promettevate troppe cose.
6. I bambini cadevano spesso.
7. Angelo vendeva biciclette.

60. 1. capivano
2. finivo
3. seguivate
4. sentivamo
5. preferivano
6. costruivate
7. apparivi
8. ubbidivano

61. 1. Sentivi il campanello?
2. Vestivate i bambini?
3. Preferivamo un gelato.
4. Capivano bene.
5. Olga soffriva molto.
6. Io seguivo i tuoi consigli.
7. Offrivi sempre il tuo aiuto.
8. Aprivamo le finestre.
9. Paolo riapriva la porta.
10. Ubbidivano alla madre.

62. 1. Sí, aprivo le porte.
2. Sí, servivamo il caffè.
3. Sí, vestivamo (vestivate) elegantemente.
4. Sí, capivo bene.
5. Sí, reagivo cautamente.
6. Sí, noi finivamo presto.
7. Sí, soffrivamo molto in ospedale.
8. Sí, Luigi seguiva molti corsi.
9. Sí, vestivamo (vestivate) i bambini.
10. Sí, gli alunni scandivano le parole.

63. 1. Stefano diceva la verità.
2. Queste fabbriche producevano pantaloni.
3. Il signor Martini faceva il dottore.
4. Io non dicevo niente.
5. Dove facevate le vacanze?
6. Questo terreno produceva molti legumi.
7. Tu non dicevi la verità.

64. 1. dicevano
2. faceva
3. produceva
4. dicevo
5. contraddicevi
6. facevano
7. conduceva

65. 1. bevevamo
2. beveva
3. bevevate
4. bevevi
5. bevevo
6. Bevevano
7. beveva
8. bevevano

66. 1. esponeva
2. ponevo
3. proponevi
4. componevano
5. posponevamo
6. ponevate
7. Supponeva
8. imponeva

67. 1. attraeva
2. traeva
3. distraevi
4. ritraevate
5. traevo
6. sottraevamo

68. 1. era
2. eravamo
3. erano
4. eri
5. era
6. eravate
7. erano
8. era

69. 1. Ero studente (-essa).
2. Maria e Carlo erano al teatro Verdi.
3. Sí, quello studente era pronto.
4. Quel signore era mio zio.
5. Sí, eravamo (eravate) bravi.
6. Sí, ero a casa spesso.
7. Sí, eravamo malati.
8. Mio padre era in Italia.

70. 1. Mio fratello arrivava sempre in ritardo.
2. Tu parlavi ininterrottamente.
3. Le studentesse andavano spesso in biblioteca.
4. Di solito Olga cenava presto.

5. La domenica andavamo al parco.
6. Di quando in quando vedevo un bel film.
7. Le mie sorelle venivano a casa tutti i giorni.
8. A volte nevicava senza sosta.
9. I bambini piangevano frequentemente.
10. Mio cugino scriveva ogni mese.

71. 1. suonava, cantavi
2. lavavamo, lavavate
3. lavoravo, giocavano
4. dormiva, studiavamo
5. telefonavi, guardava
6. scrivevamo, parlavate
7. leggevo, scrivevi
8. diceva, mentivate
9. gridava, piangeva
10. viaggiavano, stavamo

72. 1. preferiva
2. capivi
3. temevano
4. credevo
5. rifletteva
6. volevate
7. potevo, desideravo
8. odiavi
9. intuiva
10. credevamo

73. 1. La casa era grande.
2. Gli edifici erano rossi.
3. Olga era brava.
4. Gli studenti erano intelligenti.
5. La copertina del libro era verde.
6. I genitori erano pazienti.
7. Noi eravamo alti.
8. Voi eravate cattivi.
9. Le camicie erano bianche.
10. Tu eri basso.

74. 1. Che tempo faceva?
2. Quanti anni avevi?
3. Che ora era?
4. Nevicava?
5. Erano le quattro e un quarto.
6. Avevamo sedici anni.
7. Tirava vento.
8. Pietro aveva diciannove anni.
9. Era mezzanotte.
10. Pioveva.

75. 1. eravate
2. visitavamo
3. Nevicava

4. giocava
5. fumavano
6. lavoravi
7. erano
8. sapevo

76. 1. giocavano
2. andavamo
3. ascoltava
4. correvate
5. ero
6. erano
7. era; aveva
8. producevano

77. 1. Sí, dormivo sempre fino a tardi.
2. Sí, la domenica andavamo in chiesa.
3. Sí, uscivo frequentemente.
4. Sí, pioveva spesso.
5. Sí, andavamo alla spiaggia tutti i giorni.
6. Sí, Luigi arrivava sempre tardi.
7. Sí, i bambini piangevano spesso.
8. Sí, viaggiavo ogni estate.
9. Preferivamo il mare (la montagna).
10. Sí, la casa di Maria era verde.

78. 1. -arono
2. -ai
3. -ò
4. -aste
5. -asti
6. -arono
7. -ammo
8. -ò
9. -arono
10. -ai

79. 1. ascoltarono
2. invitò
3. camminammo
4. comprasti
5. pranzaste

80. 1. Noi salutammo i nonni.
2. Aspettai mio cugino.
3. Loro comprarono alcuni libri.
4. Angelo lavò l'automobile.
5. Tu portasti i regali.
6. Voi mangiaste da Carlo.
7. Gli studenti passarono gli esami.
8. Tu viaggiasti solo.
9. Io pagai il biglietto.
10. Andammo a teatro a piedi.

81.
1. gemé (gemette)
2. ripeterono
3. credemmo
4. sedeste
5. ricevesti
6. vendei

82.
1. Tu ricevesti una bella notizia.
2. Mario ripeté il corso di geografia.
3. Loro venderono (vendettero) molte cose.
4. Noi sedemmo soli.
5. Io credei a tutto.
6. Voi poteste venire presto.
7. Tu abbattesti la parete.
8. Luisa batté sul banco.

83.
1. -ii
2. -iste
3. -isti
4. -í
5. -irono
6. -immo
7. -í
8. -irono
9. -ii
10. -iste

84.
1. ubbidirono
2. capiste
3. preferii
4. dimagrí
5. finisti
6. costruimmo
7. ingrandirono
8. capii

85.
1. Gl'impiegati seguirono le istruzioni.
2. Il cuoco bollí la carne.
3. Loro sentirono il campanello.
4. Il cameriere serví le bevande.
5. Io aprii tutte le finestre.
6. Voi offriste un caffè agli amici.
7. I malati soffrirono molto.

86.
1. chiedesti
2. chiudemmo
3. rimanemmo
4. rideste
5. rispondeste
6. ponesti
7. ponemmo
8. concludeste
9. corresti
10. Scegliste

87.
1. chiusi
2. decisi
3. promisi
4. pose
5. mise
6. spese
7. composero
8. scelsero
9. risposero
10. piansero

88.
1. Sí, chiesi molte informazioni.
2. Sí, chiusi la porta.
3. Sí, decisi di rimanere qui.
4. Sí, risposi alle sue domande.
5. Sí, presi il denaro.
6. Sí, misi il libro sul tavolo.
7. Sí, volsi le spalle.
8. Sí, scelsi un vestito.

89.
1. Sí, dividemmo il premio in due.
2. Sí, rispondemmo.
3. Sí, decidemmo immediatamente.
4. Sí, chiudemmo le finestre.
5. Sí, prendemmo i passaporti.
6. Sí, mettemmo i fiori nel vaso.
7. Sí, scegliemmo dei bei regali.
8. Sí, corremmo.

90.
1. chiese
2. chiedemmo
3. conclusero
4. chiuse
5. richiusi
6. includeste
7. chiesero
8. escludesti
9. coincisero
10. rise
11. decideste
12. sorridemmo
13. divise
14. ridemmo
15. decise

91.
1. corse
2. trascorremmo
3. accogliemmo
4. scelsero
5. scelsi
6. raccolse
7. scegliemmo
8. volse

92.
1. lesse
2. eleggemmo
3. rilessi
4. correggesti
5. lessero
6. scrisse
7. descrivesti
8. iscrissi

93.
1. produsse
2. introducesti
3. tradussi
4. inducemmo
5. disse
6. maledicemmo

94.
1. trassero
2. attrasse
3. attraeste
4. traemmo
5. sottrassi
6. contraesti

95.
1. caddero
2. decadde
3. ricaddi
4. cademmo
5. tenne
6. appartennero
7. mantenesti
8. sosteneste

96.
1. bevemmo
2. bevve
3. bevvero
4. bevvi
5. beveste

97.
1. venne
2. intervenimmo
3. svenne
4. rivenisti
5. convennero
6. sovvenimmo
7. divenne

98.
1. conobbi
2. riconoscesti
3. conoscemmo
4. riconobbero
5. ruppi
6. ruppero
7. interrompeste

99.
1. nacque
2. piacemmo
3. nacqui
4. nasceste
5. dispiacque
6. piacesti
7. nacque
8. nacquero

100.
1. videro
2. rivedeste
3. previde
4. provvidero
5. intravidi
6. vedemmo
7. rivide
8. previdero

101.
1. fece
2. facemmo
3. soddisfecero
4. disfaceste
5. sopraffeci
6. rifecero
7. disfacesti
8. faceste

102.
1. ebbe
2. ebbi
3. ebbero
4. avemmo
5. avesti
6. Aveste

103.
1. fu
2. furono
3. fosti
4. fummo
5. fui
6. foste
7. furono
8. fu

104.
1. Loro stettero al bar fino a tardi.
2. Io diedi un regalo a Luigi.
3. Voi steste qui per poche ore.
4. Mario diede il biglietto a Luisa.
5. Noi stemmo a casa con i bambini.
6. Voi deste i libri alle studentesse.
7. Io stetti con mio zio.
8. Tu desti l'indirizzo al cliente.
9. Olga stette con sua cugina.
10. Tu stesti in ufficio.
11. Gli studenti diedero gli esami.

105.
1. camminarono
2. comprò
3. portaste
4. ricevesti
5. sedé
6. vendemmo
7. preferirono
8. capisti
9. finí
10. steste
11. diedi (detti)
12. fummo
13. ebbero
14. bevesti
15. bevvero

106.
1. Tu rispondesti alle domande di Mario.
2. Loro risposero bene agli esami.
3. Noi rompemmo un piatto e due bicchieri.
4. Gli studenti seppero la lezione.
5. Io scelsi un paio di pantaloni marrone.
6. Voi accoglieste gli ospiti stranieri.
7. Teresa scrisse a tutti i parenti.
8. Loro sostennero un'opinione ottimista.
9. Il circo attrasse una grande folla.
10. Io rividi i miei vecchi amici.

107.
1. arrivarono
2. morí
3. andarono
4. lessi
5. fu
6. decisero
7. passasti
8. finimmo
9. ebbi
10. veniste
11. rifiutò
12. restituiste

108.
1. Non vollero partecipare.
2. Non potemmo trovare l'indirizzo.
3. Potei partire presto.
4. Conobbe mio fratello l'estate scorsa.
5. Lo seppero poco fa.

109.
1. Lui veniva qui spesso.
2. Io lo vedevo spesso.
3. Carlo me lo ripeteva spesso.
4. Ricevevamo una lettera da lui spesso.
5. Lui mi chiamava spesso.

110.
1. Lui ci visitò due giorni fa.
2. Lei mi aiutò due giorni fa.
3. Io andai lí due giorni fa.
4. Loro me lo dissero due giorni fa.
5. Tu mangiasti in quel ristorante due giorni fa.

111.
1. Andavo a Chicago ogni mese.
2. Anche due mesi fa Maria partí per Brooklyn.
3. Mia zia fu malata per due anni.
4. Visitavo i miei cugini frequentemente.
5. Ogni tanto incontravamo dei vecchi amici.
6. Viaggiavate in Francia spesso spesso.

112.
1. Sí, lui visitò l'Europa l'estate scorsa.
2. Sí, lui andava al cinema ogni domenica.
3. Sí, lui scalò un monte nel 1965.
4. Sí, lui vedeva i nonni tutti i giorni.
5. Sí, lui faceva i bagni sempre.
6. Sí, lui ricevé (ricevette) la patente di guida ieri.
7. Sí, lui viaggiava con gli amici frequentemente.
8. Sí, lui fu malato per poco tempo.

113.
1. giocavano, studiavamo
2. suonava, entrarono
3. discutevamo, bussò
4. preparava, arrivarono
5. cominciai, cominciò
6. era, cadde
7. ascoltavano, studiavo
8. arrivammo, faceva
9. ballavano, cantavano
10. guardavate, interruppe

114.
1. giocarono, applaudirono
2. guidò, guardai
3. comprò, aspettammo
4. studiò, lesse
5. chiusi, spolverò

115.
1. giocavano, applaudivano
2. guidava, guardavo
3. comprava, aspettavamo
4. studiava, leggeva
5. chiudevo, spolverava

116.
1. porteranno
2. frequenteremo
3. arriveranno
4. canterà
5. parteciperò
6. parlerete
7. impareranno

117.
1. partiremo
2. leggeranno

3. ripeterẹte
4. venderà
5. capirẹmo
6. correrạnno
7. sentirà

118. 1. mangeremo
2. comincerạnno
3. parcheggerò
4. marcerạnno
5. noleggerại
6. viaggerẹte

119. 1. cercherẹmo
2. pagherạnno
3. sbarcherà
4. attaccherạnno
5. mancherò
6. allargherẹte
7. impaccherà
8. divagherẹmo

120. 1. darò
2. faremo
3. starà
4. darà
5. darai
6. farà
7. starạnno
8. darete
9. farạnno
10. staremo

121. 1. sarai
2. saremo
3. sarà
4. sarete
5. sarò
6. sarai
7. saremo
8. sarạnno

122. 1. andremo
2. avrete
3. potrò
4. saprà
5. andrạnno
6. avrai
7. dovremo
8. cadrà

123. 1. berrạnno
2. varrà
3. vorrạnno
4. terrà

5. vorrò
6. berremo
7. parrạnno
8. morrà (morirà)

124. 1. Saranno a casa.
2. Avrà sẹdici anni.
3. Saranno le diẹci e mezza di mattina.
4. No, non costerà molto.
5. Arriveranno alle sette di mattina.
6. Sarà a scuọla.
7. Ne avrò un centinạio.
8. Partirà alle dụe.
9. Sarà Piẹtro.
10. Sarà italiạno.

125. 1. andrò
2. arriverạnno
3. visiterại
4. nevicherà
5. farà
6. arriverò
7. vedremo
8. avremo

126. 1. I ragazzi saranno al cịnema.
2. Che ora sarà?
3. Quạndo studierại?
4. Se andrò in Itạlia, vedrò molti musẹi.
5. Quạndo arriveranno i turisti, andranno all'albergo.
6. Se visiterẹte vostra zịa, lei sarà molto contenta.

127. 1. canterẹbbero
2. camminerẹbbe
3. visiterẹbbero
4. comprerẹsti
5. arriverẹi
6. ballerẹste
7. completerẹbbe
8. preparerẹmmo

128. 1. correrẹmmo
2. leggerẹsti
3. aprirẹi
4. seguirẹbbe
5. friggerẹbbero
6. scoprirẹste
7. venderẹmmo
8. servirẹsti

129. 1. cominceremmo
2. avrẹi
3. berrebbe
4. dovreste

5. udresti (udiresti)
6. varrebbe
7. verrebbero
8. pagherei
9. mangeremmo
10. sarebbe

130. 1. abbiamo parlato
2. ha preparato
3. ha cantato
4. abbiamo accettato
5. hai pranzato
6. avete comprato
7. ho guardato
8. ha controllato
9. hanno viaggiato
10. ha chiamato

131. 1. ho perduto (perso)
2. hai ripetuto
3. hanno venduto
4. abbiamo ricevuto
5. ha conosciuto

132. 1. Loro hanno capito tutto.
2. Noi abbiamo finito il lavoro.
3. Io ho vestito il bambino.
4. Noi abbiamo servito il pranzo.
5. Maria ha finito il lavoro.

133. 1. abbiamo letto
2. ha rotto
3. hanno tratto
4. ha fatto
5. ho detto
6. hanno scritto
7. hai corretto
8. ho risposto
9. hai scelto
10. hanno vinto

134. 1. abbiamo accettato
2. hai pranzato
3. ha conosciuto
4. hanno cantato
5. avete detto
6. ha finito
7. ho letto
8. ha rotto
9. hai comprato
10. abbiamo promesso

135. 1. Luisa ha cantato bene.
2. Abbiamo letto la lettera.
3. Avete scritto molte lettere.

4. Hai chiuso la porta.
5. Ho mangiato con gli amici.
6. Hanno aperto le finestre.
7. Abbiamo finito il compito.
8. Avete aspettato Giovanni.
9. Ho lavorato fino a tardi.
10. Hai rotto il piatto.

136. 1. Maria li ha conosciuti ieri.
2. L'ho comprata in quel negozio.
3. Non le ho salutate.
4. L'ho bevuto in pochi secondi.
5. Li ho dati ieri pomeriggio.
6. L'abbiamo controllata.
7. Le hai lette?
8. Li avete finiti?
9. L'ho aperta poco fa.
10. Le hanno scritte facilmente.

137. 1. sono state
2. è arrivato
3. è durata
4. siete andati
5. sono piaciuti
6. sono usciti
7. è ritornata
8. è bastato
9. sono costati
10. siamo restati

138. 1. Marco è andato al mercato.
2. Luisa è uscita con Pietro.
3. Giuseppe e Antonio sono ritornati alle nove.
4. Olga e Maria sono entrate in un negozio.
5. Maria e Anna sono partiti per l'Italia.
6. Noi siamo stati dai nonni.
7. Le ragazze sono arrivate insieme.
8. I ragazzi sono stati a casa.

139. 1. Questa macchina (Quest'auto, automobile) è costata trentamila euro.
2. Signora Cherubini, dov'è stata ultimamente?
3. Marisa e Antonio sono andati a scuola alle otto di mattina.
4. A che ora sei arrivato oggi?
5. Ragazze, come siete arrivate, in autobus o in aereo?
6. Signori Boni, dove sono vissuti due anni fa?
7. Io sono cresciuta con i (coi) miei nonni.
8. Fausto e Anna sono morti dalla paura!
9. La mia sorellina è nata nel duemila
10. Le lenticchie sono piaciute a tutti.

140. 1. Gli aspạragi? Li ho dovuti preparare.
2. Teresa? Non l'abbiạmo potuta vedere.
3. Le scarpe? Le hai volute comprare.
4. Il televisore? L'avete dovuto portare.
5. I libri? Li ha dovuti lẹggere.

141. 1. (Io) non sono potuta andare dal dentista; (Io) non ho potuto andare dal dentista.
2. I ragazzi non hanno voluto lavare il passo carrạio.
3. Mạrio non ha potuto giocare fuọri.

142. 1. Mi sono alzato (-a) di buon'ọra.
2. I ragazzi non si sono sbarbati.
3. Ci siạmo seduti (-e) vicino alla finestra.
4. Gli amici si sono divertiti.
5. Lei si è (s'è) laureạta quest'ạnno?
6. Dottoressa, Lei si è (S'è) sentita bene?
7. Quẹlle sorelle si sono scritte spesso.
8. Mi sono (son) comprato (-a) un pạio di scarpe.
9. Quẹl ragazzo si è (s'è) lamentato sempre.
10. Ragazzi vi siẹte arrabbiạti troppo.

143. 1. sono
2. hanno
3. sono
4. hanno
5. sono
6. hanno
7. sono
8. hanno
9. sono
10. hanno

144. 1. ha veduto (visto)
2. avete fatto
3. abbiạmo comprato
4. hanno detto
5. sono arrivati
6. sono andati
7. ho letto
8. abbiạmo finito
9. ho avuto
10. siẹte venuti

145. 1. Lo vedevo spesso.
2. Parlavạmo con lui spesso.
3. Carlo mi chiamạva spesso.
4. Loro ricevẹvano una lettera da lui spesso.
5. Angelina vedeva spesso i cugini. *or* (... i cugini spesso)

146. 1. Lui mi ha visitato dụe giọrni fa.
2. Lei mi ha aiutato dụe giọrni fa.
3. Sono andato lí dụe giọrni fa.

4. Me l'hanno detto dụe giọrni fa.
5. L'hai fatto dụe giọrni fa.

147. 1. Andavo a Chicago ogni mese.
2. Iẹri Marịa è partita di mattino.
3. Ho visitato i miẹi cugini l'anno scorso.
4. Ogni tanto incontravạmo dei vecchi amici.
5. Viaggiạvi in Frạncia spesso spesso?
6. Iẹri sera abbiạmo parlato di polịtica.
7. Siạmo andati al teạtro domẹnica scorsa.
8. Loro sono andati al mercato una volta.

148. 1. Sí, la settimana scorsa sono andato alla spiạggia.
2. Sí, iẹri sera ho dormito molto.
3. Sí, stamani ho lavorato troppo.
4. Sí, andavo al cịnema ogni domẹnica.
5. Sí, viaggiạvo con gli amici frequentemente.
6. Sí, facevo delle spese ogni mattina.
7. Sí, ho parlato con lui tre giọrni fa.
8. Sí, ho veduto (visto) il film venerdí.

149. 1. nuotạvano, prendẹvano
2. parlava, sono arrivato
3. hai conosciụto, era
4. Piovẹva, siạmo usciti
5. dormivo, è squillato
6. pranzạvano, ho telefonato
7. sono arrivati, faceva
8. ballạvano, cantạvano
9. mi sono alzato, si è alzato
10. sono uscito, nevicạva

150. 1. A: Ho visitato   B: Visitại
2. A: Ho mangiạto   B: Mangiại
3. A: Hại avuto   B: Avesti
4. A: È arrivata   B: Arrivò
5. A: Siạmo usciti   B: Uscimmo
6. A: Avete letto   B: Leggeste
7. A: Sono partiti (-e)   B: Partịrono
8. A: Abbiạmo parlato   B: Parlammo
9. A: Hại scritto   B: Scrivesti
10. A: Sono ritornato (-a)   B: Ritornại

151. 1. avevạmo parlato
2. ero arrivato
3. aveva finito
4. avevạte comprato
5. eri stato
6. avẹvano creduto

152. 1. avevạmo veduto (visto)
2. avevo portato
3. eravạmo arrivati
4. avẹvano comprato

5. avevi ricevuto
6. avevano studiato

153. 1. fu arrivato
2. ebbero parlato
3. avemmo cenato
4. avemmo finito
5. fu arrivato

154. 1. avremo veduto (visto)
2. avrai avuto
3. saranno ritornati
4. avrete dato
5. avremo parlato
6. avranno giocato
7. sarà uscito
8. sarò arrivato

155. 1. saremmo usciti
2. sarei venuto
3. sarebbe arrivato
4. avreste potuto
5. avresti corso
6. sarebbero andate

156. 1. apra
2. arrivino
3. scrivano
4. cada
5. telefoni
6. seguiate
7. senta
8. descriviate

157. 1. tocchino
2. paghiate
3. cerchi
4. giochiamo
5. mangino
6. comincino

158. 1. che tu venga; che loro vengano; che voi veniate; che noi veniamo
2. che tu dica; che lui dica; che voi diciate; che loro dicano
3. che io faccia; che tu faccia; che lei faccia: che loro facciano
4. che io rimanga; che tu rimanga; che lui rimanga: che loro rimangano
5. che lui capisca; che noi capiamo; che voi capiate; che loro capiscano
6. che tu suoni; che lei suoni; che loro suonino; che io esca; che noi usciamo; che voi usciate; che loro escano
8. che io scelga; che lui scelga; che noi scegliamo; che voi scegliate

159. 1. abbiano
2. siano
3. dia
4. sappiano
5. diate
6. siate
7. stiate

160. 1. parliate; partiate; ceniate; dormiate; crediate; veniate; saliate; studiate
2. torni; esca; venga; scriva; lavori; scenda; parli; dorma
3. canti; parli; dorma; esca; parta; rida; creda; abbia ragione
4. escano; tornino; mangino; salgano; partano; cantino; studino; dormano

161. 1. Voglio che loro vengano alle nove.
2. Voglio che tu scriva una lettera.
3. Voglio che voi parliate ad alta voce.
4. Voglio che Pietro dica la verità.
5. Voglio che noi partiamo presto.
6. Voglio che lui lo sappia.
7. Ordiniamo che tu vada in biblioteca.
8. Ordiniamo che voi diciate la verità.
9. Ordiniamo che loro comprino i libri necessari.
10. Ordiniamo che Luigi rimanga a casa.
11. Ordiniamo che tu sappia la lezione.
12. Ordiniamo che voi traduciate la lettura.
13. Mi dispiace che voi siate tristi.
14. Mi dispiace che Pietro non possa venire.
15. Mi dispiace che tu scriva cosí male.
16. Mi dispiace che loro abbiano molti problemi.
17. Mi dispiace che nevichi molto.
18. Mi dispiace che voi partecipiate poco.
19. Tu insisti che io parta domani.
20. Tu insisti che i bambini dormano.
21. Tu insisti che Luisa vada a casa.
22. Tu insisti che noi studiamo.
23. Tu insisti che loro aprano le finestre.
24. Tu insisti che io sappia la lezione.

162. 1. restiate
2. parta
3. venga
4. escano
5. sappiamo
6. arriviate
7. sappiano
8. sia
9. vada
10. riportino

163. 1. prepari, riceva, legga, scriva, finisca, cerchi, paghi, sappia
2. incontriate, conosciate, riceviate, troviate, sappiate, facciate, abbiate, cerchiate
3. faccia, porti, descriva, dica, sappia, ottenga, prepari, finisca
4. venga, salga, parta, esca, legga, traduca, scii, sbagli
5. preparino, portino, finiscano, cerchino, paghino, credano, dicano, mandino

164. 1. È importante che io riceva certe lettere.
2. È giusto che paghiate il conto.
3. È probabile che ritornino tardi.
4. Bisogna che riporti i libri.
5. È meglio che usciamo presto.
6. È impossibile che parta subito.
7. Non importa che tu finisca la lettura.
8. È necessario che Paolo studi molto.
9. Speriamo che voi possiate partecipare.
10. Conviene che loro facciano i bravi.

165. 1. siano qui; arrivino presto; escano insieme; facciano i compiti
2. facciate i buoni; portiate i libri; finiate la lezione; sappiate l'indirizzo; ceniate qui; leggiate molto; abbiate pazienza; partiate presto

166. 1. Sono sicuri che vengono alle tre.
2. Non è sicura che (loro) vengano oggi.
3. Pensate che vostro fratello arrivi tardi?
4. Non dubitiamo che Loro sono sinceri.
5. Credi che Paolo lo sappia?

167. 1. sono
2. abbiate
3. sai
4. possa
5. vada
6. conosciamo

168. 1. leggiate; studiate; dormiate; facciate i compiti; scriviate una lettera; abbiate un mal di testa; siate malati; non ascoltiate
2. arrivino; finiscano; telefonino; chiamino; bussino; escano; salgano; dormano
3. scriva; venga; bussi; parli; telefoni; canti; arrivi; esca
4. sia stanco; abbia la febbre; non voglia; non possa

169. 1. sia
2. parta
3. faccia

169 (cont.) 4. abbia
5. possiate
6. siano

170. 1. Che parli con me!
2. Che partano presto!
3. Che finisca la lettura!
4. Che portino i regali!
5. Che legga il romanzo!
6. Che scrivano molto!
7. Che scii cautamente!
8. Che sappiano la domanda!

171. 1. parla italiano; scrive bene; sa formattare (to format) i documenti.
2. parli italiano; scriva bene; sappia usare l'elaboratore (word processor).

172. 1. Cerco un segretario che sappia creare un sito web (to create a web site).
2. Ho una camicia che va bene con il vestito.
3. Voglio comprare una cravatta che vada bene con la camicia.
4. Abbiamo bisogno di un dottore che abiti vicino.
5. Hai una macchina che è meravigliosa.
6. Cerco un lavoro che sia interessante.

173. 1. gioca
2. abbia
3. porti
4. ha
5. studiano
6. possa
7. sappiano
8. abbaia

174. 1. conosca
2. esista
3. abbiate
4. conoscano
5. sia

175. 1. chiami
2. capisca
3. vengano
4. abbia
5. piaccia

176. 1. aiuti
2. possa
3. venda
4. dia
5. piaccia

177.
1. Sono contenti di ẹssere con noi.
2. Antọnio spera di passare gli esami.
3. Tu suggerisci che lei arrivi presto?
4. Mi lạsciano giocare a tennis con loro.
5. Ragazzi, suggerisco che finiạte i cọmpiti.
6. Mịo padre non mi lạscia fumare.

178.
1. sịano arrivati(-e)
2. ạbbia detto
3. abbịate svelato
4. sịa stato
5. ạbbia finito
6. ạbbiano veduto (visto)

179.
1. Dụbito che voi abbịate capito.
2. Spero che Luịgi sịa arrivato presto.
3. È impossịbile che tu ạbbia letto tanto.
4. Non credịamo che loro sịano venute.
5. Ha paụra che io ạbbia sbaglịato strada.
6. Pensi che Giụlia sịa stata ammalata?

180.
1. Abbịamo paụra che Luịgi non si lạurei.
2. È probạbile che Silvana smetta d'insegnare.
3. Hai paụra che io non mi scusi?
4. Hanno l'impressịone che voi giochịate troppo.
5. Non so se lei torni oggi.
6. Pẹnsano che Lei vọglia scherzare.

181.
1. studiạssero, dicẹssero la verità, partịssero, tornạssero, dormịssero, facẹssero i cọmpiti
2. sciạssimo, traducẹssimo, uscịssimo, cantạssimo, venịssimo, fọssimo in ritardo, ripetẹssimo la domanda, bevẹssimo troppo
3. tornassi, partịssi, studiạssi, cenạssi, finịssi il lavoro, leggẹssi, scrivẹssi, dormịssi
4. capisse, sapesse, scrivesse, dicesse, facesse
5. guardaste, spiegaste, vendeste, finiste, diceste, faceste

182.
1. finissi
2. andạssero
3. tornaste
4. scrivessi
5. dicesse
6. stessi

183.
1. Insisteva che parlạssimo italiạno.
2. Avẹvano paụra che tu non lo comprassi.
3. Voleva che voi partiste.
4. Preferivi che io lo sapessi.
5. Speravạmo che Carlo arrivasse alle sẹi.

184.
1. Volẹvano che uscịssimo con loro.
2. Proibịvano che io fumassi.
3. Sperava che voi finiste il lavoro.
4. Avevo paụra che tu avessi ragịone.
5. Insistevi che io lo facessi.

185.
1. vincẹssimo
2. finịssero
3. partissi
4. studiạsse
5. visitaste
6. prendessi

186.
1. giocasse
2. avesse
3. venda
4. potesse
5. fosse
6. avesse
7. fosse
8. fosse

187.
1. Magari arrivạssimo in tempo!
2. Se solo continuạssero a studiạre!
3. Fossi fortunato!
4. Telefonạssero pure!
5. Se solo venịssero i nostri amici!
6. Magari smettesse di piọvere!

188.
1. sapesse
2. venisse
3. fosse
4. gridạssero
5. fosse
6. facesse
7. piovẹsse
8. parlạssimo

189.
1. studiạssero, partịssero per l'Itạlia, leggẹssero molto, fọssero bravi, avẹssero soldi, lavorạssero poco
2. potessi sciạre, sapessi guidare, andassi a scuọla, avessi pazịenza, stessi a casa, giocassi a tennis, lavorassi, leggessi

190.
1. fọssero arrivati(-e)
2. avẹssimo finito
3. avessi portato
4. foste partiti(-e)
5. avessi avuto
6. avẹssero fatto
7. aveste detto
8. fosse uscita

191. 1. hanno
2. fosse stato
3. facesse
4. partiamo
5. fossi
6. avesse veduti (visti)

192. 1. siate
2. sbagli
3. finisca
4. piaccia
5. fumiamo
6. facesse
7. vengono
8. partissi
9. stia
10. arrivaste

193. 1. Sí, dorma!
No, non dorma!
2. Sí, scriva!
No, non scriva!
3. Sí, ritorni!
No, non ritorni!
4. Sí, risponda!
No, non risponda!
5. Sí, arrivi presto!
No, non arrivi presto!
6. Sí, creda a tutto!
No, non creda a tutto!
7. Sí, balli!
No, non balli!
8. Sí, legga!
No, non legga!
9. Sí, guardi la televisione!
No, non guardi la televisione!
10. Sí, veda il film!
No, non veda il film!

194. 1. Sí, parlino!
No, non parlino!
2. Sí, scrivano le lettere!
No, non scrivano le lettere!
3. Sí, leggano la rivista!
No, non leggano la rivista!
4. Sí, chiudano la finestra!
No, non chiudano la finestra!
5. Sí, comprino i libri!
No, non comprino i libri!
6. Sí, guardino lo spettacolo!
No, non guardino lo spettacolo!
7. Sí, dividano i regali!
No, non dividano i regali!

8. Sí, partano alle otto!
No, non partano alle otto!
9. Sí, mandino il pacco!
No, non mandino il pacco!
10. Sí, preparino il tè!
No, non facciano il tè!

195. 1. Sí, canta!
2. Sí, torna!
3. Sí, scia!
4. Sí, cerca!
5. Sí, mangia!
6. Sí, scrivi!
7. Sí, temi!
8. Sí, dormi!
9. Sí, senti!
10. Sí, sali!

196. 1. Sí, cantate!
2. Sí, mangiate!
3. Sí, tornate!
4. Sí, sciate!
5. Sí, pensate!
6. Sí, temete!
7. Sí, scrivete!
8. Sí, dormite!
9. Sí, sentite!
10. Sí, salite!

197. 1. Da' i saluti!
2. Sta' attento!
3. Di' la verità!
4. Sappi la risposta!
5. Sii in tempo!
6. Fa' i compiti!
7. Abbi pronta la lezione!

198. 1. Fate bene il lavoro!
2. Dite tutto!
3. Sappiate i dettagli!
4. Date il benvenuto!
5. State a casa!
6. Abbiate pazienza!
7. Andate a studiare!

199. 1. Sí, parla ad alta voce!
No, non parlare ad alta voce!
2. Sí, prepara il caffè!
No, non preparare il caffè!
3. Sí, rispondi al telefono!
No, non rispondere al telefono!
4. Sí, dormi fino a tardi!
No, non dormire fino a tardi!

5. Sí, suona il piano!
   No, non suonare il piano!
6. Sí, vieni da solo!
   No, non venire da solo!
7. Sí, abbi vergogna!
   No, non avere vergogna!
8. Sí, di' la verità!
   No, non dire la verità!
9. Sí, sta' (stai) a casa!
   No, non stare a casa!
10. Sí, scrivi una lettera!
    No, non scrivere una lettera!

200. 1. Sí, tornate tardi!
   No, non tornate tardi!
2. Sí, cenate insieme!
   No, non cenate insieme!
3. Sí, date i libri a Mario!
   No, non date i libri a Mario!
4. Sí, state a casa!
   No, non state a casa!
5. Sí, credete a tutto!
   No, non credete a tutto!
6. Sí, siate cattivi!
   No, non siate cattivi!
7. Sí, abbiate pazienza!
   No, non abbiate pazienza!
8. Sí, vedete il film!
   No, non vedete il film!

201. 1. Canti bene!
2. Venga qui!
3. Sia buono!
4. Scriva la lettera!
5. Lavorino di piú!
6. Credano a tutto!
7. Mangi di meno!
8. Cerchino i bambini!
9. Restituisca i libri!
10. Rimangano qui!

202. 1. Non venga qui!
2. Non venire qui!
3. Non venite qui!
4. Non vengano qui!
5. Non parlare molto !
6. Non parli molto!
7. Non parlate molto!
8. Non parlino molto!
9. Non essere buono!
10. Non abbia pazienza!

203. 1. Grida!
2. Tagliate il foglio!

3. Sii pronto!
4. Vengano insieme!
5. Dica tutto!
6. Abbi pazienza!

204. 1. Ceniamo in quel ristorante!
2. Non balliamo molto!
3. Telefoniamo a Stefano!
4. Diciamo la verità!
5. Non usciamo tardi!
6. Prepariamo la valigia!

205. 1. sbagliando
2. salutando
3. spiegando
4. sorridendo
5. piangendo
6. lavorando

206. 1. Avendo cenato
2. Essendo partita
3. Avendo studiato
4. Essendo usciti
5. Avendo aspettato
6. Avendo visitato

207. 1. parlando, scrivendo, gridando, salendo, scendendo
2. mangiando, ascoltando, discutendo, sentendo, venendo
3. contando, piangendo, servendo il tè, leggendo, cantando

208. 1. Tu stai suonando e Pietro sta cantando.
2. Io sto dormendo e voi state studiando.
3. Loro stanno parlando e noi stiamo guardando la televisione.
4. Loro stanno arrivando e noi stiamo partendo.
5. Voi state uscendo e loro stanno entrando.
6. Noi stiamo leggendo e tu stai ascoltando la radio.
7. Io sto scrivendo e Anna sta lavorando.

209. 1. Io stavo giocando a carte.
2. Voi stavate tornando dal centro.
3. Tu stavi leggendo alcune riviste.
4. Loro stavano salendo rapidamente.
5. Olga stava studiando la lezione.
6. Io stavo girando l'Europa.
7. Voi stavate mangiando in fretta.
8. Noi stavamo vedendo un film.

210. 1. si alzano
2. vi mettete
3. si addormentano

4. mi chiamo
5. ci vestiamo
6. si laurea

211.   1. mi
2. ci
3. vi
4. si
5. si
6. ti
7. si
8. ci

212.   1. Io mi sono seduto vicino alla porta.
2. Luigi si è sbarbato con difficoltà.
3. I ragazzi si sono alzati alle sette.
4. Voi vi siete arrabbiati facilmente.
5. Ragazze, a che ora vi siete svegliate?
6. Signori, a che ora si sono alzati Loro?

213.   1. ci salutiamo
2. si sposano
3. si rispettano
4. si scrivono
5. si aiutano
6. vi salutate

214.   1. (none)
2. si
3. (none)
4. vi
5. (none)
6. ti
7. (none)
8. ci

215.   1. Gli ho parlato prima di uscire.
Gli ho parlato prima di studiare.
Gli ho parlato prima di finire.
Gli ho parlato prima di mangiare.
Gli ho parlato prima di giocare.
Gli ho parlato prima di ballare.
Gli ho parlato prima di cantare.
Gli ho parlato prima di lavorare.
2. Sono entrati senza dire niente.
Sono entrati senza parlare.
Sono entrati senza salutare.
Sono entrati senza sorridere.
Sono entrati senza dare il buongiorno.

216.   1. aver visto (veduto)
2. aver telefonato
3. aver detto
4. aver visitato
5. essere arrivato

217.   1. No, lavorare troppo non è giudizioso.
2. No, mangiare molto non è giudizioso.
3. No, parlare sempre non è giudizioso.
4. No, viaggiare ogni giorno non è giudizioso.
5. No, studiare continuamente non è giudizioso.
6. No, ballare senza sosta non è giudizioso.

218.   1. Vietato entrare!
2. Vietato tirare!
3. Vietato spingere!
4. Vietato fumare!
5. Vietato girare a destra!
6. Vietato uscire!

219.   1. Vietato fumare!
2. Vietato girare a sinistra!
3. Tenere la destra!
4. Tirare!
5. Spingere!
6. Tenersi a distanza!

220.   1. Sí, ho lasciato giocare i ragazzi.
2. Sí, ho visto studiare le studentesse.
3. Sí, ho sentito cantare il tenore.
4. Sí, ho lasciato parlare il ragazzo.
5. Sí, ho visto ballare gli studenti.
6. Sí, ho sentito leggere la ragazza.

221.   1. Ho fatto cantare il ragazzo.
2. Ho fatto cantare la canzone al ragazzo.
3. L'ho fatta cantare al ragazzo.
4. Gli ho fatto cantare la canzone.
5. Gliel'ho fatta cantare.
6. Ho fatto cantare la canzone ai ragazzi.
7. L'ho fatta cantare ai ragazzi.
8. Ho fatto cantare loro la canzone.
9. L'ho fatta cantare loro.

222.   1. Luisa lo fa fare.
2. Noi la facciamo entrare.
3. Il maestro le fa recitare.
4. Tu lo fai mandare.
5. Io me la son fatta costruire.
6. Io gliel'ho fatta tradurre.

223.   1. Un terremoto ha distrutto quel paese.
2. Olga ha composto queste poesie.
3. Noi abbiamo costruito quella casa.
4. Gli studenti hanno fatto gli scaffali.
5. Mia zia ha inviato la lettera.
6. Giovanni ha portato il pacco.

224.   1. si vede
2. Si parla

3. si dice
4. si vendono
5. si trova

225. 1. canta
2. pulite
3. parli
4. bevano
5. abbi
6. siate
7. traduca
8. vieni

226. 1. sta parlando
2. stavano cantando
3. sta arrivando
4. stanno scrivendo
5. stai facendo; sto leggendo
6. stavate facendo

227. 1. si sono seduti
2. ci siamo divertiti
3. si è addormentata
4. vi siete alzate
5. si è preparata

228. 1. Viaggiare è interessante.
2. Tenere la destra!
3. Vietato fumare!
4. Vietato sostare! (Sosta vietata!)
5. Tirare!
6. Abbiamo visto (veduto) giocare
i bambini.

Chapter 7

1. 1. Non vogliamo andare a teatro.
2. Io non conosco quei ragazzi.
3. Luisa non vuole venire adesso.
4. Non andavate alla spiaggia ogni estate.
5. Non si sveglieranno alle quattro.
6. Gli amici non portano i regali.
7. Tu non mangi troppo.
8. Non lo hanno dimenticato.
9. Non ho visto Roberto ieri sera.
10. I miei amici non visitano il museo.

2. 1. Non c'è niente sul tavolo.
2. Nessuno ti ha telefonato. (Non ti ha telefonato
nessuno.)
3. Non vedo nessuno nella stanza.
4. Mai andiamo alla spiaggia. (Non andiamo mai
alla spiaggia.)
5. Lei non ha né penna né carta?

6. Luigi mai dice la stessa cosa. (Luigi non dice
mai la stessa cosa.)
7. Non c'è nessuno in cucina.
8. Non vuole niente?
9. Carlo non parla mai con nessuno.
10. Mai leggo nessun giornale italiano. (Non leggo
mai nessun giornale italiano.)

3. 1. Non siamo mai andati a sciare. (Mai siamo
andati a sciare.)' (Non siamo andati mai
a sciare.)
2. Non ha chiamato affatto. (Non ha affatto
chiamato.)
3. Non sono ancora arrivati. (Ancora non sono
arrivati.)
4. Tu non sei neanche entrato. (Neanche tu sei
entrato.) (Tu non sei entrato neanche.)
5. Non hanno visto nessuno spettacolo.
6. Il cane non è mai tornato. (Il cane non è
tornato mai.)
7. Non abbiamo visto nessuno.
8. Non si sono ancora svegliati. (Ancora non
si sono svegliati.) (Non si sono svegliati
ancora.)
9. Mai ho visto quel film. (Non ho mai visto quel
film.) (Non ho visto mai quel film.)
10. Non abbiamo affatto cantato. (Non abbiamo
cantato affatto.)
11. Non ha scritto che poesie.

4. 1. Non mi ha telefonato nessuno ieri sera.
2. Non ho detto niente.
3. I miei amici non sono ancora arrivati.
(I miei amici non sono arrivati ancora.)
4. Non ho letto che due libri.
5. Ieri sera non ho fatto niente.
6. Non ho comprato né dischi né riviste.
7. Non l'ho visto piú. (Non l'ho piú visto.)
8. Non sono mai andato(-a) in Italia. (Non sono
andato[-a] mai in Italia.)
9. Quando è arrivato non ha detto neanche buon
giorno. (Quando è arrivato non ha neanche detto
buon giorno.)
10. Non ha mica cantato.

5. 1. Neanche lui è ricco.
2. Nemmeno le sue cugine hanno molto denaro.
3. Maria non lo sa e neppure io lo so.
4. Nemmeno Giovanni viene.
5. Neanche lui lo ha fatto.

6. 1. di non giocare qui
2. di non fumare
3. di non correre

    4. di non gridare
    5. di non sbattere
    6. di non guardare
    7. di non arrabbiarsi
    8. di non bere molto

7. 1. Marco non vuole andare a sciare.
    2. Non siamo mai andati in montagna. (Mai siamo andati in montagna.) (Non siamo andati mai in montagna.)
    3. Non ho né libri né penne.
    4. Loro non ci dicono niente.
    5. Neanche voi andate in Italia.
    6. Nessuno mi ha telefonato.
    7. Tu non leggi nessuna rivista moderna.
    8. Voi non giocate mai. (Voi mai giocate.)

8. 1. Non abbiamo mai giocato a tennis.
    (Mai abbiamo giocato a tennis.)
    (Non abbiamo giocato mai a tennis.)
    2. Non hanno lavorato affatto.
    (Non hanno affatto lavorato.)
    3. Non hai veduto nessuno.
    4. Non avete ancora finito.
    (Non avete finito ancora.)
    5. Non ho fatto nessuna telefonata.
    6. Non ha neanche salutato.
    (Non ha salutato neanche.)

9. 1. Neanche (nemmeno, neppure) tu puoi gridare qui.
    2. (Loro) non parlano tedesco, (loro) parlano spagnolo.
    3. Mia zia Paolina ci dice di non fumare.
    4. (Lei) non è tornata piú.
    5. (Lui) non ha telefonato affatto.
    6. I bambini non si sono ancora svegliati.

Chapter 8

1. 1. È arrivato alle cinque Luigi?
    (Luigi è arrivato alle cinque?)
    2. Ci sediamo qui noi?
    (Noi ci sediamo qui?)
    3. Hai paura tu?
    (Tu hai paura?)
    4. Portano il vino Loro?
    (Loro portano il vino?)
    5. Siete andati a teatro voi?
    (Voi siete andati a teatro?)
    6. Ha giocato a carte Lei?
    (Lei ha giocato a carte?)
    7. Ballano molto i giovani?
    (I giovani ballano molto?)

    8. Ha tradotto quel libro lui?
    (Lui ha tradotto quel libro?)

2. 1. I ragazzi vanno a casa.
    2. Le studentesse sono tornate.
    3. Tu hai perduto (perso) la partita.
    4. Voi vi siete alzati presto.
    5. Loro escono alle sei.
    6. Noi abbiamo ballato molto.

3. 1. Nostro fratello tornerà domani, vero?
    2. Quel vestito non costa molto, no?
    3. Ci siamo incontrati per caso, vero?
    4. Mi riporterete il mio dizionario, non è vero?
    5. Sei stato malato fino a ieri, no?
    6. Andremo in Italia insieme, non è vero?

4. 1. Quanto
    2. Quando
    3. Dove
    4. Quando; A che ora
    5. Come
    6. Quanto
    7. Quanto
    8. Perché
    9. Quando
   10. Come

5. 1. Dov'è il tuo fratellino?
    2. Come stai oggi?
    3. Come mai non sono arrivate?
    4. Perché non smette di fumare?
    5. Quanto fa sette piú quattro?
    6. A che ora arriverà?

6. 1. Chi
    2. Che
    3. che
    4. chi
    5. Che (cosa; che cosa)

7. 1. Chi
    2. Che (Cosa) (Che cosa)
    3. Che (Cosa) (Che cosa)
    4. A chi
    5. Da chi
    6. Che (Cosa) (Che cosa)
    7. Di che (Di cosa) (Di che cosa)
    8. Per chi
    9. Di che (Di cosa) (Di che cosa)
   10. Con chi

8. 1. Ragazzi, che (cosa, che cosa) fate (state facendo)?
    2. Che (cosa, che cosa) sta succedendo (succede) in questo momento?

3. Chi sono quei signori?
4. Di chi sono questi giocattoli?
5. Di che (cosa, che cosa) hanno parlato?
6. Chi è? La conosciamo?

9. 1. quale
2. Quali
3. Quale
4. Qual
5. Quali

10. 1. Quali
2. Quali
3. Quale
4. quale
5. Qual

11. 1. Quanti
2. Quante
3. Quante
4. Quanto
5. Quanta

12. 1. Compra Marco molti libri?
(Compra molti libri Marco?)
(Marco compra molti libri?)
(Marco compra molti libri, non è vero?)
2. È tuo fratello il padrone di quella casa?
(Tuo fratello è il padrone di quella casa?)
(Tuo fratello è il padrone di quella casa, vero?)
3. Arrivano sempre in ritardo i ragazzi?
(Arrivano i ragazzi sempre in ritardo?)
(I ragazzi arrivano sempre in ritardo?)
(I ragazzi arrivano sempre in ritardo,
non è vero?)
4. Va Teresa al cinema stasera?
(Va al cinema stasera Teresa?)
(Teresa va al cinema stasera?)
(Teresa va al cinema stasera, no?)
5. Andate voi a scuola in macchina?
(Voi andate a scuola in macchina?)
(Voi andate a scuola in macchina, non
è vero?)
6. Costa cinque dollari il biglietto?
(Il biglietto costa cinque dollari?)
(Il biglietto costa cinque dollari, vero?)
7. Marco compra molti libri?; Compra molti libri
Marco?
8. I signori Porta hanno tre figli?; Hanno tre figli
i signori Porta?
9. Marisa lavora in una banca?; Lavora in una
banca Marisa?
10. Tu le insegni a sciare?; Le insegni a
sciare (tu)?

13. 1. Quando
2. Chi
3. Quanto
4. Come
5. Perché
6. chi
7. Di
8. A che
9. Qual
10. cosa

14. 1. Di chi è questa valigia?
2. Quale computer hai comprato?
3. Quanto denaro avete portato?
(Quanti soldi avete portato?)
4. Quanti euro paghi per un gelato?
5. Di chi è questa e-mail?
6. Quale ragazzo gioca oggi?
7. Che (cosa, che cosa) succede (sta succedendo)
a casa?
8. A che ora può uscire (Lei)?

Chapter 9

1. 1. tu
2. Lei
3. Loro
4. voi
5. voi
6. Loro
7. voi
8. voi
9. Lei
10. Noi
11. Lei
12. Loro
13. Loro
14. Lui
15. lei
16. tu
17. Lei
18. Loro
19. Io
20. Loro

2. 1. Lui
2. Loro
3. Lei
4. Loro (Essi)
5. Loro (Esse)
6. Loro (Esse)

3. 1. lei
2. loro (esse)
3. lui
4. loro
5. noi
6. voi

4. 1. Noi cantiamo, ma lei studia.
2. Neanche loro vogliono mangiare.
3. Chi vuole giocare? Io!
4. Anche loro vanno in Italia.

5. 1. lo
2. li
3. la
4. le
5. l'
6. l'
7. li
8. le
9. la
10. lo
11. li
12. le

6. 1. Mario *le* recita.
2. Noi *la* salutiamo.
3. Teresa *li* sfoglia.
4. Il cameriere *lo* serve.
5. Arturo *le* porta.
6. Tu *la* chiami.
7. Stefano *li* saluta.
8. Tu *lo* mandi.
9. Voi *le* aspettate.
10. Loro *la* leggono.
11. Io *li* compro.
12. Noi *l'*invitiamo. (*lo* invitiamo)
13. Li usiamo spesso.
14. Eccolo!

7. 1. La
2. Le
3. Li
4. L'
5. L'
6. L'

8. 1. Signori, Li aiuto.
2. Signore, Le chiamiamo.
3. Signora, La chiamiamo.
4. Signorina, L'aspettiamo.
5. Dottore, L'aiutiamo.
6. Signor Pirri e signora Torre, Li aspettiamo.
7. Dottoressa Merini, La chiamo domani?
8. Professor Carli, La chiamo stasera?

9. 1. Sí, lo sono.
2. No, non lo credo.
3. Sí, lo dubitiamo.
4. No, non lo dubito.
5. Sí, lo crediamo.

10. 1. lo
2. lo
3. lo
4. lo
5. lo
6. lo

11. 1. Sí, i ragazzi mi chiamano.
2. No, Carlo non ci vede.
3. Sí, Mario e Teresa ci (vi) sentono.
4. No, quei signori non mi parlano.
5. Sí, Olga ci telefona.
6. No, Arturo non mi vede.
7. Sí, gli amici ci (vi) salutano.
8. No, non mi dicono tutto.
9. Sí, Stefano ci risponde.
10. No, quelle signorine non ci (vi) parlano.

12. 1. Carlo *ci* parla.
2. Maria *vi* vede.
3. Lui *c'*insegna la lezione.
4. Io *vi* saluto.
5. Loro *ci* guardano.
6. Lei *vi* risponde.

13. 1. Luisa saluta me.
2. I miei amici cercano noi.
3. Noi vogliamo vedere te.
4. Lui chiama voi.
5. Io saluto Lei.
6. Tu saluti lei.
7. Loro cercano lui.
8. Noi invitiamo loro.
9. Voi chiamate loro.
10. Io saluto Loro.

14. 1. gli
2. le
3. loro
4. Le
5. loro
6. loro
7. Le
8. Gli

15. 1. *Le* mando un regalo.
2. *Gli* scriviamo molte lettere.
3. Do *loro* l'indirizzo.
4. *Le* telefono.

5. Inviạmo *loro* un telegramma.
6. *Gli* rispondo.
7. *Le* scrivo.
8. Diạmo *loro* il benvenuto.

16. 1. loro
2. le
3. li
4. lo
5. li
6. l'
7. le
8. Gli
9. loro
10. le

17. 1. Le
2. Gli
3. Gli
4. Le
5. Le
6. Gli
7. Le
8. Le

18. 1. Sí, scrivo Loro; Sí, Gli scrivo;
   Sí, vi scrivo.
2. Sí, Le parlo; Sí, ti parlo.
3. Sí, mando Loro la ricetta; Sí, Gli mando
   la ricetta; Sí, vi mando la ricetta.
4. Sí, mando Loro la lẹttera; Sí, Gli mando la
   lẹttera; Sí, vi mando la lẹttera.
5. Sí, Le do un bel voto; Sí, ti do un bel voto.
6. Sí, mando Loro l'assegno; Sí, Gli mando
   l'assegno; Sí, vi mando l'assegno.
7. Sí, Le scrivo presto; Sí, ti scrivo presto;
8. Sí, Le restituịsco i libri; Sí, ti restituịsco i libri.

19. 1. Noi *ci* andiạmo.
2. Pietro *ci* va.
3. Luịsa *ci* sale.
4. Io *ci* resto.
5. Loro *ci* vanno.
6. Marịa *ci* vive.

20. 1. Noi non ci andiạmo
2. Pietro non ci va.
3. Luịsa non ci sale.
4. Io non ci resto.
5. Loro non ci vanno.
6. Marịa non ci vive.

21. 1. Sí, *ci* andiạmo.
2. Sí, *ci* vado.
3. Sí, *ci* resto.

4. Sí, *ci* vado.
5. Sí, *ci* vado.
6. Sí, *ci* ritorno.

22. 1. No, non ci andiạmo.
2. No, non ci vado.
3. No, non ci resto.
4. No, non ci vado.
5. No, non ci vado.
6. No, non ci ritorno.

23. 1. C*i* credo.
2. Non *ci* vede.
3. C*i* vogliạmo riflẹttere. (Vogliạmo riflẹtterci.)
4. Non *ci* sẹntono.
5. Non *ci* credo.

24. 1. Ci credi?
2. Ci vuọle troppo tempo.
3. Non ci pọssono vedere.
4. Ti assicuro che non ho niẹnte a che farci.
5. Che ci pensi?
6. È necessạrio riflẹtterci.
7. Ci mettiạmo diẹci minuti per arrivare a casa.
8. Ci puọi vedere?
9. Tu non ci stai.
10. Mi piạce perché ci tengo.
11. Ho parlato con Mạrio e lui ci sta.
12. Ti ci vuọi mẹttere? (Vuọi mẹtterci?)
13. Voi ci andate sempre.
14. (Lei) non ci pensa piú.
15. Signore, Lei ci può andare (può andarci), ma io
    non ci sto.

25. 1. *Ne* parliạmo.
2. *Ne* vẹngono.
3. *Ne* cọmprano tre.
4. *Ne* abbiạmo vọglia.
5. *Ne* ha molte.
6. *Ne* è contento.
7. *Ne* mạngia.
8. *Ne* compra una dozzina.
9. Non *ne* ho vọglia.
10. *Ne* hai dụe.
11. *Ne* abbiạmo bisogno.
12. *Ne* hanno comprati solo diẹci.

26. 1. *Ne* ritorniạmo.
2. *Ne* do a Gino.
3. *Gli* offriạmo il bigliẹtto.
4. *Le* telẹfono.
5. Invịa *loro* il pacco.
6. Tu *ci* vai.
7. *Ci* rẹstano.

8. *Ne* ricęvono pochi.

9. *Le* parliạmo.

10. *Ne* torneranno domami.

27. 1. Marịa ce la manda.

2. Giovanni ve le dà.

3. Lui te li dice.

4. Loro me le insęgnano.

5. Tu ce lo porti.

6. Antọnio ve la presta.

7. Io te lo do.

28. 1. me lo

2. ce lo

3. ce le

4. ve li

5. te la

6. me le

7. ce li

8. me la

29. 1. Gliẹla prestịamo.

2. Gliẹli hai mandati.

3. Gliẹne ho inviạte.

4. Signora, Gliẹne ho dati due.

5. Gliẹle spedisci.

6. Professore, Gliẹlo riporto.

7. Gliel'ho regalata.

8. Gliel'ho spiegata.

9. Dottore, Gliel'ho confermata.

10. Gliẹne ha causati tanti.

30. 1. Li mandịamo loro; Gliẹli mandịamo.

2. Li ho regalati Loro; Gliẹli ho regalati.

3. Tu li darại loro; Tu gliẹli darại.

4. Il maẹstro lo dà loro; Il maẹstro gliẹlo dà.

5. Lo zịo li ha portati loro.; Lo zịo gliẹli ha portati.

6. La dịamo loro.; Gliẹla dịamo.

7. La compro loro.; Gliẹla compro.

8. Signora, Gliene ho data troppa.

9. Signore, ne darò Loro alcune.; Signore, Gliẹne darò alcune.

10. Ne ho dato loro.; Gliẹne ho dato.

11. Ịeri l'ho mandata loro.; Ịeri gliel'ho mandata.

12. Signori, li abbịamo spediti Loro.; Signori, Gliẹli abbịamo spediti.

31. 1. Zịo Tommaso, come sta (Lei) oggi ? (Come state [voi] oggi)?

2. Signora Lari, si è (s'è) svegliata tardi stamani?

3. Signorina Giardino, (Lei) va al ristorante oggi?

4. Ragazzi, voi gridate quando giocate!

5. Signori, dove lavọrano (Loro)?

6. Sono andati in vacanza un mese fa.

7. Ragazzino, come ti chiạmi?

8. Lui leggeva mentre lei scriveva.

9. Di chi sono questi romanzi, di Lentrịcchia o di Sorrentino?

10. Chi vuọle farlo? (Chi lo vuọle fare?) È fạcile!

11. Se solo studịassero di piú!

12. Anche noi sịamo andati al cịnema ịeri sera.

32. 1. Giọrgio, perché non le chiụdi?

2. L'abbịamo veduta.

3. Non li vedịamo da molti anni.

4. L'ho mandata a Teresa.

5. Adesso lo compro.

6. Tu li saluti.

33. 1. Sí, ne sono sicura.; No, non ne sono sicura.

2. Sí, lo credo.; No, non lo credo.

3. Sí, lo dubitịamo.; No, non Lo dubitịamo.

4. Lo sono anch'ịo.; Io non lo sono.

5. Sí, aiutạtemi!; Sí, mi aiụtino! No, non mi aiutate (non aiutạtemi)!; No, non mi aiụtino!

6. Sí, ci hai riconosciụti.; No, non ci hai riconosciụti.; Sí, ci ha riconosciụti.; No, non ci ha riconosciụti.

7. Sí, ci scrivịamo.; No, non ci scrivịamo.

8. Carlo (*any name*) mi telẹfona spesso; Nessuno mi telefona spesso.

9. Sí, ci stịamo.; No non ci stịamo.

10. Sí, ci andịamo soli.; No, non ci andịamo soli.

11. Sí, ci sono andata sempre.; No, non ci sono mai andata.

12. Sí, ci posso crẹdere.; Sí, posso crẹderci.; No, non ci posso crẹdere.; No, non posso crẹderci.

13. Ci metto un'ora.

14. No, ne ho pochi.

15. No, ne ho bisogno poco.

16. Luịsa (*any name*) me li dà.

34. 1. Luịgi me lo da,

2. Marịa la manda loro.; Marịa gliẹla manda.

3. Il maẹstro gliẹle insegna.

4. Gliẹla presto.

5. Luịsa ce li presta.

6. Antọnio ve la regala.

7. Lo do Lọro.; Gliẹlo do.

8. Te li invịano.

9. Li comprịamo loro.; Gliẹli comprịamo.

10. Gliẹli mando.

11. Gliẹla prẹstano.

12. Il mịo amico me le manda.

13. Io te ne do.

14. Loro le comprano loro.; Loro gliele comprano.
15. Voi ce le date.
16. Signore, il vicino Gliel'ha prestato.
17. Signorina, io Gliele regalo.
18. Signori, lui Glieli manda.
19. Giovanotti, quando me lo ridate?
20. Signore (m. s.), Gliel'ho portata.

35.
1. Roberto le porterà.
2. Rosa ce la mandò.
3. Gliel'ho dato.
4. Rispondiamo loro. Gli rispondiamo.
5. Loro me lo spiegarono.
6. Stefano ve li dà.
7. Glielo darò.
8. Me l'hai portata.
9. Non ti ascoltiamo (t'ascoltiamo).
10. Gliene hai portati due.
11. Signori, Carlo le porterà Loro. Signori, Carlo Gliele porterà.
12. Professore, non li abbiamo finiti.
13. Dottore, le ha mandate loro? Dottore, Gliele ha mandate?
14. Ragazzi, portatecele!
15. Signore, li regali loro. Signore, glieli regali!
16. Ascoltiamoli!
17. Diamone loro! Diamogliene!
18. Diamone loro! Diamogliene!
19. Professoressa, non ne dia troppi loro!; Professoressa, non gliene dia troppi!
20. Maria, per piacere, portaglieli!
21. Il presidente gliene confessa molte.
22. Ragazzi, ieri ve li ho dati.
23. Quante ne hanno regalate loro i nonni? Quante gliene hanno regalate i nonni?
24. Arturo ce ne ha raccontate tante!
25. Avremmo dovuto farne molte. Ne avremmo dovute fare molte.

36.
1. Me lo possono dare.
2. Te li voglio comprare.
3. Ce li preferiscono insegnare.
4. Ve le desideriamo regalare.
5. Gliela volevo dare.
6. Me lo volevano vendere.
7. Signore (m. s.), preferisco dirGlielo.
8. Signorine, vogliamo inviarGliele.

37.
1. Luisa può aiutarmi.
2. Roberto deve parlarti.
3. Io voglio vendervela.
4. Loro possono regalarceli.
5. Tu puoi mostrargliele.

6. Noi desideriamo dartene.
7. Signori, vogliamo regalarGlieli.
8. Signora, posso prestarGlielo.

38.
1. Glieli voglio regalare. Voglio regalarglieli.
2. Ve la vogliamo mostrare. Vogliamo mostrarvela.
3. Te lo posso portare. Posso portartelo.
4. Gliele preferisco inviare. Preferisco inviargliele.
5. Maria me la vuole regalare. Maria vuole regalarmela.
6. Ce la voleva cantare. Voleva cantarcela.
7. -Signora, io Gliele voglio regalare. -Signora, io voglio regalarGliele.
8. -Signori, Glielo possiamo riportare. -Signori, possiamo riportarGlielo.
9. -Signorina, Maria Gliela deve comunicare. -Signorina, Maria deve comunicarGliela.
10. -Signore (f. pl.), Paolo Gliele desidera dare. -Signore (f. pl.), Paolo desidera darGliele.

39.
1. Roberto ci stava parlando.
2. Lui le sta portando.
3. Voi lo stavate leggendo.
4. Tu la stai preparando.
5. Noi ti stavamo scrivendo.
6. Loro gli stanno telefonando.

40.
1. Sta invitandomi.
2. Stavano scrivendovi.
3. Stanno mandandocela.
4. Stavano leggendoglielo.
5. Stanno offrendotele.

41.
1. Antonio sta comprandoli.
   Antonio li sta comprando.
2. Io sto scrivendola.
   Io la sto scrivendo.
3. Loro stanno preparandolo.
   Loro lo stanno preparando.
4. Noi stiamo portandole.
   Noi le stiamo portando.
5. Tu stai leggendola.
   Tu la stai leggendo.
6. Voi state riportandoli.
   Voi li state riportando.
7. Luisa sta prendendolo.
   Luisa lo sta prendendo.
8. Io sto lavandole.
   Io le sto lavando.
9. Pietro sta salutandolo.
   Pietro lo sta salutando.
10. Il sarto sta cucendoli.
    Il sarto li sta cucendo.

42. 1. Non me lo dare!
2. Non le fate!
3. Non la portate!
4. Non ce li prestare!
5. Non glielo mostrare!
6. Non gliele comprare!
7. Non me la mandate!
8. Non ce lo dire!
9. Non me la dire!
10. Non gliele dite!

43. 1. Mandamela!
2. Scrivetegliele!
3. Prestamelo!
4. Diteceli!
5. Compratemela!
6. Faccelo!
7. Portamele!
8. Insegnacele!
9. Vendetemelo!
10. Mostrategliela!

44. 1. Non me lo dia!
2. Non ce le diano!
3. Non me la portino!
4. Non ce li scriva!
5. Non glielo presti!
6. Non gliele mostrino!
7. Non lo faccia!
8. Non le facciano!

45. 1. Me li prestino!
2. Gliela mostri!
3. Me le diano!
4. Ce lo dica!
5. Gliele insegnino!
6. Me la scriva!
7. Glielo mandino!
8. Ce li legga!

46. 1. Compriamola!
2. Alziamoci!
3. Facciamolo!
4. Diciamole!
5. Sediamoci!
6. Mandiamoli!

47. 1. Sí, sediamoci!
No, non ci sediamo!
2. Sí, vestiamoci!
No, non ci vestiamo!
3. Sí, mettiamoci il cappello!
No, non ci mettiamo il cappello!

4. Sí, prepariamoci!
No, non ci prepariamo!
5. Sí, laviamoci le mani!
No, non ci laviamo le mani!
6. Sí, alziamoci!
No, non ci alziamo!

48. 1. mi, -e
2. mi, -ono
3. ti, -e
4. ti, -ono
5. gli, -a
6. gli, -anno
7. le, -e
8. ci, -ano
9. ci, -a
10. vi, -e
11. vi, -ono
12. Le, -a

49. 1. Sí, ci piace ballare.
2. Sí, mi occorre la macchina.
3. Sí, ci occorrono quei libri.
4. Sí, a Maria le fa male il ginocchio.
5. Sí, vi bastano questi soldi.
6. Sí, a Sandro gli duole la spalla.
7. Sí, quei ragazzi ci sembrano tristi.
8. Sí, questo vestito mi pare nuovo.
9. Sí, ci fanno male i denti.
10. Sí, mi occorre qualcosa.

50. 1. Ci piace la musica.
2. Gli piacciono le lingue.
3. Piace loro il progetto.
4. Ti piacciono i programmi.
5. Le piace l'arte moderna.
6. Piacciono Loro i concerti.
7. Ci piace l'opera.
8. Mi piace viaggiare.

51. 1. mi
2. ci
3. ti
4. vi
5. si
6. si
7. ti
8. si
9. mi
10. si

52. 1. lui
2. loro

3. lei
4. me
5. te
6. voi
7. lui
8. noi
9. lei
10. Loro

53. 1. me
2. lui
3. loro
4. noi
5. voi
6. lei
7. lui
8. loro

54. 1. nessun (alcun)
2. ogni
3. qualche
4. qualsiasi (qualunque)
5. nessun
6. Ogni
7. Alcuni
8. Alcune

55. 1. Questa è la mia.
2. La tua è piú veloce.
3. Abbiamo comprato i nostri.
4. Hanno ricevuto il loro.
5. Questi sono i miei.
6. Le nostre vivono presso di te.
7. Sto preparando la mia.
8. Dammi il tuo!
9. I miei vivono in Italia.
10. Hai portato i tuoi e i suoi.
11. Il nostro aspetta qui vicino.
12. La vostra è molto grande.
13. Ci piacciono il Suo e i Suoi.
14. Le mie arrivano domani.
15. Non voglio né la tua né la sua.

56. 1. quelli
2. questa
3. quello
4. queste
5. questi

57. 1. che
2. che
3. che
4. che

5. che
6. che
7. che
8. che

58. 1. su cui
2. di cui
3. per cui
4. a cui (cui)
5. con cui
6. da cui
7. in cui

59. 1. Coloro che arrivano sono i miei amici.
2. Colui che parla è mio zio.
3. Chi arriva e chi parte.
4. Coloro che ascoltano sono i miei studenti.
5. Colui che si siede è Antonio e colui che si alza è Marco.
6. Colei che canta è la mia amica.

60. 1. Ciò che (Quel che) dice è la verità.
2. Ciò che vogliamo è piú tempo.
3. Ciò che leggi è un ottimo romanzo.
4. Ciò che desidera comprare è un'automobile.
5. Ciò che mi fa paura è l'ignoranza.
6. Ciò che vogliono fare è un lungo viaggio.
7. Ciò che suggerite è un'ottima idea.
8. Ciò che vorrei avere è un po' di pace.

61. 1. le cui
2. il cui
3. la cui
4. i cui

62. 1. Eccoveli!
2. Eccolo!
3. EccoGliele! Eccole Loro!
4. Eccotene!
5. Eccomi!
6. Eccole!
7. Eccoli!
8. EccoGliela!
9. Eccoci!
10. Eccone!
11. EccoGliene! Eccone Loro!
12. EccoGlielo!
13. Eccoveli!
14. Eccomene!
15. Eccocele!

63. 1. Signore, eccoLe la posta!
2. Signora, eccoGlieli!
3. Rosetta, eccotelo!

    4. Tito e Marcello, eccovele!

    5. Eccoglieli!

    6. Signori, eccoGliela! Eccola Loro!

64. 1. Loro studiano ogni giorno.

    2. Tu le leggi.

    3. Le diamo il regalo.

    4. Loro ci scrivono.

    5. Ci saliamo.

    6. Ne comprate.

    7. Ne ha due.

    8. Ti piacciono gli sport.

65. 1. che

    2. di cui

    3. Chi (Colui che)

    4. Ciò che (Quel che)

    5. eccomi

    6. niente

66. 1. ci

    2. Ne

    3. io

    4. te

    5. Gli

    6. Lei

    7. Ci

    8. mi

    9. vi

    10. me

Chapter 10

1. 1. dalla

    2. nello studio

    3. delle

    4. nell'armadio

    5. sugli

    6. per i (*rare*: pei)

    7. con i. (also: coi)

    8. dal

    9. dai

    10. dalla

    11. dell'

    12. Nei

    13. per il

    14. dello, sul

    15. con la

    16. alla, dei

2. 1. in

    2. a, in

    3. a

    4. a

    5. a

    6. in, negli

    7. in

    8. a, in, a

    9. in

    10. a

3. 1. I turisti sono in Sicilia.

    2. Io vado a scuola a piedi.

    3. La ragazza abita a Firenze.

    4. Le studentesse studiano in biblioteca.

    5. Andate voi in Spagna ogni anno?

    6. Mio padre abita a Milano.

    7. Giovanna va in città in bicicletta.

    8. Gl'invitati sono in salotto.

    9. La zia di Laura è in chiesa.

    10. I giovani vogliono andare nel Messico.

4. 1. D'

    2. della

    3. Da

    4. dal

    5. dei, dal

    6. Da

    7. Da

    8. d'

    9. di

    10. di

    11. di

    12. di

    13. da

    14. da

    15. da

    16. da

    17. da

    18. dai

    19. da

    20. da

5. 1. Abbiamo molto da mangiare.

    2. Hanno poco da vendere.

    3. Non ho niente da fare.

    4. Hai qualcosa da bere?

    5. Non avete nulla da discutere?

    6. Avete troppo da leggere.

6. 1. (none)

    2. di

    3. a

    4. (none)

    5. di

    6. (none)

    7. a

    8. a

9. di

10. di

11. (none)

12. di

13. (none)

14. (none)

15. a

16. a

17. (none)

18. di

19. di

20. a

7. 1. in

2. in

3. in

4. a

5. a, da

6. a, di

7. in, di

8. della

9. in, in, da

10. di

11. di

12. di, di

13. della

14. da

15. da

16. da

17. da

18. da

19. da

20. da

21. di

22. da

23. da

24. da

25. da

8. 1. Franco è degli Stati Uniti.

2. Siamo andati in città da noi.

3. Abbiamo molto da fare oggi.

4. Mi occorre un nuovo spazzolino da denti.

5. Lei ha una casa da vendere.

6. C'è qualcosa da mangiare?

7. Da bambino (bambina) mi piaceva andare in montagna.

8. Non c'è un momento da perdere.

9. Da giovane, ero molto bello.

10. In autunno, andavamo in campagna in treno.

9. 1. a

2. a

3. (none)

4. a

5. di

6. a

7. (none)

8. di

9. di

10. a

11. (none)

12. di

13. di

14. a

15. (none)

Chapter 11

1. 1. hanno

2. abbiamo

3. ha

4. ha

5. avete

6. hai

7. hanno

8. ho

2. 1. Ho fame.

2. Hai sonno?

3. Luisa ha freddo.

4. Abbiamo sete.

5. 1 bambini hanno voglia di uscire.

6. Avete fame.

7. Ho vergogna di parlare.

8. Ha mal di testa.

9. Ho mal di denti.

10. Hai mal di gola?

3. 1. Le devo

2. Hanno dovuto aspettare

3. Siete stati

4. Devono essere; (saranno)

5. Dovresti finire di

6. Dovranno arrivare

7. Deve essere

8. È stata

4. 1. hanno voluto

2. non avete voluto

3. (Lei) dovrebbe

4. non siamo potuti; Non abbiamo potuto

5. non so suonare

6. l'ho saputo

7. potrebbero essere

8. doveva preparare

5. 1. Non hanno voluto farlo.
2. L'abbiamo saputo alcune ore fa.
3. È voluta venire presto.
4. Sa suonare la chitarra.
5. Non saprei ripeterlo.
6. Hanno potuto convincermi.
7. Avrebbero potuto leggerlo.
8. Avreste dovuto studiare di piú.
9. Dovrebbe telefonare.
10. Doveva partire con noi.
11. Le dobbiamo dieci dollari.
12. Hanno dovuto finire gli esami.
13. Avrei potuto aiutarli.
14. Deve riportate i libri in biblioteca.
15. Devono essere malati. (Saranno malati.)

6. 1. fa bel tempo
2. farà cattivo (brutto) tempo
3. fa freddo
4. fa caldo
5. ha fatto paura
6. farà tardi
7. faremo cena
8. abbiamo fatto una partita
9. fate attenzione
10. hai fatto la prima colazione

7. 1. giocate
2. suoni
3. giocano
4. suonare (sonare)
5. gioca
6. giocare
7. suona
8. giocano

8. 1. a
2. dell'
3. ai

4. di, dei
5. a
6. alla, alle

9. 1. servirà
2. si servono
3. servirti di
4. serve
5. si serve da

10. 1. sono tornati (-e) (sono ritornati (-e))
2. riporti
3. restituita
4. torneranno (ritorneranno)
5. restituisco

11. 1. hanno fame
2. ha ragione
3. Ho sete
4. ha freddo
5. devo
6. giocare, suonare
7. fare una domanda
8. fare presto

12. 1. Oggi non possono andare a scuola perché hanno mal di gola.
2. Ho molta fame; vorrei comprare un panino.
3. Giorgio, ti devo la mia gratitudine.
4. Avremmo dovuto vedere i nostri nonni la settimana scorsa.
5. Hanno potuto spedire il pacco due ore fa.
6. Mario non ha voluto comprare i biglietti per la partita.
7. Io dovevo giocare a carte con lui.
8. Vorremmo fare una passeggiata stasera.
9. Maria suona il piano e la chitarra.
10. Adesso che sono lontano(-a) dalla mia città, penso ai miei amici (alle mie amiche).

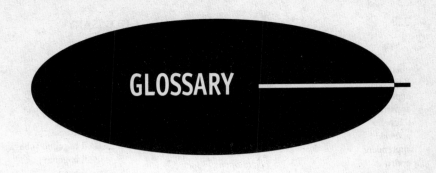

GLOSSARY

GLOSSARY: ITALIAN – ENGLISH
GLOSSARIO: ITALIANO – INGLESE

A

abbastanza	*enough*
abbracciarsi	*to hug one another*
abitare	*to live*
l'abito	*suit*
acerbo	*sour, unripe*
l'accaduto	*event, fact*
accendere	*to light up, to turn on (the radio, the light, etc.)*
l'accento	*accent*
l'accento acuto	*acute accent*
l'accento grafico	*written accent*
l'accento grave	*grave accent*
l'accento tonico	*stress accent*
accludere	*to enclose*
accogliere	*to welcome*
l'acconto	*down payment*
accorgersi (di)	*to notice*
accusare ricevuta	*to acknowledge receipt*
l'acquirente	*buyer*
l'acqua	*water*
l'acqua minerale	*mineral water*
adesso	*now*
l'addetto alla vendita	*salesperson*
addormentarsi	*to fall asleep*
l'aereo	*airplane*
afoso	*sultry*
l'affare	*affair, event*
gli affari	*business*
affinché	*in order that*
l'affittacamere	*landlord*
affittare	*to rent*
affollato	*crowded*
l'affrancatura	*postage*
affrettarsi	*to hurry up*

l'agente pubblicitario	*advertising agent*
l'agenzia pubblicitaria	*publicity agency*
agghiacciare	*to freeze*
aggiustare	*to fix*
aiutare	*to help*
aiutarsi	*to help one another*
l'albergo	*hotel*
l'albero	*tree*
l'altoparlante	*loudspeaker*
l'alunno	*pupil*
allargare	*to widen*
l'allegato	*enclosure*
allegro	*happy*
allungare	*to lengthen*
alto	*tall, high*
altrove	*elsewhere*
l'altro ieri	*two days ago*
alzare	*to raise*
alzarsi	*to get up*
amare	*to love*
ammettere	*to admit*
l'amica	*friend*
l'amico	*friend*
l'amore	*love*
ampio, ampia, ampi, ampie	*wide*
ancora	*still*
(non)ancora	*not yet*
andare	*to go*
anteriore	*previous*
antico	*ancient*
l'anno	*year*
l'anno scorso	*last year*
annoiarsi	*to get bored, to bore one another*
anziché	*instead*

aperto	open
l'apricastole	can opener
apparire	to appear
appartenere	to belong
l'appello	roll call
appena	as soon as
apprendere	to learn
aprire	to open
arancione (inv.)	orange
l'arcivescovo	archbishop
l'arcobaleno	rainbow
l'armadio	closet
arrabbiarsi	to get mad
arrischiare	to risk
ascoltare	to listen
aspettare	to wait
assaggiare	to taste
l'assegno	check
astenersi di	to abstain from
attaccare	to attack, to glue
attaccare il ricevitore	to hang up the telephone
attendere un momento	to wait a moment
(un minuto, un attimo)	
attestare	to testify
l'attivo	assets
attraversare	to cross
anche	also; too
l'aula	classroom
l'aumento	increase
augurarsi di	to hope to
l'auto (le auto)	car
l'autoservizio	car service
l'autore	author (m.)
l'autrice	author (f.)
l'autunno	fall
avere	to have
avere … anni	to be … years old
avere bisogno di	to need
avere caldo	to be hot (said of a person)
avere fame	to be hungry
avere freddo	to be cold
avere fretta	to be in a hurry
avere l'aria di	to seem
avere luogo	to take place
avere mal di gola	to have a sore throat
avere mal di pancia	to have a stomach ache
avere mal di testa	to have a headache
avere paura (di)	to be afraid (of)
avere ragione	to be right
avere sete	to be thirsty
avere sonno	to be sleepy
avere torto	to be wrong
avere vergogna (di)	to be ashamed (of)
avere voglia (di)	to feel like (doing something)
avvertire di	to warn, to caution
avvenire	to happen
l'avventora (le avventore)	customer (f.)
l'avventore (gli avventori)	customer (m.)
avvocatessa	attorney (f.)
l'avvocato	attorney
azzurro	blue

B

il babbo	dad
il bacio	kiss
baciarsi	to kiss one another
badare a	to take care of
il bagaglio (i bagagli)	luggage
il bagnino	lifeguard
il bagno	bath
ballare	to dance
il bambino	baby, child
la banca (le banche)	bank
la banconota	currency
il banco (i banchi)	bench
il bancone	counter
la bandiera	flag
la barca (le barche)	boat
basilare	basic
basilarmente	basically
basso	low, short
basta	enough
bastare	to be enough
battere	to beat, to hit
il baule	trunk
bello, -a, -i, -e	handsome; beautiful
bene	well
beneficiario, beneficiari; beneficiaria, -e	beneficiary
beni di consumo	consumer goods
il benvenuto	welcome
benché	although
bere	to drink
la bevanda	drink
bianco, bianchi; bianca, bianche	white
la bibita	drink
la biblioteca	library
il bicchiere	glass
bigio, bigi; bigia, bigie	grayish
il biglietto	ticket
il bilancio, i bilanci (saldo)	balance
il bimbo	child
biondo	blond
bisognare	to need
il boccaporto	hatch
bollire	to boil
bonario, bonari; bonaria, bonarie	good-natured
il bosco, i boschi	woods
il braccio, le braccia; i bracci	arm
bravo	good, able
il brindisi, i brindisi	cheer
bruciarsi	to burn oneself
brutto	ugly
il buco (i buchi)	whole
la bugia (le bugie)	lie
buongiorno (buon giorno)	good morning
bussare	to knock
buono, -a, -i, -, -e	good
la busta	envelope

C

la cabina telefonica	phone booth
cadere	to fall

il caffè	coffee
caffé	bar, caffé
il calciatore	soccer player
il caldo	heat
caldo	hot
la calza	sock
cambiare	to change
la camera da letto	bedroom
il cameriere	waiter
la camicia (le camicie)	shirt
il camion (i camion)	truck
commettere	to commit
il cammino	path
la campagna	countryside
il campanello	bell
il campo	field
cancellare	to erase
il cane	dog
condurre	to drive, to conduct
il canottaggio	canoeing
la carne	meat
il/la cantante (i/le cantanti)	singer
cantare	to sing
il canto	song
la canzone	song
capace	able
il capello	hair
capirci	to understand something about it
capire	to understand
il cappello	hat
il cappotto	overcoat
il capofila (i capifila)	head of a line
il capogiro	dizziness
il capoluogo (i capoluoghi)	capital of province
il caporeparto (i capireparto)	section head
il capostazione (i capistazione)	station master
il caposquadra (i capisquadra)	team captain
la caramella	candy
il carbone (i carboni)	coal
il carico (i carichi)	load
carico (-a, -chi, -che)	loaded
carino	cute
la carità	charity
caro	dear
la carta	paper, card
la carta telefonica (scheda telefonica, scheda magnetica)	phone card
la cartolina	card
la casa	house, home
il casco	helmet
il caso	case
la cassa	cash register
la cassaforte	safe
il cassetto	drawer
cattivo	bad, mean
i ceci	garbanzos
cedere	to give in
la cena	supper
certe volte	sometimes
cessare (di)	to stop
centesimo (-a, -i, -e)	hundredth
(un) centinaio (centinaia)	about one hundred
cento	one hundred
il/la centralinista	telephone operator
il centralino	telephone switchboard
il centro	downtown, center
cercare	to search for, to look for
chi	one who, who, whom
chiamare	to call
chiamarsi	to be named, to call one another
chiaro (-a, -i, -e)	clear
la chiave (le chiavi)	key
chiedere	to ask
la chiesa	church
il chilo	kilo
la chimica	chemistry
il chirurgo	surgeon
Chissà!	Who knows!
chiudere	to close
chiunque	whoever
chiuso	closed
ciascuno	each
il cibo	food
il cielo	sky
il ciglio (le ciglia; i cigli)	eyelash, border
la cinepresa	movie camera
il Cinquecento	sixteenth century
cinquantesimo (-a, -i, -e)	fiftieth
ciò	that which
ciò che	what
cioè	that is
la cipolla	onion
il circolo	club
la città (le città)	city
la civiltà (le civiltà)	civilization
il/la cliente(i/le clienti)	client, customer
il clima	climate
cogliere	to gather, to pick
il cognome	surname
colei che	she who
coloro che	those who
il colpo	blow
(di colpo)	suddenly
colui che	he who
la collana	necklace
il/la collega	colleague
come mai	how come?
come no!	of course
cominciare (incominciare)	to begin
il comitato	committee
il comò	chest of drawers
comodo (-a, -i, -e)	comfortable
la compagnia	company
la compagnia di assicurazioni	insurance company
compiacere	to gratify, to please
la commedia	play, comedy
il commerciante al minuto	retailer
commissionare	to place an order
il compagno	mate, partner
comparire	to appear, to cut a good figure
il compleanno	birthday
il componimento	composition
comporre	to compose

comprare	to buy	a cui	to whom, to which
il concessionario	franchised dealer	il cuore	heart
il/la concorrente (i/le concorrenti)	competitor	con cui	with whom, with which
il concorso	competition	di cui	of whom, of which
condannare	to condemn	da cui	from whom, from which
le condizioni di pagamento	terms of payment	in cui	in whom, in which
la conferenza	meeting, conference	per cui	for whom, for which
il conferenziere	lecturer	su cui	on whom, on which
confermare	to confirm		
confondere	to confuse		
conglomerare	to conglomerate	**D**	
la colazione	breakfast, lunch	dannoso (-a, -i, -e)	harmful
il coltello	knife	dappertutto	all over
il condizionale	conditional	dare	to give
il congiuntivo	subjunctive	la data	date (as in calendar)
la/il coniuge (le/i coniugi)	spouse	decadere	to decline
conoscere, sapere	to know	decimo (-a, -i, -e)	tenth
consentire	to agree, to allow, to permit	decidere di	to decide to
consigliare di	to advise	decidersi	to make up one's mind
il consiglio	advice	dedicarsi	to devote oneself
il consiglio dei ministri	council of ministers	dedurre	to deduce
consolarsi di	to take comfort	la delusione (le delusioni)	disappointment
il/la consorte (i/le consorti)	spouse	il dente	tooth
contenere	to contain	il/la dentista; i dentisti; le dentiste	dentist
il conto	bill, check	dentro	inside
contrarre	to contract	derivare	to derive
il contratto di manutenzione	maintenance contract	il desiderio	desire, wish
il contratto di vendita	contract sale	a destra	to the right
contravvenire	to contravene	la destra	right
il controsenso	nonsense	determinare di	to determine to
convenire	to convene	detrarre	to detract
la coperta	bedspread	il dettaglio	detail
la copertina	cover	il dí, il giorno, la giornata	day
la coppa	goblet	la dichiarazione	declaration
la coppa del mondo	World Cup	diciannovesimo	nineteenth
la coppia	couple	diciassettesimo	seventeenth
coprire	to cover	diciottesimo	eighteenth
coricarsi	to go to bed	differire	to differ, to be different
correggere	to correct	difficile	difficult
correntemente	currently, fluently	la diga	dam
correre	to run	dimagrire	to lose weight
il corridoio (i corridoi)	hall	dimenticare	to forget
per cortesia	please	dimenticarsi	to forget, to forget one another
cosa (che, che, cosa)	what		
la cosa	thing	dipingere	to paint
cosí	so	il dipinto	painting
cosí ... come	as ... as ...	diplomarsi	to get a diploma
costare	to cost	dire	to say
costoso	expensive	il discorso	speech (as in to give a speech)
costringere	to compel, to force	disporre	to dispose
costruire	to build	discutere	to discuss
la cravatta	tie	il dio (gli dèi)	god
la credenza	sideboard	disdire	to retract
credere	to believe	disfare	to undo
crederci	to believe in something	distrarre	to distract
il credito	credit	distribuzione (vendita)	marketing
crescere	to grow	distribuire	to distribute
cucire	to sew	distrutto	destroyed
cucinare	to cook	il dito	finger
la cugina	cousin	la ditta	company (business)
il cugino	cousin	il dittongo	diphthong
cui	whom, which	il divano	sofa, couch

divagare	*to amuse*	la famiglia	*family*
divenire	*to become*	fantasioso	*fantastic*
diventare	*to become*	fantasticare di	*to imagine to*
divertente	*fun*	la farina	*flour*
divertirsi	*to have fun, to enjoy oneself*	fare	*to do, to make*
divulgare	*to divulge*	fare:	
il dizionario	*dictionary*	fa caldo	*it's hot*
la doccia, le docce	*shower*	fa freddo	*it's cold*
dodicesimo (-a, -i, -e)	*twelfth*	fa bel tempo	*the weather is good*
il dolore	*pain*	fa cattivo tempo	*the weather is bad*
la domanda	*question*	fa brutto tempo	*the weather is bad*
domani	*tomorrow*	fare attenzione (a)	*to pay attention (to)*
domenica, le domeniche	*Sunday*	fare cena	*to have supper*
il dono (il regalo)	*gift*	farsi la barba	*to shave*
la donna	*woman*	fare colazione	*to have lunch*
dopo	*after*	farsi la doccia	*to take a shower*
doppio	*double*	fare domanda	*to apply*
dormire	*to sleep*	fare paura (a)	*to frighten (someone)*
il dottore	*doctor*	fare presto	*to hurry up*
la dottoressa	*doctor*	fare una domanda	*to ask a question*
dove	*where*	fare un regalo	*to give a gift*
dovere	*to have to (must)*	fare un viaggio	*to take a trip*
dovunque	*wherever*	fare una visita	*to visit*
la dozzina	*dozen*	farsi il bagno	*to take a bath, to*
il Duecento	*Thirteenth Century*		*bathe oneself*
il dubbio	*doubt*	fare la prima colazione	*to have breakfast*
dunque, allora	*then*	fate le valige	*to pack (a suitcase, suitcases)*
duro (-a, -i, -e)	*hard*	fare male (a)	*to hurt (someone)*
		farsi male	*to hurt oneself, to get hurt*
E		fare tardi	*to be late*
		fare torto	*to do wrong*
è (essere)	*is*	fare una passeggiata	*to take a walk*
e	*and*	il fatto	*fact*
ecco	*here is, here are, there is,*	il fattorino	*messenger, delivery boy*
	there are	il fazzoletto	*kerchief*
Eccome!	*And how!*	la febbre	*fever*
l'edificio	*building*	felice, contento	*happy*
l'editrice	*publishing house*	feroce	*fierce, ferocious*
educato	*polite*	fermare	*to stop*
egli (lui)	*he*	fermarsi	*to stop (oneself)*
eleggere	*to elect*	fermo	*still, motionless*
ella (lei)	*she*	il Ferragosto	*August 15th holiday*
entrarci	*to have something to do with it*	il ferro	*iron*
l'entrata	*entrance*	il ferro da stiro	*iron (for clothes)*
egregio	*distinguished (form of address)*	ferrovia	*railroad*
eseguire un ordine	*to carry out an order*	ferroviario (-a, ferroviari, -e)	*(about the) railroad*
esigere	*to demand*	la festa	*feast*
esitare	*to hesitate*	la fetta	*slice*
esporre	*to expose, to show*	il fiato	*breath*
essa (lei)	*she*	fidanzarsi	*to get engaged*
essere	*to be*	fidarsi (di)	*to trust*
l'estate	*summer*	la fiducia	*confidence*
estrarre	*to extract*	la figlia (figlie)	*daughter*
estivo	*summer (adj.)*	il figlio (figli)	*son*
l'euro (gli euro)	*euro*	la fila	*row, file, line*
		il filo	*thread*
		la fine	*end*
F		la finestra	*window*
		finché	*till*
la fabbrica (le fabbriche)	*factory*	fingere	*to pretend, to feign*
falciare	*to cut, to mow (the grass)*	finire	*to finish, to end*
il fallimento (la bancarotta)	*bankruptcy*	il fiore	*flower*
la fame	*hunger*		

firmare	*to sign*
il fiume	*river*
flebile	*feeble*
la foglia	*leaf*
la folla	*crowd*
il fonema (i fonemi)	*phoneme*
il fondo	*bottom*
la forchetta	*fork*
la foresta	*forest*
il formaggio, i formaggi	*cheese*
formare	*to form*
formare il numero	*to dial the number*
fornito	*furnished*
il fornitore	*supplier*
forte	*strong*
forzare	*to force*
il francobollo	*stamp*
il fratello	*brother*
il Frate	*Brother (for a monk)*
freddo	*cold*
fresco	*cool, fresh*
la fretta	*hurry, haste*
frequentare	*to frequent*
frugare	*to rummage*
fuggire	*to flee*
fumare	*to smoke*
il fumo	*smoke*
funzionare	*to function*
il fuoco, i fuochi	*fire*
fuori	*outside*

G

la garanzia	*guarantee*
Gentilissimo	*Kindest, Most Kind (form of address)*
il ghiaccio, i ghiacci	*ice*
già	*already*
il ginocchio, le ginocchia; i ginocchi	*knee*
il giornale, -i	*newspaper*
il/la giornalista (i giornalisti, le giornaliste)	*journalist*
la giornata	*day*
il giorno, il dí (i dí), la giornata	*day*
giovane	*young*
il giovane	*young man*
la giovane	*young woman*
glabro (liscio)	*smooth*
la gola	*throat*
la gomma	*tire*
grandissimo	*very big*
il grattacielo	*skyscraper*
grazie	*thanks*
il grido	*cry*
grigio	*grey*
il grossista	*wholesaler*
grosso	*large, thick*
il guardasigilli	*minister of justice*
la guida telefonica	*telephone (phone)book*
guidare	*to drive*
gustoso	*tasty*

H

ho (io)	*I have*
hai (tu)	*you have*
ha (lui/lei)	*it/he/she has*
ha (Lei)	*you (formal s.) have*
hanno (loro)	*they have*
hanno (Loro)	*you (formal pl.) have*

I

lo iato (gli iati)	*hiatus*
ieri	*yesterday*
Illustre	*Illustrious (form of address)*
Illustrissimo	*Most Distinguished (form of address)*
l'imballaggio per esportazione	*export packing*
immagazzinare	*to store, to stock*
impaccare, impacchettare	*to pack*
l'importatore, l'importatrice (gli/gl'importatori, le importatrici)	*importer*
l'indagine del mercato	*market survey*
l'indirizzo	*address*
l'inizio (gli/gl'inizi)	*beginning*
l'inserzione	*ad, advertisement*
l'italiano degli affari	*business Italian*
l'ipoteca	*mortgage*
l'inverno	*winter*

L

largo	*wide*
lasciare	*to leave (behind)*
il latte	*milk*
laurearsi	*to graduate (from college)*
la lavagna	*blackboard*
legare	*to tie*
leggere	*to read*
lei (ella, essa)	*she*
il lenzuolo, i lenzuoli; le lenzuola	*sheet*
lento	*slow*
la lettera pubblicitaria	*promotional letter*
il libro	*book*
il libro maestro	*ledger*
la linea libera	*dial tone*
la linea occupata	*busy signal*
la lineetta	*dash*
liscio (liscia, lisci, lisce), glabro	*smooth*
il listino dei prezzi	*price list*
loro (essi, esse)	*they*
luglio	*July*
lui(egli)	*he*

M

ma	*but*
la macchina (l'auto; l'automobile), (le auto; le automobili)	*car*
la maestra	*teacher*
il maestro	*teacher*
Magari!	*If it were only so!*
maggio	*May*
il/la maggiore	*eldest*

mai	*never*
maiuscolo	*upper case, capital*
la maglia	*sweater*
il maglione	*sweater*
la mancia	*tip (money)*
mandare	*to send*
la mano (le mani)	*hand*
manutenzione	*maintenance*
il marchio registrato	*registered trade mark*
il mare	*sea*
marrone (inv.)	*brown*
la mattina, il mattino	*morning*
il medico, i medici	*doctor*
meglio (adv.)	*better*
il meglio (adv.)	*best*
mentre	*while*
il mercato	*market*
la merce	*merchandise*
la merce difettosa	*defective goods*
mercoledí	*Wednesday*
meridionale (-i)	*southern*
mettere	*to put, to place*
la mezzanotte	*midnight*
mezzo, -a	*half*
il mezzogiorno	*noon*
mi	*me, to me*
mia (mie)	*my*
il miglio (le miglia)	*mile*
milionesimo, -a, -i, -e	*millionth*
millesimo, -a, -i, -e	*thousandth*
il minerale	*mineral*
la minestra	*soup*
il ministro	*minister (government)*
il/la minore, i/le minori	*minor*
mio (miei), mia, (mie)	*my*
modico, -a, -i, -e	*reasonable*
molto, -a, -i, -e	*a lot of (pl. many)*
mondiale, -i	*world (adj.)*
il mondo	*world*
la moto (le moto;	*bike, motorcycle*
from motocicletta)	
il motorino	*motor bike*
muoversi	*to move*
il muro	*wall*

N

nascere	*to be born*
nemmeno (neanche, neppure)	*not even*
né ... né	*neither... nor*
il negozio	*store*
nessuno	*no one*
niente (nulla)	*nothing*
il/la nipote, i/le nipoti	*nephew / niece*
il/la nipote, i/le nipoti	*grandson / granddaughter*
noleggiare	*to rent (a car, a tuxedo, etc.)*
non affatto, non ... affatto	*not at all*
non ancora, non ... ancora	*not yet*
non ... mai, mai	*never*
non piu, non ... piú	*no longer*
nonostante	*even though*
novantesimo, -a, -i, -e	*ninetieth*

il Novecento	*Twentieth Century*
il numero interno	*extension number*
il numero telefonico	*telephone number*
nuotare	*to swim*
il nuoto	*swimming*

O

obbligare	*to force, to oblige*
l'obbligo (gli obblighi)	*duty*
l'occasione	*opportunity*
l'occhio (pl. gli occhi)	*eye*
occidentale (-i)	*western*
occorrere	*to be necessary, to be lacking*
occuparsi (di)	*to attend to*
ogni	*every (m. & f. s.)*
ogni tanto	*once in a while*
l'onomatopea (-eia)	*onomatopoeia*
onorevole	*honorable (member of parliament; Your Honor/ His Honor)*
l'ora	*hour*
ora, adesso	*now*
l'orario	*schedule, time, hour*
l'orecchio (gli orecchi, le orecchie)	*ear*
ottantesimo, -a, -i, -e	*eightieth*
l'Ottocento	*Nineteenth Century*
ovunque, dovunque	*everywhere, wherever*

P

il padre	*father*
la padrona	*boss, owner*
il padrone	*boss, owner*
il paese, i paesi	*town, country*
il pagamento	*payment*
il pagamento alla consegna	*cash on delivery (COD)*
pagare	*to pay*
il palazzo delle Poste	*main post office*
il parabrezza	*windshield*
parcheggiare	*to park*
il/la parente, i/le parenti	*relative*
parere	*to seem*
la parete	*wall (of a room)*
parlare	*to speak*
la parola	*word*
partire	*to leave*
passare la linea	*to put one through (a phone call)*
la patente di guida	*driver's license*
peggio (adv.)	*worse (adv.)*
il peggio (adv.)	*the worst (adv.)*
passeggiare	*to stroll*
pensare	*to think*
la percentuale	*percentage*
perché	*why, because*
perdere	*to lose*
pesare	*to weigh*
il peso lordo	*gross weight*
il peso netto	*net weight*
piacere	*to like*

(per) piacere (per cortesia, per favore)	*please*	quasi	*almost*
il piano	*floor (1st, etc.)*	il Quattrocento	*Fifteenth Century*
il piano	*piano (instr.)*	quel che	*what, that which*
piano	*slow, low (in sound)*	quello	*that, that one*
piccolo	*small*	questo, -a, -i, -e	*this, this one*
(a) piedi	*on foot*	quindi	*therefore*
pieno, -a, -i, -e	*full*	quotidianamente	*daily*
piovere	*to rain*		
il pittore (i pittori)	*painter (m.)*	**R**	
la pittrice (le pittrici)	*painter (f.)*	raccogliere	*to collect, to pick up*
piú	*more*	racconciare	*to mend*
piú di, piú … di	*more than*	raccontare	*to tell a story*
un po'	*a little*	racconto	*tale*
poco fa	*a little while ago*	radersi	*to shave (oneself)*
la polizza di assicurazioni	*insurance policy*	il raffreddore	*cold, (n.)*
il pomeriggio	*afternoon*	la ragazza	*girl*
la poltrona	*easy chair*	il ragazzo	*boy*
porgere	*to extend*	raggiungere	*to reach*
porre	*to put*	la ragioniera	*accountant (f.)*
portare	*to bring, to take*	il ragioniere	*accountant (m.)*
il portabandiera	*flag bearer*	il reclamo	*claim*
il portafoglio	*wallet*	regalare	*to give as a gift*
il portalettere	*letter carrier*	il regalo, il dono	*gift*
la posta	*mail*	reggere	*to sustain*
posto che	*supposing that*	restare in linea	*to hold on (phone)*
potere	*to can, to be able*	restituire	*to give back, to return*
povero	*poor*	la rete di distribuzione	*distribution network*
pranzare	*to dine*	ricevere	*to receive*
il prato	*lawn, meadow*	la ricevuta	*receipt*
predire	*to foretell*	la richiesta	*demand*
prendere	*to take, to have*	ricordare	*to remember*
la prenotazione	*reservations*	ridere (ridere a crepapelle)	*to laugh (to roar with laughter)*
presso	*near*	rimettere	*to remit*
prestare	*to borrow, to loan*	riportare	*to carry forward (the balance)*
presto	*early, quickly*	riportare	*to give back, to return (something)*
il prezzo	*price*		
il prezzo al minuto	*retail price*	riposare (riposarsi)	*to relax, to rest*
il preventivo di spesa	*estimate*	rifare	*to redo, to remake*
prima	*before, first (adv.)*	la rimessa (il garage)	*garage*
la primavera	*spring*	ringraziare (di)	*to thank*
primo (-a, -i, -e)	*first*	ripetutamente	*repeatedly*
la produzione in serie	*mass production*	il risarcimento danni	*compensation*
Pronto, chi parla?	*Hello, who's speaking?*	risarcire	*to compensate*
i proventi (le/ l'entrate)	*receipts (income)*	riuscire	*to succeed*
purché	*unless*	la rivista	*magazine*
purtroppo	*unfortunately*	il romanzo	*novel*
		rompere	*to break*
		rotto, -a, -i, -e	*broken*
Q		rosa (inv.)	*pink*
qua (qui)	*here*	rosso	*red*
il quaderno	*notebook*	il rullino	*film roll*
qualche	*some*	rumoroso, -a, -i, -e	*noisy*
quale	*which, which one*		
qualora	*in case, if*	**S**	
qualunque	*whatever, whichever, any*		
quando	*when*	lo sbaglio	*mistake*
(di) quando in quando, ogni tanto	*from time to time*	la scala	*stairs, ladder*
la quantità	*quantity*	la scarpa	*shoe*
quanto	*as much, how much*	scendere	*to come down*
quantunque	*although*	la scheda magnetica	*telephone card*

la scheda telefonica	telephone card
lo schema	diagram
lo scherzo	joke
la schiena	back (anat.)
lo sci	skiing
sciare	to ski
lo sciopero	strike
la sciovia	ski lift
lo sconto	discount
la scopa	broom
la scrivania	desk
scrivere	to write
la sdraia	deck chair
sdrucire (strappare)	to tear
il segretario di stato	secretary of state
semplicemente	simply
sempre	always
sentirsi bene	to feel well
sentirsi male	to feel ill
la sete	thirst
settentrionale	northern
la settimana	week
sfogliare	to leaf through
lo sgabello	footstool
(a) sinistra	to the left
lo sloggio	moving, eviction
la smania	frenzy
snidare	to flush, to drive out
sonare (suonare)	to play (an instrument)
il sonno	sleep
la sorella	sister
sosta vietata	no parking, no standing
lo spazzolino da denti	toothbrush
spedire	to mail
la spesa	food shopping
la spese	shopping
la spiaggia	beach
gli spiccioli	change, coins (money)
squillare	to ring
stabilire (di)	to agree to
staccare il ricevitore	to pick up the receiver
stamani	this morning
stancarsi (di)	to get tired of/to
la stanza, la camera	room
la stanza da bagno	bathroom
stare	to stay, to be
la stazione	station
la stazione ferroviaria	railroad station
lo stipendio	salary
la strada	road, street
suonare (sonare)	to play (an instrument)
lo svantaggio	disadvantage
svegliarsi	to wake up
sveglio	awake, alert
svendere	to undersell

T

tanto ... quanto	as ... as, as much ... as
il tappo	cork, stopper
la tariffa	tariff

la tazza	cup (for coffee, tea, etc.)
il tè	tea
il telecomando	remote control
il/la telecronista	broadcaster
telefonare	to telephone
telefonarsi	to telephone one another
la telefonata	telephone call
la telefonata a carico del destinatario	collect call
la telefonata con preavviso	person-to-person call
la telefonata internazionale	international call
la telefonata interurbana	long-distance call
la telefonata locale (urbana)	local call
il telefonino (il cellulare)	cellular phone
il telegiornale	TV news
il televisore	TV set
Tenere la destra!	Keep right!
Tenere la sinistra!	Keep left!
il totocalcio	soccer lottery
tranne	except
trattare (di)	to deal with, to bargain to
troppo	too much
trovare	to find

U

udire	to hear
ultimo, -a, -i, -e	last
l'uomo (pl. gli uomini)	man
uscire	to go out
l'uscita	exit
utile	useful

V

valere	to be worth
la valigia (pl. -ge & -gie)	suitcase
la vecchia	old woman
il vecchio (pl. vecchi)	old man
vedere	to see
vedersi	to see one another
la veduta	view
veloce	fast
vendere	to sell
la vendita forzata	compulsory sale
verde, -i	green
venire	to come
la verdura	greens
la veste	dress
vestire	to dress (the baby, etc.)
vestirsi	to get dressed
la via, le vie	street, way
il viaggio, i viaggi	trip, journey
vicino	nearby, close
la vicina	neighbor
il vicino	neighbor
Vietato entrare!	No entrance!
Vietato fumare!	No smoking!
Vietato girare a destra!	No right turn!
Vietato girare a sinistra!	No left turn!
Vietato parlare!	No talking!

Vietato sostare!	*No parking!, No standing!*
vincere	*to win*
il vino	*wine*
viola (inv.)	*purple*
vivere	*to live*
volere	*to want*
volersi bene	*to like one another*
volgere	*to turn*
vuoto, -a, -i, -e	*empty, vacant*

Z

lo zaino, gli zaini	*knapsack*
la zia	*aunt*
lo zio	*uncle*
lo zoo, gli zoo (il giardino zoologico), i giardini zoologici	*zoo*
lo zucchero, gli zuccheri	*sugar*

GLOSSARY: ENGLISH–ITALIAN
GLOSSARIO: INGLESE–ITALIANO

A

able, good	*bravo, capace*
(to) abstain from	*astenersi di*
accent	*l'accento (gli accenti)*
acute accent	*l'accento acuto*
grave accent	*l'accento grave*
stress accent	*l'accento tonico*
written accent	*l'accento grafico*
accountant	*il ragioniere (i ragionieri), la ragioniera*
(to) acknowledge receipt	*accusare ricevuta*
ad, advertisement	*l'inserzione (le inserzioni)*
address	*l'indirizzo (gli/gl'indirizzi)*
(to) admit	*ammettere*
advertising agency	*l'agente pubblicitario*
advice	*il consiglio (i consigli)*
(to) advise (to)	*consigliare (di)*
affair, event	*l'affare*
after	*dopo*
afternoon	*il pomeriggio*
(to) agree	*consentire*
(to) agree	*stabilire (di)*
airplane	*'aereo*
all over	*dappertutto*
(to) allow, to permit	*consentire*
almost	*quasi*
already	*già*
also	*anche*
although	*quantunque, benché, sebbene*
always	*sempre*
(to) amuse	*divagare*
ancient	*antico, -ca, -chi, -che*
and	*e*
And how!	*Eccome!*
(to) appear	*apparire*
(to) appear, to cut a good figure	*comparire*
(to) apply	*fare domanda*
archbishop	*l'arcivescovo (gli arcivescovi)*
arm	*il braccio, (le braccia & i bracci)*
as ... as	*cosí ... come*
as ... as, as much as	*tanto ... quanto*
as soon as	*appena*
(to) ask	*chiedere*

(to) ask a question	*fare una domanda*
assets	*l'attivo (gli attivi)*
(to) attack, to glue	*attaccare*
(to) attend to	*occuparsi di*
attorney	*l'avvocato (gli avvocati), l'avvocatessa (le avvocatesse)*
August 15th holiday	*il Ferragosto*
aunt	*la zia*
author	*l'autore (m.) (gli autori)*
author	*l'autrice (f.) (le autrici)*
awake, alert	*sveglio, -a (svegli, sveglie)*

B

baby, child	*il bambino, la bambina, il bimbo, la bimba*
back (anat.)	*la schiena*
bad, mean	*cattivo*
balance	*il bilancio (il saldo), (i bilanci)*
bank	*la banca*
bankruptcy	*il fallimento, la bancarotta*
bar, café	*il bar, il caffè (i bar, i caffè)*
basic	*basilare, m. f. s.*
basically	*basilarmente*
bath	*il bagno*
bathroom	*la stanza da bagno*
(to) be	*essere, stare*
(to) be afraid, (of, to)	*avere paura (di)*
(to) be ashamed	*avere vergogna (di)*
(to) be born	*nascere*
(to) be cold	*avere freddo*
(to) be enough	*bastare*
(to) be hot	*avere caldo*
(to) be hungry	*avere fame*
(to) be in a hurry	*avere fretta*
(to) be late	*fare tardi, essere in ritardo*
(to) be named	*chiamarsi*
(to) be necessary,	*occorrere*
(to) be lacking	
(to) be right	*avere ragione*
(to) be sleepy	*avere sonno*
(to) be thirsty	*avere sete*
(to) be wrong	*avere torto*
(to) be ... years old	*avere ... anni*

beach	*la spiaggia (le spiagge)*	candy	*la caramella*
(to) beat, to hit	*battere*	canoing	*il canottaggio*
beautiful, handsome	*bello, -a, -i, -e*	can opener	*l'apriscatole (gli apriscatole)*
(to) become	*divenire, diventare*	capital of a province	*il capoluogo (i capoluoghi)*
bedroom	*la camera (stanza) da letto*	car (automobile)	*l'auto, f. s. (pl. le auto),*
bedspread	*la coperta*		*la macchina, l'automobile*
before, first (adv.)	*prima*		*(le automobili)*
(to) begin	*cominciare, incominciare*	card (that one mails)	*la cartolina*
beginning	*l'inizio (gli/gl'inizi)*	(to) carry forward (the balance)	*riportare*
(to) believe	*credere*	(to) carry out an order	*eseguire un ordine*
(to) believe in something	*crederci*	car service	*l'autoservizio (gli autoservizi)*
bell	*il campanello*	case	*il caso*
(to) belong	*appartenere*	(in) case	*qualora*
bench	*il banco (i banchi)*	cash on delivery (COD)	*il pagamento alla consegna*
beneficiary	*il beneficiario, la beneficiaria;*	cash register	*la cassa*
	i beneficiari, le beneficiarie	cellular phone	*il telefonino, il cellulare*
			(i cellulari)
better (adv.)	*meglio*		
best (adv.)	*il meglio*	cold	*freddo*
bike	*la moto (le moto)*	center (downtown)	*il centro*
(very) big	*grandissimo*	change, coins (money)	*gli spiccioli, la moneta*
bill, check	*il conto*	(to) change	*cambiare*
birthday	*il compleanno*	charity	*la carità (le carità)*
blackboard	*la lavagna*	check	*l'assegno*
blond	*biondo. –a, -i, -e*	check (bill)	*il conto*
blow	*il colpo*	cheer	*il brindisi (i brindisi)*
blue	*azzurro, blu (inv.)*	cheese	*il formaggio (i formaggi)*
boat	*la barca (le barche)*	chemistry	*la chimica*
(to) boil	*bollire*	chest of drawers	*il comò, la cassettiera*
book	*il libro*	child	*il bimbo; la bimba, il bambino,*
border (of a crater, etc.)	*il ciglio (i cigli)*		*la bambina*
(to) borrow, to loan	*prestare*	church	*la chiesa*
boss, owner	*la padrona*	city	*la città (le città)*
boss, owner	*il padrone (i padroni)*	civilization	*la civiltà*
bottom	*il fondo*	claim	*il reclamo*
boy	*il ragazzo*	classroom	*l'aula (pl. le aule)*
(to) break	*rompere*	clear	*chiaro, -a, -i, -e*
breakfast	*la prima colazione*	client (customer)	*il/la cliente (i/le clienti)*
breath	*il fiato*	climate	*il clima (i climi)*
(to) bring, to take	*portare*	(to) close	*chiudere*
broadcaster	*il/la telecronista (i telecronisti,*	closed	*chiuso, -a, -i –e*
	le telecroniste)	closet	*l'armadio (gli armadi)*
broken	*rotto*	club	*il circolo*
broom	*la scopa*	coal	*il carbone (i carboni)*
brother	*fratello*	coffee	*il caffè (i caffè)*
brother (rel.)	*Frate, Fratello (for a monk),*	cold	*freddo, -a, -i, -e*
	(i Frati)	cold (illness)	*il raffreddore (i raffreddori)*
brown	*marrone (inv.)*	colleague	*il/la collega (i colleghi;*
(to) build	*costruire*		*le colleghe)*
building	*l'edificio*	(to) collect, to pick up	*raccogliere*
(to) burn oneself	*bruciarsi*	collect call	*la telefonata a carico del*
business	*gli affari*		*destinatario*
business Italian	*l'italiano degli affari*	(to) come	*venire*
busy signal (telephone)	*la linea occupata (telefono)*	(to) come down	*scendere*
but	*ma*	comfortable	*comodo, -a, -i, -e*
(to) buy	*comprare*	company	*la compagnia*
buyer	*l'acquirente, m. & f.s.*	company (business)	*la ditta, l'impresa (le imprese)*
	(gli acquirenti; le acquirenti)	(to) compel (to force)	*costringere, forzare*
		(to) compensate	*risarcire*
		compensation	*il risarcimento danni*
C		competition	*il concorso*
		competitor	*il/la concorrente*
café, bar	*caffè, bar*		*(i/le concorrenti)*
(to) call	*chiamare*		
(to) can, to be able	*potere*		

(to) compose	*comporre*	(to) decline (in power)	*decadere*
composition	*il componimento*	(to) deduce	*dedurre*
compulsory sale	*la vendita forzata*	defective goods	*la merce difettosa (le merci ...)*
(to) condemn	*condannare*	dial tone	*la linea libera*
conditional	*condizionale*	(to) dine	*pranzare*
(to) conduct (an orchestra), to lead	*dirigere (un'orchestra)*	(to) do, to make	*fare*
(to) conduct (or run an investigation)	*gestire*	demand	*la richiesta*
		(to) demand	*esigere*
confidence	*la fiducia*	dentist	*il/la dentista (i dentisti;*
to confirm	*confermare*		*le dentiste)*
(to) confuse	*confondere*	(to) derive	*derivare*
(to) conglomerate	*conglomerare*	desk	*la scrivania (le scrivanie)*
consumer goods	*i beni di consumo*	destroyed	*distrutto. -a, -i, -e*
(to) contain	*contenere*	detail	*il dettaglio (i dettagli)*
contract sale	*il contratto di vendita*	(to) detract	*detrarre*
(to) contract	*contrarre*	(to) devote oneself	*dedicarsi*
contravene	*contravvenire*	diagram	*lo schema (gli schemi)*
(to) convene	*convenire*	(to) dial the number	*formare il numero*
(to) cook	*cucinare*	dictionary	*il dizionario (i dizionari)*
cool (fresh)	*fresco, -a (pl. freschi, freshe)*	(to) differ, to be different	*differire*
cork, stopper	*il tappo*	difficult	*difficile*
(to) correct	*correggere*	diphthong	*il dittongo (i dittonghi)*
council of ministers	*il Consiglio dei Ministri*	disadvantage	*lo svantaggio*
counter	*il bancone*	disappointment	*la delusione (le delusioni)*
countryside	*la campagna*	discount	*lo sconto (gli sconti)*
(to) cost	*costare*	(to) discuss	*discutere*
couple	*la coppia*	(to) dispose	*disporre*
(of) course!	*come no!*	Distinguished (form of address)	*Egregio*
cousin	*la cugina; il cugino*	(to) distract	*distrarre*
cover	*la copertina*	(to) distribute	*distribuire*
(to) cover	*coprire*	distribution network	*la rete di distribuzione*
(to) cost	*costare*	(to) divulge	*divulgare*
crane	*la gru*	dizziness	*il capogiro*
credit	*il credito*	(to) do, to make	*fare*
(to) cross	*attraversare*	(to) do wrong	*fare torto*
crowd	*la folla*	doctor	*la dottoressa, il dottore,*
crowded	*affollato, -a, -i, -e*		*il medico (i dottori)*
cry	*il grido (i gridi & le grida)*	dog	*il cane (i cani)*
cup (of coffee, etc.)	*la tazza*	donkey	*asino, somaro*
currency	*la banconota*	double	*doppio, doppia*
currently, fluency	*correntemente*		*(doppi; doppie)*
customer	*l'avventora (f.); l'avventore (m.),*	doubt	*il dubbio (i dubbi)*
	(le avventore; gli avventori)	down payment	*l'acconto (gli acconti)*
(to) cut (to mow)	*falciare (ex. falciare l'erba)*	downtown, centre	*il centro*
cute	*carino, -a, -i, -e*	dozen	*la dozzina*
		drawer	*il cassetto*
D		dress	*la veste (le vesti)*
		(to) dress (the baby, etc.)	*vestire*
dad	*il babbo*	(to) drive	*condurre, guidare*
daily	*quotidianamente*	dear	*caro*
dam	*la diga (le dighe)*	drink	*la bevanda, la bibita*
(to) dance	*ballare, dansare*	(to) drink	*bere*
dash	*la lineetta*	(to) drive	*guidare*
date (as in a calendar)	*la data*	(to) drive, to conduct	*condurre*
daughter	*la figlia (pl. le figlie)*	driver's license	*la patente di guida*
day	*il dí, il giorno, la giornata*		*(le patenti di guida)*
	(i dí)	duty	*l'obbligo, gli obblighi*
(two) days ago	*l'altro ieri, due giorni fa*		
(to) deal with, to bargain (to) take in dear	*trattare (di)*	**E**	
(to) decide	*decidere*	each	*ciascuno, ciascheduno*
deck chair	*la sdraia, (le sdraie)*		*(ciascuna, ciascheduna)*
declaration	*la dichiarazione*		

ear	*l'oręcchio, l'oręcchia*
	(gli oręcchi, le oręcchie)
early, quickly	*presto*
easy chair	*la poltrona*
eighteenth	*diciottęsimo, -a, -i, -e*
eightieth	*ottantęsimo, -a, -i, -e*
eldest	*il/la maggiọre (i maggiọri;*
	le maggiọri)
(to) elect	*elęggere*
elsewhere	*altrove*
empty, vacant	*vuọto, -a, -i, -e*
(to) enclose (in an envelope, etc,)	*acclụdere*
enclosure	*l'allegato (gli allegati)*
end	*la fine (le fini)*
enough	*abbastanza*
Enough!	*Basta!*
entrance	*L'entrata (le/l'entrate)*
(no) entrance!	*Vietato entrare!*
envelope	*la busta*
(to) erase	*cancellare*
estimate	*il preventivo di spesa*
euro	*l'ęuro (pl. gli ęuro)*
(not) even	*neạnche, nemmeno, neppure*
event, fact	*l'accaduto (gli accaduti)*
even though	*quantụnque*
every	*ogni, m. & f. s.*
everywhere, wherever	*ovụnque, dovụnque*
except	*tranne*
exit	*l'uscita (le uscite)*
expensive	*costoso, caro, -a, -i, -e*
export packing	*l'imballạggio per esportazịone*
	(gli/gl'imballaggi ...)
(to) expose, to show	*esporre*
(to) extend (one's regards, etc,)	*pọrgere*
extension number	*il nụmero interno*
extract	*estrarre*
eye	*l'ọcchio (gli occhi)*
eyelash	*il ęiglio, le ęiglia*

F

fact	*il fatto*
factory	*la fạbbrica, (le fạbbriche)*
fall, autumn	*l'autunno (gli autunni)*
(to) fall	*cadere*
(to) fall asleep	*addormentarsi*
family	*la famịglia (le famịglie)*
fantastic	*fantasiọso*
fast	*veloce*
father	*il padre, i padri*
feast	*la festa*
feeble	*flębile, flebili*
(to) feel ill	*sentirsi male*
(to) feel like ...	*avere vọglia di ...*
(to) feel well	*sentirsi bene*
fever	*la febbre*
field	*il campo*
fierce	*feroce, feroci*
Fifteenth Century	*Il Quattrocento*
fiftieth	*cinquantęsimo, -a, -i -e*
film roll	*il rullino*
(to) find	*trovare*

finger	*il dito (le dita & i diti)*
(to) finish, to end	*finire (-isc verb)*
fire	*il fuọco (i fuọchi)*
fireplace	*il camino*
first	*primo, -a, -i, -e*
(to) fix	*aggiustare*
flag	*la bandiẹra*
flag bearer	*il portabandiẹra*
	(i portabandiẹra)
	il vessillifero (i vessilliferi)
flame	*la fiạmma*
(to) flee	*fuggire*
floor (as in 1st floor, etc.)	*il piạno*
flour	*la farina*
flower	*il fiọre (i fiọri)*
fluently, currently	*correntemente*
(to) flush, to drive out	*snidare*
food	*il cibo*
food shopping	*fare la spesa*
(on) foot	*a piędi*
footstool	*lo sgabello*
(to) force, to oblige	*obbligare, forzare*
forest	*la foresta*
(to) foretell	*predire*
(to) forget	*dimenticare, dimenticarsi di*
fork	*la forchetta*
(to) form	*formare*
franchised dealer	*il concessionạrio*
	(i concessionari)
(to) freeze	*agghiacciạre*
frenzy	*la smạnia*
(to) frequent	*frequentare*
friend	*l'amico, l'amica (gli amici;*
	le amiche)
(to) frighten (someone)	*fare paụra (a)*
fruit dealer	*il fruttivẹndolo*
full	*pięno, -a, -i, -e*
fun (adj.)	*divertente*
(to) function	*funzionare*
furnished	*fornito*

G

garage	*il garage, la rimessa*
garbanzos	*i ceci*
(to) gather	*cọgliere, raccọgliere*
(to) get a diploma	*diplomarsi*
(to) get bored, to bore	*annoiạrsi*
one another	
(to) get dressed	*vestirsi*
(to) get engaged	*fidanzarsi*
(to) get hurt	*farsi male*
(to) get mad	*arrabbiạrsi*
(to) get tired of	*stancarsi di*
(to) get up	*alzarsi*
gift	*il regalo, il dono*
girl	*la ragazza*
(to) give	*dare*
(to) give a gift	*fare un regalo*
(to) give as a gift	*regalare*
(to) give back, to return	*restituịre, a riportare*
(to) give in	*cędere*

glass	*il bicchiẹre*	(to) have something to do with it	*entrarci*
(to) glue	*attaccare*	(to) have supper	*fare cena*
(to) go	*andare*	(to) have to, to must	*dovere*
(to) go out	*uscire*	(to) have, to take	*prẹndere*
(to) go to bed	*coricarsi*	he	*lui, egli*
goblet (glass)	*la coppa*	head of the line	*il capofịla, i capifịla*
god	*il dịo (pl. gli dèi)*	(to) hear	*udire*
good, able	*bravo, -a, -i, -e*	heart	*il cuọre*
good	*buọno, -a, -i, -e*	heat	*il caldo*
goods	*la merce (le merci)*	hello, hi, goodbye	*ciạo*
defective goods	*la merce difettosa*	he who	*colụi che*
good morning	*buongiọrno, buon giọrno*	Hello, who's speaking?	*Pronto, chi parla?*
good-natured	*bonạrio, -a, -i, -e*	helmet	*il casco*
(to) go to bed	*coricarsi, andare a letto*	(to) help	*aiutạre*
glossary	*il glossạrio (pl. i glossari)*	(to) help one another	*aiutạrsi*
(to) graduate (from college)	*laureạrsi*	here	*quạ, quị*
grammar	*la grammạtica*	here is ..., here are ...	*ecco ...*
granddaughter	*la nipote (le nipoti)*	(to) hesitate	*esitare*
grandson	*il nipote (i nipoti)*	hiatus	*lo ịato, gli ịati*
(to) gratify, to please	*compiacẹre*	(to) hold on (on the phone)	*restare in lịnea*
grayish	*bịgio, -a,-i -ie*	honorable (Your Honor,	*Onorẹvole (Member of*
grass	*l'erba*	his Honor, etc.)	*Parliament), pl. onorẹvoli*
green, adj.	*verde, verdi*	(to) hope to	*augurare di, augurạrsi di*
greens	*la verdura*	hot	*caldo, -a, -i, -e*
grey	*grịgio (grịgia, grigi, grịgie)*	(it's) hot	*fa caldo*
gross weight	*il peso lordo*	hotel	*l'albergo (pl. gli alberghi)*
(to) grow	*crẹscere*	hour	*l'ora (le ore)*
guarantee	*la garanzịa*	house, home	*la casa*
		(and) how!	*Eccọme!*
		How come?	*Come mại?*
H		(to) hug one another	*abbracciạrsi*
		(about one) hundred	*un centinạio (pl. centinạia)*
hair	*i capelli*	(one) hundred	*cento*
half (adj.)	*mezzo,-a*	hundreth	*centẹsimo, -a, -i, -e*
half (n.)	*la metà (pl. le metà)*	hunger	*la fame*
hall	*il corridọio, i corridọi*	hurry, haste	*la fretta*
hand	*la mano (pl. le mani)*	(to) hurry up	*affrettarsi, fare presto*
handle	*il mạnico (pl. i mạnichi &*	(to) hurt	*dolere*
	i mạnici)	(to) hurt oneself	*farsi male*
handsome, beautiful	*bello, -a, -i, -e*	(to) hurt (someone)	*fare male (a)*
(to) hang up (the telephone)	*attaccare (il ricevitore)*		
(to) happen	*avvenire, succẹdere*		
happy	*allegro, contento, felice*	**I**	
hard	*duro. -a, -i, -e*		
harmful	*dannoso, -a, -i, -e*	ice	*il ghiạccio (i ghiạcci)*
hat	*il cappello*	if, in case	*se, qualora*
hatch	*il boccaporto*	If it were only so!	*Magari!*
(to) have	*avere*	Illustrious (Form of address)	*Illustre, -i*
I have	*(io) ho*	(to) imagine	*fantasticare (di)*
you have	*(tu) hại*	importer	*l'importatore (gli/gl'importatori),*
he/she/it has	*(lui/lei/) ha*		*l'importatrice (le importatrici)*
you (formal s.)	*(Lei) ha*	increase	*l'aumento, gli aumẹnti*
we have	*(noi) abbiạmo*	inside	*dentro*
you have	*(voi) avete*	instead	*anziché*
they have	*(loro) hanno*	insurance company	*la compagnịa di assicurazịoni*
you (formal pl.)	*(Loro) hanno*	insurance policy	*la pọlizza di assicurazịoni*
(to) have a headache	*avere mal di testa*	international (phone) call	*la telefonata internazionạle*
(to) have a sore throat	*avere mal di gola*	in order that	*affinché*
(to) have a stomachache	*avere mal di pạncia*	iron (mineral)	*il ferro*
(to) have breakfast	*fare la prima colazịone*	iron (for clothes)	*il ferro da stiro*
(to) have fun (to enjoy oneself)	*divertirsi*	is (ẹssere)	*è*
(to) have lunch	*fare colazịone*	it's cold	*fa freddo*
(to) have supper	*fare cena, cenare*	it's hot	*fa caldo*

J

joke	*lo scherzo (gli scherzi)*
July	*luglio*
journalist	*il/la giornalista (pl. i giornalisti; le giornaliste)*
jacket	*la giacca*

K

Keep left!	*Tenere la sinistra!*
Keep right!	*Tenere la destra!*
kerchief	*il fazzoletto*
kernel	*il gheriglio*
key	*la chiave (le chiavi)*
kindness	*la gentilezza*
kiosk	*l'edicola, il chiosco*
kiss	*il bacio, i baci*
(to) kiss one another	*baciarsi*
knapsack	*lo zaino (gli zaini)*
knee	*il ginocchio (i ginocchi, le ginocchia)*
(who) knows!	*Chissà!*
(to) knock	*bussare*
(to) know	*conoscere, sapere*
kilo	*il chilo (kg)*
Kindest, Most kind (form of address)	*Gentilissimo*

L

landlord, landlady	*l'affittacamere (m. & f.s.) (pl. gli affittacamere, le affittacamere)*
large, thick	*grosso*
last	*l'ultimo, l'ultima (gli ultimi; le ultime)*
(to) last	*durare*
last year	*l'anno scorso (gli anni scorsi)*
(to) laugh (to roar with laughter)	*ridere (ridere a crepapelle)*
(to) laugh	*ridere*
lawn, meadow	*il prato*
leaf	*la foglia, le foglie*
(to) leaf through	*sfogliare*
(to) learn	*imparare, apprendere*
(to) leave	*partire*
(to) leave (behind)	*lasciare*
lecturer	*il conferenziere, -i; la conferenziera, -e*
ledger	*il libro mastro*
(to the) left	*a sinistra*
(No) left turn!	*Vietato girare a sinistra!*
(to) lengthen	*allungare*
letter carrier	*il portalettere, il postino (i portalettere)*
library	*la biblioteca*
lie	*la bugia, le bugie*
lifeguard	*il bagnino*
(to) light up	*accendere*
(to) like	*piacere*
(to) like one another	*volersi bene*

(to) listen	*ascoltare*
(a) little	*un po'*
(a) little while ago	*poco fa*
(to) live	*abitare, vivere*
load (n.)	*il carico*
(to) load (v.)	*caricare*
loaded (adj.)	*carico, -a, -i, -e*
(to) loan, to borrow	*prestare*
local call	*la telefonata locale (urbana)*
long-distance call	*la telefonata interurbana*
(to) look for (to search)	*cercare*
(to) lose	*perdere*
(to) lose weight	*dimagrire*
(a) lot (of)	*molto, -a, -i, -e*
loudspeaker	*l'altoparlante, gli altoparlanti*
(to) love	*amare*
love	*l'amore, gli amori*
low, short	*basso, -a, -i, -e*
luggage	*il bagaglio, i bagagli*

M

magazine	*la rivista*
mail	*la posta*
(to) mail	*spedire*
Main Post Office	*il palazzo delle Poste*
maintenance	*la manutenzione*
maintenance contract	*il contratto di manutenzione*
(to) make, to do	*fare*
(to) make up one's mind	*decidersi*
man	*l'uomo (gli uomini)*
(old) man	*il vecchio (i vecchi)*
(young) man	*il giovane*
market	*il mercato*
market survey	*l'indagine del mercato (le indagini)*
marketing	*la distribuzione, la vendita*
mass production	*la produzione in serie*
mate, partner	*il compagno*
May	*maggio*
me, to me	*mi*
meat	*la carne, le carni*
meeting, conference	*la conferenza*
(to) mend	*racconciare*
merchandise	*la merce, le merci*
messenger (delivery boy)	*il fattorino*
midnight	*la mezzanotte*
mile	*il miglio (pl. le miglia)*
milk	*il latte*
millionth	*milionesimo, -a, -i, -e*
mineral	*il minerale, i minerali*
mineral water	*l'acqua minerale, le acque minerali*
minister (gov't)	*il ministro*
Minister of Justice	*il guardasigilli, i guardasigilli*
minor	*il/la minorenne, i/le minorenni; il/la minore, i/le minori*
mistake	*lo sbaglio (gli sbagli)*
Monday	*lunedí*
moon	*la luna*
more	*piú*

more than	*piú di, piú … di*	open	*aperto, -a, -i, -e*
morning	*la mattina, il mattino*	opportunity	*l'occasione, le occasioni*
(this) morning	*stamani*	orange (adj.)	*arancione (inv.)*
mortgage	*l'ipoteca (le ipoteche)*	orangeade	*l'aranciata, le aranciate*
Most Distinguished	*Illustrissimo, -a, -i, -e*	(in) order that	*affinché*
(form of address)		outside	*fuori*
mother	*la madre*	oven	*il forno*
motor bike	*il motorino*	(all) over	*dappertutto*
(to) move	*muoversi*	ovecoat	*il cappotto*
movie camera	*la cinepresa*		
moving, eviction	*lo sloggio (gli sloggi)*	**P**	
(as) much, how much	*quanto (quanta)*		
mushroom	*il fungo (pl. i funghi)*	(to) pack	*impaccare, impacchettare*
(to) must, to have to	*dovere*	(to) pack one's suitcase(s)	*fare le valige (-gie)*
my	*mio, mia (pl. miei, mie)*	pain	*il dolore, i dolori*
		(to) paint	*dipingere*
N		painter. (f. + m.)	*la pittrice (le pittrici),*
			il pittore (i pittori)
near (adv.)	*presso, vicino*	painting	*il dipinto*
nearby (adj.)	*vicino. -a, -i, -e*	paper	*la carta*
(to be) necessary	*occorrere*	(to) park	*parcheggiare*
necklace	*la collana*	(No) parking! No standing!	*Vietato sostare!*
(to) need	*avere bisogno (di)*		*Sosta vietata!*
(to) need	*bisognare (used with ind. obj. pr.*	partner, mate	*il compagno*
	like the verb 'piacere')	path	*il cammino*
neighbor	*il vicino, la vicina*	(to) pay	*pagare*
neither … nor	*né … né*	payment	*il pagamento*
nephew	*il nipote (i nipoti)*	(to) pay attention (to)	*fare attenzione (a)*
net weight	*il peso netto*	(to) pay someone a visit	*fare una visita*
never	*mai, non … mai*	people	*la gente*
newspaper	*il giornale (i giornali)*	percentage	*percentuale*
niece	*la nipote (le nipoti)*	person-to-person call	*la telefonata con*
nineteeth	*diciannovesimo, -a, -i, -e*		*preavviso*
Nineteeth Century	*l'Ottocento*	piano	*il piano (instr.)*
ninetieth	*novantesimo, -a, -i, -e*	(to) pick up the receiver	*staccare il ricevitore*
noisy	*rumoroso, -a, -i, -e*	(to) pick, to gather	*cogliere, raccogliere*
no longer	*non piú, non … piú*	pink	*rosa (inv.)*
nonsense	*il controsenso*	phone booth	*la cabina telefonica*
no one	*nessuno, nessuna*	phoneme	*il fonema (i fonemi)*
noon	*il mezzogiorno*	place	*il luogo*
northern	*settentrionale, -i*	(to) place, to put	*mettere*
not at all	*non affatto, non … affatto*	(to) place an order	*commissionare*
not even	*nemmeno, neanche, neppure*	play	*la commedia*
not yet	*non ancora, non … ancora*	(to) play (an instr.)	*suonare, sonare*
notebook	*il quaderno*	please	*per cortesia, per favore,*
nothing	*niente, nulla*		*per piacere*
(to) notice	*accorgersi (di)*	polite	*educato, -a, -i, -e*
novel	*il romanzo*	poor	*povero, -a, -i, -e*
now	*adesso, ora*	postage	*l'affrancatura*
		(to) pretend, to feign	*fingere*
		previous	*anteriore, -i*
O		price	*prezzo*
		price list	*il listino dei prezzi*
oenologist	*l'enologo, -a; gli enologi;*	promotional letter	*la lettera pubblicitaria*
	le enologhe	publicity agency	*l'agenzia pubblicitaria*
of course	*Come no!*	publishing house	*l'editrice, le/l'editrici*
omelet	*la frittata*	pupil	*l'alunno, -a (gli alunni,*
once in a while	*ogni tanto, di quando in quando*		*le alunne)*
one hundred	*cento*	purple	*viola (inv.)*
onion	*la cipolla*	(to) put, to place	*mettere, porre*
onomatopoeia	*l'onomatopea, -eia*	(to) put one through (a phone call)	*passare la linea*
(to) open	*aprire,*		

Q

quay	*il molo*
question	*la domanda*
quality	*la qualità, le qualità*
quantity	*la quantità, le quantità*
quarterly	*trimestrale*
queen	*la regina*
question	*la domanda*
quick	*rapido, veloce*
quickly	*presto*
quiet	*quieto, silenzioso*

R

railroad	*la ferrovia*
(about the) railroad (adj.)	*ferroviario*
railroad station	*la stazione ferroviaria*
(to) rain	*piovere*
rainbow	*l'arcobaleno (gli arcobaleni)*
(to) raise	*alzare*
(to) reach	*raggiungere*
(to) read	*leggere*
reasonable	*modico*
receipt	*la ricevuta*
receipts (income)	*i proventi (le/l'entrate)*
(to) receive	*ricevere*
red	*rosso, -a, -i, -e*
(to) redo, to remake	*rifare*
registered trade mark	*il marchio registrato (marchi)*
relative	*il/la parente (i/le parenti)*
(to) relax, to rest	*riposare, riposarsi*
(to) remember	*ricordare*
(to) remit	*rimettere*
remote control	*il telecomando*
(to) rent (an apartment, etc.)	*affittare*
(to) rent (a car, etc.)	*noleggiare*
repeatedly	*ripetutamente*
reservation	*la prenotazione, -i*
retail price	*il prezzo al minuto*
retailer	*il commerciante al minuto*
(to) retract	*disdire*
right	*la destra*
(to the) right	*a destra*
(No) right turn!	*Vietato girare a destra!*
(to) ring	*squillare*
(to) risk	*arrischiare*
river	*il fiume*
road, street, way	*la strada, la via*
roll call	*l'appello, gli appelli*
room	*la camera, la stanza*
row (file, line)	*la fila*
ruined	*guasto*
(to) rummage	*frugare*
(to) run	*correre*
rustle	*il fruscio*

S

safe	*la cassaforte, le casseforti*
salary	*lo stipendio (gli stipendi)*
salesperson	*l'addetto alla vendita*
(to) say	*dire*
schedule (time, hour)	*l'orario (gli orari)*
sea	*il mare, i mari*
(to) search for, to look for	*cercare*
Secretary of State	*il segretario di stato*
section head	*il caporeparto, i capireparto*
(to) see	*vedere*
(to) see one another	*vedersi*
(to) seem	*avere l'aria di, parere, sembrare*
sell	*vendere*
send	*mandare, inviare*
seventeenth	*diciassettesimo, -a, -i, -e*
(to) sew	*cucire*
(to) shave	*farsi la barba, radersi, sbarbarsi*
she	*lei (ella, essa)*
she who	*colei che*
sheet	*il lenzuolo (i lenzuoli & le lenzuola)*
shirt	*la camicia (le camicie)*
shoe	*la scarpa*
shopping	*le spese*
short, low	*basso, -a, -i, -e*
shower	*la doccia, le docce*
sick	*ammalato*
sideboard	*la credenza*
(to) sign	*firmare*
simply	*semplicemente*
(to) sing	*cantare*
singer	*il/la cantante (pl. i/le cantanti)*
sister	*la sorella*
Sixteenth Century	*il Cinquecento*
(to) ski	*sciare*
skiing	*lo sci*
ski lift	*la sciovia*
skirt	*la gonna*
sky	*il cielo*
skyscraper	*il grattacielo*
sleep	*il sonno*
(to) sleep	*dormire*
slice	*la fetta*
slow	*lento, -a, -i, -e*
slow, low (in sound), (adv.)	*piano*
small	*piccolo, -a, -i, -e*
smoke	*il fumo*
(to) smoke	*fumare*
(No) smoking!	*Vietato fumare!*
smooth	*liscio, -a, lisci, lisce; glabro, -a,-i, -e*
so	*così*
soccer lottery	*totocalcio*
soccer player	*il calciatore, -i*
sock	*la calza*
sofa, couch	*il divano*
some	*qualche (s. only)*
sometimes	*a volte, di quando in quando, qualche volta*
son	*il figlio (pl. i figli)*
song	*la canzone, il canto*
(as) soon as	*appena*

soup	*la minestra, la zuppa*	tasty	*gustoso, -a, -i, -e*
sour, unripe	*acerbo, -a, -i, -e*	tea	*il tè (tè), il thè(i thè)*
southern	*meridionale, -i*	teacher	*la maestra, il maestro*
(to) speak	*parlare*	team captain	*il caposquadra, i capisquadra*
speech	*il discorso*	(to) tear, to rend	*sdrucire, strappare*
spouse	*il/la coniuge (pl. i/le coniugi),*	(to) telephone	*telefonare*
	il/la consorte (pl. i/le consorti)	(to) telephone one another	*telefonarsi*
spring	*primavera*	telephone book	*la guida telefonica*
stairs, ladder	*la scala*	telephone booth	*la cabina telefonica*
stamp	*il francobollo*	telephone call	*la telefonata*
(No) standing! No parking!	*Vietato sostare!*	telephone card (phone card)	*la carta telefonica, la scheda*
station	*la stazione*		*telefonica, la scheda magnetica*
station master	*il capostazione, i capistazione*	telephone number	*il numero telefonico, i numeri*
(to) stay, to be	*stare*		*telefonici*
still, motionless	*fermo, -a, -i, -e*	telephone operator	*il/la centralinista, i centralinisti,*
still (adv.)	*ancora (non ancora = not yet)*		*le centraliniste*
(to) stop (+ -ing)	*cessare (di)*	telephone switchboard	*il centralino*
(to) stop (something, someone)	*fermare*	(to) tell a story	*raccontare*
(to) stop (oneself)	*fermarsi*	tenth	*decimo, -a, -i, -e*
store	*il negozio (i negozi)*	terms of payment	*le condizioni di pagamento*
(to) store, to stock	*immagazzinare*	(to) testify	*attestare*
street, way, road	*la via, la strada*	(to) thank	*ringraziare di*
strike	*lo sciopero, gli scioperi*	thanks	*grazie*
(to) stroll	*passeggiare*	that, that one	*quello, quella (quelli, quelle)*
strong	*forte, -i*	that is	*cioè*
subjunctive	*il congiuntivo*	that which, what	*ciò che*
succeed	*riuscire*	then	*allora, dunque*
suddenly	*di colpo, all'improvviso*	therefore	*quindi*
sugar	*lo zucchero*	they	*loro, essi, esse*
suit	*l'abito, gli abiti*	thick, large	*grosso, -a, -i, -e*
suitcase	*la valigia (le valige &*	thigh	*la coscia, le cosce*
	le valigie)	thing	*la cosa*
sultry	*afoso, -a, -i, -e*	(to) think	*pensare*
summer	*l'estate (pl. l'/le estati)*	Thirteenth Century	*Il Duecento*
summer (adj.)	*estivo*	thirst	*la sete*
Sunday	*domenica*	this, this one	*questo, questa, questi, queste*
sunflower	*il girasole, i girasole*	this morning	*stamani*
supper	*la cena*	those who	*coloro che*
supplier	*il fornitore, -i*	thousandth	*millesimo, -a, -i, -e*
supposing that	*posto che*	thread	*il filo (i fili, le fila)*
surgeon	*il chirurgo (i chirurghi &*	throat	*la gola*
	i chirurgi)	ticket	*il biglietto*
surname (last name)	*il cognome, -i*	(to) tie	*legare*
(to) sustain	*reggere*	tie	*la cravatta*
sweater	*la maglia, il maglione*	till	*finché*
(to) swim	*nuotare*	(from) time to time	*di quando in quando, ogni tanto,*
swimming	*il nuoto*		*a volte*
		tip (money)	*la mancia, le mance*
		tire	*la gomma*
T		tomorrow	*domani*
(to) take, to have	*prendere*	too much	*troppo*
(to) take a bath, to bathe oneself	*farsi il bagno, fare il bagno*	tooth	*il dente, i denti*
(to) take a shower	*farsi la doccia*	toothbrush	*lo spazzolino da denti*
(to) take a trip	*fare un viaggio*	town, country	*il paese, i paesi*
(to) take a walk	*fare una passeggiata*	tree	*l'albero, gli alberi*
(to) take care of	*badare a*	trip	*il viaggio (i viaggi)*
(to) take comfort (in)	*consolarsi (di)*	trouble	*il guaio (pl. i guai)*
(to) take place	*avere luogo*	(to) turn on (the radio,	*accendere (la radio, ecc.)*
tale	*il racconto*	the light, etc.)	
tall, high	*alto, -a, -i, -e*	truck	*il camion (pl. i camion)*
tariff	*la tariffa*	trunk	*il baule, i bauli*
(to) taste	*assaggiare*	(to) trust	*fidarsi (di)*

(to) turn, to turn oneself	*volgere, volgersi*
TV news	*il telegiornale, -i*
TV set	*il televisore, -i*
twelfth	*dodicesimo, -a, -i, -e*
Twentieth Century	*Il Novecento*
two days ago	*due giorni fa, l'altro ieri*

U

ugly	*brutto*
uncle	*lo zio (gli zii)*
(to) undersell	*svendere*
(to) undo	*disfare*
(to) understand	*capire*
(to) understand something about it	*capirci*
unfortunately	*purtroppo*
unless	*purché*
upper case, capital	*maiuscolo*
useful	*utile*

V

vacant, empty	*vuoto, -a, -i, -e*
view	*la veduta*
(to) visit (a place, a patient, etc.), to inspect	*visitare (un luogo, i malati, ecc.)*
(to pay someone a) visit	*fare una visita a qualcuno*

W

(to) wake up	*svegliarsi*
(to) wait	*aspettare*
(to) wait a moment (a minute, etc.)	*aspettare un momento (un attimo, un minuto, ecc.), attendere (un attimo, ecc.)*
waiter	*il cameriere, -i*
wall	*il muro*
wall (of a room)	*la parete, le pareti*
wallet	*il portafoglio, i portafogli*
(to) want	*volere*
war	*la guerra*
(to) warn (about, to, not to, etc.)	*avvertire (di)*
water (mineral water)	*l'acqua (l'acqua minerale), le acque minerali*
(the) weather is bad	*fa cattivo tempo, fa brutto tempo*
(the) weather is good	*fa bel tempo*
Wednesday	*mercoledí*
week	*la settimana*
(to) weigh	*pesare*
welcome	*il benvenuto*
(to) welcome	*accogliere, dare il benvenuto*
well (adv.)	*bene, allora, dunque*
western	*occidentale*
what	*che, cosa, che cosa*
what, that which	*ciò che, quel che*
whatever, whichever, any	*qualunque (s. only)*

when	*quando*
where	*dove*
wherever	*dovunque, ovunque*
which, which one	*quale, -i*
while	*mentre*
white	*bianco, -a (pl. bianchi, bianche)*
who, one who, whom	*chi*
whoever	*chiunque (s. only)*
whole	*il buco, i buchi*
wholesaler	*il grossista (i grossisti), la grossista (le grossiste)*
who, whom, one who, which	*chi*
Who knows!	*Chissà!*
for whom, for which	*per cui*
from whom, from which	*da cui*
in whom, in which	*in cui*
of whom, of which	*di cui*
on whom, on which	*su cui*
to whom, to which	*cui, a cui*
with whom, with which	*con cui*
why, because	*perché*
wide	*ampio, largo (ampia, ampi, ampie; larga, larghi, larghe)*
(to) widen	*allargare*
(to) win	*vincere*
window	*la finestra*
windshield	*il parabrezza (i parabrezza)*
wine	*il vino*
wing	*l'ala (pl. le ali & le ale)*
winter	*l'inverno (gli inverni & gl'inverni)*
woman	*la donna*
(old) woman	*la vecchia (le vecchie)*
(young) woman	*la giovane, -i*
wood	*il legno*
woods	*il bosco (i boschi)*
word	*la parola*
world (adj.)	*mondiale*
world	*il mondo*
World Cup	*la coppa del mondo*
worse (adv.)	*peggio*
worst (adv.)	*il peggio*
(to) write	*scrivere*

Y

year	*l'anno (pl. gli anni)*
(last) year	*l'anno scorso*
yesterday	*ieri*
(not) yet	*non ancora, non … ancora*
young, adj.	*giovane, giovani*
young women	*la giovane, le giovani*

Z

zoo	*lo zoo, il giardino zoologico*

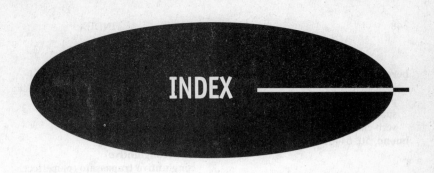

INDEX